EDVARD GRIEG

EDVARD GRIEG

BY

DAVID MONRAD-JOHANSEN

TRANSLATED FROM THE NORWEGIAN

BY

MADGE ROBERTSON

TUDOR PUBLISHING COMPANY
NEW YORK

CONTENTS

CONTENTS

TWO CULTURAL BACKGROUNDS

TWO CULTURAL BACKGROUNDS

TO learn to understand a period one must study its art. Not only are general tendencies reflected there but also that chequered multiplicity of detail which is essential to the completeness of the picture.

The years that have passed since Edvard Grieg died in the Bergen hospital on September 4, 1907, may be characterized as a revolutionary period in every form and field of development; not least in the domain of the mind. The World War, with all the violence and inevitability of a natural catastrophe, provided the external occasion for change; and, just as the foundation for this catastrophe had been laid in the political and social life of the nations, so too the revolution in the life of the mind and spirit had its natural cause. There also the ground had been prepared— especially perhaps as regards the art of music.

If we consider the history of music throughout the last two hundred years, we see that harmony, the cultivation of the purely colorful, has developed with startling rapidity. The harmonic values that have been gained through romanticism and impressionism seem almost miraculous. The Slavs and the Scandinavians contemporaneously have enriched world music with new melodic and rhythmic elements. The art of line, on the contrary, counterpoint as it is called, has in this epoch remained stationary; no development in counterpoint can be traced from the time of Bach and Handel to our own day. But now a crisis has been reached; with impressionism the last harmonic intrenchment was stormed, and it is on its smoking ruins that most modern composers stand and gaze perplexed over the conquered land.

But there were those who saw more deeply than their fellows, who not only were alive to the threatening crisis but with steady, self-denying labor set themselves to work out a solution of the greatest problem that the art of music has presented for a long time—how to create a counterpoint that, in addition to its own special task of forming the structure of the edifice, would allow free play to all the countless shades of color which the newly gained knowledge of the whole harmonic system has placed at our disposal. Even if it is still too early to form a well grounded opinion upon the new movement in music, there are at least signs that we are standing on the brink of a new period, a new epoch, perhaps the most significant for some hundreds of years.

It may reasonably be assumed, therefore, that we are today better qualified to make an objective and fruitful appraisal of Edvard Grieg than was possible in his own time. We can see him in the deep perspective which the tension between two epochs has brought into being. But for an intimate understanding of Edvard Grieg's personality one thing is and always will be essential: to understand the cultural foundations for his life's work, and here certain phenomena of Norwegian intellectual life must be examined.

Is there really anything in the idea that there are two cultural backgrounds in Norway? Is it not just a phantom, a ghost conjured up by chauvinists or others whose spiritual horizon never extends beyond the narrow bounds of the parish, much less the nation? Or is it a fact which no one can ignore—least of all when passing in review the intellectual life of Norway in the last hundred years? Are they perhaps right—those men, who, out of a deep sense of reality and in the strength of their own bitter experiences, claim that Norway's old culture, the mental and spiritual values of our great period, did not crumble to dust when the country lapsed into political impotence; that it continued to live in the people, and not only survived but underwent a rich development, steadily incorporating new ideas? What has been called the National Revival of about a hundred years ago was not a renaissance of moribund powers among the people; in the people they had never died, but had continued to grow and to develop. The so-called National Revival was the first encounter of the genius of the people with the official culture of the country as represented by the rich, patrician families in the towns, by the civil service, and by a few rationalistic writers. That culture derived its vital impulses from abroad; it showed the influence of Norwegian inspiration and had some Norwegian elements, but it was a culture without roots in the land.

It is evident that a conflict like this between two cultures, both of which claim domicile in the country (and with some reason) may be exceedingly fruitful where art is concerned. A glance at Norway's literary history—the Wergeland period, for example—shows this clearly, not to speak of the last fifty years when the policy of

Norwegianism not only has made good its claim purely on the ground of contents but has abetted the struggle over the language which is being actively waged even today. Here, as always, nature demands her rights and, if they are not granted, spiritual life becomes stunted, stifled, dies out. For what is the deep foundation on which nationalism is built? It is simply that in a people, a nation, there lies a wealth of spiritual forces, a motley multiplicity of thoughts, ideas, feelings, visions—the unity and the diversity of the people's soul—but it lies *locked up* since it lacks the means of artistic expression dictated by and springing from its own inner law and compulsion. Even other related cultures can only be imperfect media here. This, among others, is the basic reason for the language movement, "this so inevitable historic movement" as Arne Garborg expresses it in a letter to Edvard Grieg.

If we look at the art of music, Norway's short and easily reviewed musical history shows even more plainly than in the case of literature the antagonistic relationship between our own and foreign cultures. For irrefutable evidence of the fissure in our cultural life we have only to study Edvard Grieg's life work.

There the clashes are so fierce as to sweep away all doubt. In his art the battle was fought out and he throws light on the problem as much through what he *did not* as through what he *did* achieve. Looked at from this point of view, Edvard Grieg is still a living, fighting, and suffering personality and above all a man who counts today.

Edvard Grieg was the fine flower of a stock that had attained a very high degree of cultivation. So delicately adjusted was his mind that, when it burst into bloom, it was not only talents and powers latent in his stock that found release. These would no doubt have made of him a fine artist of importance in himself, but they would not have made him of importance to the intellectual and spiritual life of Norway. The momentous, the crucial thing was that his mind, through generations of cultivation, was tempered to so high a degree of fineness that the thoughts of his age found in it an adequate and to the last degree sensitive vehicle of expression. As the wind, sighing through the strings of the Aeolian harp, makes music, so the Norway of his time found utterance through Edvard Grieg.

Nor was it only his own time that found expression in Grieg's art; he bridged the gaps in Norway's history and showed that there was an unbroken connection between past and future in Norwegian culture. Because in his art he was so deeply anchored in the soul of the people and was, like it, the product of centuries of growth, he, a man of modern culture, was able to become one of the noblest representatives the genius of the nation has to show.

He was not one of these so lamentably misunderstood "liberal minded" artists who are for ever shouting "windows up towards Europe," who, in their feeling of inner poverty and emptiness, cling to foreign cultures in order to have some substance in their lives. Edvard Grieg was not like that. He was interested in everything around him, including all that happened at home, but he viewed all his experiences both at home and abroad in relation to his own personality. For that reason his reactions were particularly fruitful for his art and for the spiritual life of Norway.

When we consider the work of restoration that has been going on for over a century now, the awakening to self-consciousness of a people who were not, as Ibsen said, in danger of being "to themselves enough," but whose curse it was rather to be forced into being something they were never meant to be—when we think of all who have helped in this difficult task, Edvard Grieg stands in the front rank.

He has awakened in Norwegians the consciousness that as a nation they too are capable of creating for themselves a strong, clear-cut individuality. He has set in motion forces which will not easily be checked. He has stimulated the flow of blood in a people who were sickening because violence had been done to their natural functions. He has made it possible for the fresh blood to flow out once more from the heart through the whole organism. This connection with the heart of the people is precisely what was lacking in the Norwegian-Danish culture—that heart of the people which is the fountain of life and the origin of art.

If today these things seem more obvious, more natural, and the real facts of the case are more apparent; if Norwegians feel their hard fate more plainly and therefore find it easier to devise remedies; if the day is perhaps not far off when the Norwegian people will again have conquered their land and will have a national culture which has sprung from a folk culture as in every sound and truly living country, then to Edvard Grieg is due the deepest gratitude. He was not only a musician, an artist, an individualist, he was before all a servant of the people, a servant of that "half wild land, heavy with substance," as he loved to call Norway. And he saw so deeply into the Norwegian problem that he could often cut down his own contribution to permit of the fuller realization of the great possibilities he intuitively sensed in Norwegian musical art, possibilities so enormous that his own work appeared to him merely as a glimpse into the promised land. It is because of this that Edvard Grieg has today such an arousing influence; to this his work owes its unparalleled freshness and youthfulness. On this account his work involves great obligations, since it waits upon a posterity that will complete what he has begun. And for this reason the banner of the future waves over his life's work.

ANCESTRY

ANCESTRY

GRIEG'S ancestors were immigrants from Scotland. The reasons for their going into exile were political. In the war of the Stuarts with the English the latter won so overwhelming a victory at Culloden in 1746 that they availed themselves of their opponents' defenselessness, not only to hang one man in every twenty, but to exploit the Scots financially to such an extent that for a large number of people the position became untenable, and many tradesmen decided to emigrate. Among them was an Alexander Greig, born in Aberdeen in 1739, son of John Greig who also was a merchant. Exactly when Alexander Greig came to Bergen is not known with certainty, but he attained Norwegian citizenship in 1779 and was at this time already in full swing with his business of exporting lobsters to England. He had small schooners designed for this purpose built for him, and it soon became evident that the business was a very paying one. Alexander Greig gradually became a very prosperous man. There is clear proof of the high position he had in a short time achieved in his new country in the fact that before his death in 1803 he was appointed English consul general in Bergen. To get the correct English pronunciation of his name he transposed two letters and wrote himself "Grieg," which has since become the family name in Norway.

When Alexander Grieg died, his son John Grieg took over the business and followed in his father's footsteps. John Grieg too became English consul in Bergen. With his marriage to Maren Regine Haslund a new element, which has not perhaps been without importance for Norwegian music, came into the family. Maren Regine's father, Niels Haslund, was among those who played a large part in the musical life of old Bergen. He was born in 1747 in Aalborg, Denmark, and in 1770 was appointed director of the Harmonic Society established in the previous year. What he accomplished in this position may really be called remarkable. In his book *The Harmonic Society and its Directors*, Emil Jessen writes of him as follows: "In a little town of about 14,000 inhabitants, in a remote corner of the world, he organized and kept going for fifteen years, with never-slackening interest on the members' side, a society which had orchestral music as its principal object. In recognition, he was then awarded a gold medal, struck for him by the society, and on his death the *Advertiser* wrote: 'Among us he had earned—and with justice—the name of an artist. Not only because of his remarkable proficiency in music, but even more because of his clear intellect and his good taste.' "

That marriage with the daughter of such a man should lead to the awakening of John Grieg's interest in music was natural enough, and now, for the first time, we find the name of Grieg mentioned in connection with music. John Grieg was an active member of the Harmonic Society's orchestra and once, when the Dramatic Society called upon the Harmonic for assistance, we find John Grieg among the seven who gave their services.

Alexander Grieg (1806-1875), one of their children, married Gesine Judith Hagerup (1814-1875). These were Edvard Grieg's parents.

As the daughter of Stiftamtmann[1] Hagerup, Edvard Grieg's mother belonged to a family which in various ways has played a prominent part in the official life of Norway. Gesine Hagerup grew up in a well-to-do home. Not only had her father, the Stiftamtmann, a high position socially—he was a member of the Storting (the Norwegian parliament) for Bergen in the years 1814-1824 and 1827-1828, the last year as president of the Lagting (one of its two houses), and in 1836 he was offered a seat in the Cabinet, which, however, he declined—but through marriage and inheritance he had come into possession of much landed property, which at his death went to his children. To Gesine Grieg went the gloriously situated Landås, a big house built in a fine manorial style and with land belonging to it.

No wonder, then, that Stiftamtmann Hagerup was anxious to procure for his children the best possible education. Gesine, who from her early years had shown a decided talent for music, was given not only the best instruction that could be obtained for her in Bergen, but was permitted also to go abroad to continue her education—an exceptional privilege at that time in the case of a young girl. She was sent to Hamburg and studied piano playing, singing, and the theory of music under the well known conductor Albert Methfessel. Later, she played an important part in the musical life of Bergen, often appearing as soloist and taking part

[1] Stiftamtmann = Provincial governor, an office of high rank in the Norwegian Civil Service.

in the performances of chamber music. As late as 1869, she appeared at the Harmonic Society's centenary jubilee concert, where, with August Fries, she played her son's gavotte and minuet (from the first violin sonata).

In one direction only was Stiftamtmann Hagerup unwilling to let his gifted daughter have her own way and that was in a matter which to a young woman was of supreme importance for her whole life. It is said that Gesine Judith had given her heart to a young sailor and him she would have, cost what it might. But it was not to be. Stiftamtmann Hagerup considered the match unsuitable, and, as everyone knows, the choice in such matters lay in those days, according to the good old custom, with the parents; it was they who knew who would make fitting life partners for the young daughters. In Gesine's case the choice fell on Alexander Grieg, son of the prosperous merchant, and to him she was married on November 8, 1836.

Since Edvard Grieg's mother is described by everyone as a woman of strong personality with a somewhat stern and reserved nature, it seems not at all unlikely that this serious youthful experience marked her for life. Her daughter-in-law, Marie Grieg, described her as of a nature at once reflective, critical, and reserved, austere and masterful, with a great sense of order and good management in pecuniary matters. Edvard Grieg himself remembered his mother with a mixture of great respect and warm devotion and love. In a letter to a friend he writes: "Here energy is what's needed, and I shall work till my back breaks. I have that from my mother, my noble mother."

When John Paulsen, in a biographical sketch of Grieg and his art, stated that "Gamle Mor" (The Old Mother), written to Vinje's poem, was composed on the occasion of Grieg's mother's death, Grieg corrected this. "The Old Mother," he said, "was not written when my mother had just died. She was still alive (aged 73) in Sandvigen where I brought her the song which had sprung out of thoughts of her who, with unconquerable energy and sense of duty, had toiled and suffered till she dropped."

When Edvard Grieg married and his mother sent him a quantity of things to help in the furnishing of the new home, among them her own grand piano, she wrote in a letter to her son as follows: "The grey stockings are the sixth pair I have found time to knit this autumn to fit you out at starting. The striped ones I thought might be the wedding socks, if you have nothing better. Fine they are not, but I don't know what your demands are in this respect. My prayers and good wishes are knitted into them." She finishes the letter with the hope that her son will "feel that necessity for and happiness in childlike faith and confiding love which have made me strong and glad so many times."

"Yes, God has been good to the boy," was her constant refrain when she spoke of her gifted son. Her steadfast Christian faith was a help and support to her in all life's difficulties, and she submitted herself in piety and trust to fate and the will of God.

Alexander Grieg seems in many ways to have been her exact opposite. A round, comfortable, and genial man, ardent and impulsive, jovial and easy, he was a favorite and held in affection by all. His letters to his son bubble over often with good humor and lively fancies, even in the later years, when constantly increasing illness and a steady deterioration of his financial position damped his spirits. Alexander Grieg, too, was musical and played the piano, often duets with his wife. On his many business trips to foreign countries, especially to London, he never missed going to good concerts. In the last year of his life, he wrote to his son that he envied him all the music he had the opportunity of hearing. "But that does me no good," he goes on, "and so I put it out of my head and rejoice in the memories of what I have enjoyed in earlier days, which evenly distributed might seem enough for a whole lifetime. . . . Music has been my greatest enjoyment all my life through, and the love of it will certainly follow me to the grave," he ends the letter.

How deep this interest in music really went, it is not easy to know. In his many letters to his son he very seldom touches on questions of music, and when he writes from Bergen about concerts, it seems to be chiefly the size of the audience that has interested him and how much the artist concerned can have made or lost.

When Edvard had begun his own subscription concerts in Christiania, his father wrote to him: "It pleased me more than I can say to hear from your own hand that the concerts have paid well and that you have won a public for yourself, for I must own I don't put much faith in newspaper statements." Surely a very sensible reservation that might apply to all periods and in all situations.

Gesine and Alexander Grieg, Parents of Edvard Grieg

On the other hand, it must not be forgotten that Alexander Grieg showed himself very self-sacrificing in the matter of securing for Edvard a thorough musical education. Not only did he support him for four years at the Conservatory in Leipzig, but he let him continue his studies in Copenhagen and even made it possible for him to undertake the first visit to Rome in the autumn and winter of 1865-1866. Even after his return to Denmark in the spring of 1866, his father helped him with money, though his own financial position had by this time begun to deteriorate very much. Altogether, he followed his son's first difficult steps on the thorny and uncertain path he had chosen with warm and eager interest. "If only I could help you to a living," he wrote to Edvard after his return from his first stay in Rome. And in the straitened years in Christiania, when for Edvard it was not merely a question of a struggle to achieve a position as an artist, but as often perhaps a question of daily bread, his father wrote: "Poor you, who must be always slaving and toiling and get so little return for all your hard work."

But so much greater was the joy when Edvard could announce a victory after his first concert in Christiania. In a letter of October 19, the younger sister, Elisabeth, wrote to Edvard: "I have never seen father and mother so happy; father rushed like a boy with the telegram first into the kitchen to mother, then up to John and then to the back drawing-room and finally to the attic, to tell everyone in the house himself. It was a happy day—happier than our house has known for a very long time."

Naturally enough too, Alexander Grieg took a lively interest in everything English. But it was certainly not due entirely to his Scotch ancestry that, in his enthusiasm for all things English, including questions of art and literature, he was said to set up the English as unquestionably first, and that Dickens was his favorite author. In his letters to his son there are touches that in their sly humor could easily find their place in a Dickens novel and that disclose kinship of spirit with the English author.

The father too embellished his letters with sentiments of a religious nature, and he also sought comfort in religion when life's reverses might well have given cause for bitterness. When Edvard and Nina in the autumn of 1869 had had a great success and been much fêted after a concert in Copenhagen, he wrote to them: "I hope you never let yourselves be carried away by all the incense that has been burned before you of late, but that you both gratefully give all the glory to God. For it is only through Him that we can accomplish anything."

The joint life of the married pair was good and harmonious, even though Fru Gesine Grieg often lived more in a world of her own than in the one in which fate had placed her to live together with her husband.

They had five children, Maren, born 1837, Ingeborg Benedicte, born 1838, John, born 1840, Edvard Hagerup, born June 15, 1843, and Elisabeth Kimbell, born 1845.

CHILDHOOD
1843-1858

FAR out in Strandgaten, No. 152, lay the home of Edvard Grieg's childhood. Even today, wandering along the narrow, crooked street where, should one meet in the living flesh all Holberg's motley portrait gallery, it would cause not a moment's surprise, one gets the feeling of the small, comfortable activities and snugnesses of a bygone time.

Just below is the harbor, with its swarming life of ships and boats, and not far off the Triangle, with the fish market where retorts are exchanged between buyer and seller which could serve as models of pregnant and exact expression. The capacity of concentrating one's views upon a given subject to an essence, as it were, of letting teeming thoughts and reflections stream together and crystallize in a sharp repartee seems to be developed here to a quite unusual degree.

How very closely Grieg felt himself bound to his surroundings in Bergen, to its scenery and the life of its people, he has expressed time after time. He responded to it all with the intimate joy of recognition. Even its smell of fish could throw him into an ecstasy. One of his good friends, Director Johan Bögh, relates that one day he crossed the market with Grieg. It was in full swing and a rank smell of fish was coming from the harbor. Bögh couldn't refrain from exclaiming, "What a disgusting smell of fish!" But Grieg was up in arms and answered vehemently, "Call that disgusting, you idiot—it's simply inspiring!" On which Bögh remarked quietly, "Aha—so that's where you get your inspiration?" "Yes—among other places," was Grieg's quick response.

In his speech on his sixtieth birthday, Grieg said: "It is not only from Bergen's art and science that I have sucked nourishment; it is not only from Holberg or Welhaven or Ole Bull that I have learned. No, the whole Bergen milieu surrounding me has been my material. Bergen's environment—the life of its people, Bergen exploits and enterprises of every kind have inspired me."

If it can be said for most men that environment and education in childhood play a part of vital importance, how much more does this apply to the artist with his highly sensitive mind and disposition, so emotional and open to all impressions? Edvard Grieg grew up in conditions well fitted to provide food for the imagination and, what was of immense importance, he was allowed to give himself up to the pleasures towards which he felt a natural inclination, even though they were at times of a rather unusual kind; he was allowed to feed his boyish fancy on the nourishment it craved. He had in this sense "modern" parents, not hemming him in in all directions with prohibitions; and any maladjustments or complexes in his young mind can certainly not be blamed on a too strict upbringing.

In an autobiographical sketch, "My First Success," which he wrote at Voksenkollen in December 1903, and which has been published in various foreign periodicals, but curiously enough never in its original tongue, he dwells in detail on his childhood, his school days, and later student years in Leipzig. We feel here with what extreme sensitiveness he reacted towards warmth and affection or harshness and coldness. This remained characteristic of him, moreover, all his life through.

The following extract from this article is taken from the original manuscript, which was found among Grieg's papers after his death. He writes: "I could go very far back, to the earliest years of childhood, for who is so keenly alive to appreciation as a child. This kind of sensitiveness the parsons would be likely to call 'the old Adam.' I should call it the craving for sunshine and mildness in life rather than for gloom and austerity. The development of the nascent art life depends very largely upon how this childish need is satisfied. I could name many small triumphs from these years that worked decisively on my imagination. As when, for example, as a little boy I was allowed to see a funeral, to go to auctions, and so on, in order, let it be understood, to detail my impressions afterwards at home. If I had been forbidden to do these things, to follow my childish instincts, who knows whether imagination might not have failed in these early years or taken quite another direction, away from nature."

One gets a vivid impression in these articles of how great an importance he attaches to first impressions from the early golden years of childhood. And he finds it difficult to emphasize one experience at the expense of another; they have all played their part, he feels, in building up his personality.

"When I rummage in my brain among memories from days long gone by," he writes, "to find something that might be called a success, I am at once in the midst of my childhood when life with its many future possibilities lay like one single great success before me, feeling my way in a veritable jungle of many shoots all seeking the light. Half-forgotten memories of childhood stretch out their arms to me. Youthful dreams that were never realized, ideas I should have thought out to an end accuse me like the 'balls' in *Peer Gynt*. But I remember also dim guesses at a happiness I hardly dared believe in but which came to complete fulfilment. Shadows, longings, high hopes in a motley confusion appear and whisper, 'Here am I—and I—and I!' All have claims to be heard. All will have contributed to the early successes. Not the noisy, outward ones. Of these, in any case, there were not many. But the quiet, intimate ones from which was born belief in myself. And if I should choose to distinguish one success at the expense of another, I hear like a far-off childish sobbing, 'Will you deny me—and me —and me! You wouldn't have the heart to do it!' So what shall I do? Draw a thick line through them all as not worthy of notice? No—that I neither will nor can do. For all these small appreciations and feelings of happiness from the years of childhood have had their value, since they contributed to the development of character."

Very interesting is Grieg's account of his first fumbling attempts at the piano. Children, as a rule, like to try to pick out some melody they have heard. If they get as far as harmonies, they seldom go beyond triads. Chords of the seventh and fourth appear to them "false" and chords of the ninth and fifth need, as a rule, a certain musical ripeness before they give one pleasure. It is, therefore, extremely characteristic that Grieg, the creator of the harmony of the future, was, from the very beginning, enraptured with the complex tone combinations which later he knew how to use with such mastership in his art. But now let Grieg speak for himself. "What a rest for thought to follow memory back to the first early dawn of morning. And why not go right back? Why not begin with remembering the marvellous mystic satisfaction achieved by reaching one's arms up to the piano and finding—not a melody. Far from it! No—it had to be a harmony. First a third—then a triad, then a fourth. And at last—with both hands to help—oh glorious!—a fifth, a chord of the ninth. When I had found them out my delight knew no bounds. That was a triumph! No later one has been able to intoxicate me like that one. I must have been about five years old then. A year later, I was given lessons in piano playing by my mother. Little did I guess that here already disappointments lay in wait. Only too soon I realized that I didn't like practising the things I ought to. And my mother was strict. Inexorable. If perhaps, in reality, it gladdened her mother's heart that I would sit trying to find out a little of everything, because in my attempts a musical nature could be perceived, she appeared at all events to take no notice of it. Quite the contrary. It was no matter for jesting with her if I idled my time away in dreaming at the piano instead of getting on with my task. And when I had to apply myself to my scales and exercises and all the rest of the technical devilment, which to my childish longings were stones for bread, it might well happen that she would check me, even if she were not in the room. One day there rang out threateningly from the kitchen where my mother was busy over the midday meal: 'But fie! Edvard, F sharp, F sharp—not F.' I was completely overawed by her wonderful cleverness. If I had then been more diligent and followed more willingly my mother's loving though strict guidance, I should later have come more easily through very much. But my unpardonably dreamy nature had begun even then to prepare for me the same difficulties that followed me far on in my life. If I had not, besides my talent for music, inherited also from my mother indomitable energy, I should certainly never at any point have taken the step from dreams to deeds."

SCHOOL DAYS

IF, AS would seem from his account, Grieg remembered his schooldays with little happiness, the reason was that, as later with the Conservatory in Leipzig, he found little or no food for his imagination, little or nothing that could satisfy his longings and dreams. He states that at school he was at least as lazy as he was with the piano, and he sums up his impressions from these years in the following words: "School life was to me deeply unsympathetic; its materialism, harshness, and coldness were so contrary to my nature that I would think out the most incredible things to be quit of it even if only for a little while. And that this was not only the child's but at least as much the school's fault, I see now. At that time I saw in school life only a boundless unhappiness, and I could not explain to myself the necessity for all these child agonies. I have no doubt at all that school developed the evil in me and let the good lie fallow."

It may be of interest to quote here a few scattered impressions from Grieg's own narrative, since, besides showing his increasing dislike of school, they may perhaps explain also how it was that he came gradually to regard it with hatred.

"From my tenth year my parents lived at the delightful country house Landås, a couple of kilometers from Bergen," writes Grieg. "Every single morning I, with my elder brother, had to start off for school in the famous Bergen downpour. But I made use of this downpour for what I think myself was a neat piece of boyish generalship. At school there was a rule that no boy who came late should be allowed into class but, as a punishment, should stand outside till the end of the lesson. So if on one of these days of pouring rain I started off—as happened often—with none of my lessons prepared, I didn't get myself out of my difficulty only by coming a little late—I used also to go down the street and place myself under the rain spout of a house until I was wet to the skin. When at last I reached the classroom, such a stream of water would run from my clothes on to the floor that the master, both for the sake of my fellow pupils and myself, could not be responsible for keeping me but would send me home immediately to change my clothes—which, on account of the long distance, was the same as letting me off morning school. That I repeated this experiment fairly often was already risky, but when at last I carried things to such an extent that one day when it hardly rained at all I arrived wet through, suspicions were roused and a watch was set. One fine day I was caught and then I made a forcible acquaintance with 'percussion instruments.' "

In this account of his schooldays Grieg tells also of his first composition—variations on a German melody—which he took with him to school and which there met with a reception not calculated to tempt him to further endeavors. Grieg writes of it: "It happened at last one day—I must have been about twelve or thirteen years old—that I brought with me to school a sheet of music written by myself, on the title page of which I had printed in magnificent capitals: 'Variations on a German Melody for the Piano by Edvard Grieg, Opus I.' I greatly enjoyed showing this to a schoolmate who was very interested in me. But what happened? In the middle of the German lesson this same friend was heard to mumble some incomprehensible words, causing the teacher to ask half unwillingly: 'What's that you're saying down there?' There was another indistinct mumbling in response, which brought another sharp question from the teacher. Then there came in a low voice: 'Grieg has something.' 'What do you mean by Grieg has something?' 'Grieg has composed something!' The teacher, with whom for the very good reasons I have described I was not at all popular, got up, came over to me, looked at the sheet of music and said in a characteristically ironical but not ungracious tone: 'So—so, the young rascal is musical—the young rascal composes. Let's have a look at this!' With which he opened the door to the next classroom, brought the teacher from it in to us and went on: 'Just look at this —that young scamp there is a composer.' Both teachers turned over the pages of my music with interest. There was general excitement in both classes. I felt myself already sure of a great success. But one mustn't be too confident. For no sooner was the visitor gone than our own teacher suddenly changed his tactics, grabbed me by the hair, so that everything went black before my eyes, and snapped abruptly: 'Another time he will have the German dictionary with him as he should and leave such trash at home.' Oh, misery! So near the peak of happiness and then in a moment down in the depths! How often has it been like that for me in life. And every time my thoughts have gone back involuntarily to this first time.

"Almost opposite the school buildings there lodged a young lieutenant who was a passionate lover of music and a good pianist. To him I betook myself with my attempts at composition, which interested him so much that I had always to copy them out for him. That was a success which I was not a little proud of.

"I had the good fortune later to be able to wrest these copies from him to consign them to the wastepaper basket where they belonged. I have often sent my friend the lieutenant—who has since become a general—grateful thanks for the encouraging reception he gave to my first spirit children. For my child nature it was a salutary counter-balance to all the hard words and scoldings I constantly received at school.

"Even now I had never for a moment thought that I might become an artist. And if the idea did on any occasion cross my mind, I dismissed it instantly as something unattainable—quite unthinkably high. If I was asked what I was going to be, I answered dutifully, 'A pastor.' Such a black-clad shepherd of souls my imagination furnished with the most alluring qualifications I could conceive. To be allowed to preach or discourse to a listening crowd seemed to me a great thing. Prophet—proclaimer of the glory of God—that was something for me. And how I declaimed in season and out of season to my poor parents and brothers and sisters! I could recite all the poems in our reader by heart. And every day, after dinner, when my father was longing for a rest in his easy chair, he could get no peace for me, who, standing behind a chair for a pulpit, went at it irrepressibly. I kept my eye on father who was, to all appearances, dozing. But he couldn't help smiling now and again. Then I was happy. That was recognition. And how I could go on plaguing father! 'Oh, just one other little piece!'—'No, you've done enough now.'—'Just one more!'—Ah, childish ambition! It knows to a nicety how stimulating is the sensation of making a success."

But there is one thing of which Grieg in this narration never says a word and that is the musical impressions he had already, as a child, received in his own home.

Fru Gesine Grieg not only took a prominent part in the public musical life of Bergen, where she played as soloist at the Harmonic

Society and at other concerts, she also cultivated chamber music and acted as accompanist. To make up for the lack of opportunity to hear dramatic works, she gathered together at her home enthusiastic amateurs, male and female, made up a choir, and practised operatic parts—especially from Mozart and Weber—holding performances at weekly gatherings in her own home. At these she would herself sit at the piano and direct the whole.

Everyone who has experienced the rare delight and enrichment that lies in the practice and production of good music in this manner within the four walls of home can realize the importance of this for the young Edvard. What such performances may lack on the purely technical side is made up for many times over by the close and fervent relationship one comes into with the works performed—a relationship for which the brilliant model performances of the concert hall provide no substitute.

It almost seems like an irony of fate to know that in the home of Edvard Grieg's childhood, where the practice of music went on regularly and often, *Norwegian* music was an unheard-of conception. Grieg has himself told his American biographer, Finck, that when he wrote his first piano pieces and songs he did not know his own country's folk music. Even when he wrote the "Humoresques" —in his twenty-second year—he was unacquainted with Norwegian folk music.

Even in music the "cultivated" classes in Norway lived only on what they could get from abroad.

OLE BULL

BUT there was one person who, even at this time, had clarity of vision regarding Norwegian music, and that was Ole Bull. At Osteröy, where his parents lived in summer, he had learned from childhood to know many clever fiddle players. With Einlidskarden especially, who had learned from the celebrated Nils Rekve of Voss, and who, through talks with Henrik Wergeland, had been strengthened in his belief in the great natural riches of Norway in regard to "the things of the spirit," he spent much time. What Ole Bull had himself been striving after, to give expression in music to his rapturous feeling for nature, the fascination Norway and everything Norwegian had for him, he found these fiddlers had accomplished with a degree of strength and refinement that only tradition and culture could explain. And there can be no doubt that Ole Bull's view of Norwegian music which found expression, among other things, in his great plan for a Norwegian academy of music, contributed to the realization of the first national theater, which was opened in Bergen on January 2, 1850, and whose motto was: "Norwegian plays, Norwegian actors, Norwegian music, and a Norwegian ballet." It may be of interest here to quote a short extract from Ole Bull's long and elaborate invitation to establish a Norwegian academy of music, because it shows how instinctively deep and right his views were. And even though at that time he spoke to deaf ears, his ideas lived and spread, rose up again, and bore fruit in men like Nordraak and Grieg.

In this invitation, Ole Bull writes as follows: "My business in the world is Norwegian music. I am not a painter, not a sculptor, not a literary man. I am a musician. And as such my nation must believe me when I say that I hear a wonderfully deep and characteristic sounding board vibrating within its breast. The aim of my life has been to draw strings across it and enable it to speak out, so that its deep voice can resound in the hall of the temple and, as Norway's own church music, carry the preacher's word to the hearts of the people; so that, on the battlefield, it may bring the nation's hearths and homes to the minds of our country's defenders; so that it may sound out from orchestras to build up our

Norwegian art on a sure foundation; so that it may ring out from pianos all over the country into family life, where these notes will speak to the feelings, shaping and elevating more than all the speech in the world—unsurpassable in charm and clarity. I have spent my life in the endeavor to scale the same grey peak as have the other Norwegian artists, to overcome our denationalized musical sense."

Ole Bull's sister-in-law, Marie Bull, née Midling, writes in her *Memories of Bergen's First National Stage*: "Bull had a living faith that Norwegian art, just as it lived among the peasants, had only to be brought out of its obscurity to be adopted by those interested in art among the general public of the towns—so surely as national feeling and genuine understanding of art existed among the people. Therefore, he arranged for the Norwegian ballet, which consisted of genuine country dancers, to take part in Wergeland's *Fjeldstuen* (The Mountain Hut) and brought the celebrated fiddler Torgeir Audunsön, 'Möllargutten,' to Bergen to show the people of Bergen something still more remarkably national than the peasant dances in *The Mountain Hut*. And both were a great success. With Möllargutten, Ole Bull gave a concert in Norway's national theater and, though it was not much advertised, all the tickets were sold out by 3 o'clock and the house in a state of great national enthusiasm.

"On the stage the scenery for the last act of *The Mountain Hut* was set up and from the low door of the hut Torgeir stepped out, led by Ole Bull, and came forward to the footlights. There was wild applause lasting for a full minute. Torgeir sat down on a stool in the foreground and Ole Bull remained standing by his side, looking down in admiration on the fiddler, who sat, a little bent over, sawing away with his bow—his body swaying in time with the tunes and his foot tapping the floor mechanically. Six numbers he played altogether. I remember that one of them was called 'Abildhaugen,' another 'Grungedalen'; 'Sævelien' he gave also, and the famous 'Kivlemöyarne.' When he had finished the applause broke out like a hurricane. He had to come back and play a tune over again.

"On the grass outside, people stood as packed as on May 17— Ole Bull and Möllargutten went from the theater like two demi-gods. I have never seen anything to equal the enthusiasm. And yet, if one asked people what they thought of Torgeir's playing, they

said, 'Well, I didn't understand it.' But there were few brave enough
to admit that, for in those days it was said in full seriousness, 'If
one isn't an enthusiast for Möllargutten's playing, one is no true
Norwegian.' But the newspapers said, 'The best of Möllargutten's
concert was Ole Bull's performance of *A Visit to the Sæter.*"

But this was but a little glimpse into that wonderland called
Norwegian Music, and for Edvard Grieg not even a glimpse—he
had not yet completed his seventh year. It was not till the last
year of his life that Edvard Grieg met Möllargutten, not in the
flesh but in the spirit, since he took a number of his splendid folk-
dance tunes and transcribed them for the piano.

Ole Bull soon went on his way and for the time being that was
an end of glimpses of the Norwegian element in music. But in the
summer of 1858, he was again in Bergen and it was now that he
interfered decisively in Edvard Grieg's destiny.

In the article already mentioned, Grieg tells about his first meeting with Ole Bull. "The end of my school days, and with it farewell to my home, came more abruptly than I expected. I was
almost fifteen but had not nearly reached the highest class at
school. Then one summer day at Landås, a rider came galloping
at full speed along the road. He approached, stopped his splendid
Arab, and jumped off. It was he—the fairy-tale hero I had dreamt
of but never seen before. It was Ole Bull. There was something in
me that didn't quite like the hero to jump down with no further
ado and behave like an ordinary man; to come into the room and
greet us all smilingly. I remember vividly that when his hand
touched mine something like an electric shock went through me.
But bye-and-bye the hero began to make jokes and then it became
plain to me—at bottom to my quiet sorrow—that he was only a
man after all. His violin, alas, he hadn't with him. But he could
talk. And talk he did. We listened breathlessly to his hair-raising
stories of his journeys in America. That was something for a
child's imagination. When he got to know that I was keen on composing and improvising, there was no saying him nay: I must to
the piano. I do not understand what Ole Bull could find at that
time in my naïve childish notes, but he grew serious and talked in a
low voice with my parents. The result of this discussion was not to
my disadvantage. For suddenly Ole Bull came over to me, shook
me in his own characteristic fashion and said: 'You are to go to

Leipzig and become a musician.' Everyone looked at me affectionately, but I grasped only one thing, that a kind fairy was stroking my cheek and that I was happy. And my parents! Not a moment's opposition or even hesitation. Everything was decided. And I thought it all the most natural thing in the world and did not realize till long afterwards all the gratitude I owed to my parents and to Ole Bull. The spirit of adventure had cast its spell upon me and nothing else could move me.

STUDENT DAYS IN LEIPZIG
1858-1862

STUDENT DAYS IN LEIPZIG

WE ARE again so fortunate as to have Grieg's own account of his student period at the Conservatory. Here, as in the case of school at Bergen, we observe that anything that smacked of compulsion, all that might be called task work and systematic study was absolutely foreign to his nature. Now, too, he demanded, first and foremost, food for his imagination and his special disposition, such things as satisfied his dreams and longings. To one starting with such expectations, study at the Conservatory naturally offered many disappointments.

But we shall let Grieg himself tell about his departure from home and his first impressions of Leipzig. It was not many months after Ole Bull's visit to Bergen that the fifteen-year-old Edvard was sent abroad.

"It is not only by chance that the expression 'was sent' comes to my pen," writes Grieg. "I felt like a parcel stuffed with dreams. I was sent under the care of an old friend of my father's. Over the North Sea we went to Hamburg, and after staying a day there, went on southward by train to mediaeval Leipzig, whose dark, gloomy high houses and narrow streets fairly took my breath away. I was delivered at a pension. Father's old friend said goodbye, the last Norwegian words I heard for a long time, and there stood I, a fifteen-year-old boy, alone in that strange land among strange people. Homesickness seized me—I went into my room where I sat and cried without stopping till I was fetched for the midday meal by my hosts. The husband, a worthy Saxon Oberpostsecretär, tried to comfort me. 'See, my dear Herr Grieg, we have the same sun, the same moon, the same good God here that you have at home.' Very well meant. But neither sun nor moon nor der liebe Gott could make up for my father's friend, now receding from me, the last link binding me to home.

"But the moods of childhood change rapidly. Soon I got over my homesickness and, though I hadn't a scrap of understanding of what it really meant to study music, I was perfectly sure the miracle would happen—that at the end of my three years of study I should come home again a wizard in the kingdom of sound! This is the best proof of my great naïveté, that it was the child in me that ruled completely. And I do not wish to be regarded as anything but a child conservatory student, since that is what I was, even to my clothes. I wore a short blouse belted at the waist, such as boys at home wore. My fellow pupils looked me up and down at first; there was indeed a violin player who amused himself by taking me on his knee, which reduced me to desperation. But all that was soon over."

It was always with a certain bitterness that Grieg in after life spoke of the Leipzig Conservatory. To his first biographer, Aimar Grönvold, he wrote in 1881 that he, in contrast to Svendsen, might say that he left the Conservatory as stupid as when he came to it. In a letter to Julius Röntgen three years later, he complained about his lack of technique, adding that "for this it is not only I who am to blame, but chiefly that damned Leipzig Conservatory where I learnt *absolutely* nothing." As late indeed as 1901 he wrote to Johan Halvorsen lamenting that he had learned so little. "How I do hate that Conservatory in Leipzig!" Constantly in his letters he comes back to the same thing. Every time his want of technique hampered him, every time he felt his powers fail him when he had great problems to solve, it was always the Leipzig Conservatory which was responsible.

Without realizing it, Grieg was in all probability not a little unjust towards the seat of learning, which after all had sharpened his understanding of what the technique of composition really was. For what did Grieg, like everyone, acquire at the Conservatory? He became practised in the fundamental harmonic relations of the art of music, and in his work on counterpoint and fugue obtained an insight into a species of composition through which the highest revelations of genius in the art of music have found expression. That these harmonic and stylistic relationships were foreign to his nature, and therefore could not directly foster and release what was in him, but perhaps rather had a stultifying effect on the development of his special talents and powers, is quite another matter.

It would seem, however, from Grieg's own account that the teaching at the Leipzig Conservatory was at that time unusually dry and uninspiring. There was (and still is) a way of teaching the theory of harmony that probably brought others besides Grieg to despair—a way of concentrating wholly on the pointing out of faults without explaining the reasons for which certain harmonic combinations and voice-leadings are to be condemned. All sorts of rules and prohibitions are imposed without the student's being first convinced of their justification. One has only to submit to unimpeachable authority to find oneself on sure ground. But at the same time, one sees how these theoretical rules and prohibitions are altogether ignored by the masters one most admires. How can these things be reconciled?

Nor was it only the teaching of theory that Grieg found dry and boring. In his piano lessons, too, he was, as he writes himself, given stones for bread. His first piano teacher, Louis Plaidy, does not seem to have had exactly a stimulating effect on the young pupil. "His method of teaching was about the driest imaginable," writes Grieg. "As he sat during the lesson hour planted close beside the piano, a little fat, bald man, listening to his pupil's playing, his right forefinger behind his ear, he would repeat continually till one nearly died of boredom, the words, 'Immer langsam, stark, hochheben, langsam, stark, hochheben!' It was enough to drive one crazy."

Besides, since he only allowed his pupils to play Czerny, Kuhlau, and Clementi, all of whom Grieg hated, it is not to be wondered at that, as he said himself, he grew desperately dull and stale. At last it was more than he could stand. He went to the director of the Conservatory and asked to be allowed to have another teacher, and his request was actually granted. He was put under Ernst Ferdinand Wenzel, Schumann's brilliant friend, whom he soon grew to love and admire. "He had a masterly way of imparting to me his interpretations," writes Grieg; "he could explain a bar in detail with far more penetration than Plaidy and, above all, there was music behind his words." Later Grieg became a pupil of the celebrated Ignaz Moscheles and under the influence of these two teachers all his sluggishness was blown away.

"Hard things are said of old Moscheles as a teacher. I must defend him with the utmost warmth," writes Grieg. "It is true that he was naïve enough to believe that he could impress us when during lessons he set himself on all possible occasions to run down Chopin and Schumann, whom in secret I loved. But he could and did play beautifully, sometimes for almost the whole of the lesson. Specially fine were his renderings of Beethoven, whom he adored.

They were faithful, full of character, and noble without any striving after effect. I studied with him dozens of Beethoven's sonatas.
Often I had not played four bars before he would lay his hands
over mine, push me gently off the stool and say, 'Now listen to
what I make of it.' In this way I was initiated into many small
technical secrets and learned to appreciate to the full his brilliant
interpretations.

"It was said at the Conservatory—though as luck would have it
I did not witness it myself—that during lessons he would give his
pupils the following advice: 'Play diligently the old masters,
Mozart, Beethoven, Haydn—and me.' I cannot vouch for the
truth of this, but mention it because at his desire I grappled with
his twenty-four Studies, Opus 70, which I do not regret having
studied with him indefatigably from beginning to end. I liked them
and did my best to satisfy both him and myself. He may have
taken note of that, since he became steadily more sympathetic
towards me. And a quite simple, to be sure, but for me momentous
'success' it was when one day, after I had played one of his studies
without having been stopped once, he turned to the other pupils
and said, 'See, gentlemen, that is musical piano playing.' How
happy I was! That day the whole world was bathed in sunshine for
me."

At the same time Grieg studied the theory of harmony under
E. F. Richter, the celebrated author of the text-book. But it seems
to have been difficult for the young Norwegian to submit himself
to Richter's strict rules. Instead of writing the harmonies called for
by the score of the thorough bass, Grieg tells us that he wrote
rather harmonies the musical effect of which appealed to him. "I
did not yet realize that what I had to learn was: to restrain myself,
to obey orders, as it says in the introduction to his *Theory of
Harmony*, not to ask 'Why?' All the same, we were never un-
friendly. He only smiled indulgently at my stupidities and with a
'No—false!' would score them out with a thick stroke of his pencil,
which, to tell the truth, left me as much in the dark as ever. But
we were many at a lesson and Richter could not give individual
attention to each."

Grieg had besides lessons in harmony from Dr. Robert Pappernitz, who gave him a freer rein. "The result was that I moved so
far out of the beaten track that in my choral works I brought

chromatic passages into my scoring whenever I possibly could,"
Grieg relates. "One day he broke out, 'Aber diese Cromatik! Sie
werden ja der zweite Spohr!' And as Spohr to me was an academic
stockfish of the first order, I was not at all delighted with this pronouncement.

"Finally, I had lessons from Moritz Hauptmann, and I still
thank that dear old man for all he taught me through his fine and
intelligent observations. In spite of all his learning, he represented
for me the absolute anti-scholastic. For him rules signified nothing
in themselves but were an expression of nature's own laws. An
episode that in a weak moment I might call a 'success,' I will put
in here. Before I knew Hauptmann—I was not yet sixteen and still
wore my child's blouse—I had attained in Privat-Prüfung (a kind
of yearly private examination in which all the pupils, without exception, had to take part) the honor of being allowed to play a
piano piece of my own composition. When I had finished and had
left the piano, I saw to my great surprise an elderly gentleman get
up from the teacher's table and come towards me. He laid his hand
on my shoulder and said only, 'Good day, my boy. We must be
good friends.' It was Hauptmann. Naturally I loved him from that
moment. Ill as he was in the last year of his life, he gave lessons at
his home, the Thomas Schule, Sebastian Bach's old residence. Here
I had the happiness of getting to know him more intimately. I
remember him on his sofa in dressing-gown and slippers, his spectacles almost touching my book of studies, which still retains more
than one spot of the yellow brown snuff that was always dripping
from his snuffy nose. He used to sit with a big silk handkerchief in
his hand so as to forestall the drops. But he had no luck. Then it
was used as a cloth to wipe the book of studies, where its traces are
still plain to see."

There was a questionable custom at this time at the Conservatory of letting the students have lessons in the same subject from
different teachers. That might lead—in piano playing, for instance
—to the handicap of one's having to work according to two opposing methods and in case of the theory lessons, the pupils had more
to do than they could manage. "Especially when we got so far as
to have to write complicated fugues with two or three subjects for
both masters," says Grieg. "I presume that other pupils did as I
did: showed the same piece to both teachers. That, as it happened,
led to a 'success' for me. A fugue on the name GADE which had

not found favor in Richter's eyes aroused so much admiration in
Hauptmann that, after having read it through and lingered over
the details of my work, he exclaimed, contrary to all custom,
'That must sound very fine. Let me hear it.' When I had finished,
he said to me with his kind, lovable smile, 'Very good—very
musical!'

"In my last year at the Conservatory I had lessons in composition from Carl Reinecke, who had then just entered upon his new
duties as conductor at the Gewandhaus concerts and master at the
Conservatory. To illustrate how things went at those lessons, I will
only say that I who had announced that I knew nothing whatever
either of the theory of form or the technique of string instruments
was ordered to write a string quartet. I felt that a thing like that
might as well have been proposed to me by our porter N.N.—
so utterly absurd I thought it. It made me think of my old nurse.
If she wanted me to do something I didn't feel able to and I
objected, 'I can't,' she would answer, 'Put can't away from you
and take hold with both hands.' This saying, which has many a
time put courage in me, did it here too. What Reinecke did not
teach me I tried to pick up for myself from Mozart and Beethoven,
whose quartets I studied diligently on my own initiative. I got
through my task in some kind of a way, the parts were written out
and were played by my fellow students at one of our private en-
sembles. The director of the Conservatory was in favor of the performance of the quartet at a Haupt-Prüfung (public performance
of the best works of the students). But Ferdinand David, the distinguished violinist and teacher, who was present at the rehearsal,
thought otherwise. He took me aside and gave me the advice—as
well meant as it was wise—not to let the quartet be performed. 'Die
Leute werden sagen, es ist Zukunftmusik!' he said. In thinking it
Zukunftmusik he was, however, mistaken. It went the Schumann-
Gade-Mendelssohn way. But that it was an utterly undistin-
guished piece of work I realized very soon and have been extremely
grateful to David for preventing its performance.

"After the negative 'success' meted out to my first string
quartet, Reinecke said, 'Next you must write an overture!' I, who
hadn't a notion either of orchestral instruments or of orchestration, was to write an overture! Again I thought of our porter N.N.
and of—my nurse. I set to work with the reckless abandonment of

youth. But this time I was defeated. I sat literally stuck fast in the middle of the overture and could not get any further.

"It was fortunate for me that I heard so much fine music in Leipzig, especially orchestral and chamber music. That compensated for the instruction in the technique of composition which I did *not* get at the Conservatory. It developed my mind and my musical critical sense to the highest degree, but at the same time it confused the relationship between what I wanted to do and what I was capable of doing, and this confusion was the result of my stay in Leipzig. It would have seemed to me quite natural if neither the director of the Conservatory nor the teachers had taken any interest in me, for in the three or four years I was there I achieved nothing that could awaken expectations of a future. When, therefore, in these glimpses of the Conservatory I have had to find fault with several things, both in persons and in the institution, I hasten to add that I take it for granted that it was, first and foremost, my own nature that led to my going out of the Conservatory almost as ignorant as when I went in. I was a dreamer with no turn for competition. I was heavy, not very communicative, and anything but quick to learn. We Norwegians develop, as a rule, too slowly to be able to show fully at eighteen what we are capable of. However that may be, I didn't in the least know how to deal with myself."

Even when looked at solely from the point of view of the technique of composition, the Leipzig Conservatory was not so altogether without importance for Grieg. To this the songs and piano pieces, for example, that he composed at this time bear witness. These were published as Opus 1 and 2 respectively. The piano pieces he played himself at the public "Prüfung" in the Gewandhaus. "It was at Easter time, 1862, before I left the Conservatory that I attained the very special honor of being included among the elect who were allowed to perform there," he writes himself in his narrative.

What sort of certificate did he get from the Conservatory? After what has been said one would have expected his testimonials to be rather mediocre, perhaps in some subjects actually poor. Grieg writes: "It cannot be denied that it hurt me to see the way in which I was outdistanced by my fellow pupils who made tremendous strides and only had tasks they were able to accomplish." When, therefore, his certificate was found a few years ago in the

Grieg collection in Bergen and published in a musical paper, it caused something of a sensation. It must be agreed, as was said by a college principal who read it, "This is indeed a real *praeceteris-testimonium.*"

Nor is it only the certificate that conflicts with his account. When he says that in the harmony problems set by Richter he always wrote the harmonies he himself liked instead of those required by the thorough bass, and adds besides that "I defied him persistently and went on in my own way," he exaggerates more than a little. His composition books are to be found in the public library in Bergen, and they tell a different story. In them one can follow him from lesson to lesson through the whole three years from the time when he begins with elementary theory of music till he finishes with transcriptions of chorales and fugues; and almost all the compositions show Edvard Grieg as a very conscientious, diligent pupil. The faults of which he accuses himself are those one usually finds in every student. These are parallel motion, false relations, and too great intervals, just the things a strict style does not permit.

When he states that in his lessons with Dr. Pappernitz, who gave him a freer hand, he went so far out of the beaten track as to bring in chromatic intervals in the voice-leadings wherever possible in his transcriptions of chorales, the composition books here also bear witness against Grieg's statement.

No—Grieg did not at that time entertain revolutionary ideas. He was a young modest pupil with a strong belief in and respect for authority. The cause of his disappointment with the Conservatory was rather that Grieg, like every young student, had gone there in the belief that he would be furnished with the technical equipment his nature demanded. The technical exercises were to meet and satisfy his innermost longings and dreams so that at the end of his studies he would return home a wizard in the kingdom of sound as in his childish imaginings he had pictured it. In addition, Grieg's whole disposition was strongly lyric-romantic, and because of this he felt himself straight-jacketed by the austere exercises in composition on which the school insisted. He obtained through the school what one might call a classical education in the art of music. It was his own affair to make the best use he could indirectly of this education.

One thing Grieg does not mention in his very full account of his stay in Leipzig, even though it not only threatened to put an end to his studies but inflicted a lasting injury upon his constitution.

In 1860 he had a very serious attack of pleurisy. Fru Gesine Grieg came down to Leipzig to nurse her suffering son and, when he was well enough for it to be safe, took him home with her to Bergen, where he remained through the summer. But Grieg was impatient to continue his studies and, against the doctor's advice, went back in autumn to Leipzig, where he completed his course in the spring of 1862.

It may be of interest to put in here the official statement his friend and doctor of many years' standing, Dr. Klaus Hanssen, made after Grieg's death with regard to his health: "When sixteen years old, Edvard Grieg had an attack of pleurisy that led to collapse of his left lung, which never expanded again. It was permanently useless and the whole of the left half of the chest fell in. Although the shortness of breath resulting from this was a permanent inconvenience to him, he was, nevertheless, an enthusiastic mountaineer and in his earlier days a frequent visitor to the Jotunheim. On the whole, he had good health and a remarkable capacity for work. His exceptional energy was the main factor here. In the last three years his shortness of breath increased very much and his strength failed. This curtailed his mountain wanderings, but did not stop his work. Even in these years he made his strenuous concert tours. The nervous excitement of these concerts enabled him to forget his body and carried him through."

RESULTS OF LEIPZIG
1862-1863

THE FIRST PIANO PIECES AND SONGS

A S WE have seen, it was rather against his will that Grieg
adopted the severe classical style the Leipzig Conservatory
required of its pupils. But there was another way of expression, another technique which he acquired much more easily
during his residence in Leipzig, the style that originated with the
romantics of the period. Schumann, Mendelssohn, and also Chopin
had just at this time made themselves heard among the people in
Germany. The melodic richness of these masters, their luxuriant
harmonies and short mosaic-like forms satisfied the needs of
Grieg's disposition to the full and made up to him for the dryness
and dullness of the Conservatory. It is to his enthusiasm for the
ideals of the romantics that Grieg owes the first fruits of his genius.
So unreservedly, indeed, did he give himself up to German romanticism that his art was influenced by it for a long time,
indeed, as regards musical form, for the whole of his life.

Besides the masters named, the works of Wagner had already
kindled Grieg's enthusiasm. When Gerhard Schjelderup in his
biography assumed that Grieg, while at the Conservatory, had no
opportunity of getting to know Wagner's works, Grieg wrote to
correct this: "Not the later Wagner, whom at that time few or
none knew. But by 1858 *Tannhäuser* had appeared, and it impressed me so much that I heard it fourteen times running."

In the four pieces for the piano, Opus 1, which he dedicated to
his teacher Wenzel, and still more in the four songs for an alto
voice, Opus 2, Grieg affiliates himself very closely indeed with the
German romantics. So well indeed was he disguised in the German
romantics' garb, in which traits from Chopin could also be
seen, that it is difficult to detect the man beneath the robes. But
he is there. We see the youthful fire, enthusiasm, intensity of expression that bear witness to a character of great vitality and
strength of feeling which demands utterance, cost what it may.

What is amazing in the piano piece is the technical skill of the
barely eighteen-year-old composer. A rich and comprehensive
utilization of the instrument, harmonic elaboration, and sureness
in musical form distinguish these, his first tone poems for the piano.
Towards the end of the fourth piece there breaks through one of

the shrill dissonances we learn later to recognize as a characteristic feature of his mode of expression. But apart from this, it is naturally enough Schumann, Chopin, and Mendelssohn who have been his helpers, both as regards style and form and utilization of the instrument.

As happens so often with great artists, Grieg disowns these first youthful works. In the already mentioned article, "My First Success," he writes of them: "Goodness knows they betoken the fumbling pupil and I blush to think that they are printed and figure as my Opus 1."

Of the five songs for alto voice, the two written to poems of Heine's are the most interesting. "Eingehüllt in graue Wolken" has a greatness of design, a grotesque-dramatic character and, above all, a strength of feeling for nature worthy of a master. In "Ich stand in dunkeln Träumen" there is a sustained certainty in characterization combined with intensity in feeling, and Grieg's pictorial powers are very evident. It is not only the thought of the poem and its emotional content that find expression, the poetical images too are conjured up with vivid imagination in the richly colored piano accompaniment. That Schubert has been Grieg's teacher, both here and in "Die Müllerin" to words of Chamisso's, is plain enough. That is perhaps the real reason why Hugo Riemann and with him other German writers on music, who cannot exactly be accused of having been specially favorable to Grieg, admire just these songs. Riemann, indeed, sets them so high as to say, "They reveal a mastery in musical language that makes one think of Schubert in his great moments."

It is not difficult to understand why Riemann favors precisely these compositions of Grieg's. He represented, in respect to Grieg, an opinion that in his time was fairly widespread in Germany and which found its classical expression in the famous criticism in Riemann's lexicon, where he deplores the fact that Grieg limited himself to national characterization instead of writing works of permanent significance in the diction of international music. Riemann belonged to the group of German writers on music who with their uncomprehending estimate helped to embitter Grieg's last years. Things went so far, indeed, that at his last concerts in Berlin, in the spring of 1907, Grieg refused admission to the critics. But naturally, they came all the same and did their work. In a letter to Frants Beyer, of May 3, 1907, Grieg writes: "Marvellous

dvard Grieg When He Had Completed His Studies in the Leipzig Conservatory

this tour has been. I have had the public on my side. They have applauded my art as never before. But the critics both in Munich and Berlin have told me plainly that I am a dead man."

The diction of international music! How would composers such as Debussy, Mussorgsky, or Stravinsky fare if they should be measured by the Riemann yardstick?

Since that time, however, Germany has lived through World War and revolution. Hugo Riemann and with him many who indulged in imperialistic dreams in music are gone; and now one can find, even in the later editions of Riemann's own lexicon, an estimate more in accordance with facts both of Grieg and of other composers who stood in opposition to German music.

THE FIRST PUBLIC PERFORMANCE

IN THE spring of 1862 Grieg left Leipzig and came home to Bergen. He came, indeed, by no means as the wizard in the kingdom of music that he had imagined but, on the other hand, he did not come empty-handed. Besides the piano pieces and songs already mentioned, he brought his string quartet written at the Conservatory and, in addition, he had, during his years of study, acquired considerable technical proficiency as a pianist.

Soon after his return home he gave his first independent concert, in Bergen. The programme for this event, which took place in the great hall of the Workers' Society, was unusually rich and varied. In *Bergensposten* of May 23, 1862, a short notice of the concert is to be found. It runs as follows: "The high reputation which had preceded him does not seem to have been exaggerated. His compositions were singularly pleasing and it would seem that Herr Grieg has a great future before him as a composer. As an executant also he won universal applause, especially in the Schumann quartet for piano and strings which might be called the crowning feature of the concert."

But what now?—In spite of successes both at the Conservatory and in the town of his birth, Grieg felt himself far from fully trained, far from being fully equipped, and the dream he had cherished in his mind like a precious treasure seemed now more difficult to realize than ever before. The essential thing now was to get out into the great world and see and hear and learn more, then perhaps the miracle would happen. But now it seemed to Alexander Grieg that he had spent enough on his two sons. Edvard's elder brother John, too, he had kept for some years at the Leipzig Conservatory, where he had studied as a cellist. The only way, then, was to seek help in high places, write to the government, to the King, or whoever it was that had a duty towards that indefinable thing called the cultural life of the country or that of which it is often even more difficult to define the "use," the art of the country. So after much consideration and discussion an application for a stipend[1] was sent to The Royal Ecclesiastical and Educational Department.

But, very naturally, there was no stipend to be had. Edvard Hagerup Grieg, who was he? A youngster of nineteen with good testimonials from a music school, but otherwise a blank page.

Then he must manage for himself. Out of the margin of profit from the concert, Grieg bought a large number of orchestral scores, and the systematic education in the playing of such scores, in orchestration and in the principles of musical form which he had not received at the Leipzig Conservatory, he tried now to acquire for himself by private study.

Otherwise this year spent at home in Bergen was a year of uncertainty. The only thing composed was a little work for choir and piano, "Rückblick," which was performed at the Harmonic Society on April 27, 1863. A month before, at a Harmonic Society concert, Grieg, with the Society's Polish conductor, A. Maezewsky, had played Beethoven's sonata in C minor for piano and violin.

Grieg now bent all his energies towards getting away again. According to what he said in a later application for a stipend, his father did not see his way to spend any more upon him. He obtained, however, a loan from his father and was in this way enabled to go out again into the world to continue his studies. This time he did not go to Germany, but to Denmark, where the voices of Gade and Hartmann called so promisingly. "I was simply wrecked after my stay in Leipzig. I did not know which way to turn when an indefinable longing drove me towards Copenhagen," wrote Grieg in a letter to Iver Holter.

[1] The Norwegian government sometimes makes grants of money to persons of special talent for purposes of study or travel for the sake of study.

YOUTHFUL YEARS IN DENMARK
1863-1866

MEETING WITH GADE—DANISH FRIENDS
AND COLLEAGUES

IN MAY 1863 Grieg came to Copenhagen to seek Gade, the great man of Northern music, the master held in very high respect at that time. With his Ossian overture and his first symphony, Gade, at the age of twenty-five, had already won European fame. The leading musicians of Germany, Mendelssohn and Schumann in the van, had greeted him as a bringer of new life to music, his Northern tone color created a sensation, they spoke even of his "imagination kindling the Northern Lights." He became Mendelssohn's friend and colleague—even his successor at the famous Gewandhaus concerts at Leipzig, and for a short time was one of the leading figures in the musical life of Europe. In 1848, on account of the war, he went back to Copenhagen and from that time dedicated his talents to the musical life of Denmark, as conductor, among other things, in the Musical Society during forty years.

Gade had won honor and renown in foreign lands, but surely Charles Kierulf is right when, in his Gade biography, he asserts that he came in the end to "suffer for his glory" and paid no small price for it. The close and cordial encounter with German romanticism and especially with Mendelssohn was fateful for Gade as for so many Northern artists. Instead of his Leipzig period strengthening and developing his own individuality, his works from this time show how his first great inner originality was slowly blurred, smoothed down, and melted away, writes Kierulf. Even after he had settled down in Copenhagen, Mendelssohn and his art had so got into his blood that, to put it shortly, they destroyed "the original grand, broad Northernism that had such great possibilities in it."

It was natural enough then that Gade, at the time Grieg came to Copenhagen, should take so indifferent an attitude towards the nationalist movements in music. Perhaps, though he did not realize it, it was to some extent a bad conscience that brought him in the end to regard the movement mainly as a limitation, a mannerism, a danger. "There is nothing more to be got out of it,"

Angul Hammerich reports him as saying when he touched upon the subject.

When, therefore, Grieg came to Gade seeking for something specifically Northern, it was the spirit of Leipzig he met again, the very thing he was doing all he could to get away from. "I was longing to find expression for something of the best in me that lay a thousand miles from Leipzig and its atmosphere," he wrote in a letter.

Gade's first question to him was, "Have you written anything?" To which Grieg answered modestly that he had done nothing of importance. "Then go home and write a symphony," came the curt command. It was just as if he heard again Reinecke's, "Jetzt schreiben Sie mal eine Ouverture, ein Streichquartett." It is not at all unlikely that Grieg thought once again of N.N. the porter and of his nurse. At any rate, this time too he put "can't" away from him, went home and set to work with embittered energy, and a fortnight later was able to show Gade the first movement of the symphony, fully orchestrated. Gade was pleased with his work and exhorted him in his best manner to continue. Considering in what a dogmatic manner Gade reacted later towards several of Grieg's best works, one can only find it droll that this particular symphony should win his applause. True, there was nothing that should terrify him by new thoughts or put him off by nationalist tendencies in this youthful attempt. But the movement has a certain captivating freshness and, both as regards form and style, all is in order, and this last was very probably decisive with Gade. Only in one place, in a little side theme, there springs up a genuine, original note, one of these plaintive chromatic passages to a tenaciously held note that we know so well as a typical Grieg expression. The passage has a direct connection with "Borte" (Gone), the song to Ibsen's words which was written thirteen years later. Otherwise the piece is derivative, both in invention and form.

That Grieg was not himself mentally stimulated by his work is shown by the fact that he took almost a year to finish and write down the remaining parts. The manuscript was found among Grieg's papers after his death and is displayed in the Public Library in Bergen. It is dated May 2, 1864. The adagio and the intermezzo were published later as a piano duet under the opus number 14.

To Gerhard Schjelderup, who in his Grieg biography assumed that the symphony was never finished, Grieg wrote: "The symphony was completed—it was completed before the two middle parts were performed in Euterpe. But it has never satisfied me and therefore I have never allowed it to be printed or performed in full." But performed it certainly has been, not only once but several times, so Grieg's memory has misled him here. In an interview in *The Woman at Home* for January 1894, Grieg says that old Lumbye had it performed in the Tivoli in Copenhagen, he thought it was in 1864. On the Harmonic Society's programmes in Bergen it figures both on January 1, 1865, and November 28, 1867. In addition, Grieg himself performed three of the movements when in 1867 he conducted the Philharmonic Society in Christiania. But from that year, the year in which Johan Svendsen made his tremendous success with his brilliant D major symphony, Grieg's work is no longer to be found on concert programmes. That his first and only attempt at writing a symphony did not satisfy him one can well believe. On the title-page he has written later: "Is never to be performed. E.G."

Though his association with Gade in the first year was only a continuation of Leipzig, yet Grieg at Copenhagen came into connection with a number of Scandinavian musicians and artists who were not without importance in his development.

In Leipzig he had already met the two years older Danish composer, Emil Hornemann. In Copenhagen he had, besides, the young composers August Winding and Gottfred Matthison-Hansen as his daily companions and friends. Of not least importance for his understanding of Danish nature, the Danish disposition and spirit, was it that he came to know the man who more than any other epitomized the very spirit of the land in his own personality—Hans Christian Andersen. Grieg in his youth wrote, in all, fifteen songs to poems by Andersen, and, during a stay in London in 1889, he told an English newspaper that one of the first who understood how to estimate his work was the great Danish poet, Hans Christian Andersen. Two others must also be named here, the singer Julius Stenberg, and Benjamin Feddersen, both of whom were Grieg's faithful friends throughout the years to come.

NINA HAGERUP AND THE COMPOSITIONS FROM THE FIRST YEAR IN COPENHAGEN

THERE was one factor, a not unimportant factor, that was instrumental in making Grieg's youthful years in Denmark so happy and unforgettable, and that was his association with Nina Hagerup.

Grieg at this time was twenty, she eighteen. They were closely related, since her father, Herman Hagerup, was the brother of Edvard Grieg's mother. In other words, Edvard and Nina were first cousins. Nina too had been born in Bergen, but when she was eight years old her parents had removed to Denmark, where they lived on the Kronborg Castle farm, near Helsingör. Here the young people had met each other for the first time when Edvard, on his way to Leipzig, had visited his relations. Nina's mother was the well known Danish actress, Madame Werligh, from whom Nina inherited her dramatic gifts. Madame Werligh's first husband had been the actor Werligh, in whose theatrical company she had held the highest place.

Nina showed, even as a young girl, an unusual aptitude for music. She had a beautiful voice and a rare dramatic talent, both of which had been developed under the noted teacher of singing, Carl Helsted. Her voice must originally have been of an exceptionally melodious and beautiful quality, such indeed as to enable her to attempt the most difficult tasks, even in a purely vocal sense. And Nina filled her home with song. She sang anywhere and everywhere and everyone was enraptured. She never thought of sparing herself—either then or later. But this want of care was to have its revenge. As quite a young girl she sang once in a big hall at Copenhagen without paying heed to the fact that she had not yet completely recovered from an attack of whooping cough. She had a huge success, but from that time her voice had never the same power and splendor as before. But her dramatic powers developed all the more and, according to the contemporary verdict—and not least Grieg's own—what she could do in this direction must have been altogether exceptional. "What was the special characteristic of her singing?" writes Julius Stenberg. "In a way she made her own school. It was by no means the conventional one, called by Wagner 'the criminal'—her songs were more like vividly dramatic recitative. Not only did she catch the essential mood of a poem, but dug, as it were, into the single words so that they took on deeper and more characteristic colors than when read."

We find striking and interesting testimony to the importance of her influence on Grieg's development as a composer of romances in the autobiographical notes written by him in 1900 at the request of his American biographer, Mr. Finck. Like all Grieg's foreign correspondence, this article was written in German, but the extract, which is here published for the first time, is given in translation. The original manuscript is to be found among Grieg's posthumous papers. Among other things, he writes: "I do not think I possess more talent for song writing than for any other kind of music. How comes it then that romances in particular play such a prominent part in my productions? Quite simply because I too, like other mortals, once in my life (to speak with Goethe) had genius. The genius was: love. I loved a young girl with a wonderful voice and an equally wonderful dramatic talent. This girl has been my wife, has been my life's companion until this day. She has become for me—I can say with truth—the only true interpreter of my songs.

"While I was acting as conductor in Christiania in 1866-1874 (her voice just at this time reached the height of its glory) she performed many times. The audiences of that time, had, however, a very primitive outlook and their conception of art was too brutal for them to appreciate renderings which laid emphasis mainly on the inner spiritual life. In the end it came to be that we made music only at home for ourselves or in the company of friends. But in Copenhagen, where I gave concerts almost every year, my wife was the darling of the artists and of the music-loving public. All my songs from this time on came into being with the inevitability of a law of nature and were all written for her. To give my feelings expression in romances became from now on a condition of existence, as necessary as breathing. In the songs from my second period(from about Volume III in the Peters edition) the connoisseur will be able to observe a greater tendency towards contemplation, towards digging deeper into myself. My wife's interpretation became by degrees correspondingly spiritualized.

"The third, the present, period seems to me almost like a combination of the two earlier ones. 'On revient toujours'—etc. N.B.: with the addition of one's experience of life.

"In laying such stress on my wife's great influence on my songs and emphasizing her contributions in so partial a manner, I know very well that I am running the risk of your getting the impression: This is the husband writing up his wife. But I will take the risk. I feel it as a duty, both towards you and the task you have set me, to express myself in regard to this matter with ruthless candor and without any petty sentimentality."

Among the compositions from this first year in Christiania (1863-1864), where Grieg, besides the symphony, wrote a series of songs and pieces for the piano, songs are found to preponderate greatly. While on the piano is bestowed the *Poetic Tone-pictures*, Opus 3, six songs in all were written this year.

That Grieg was still clinging to German romanticism, both his choice of poems and his musical diction show. It is clear, nevertheless, that the composer was moving towards the North. His association with Northern artists, the study of Northern sagas and folk life seem to have evoked a need for more lively coloring and stronger color contrasts than the German romantic school considered permissible.

This is noticeable already in the first part of the *Poetic Tone-pictures*. While No. 2 shows the influence of Schumann, No. 4 stands in close relationship to Chopin, and in No. 6 can be traced an easily understandable enthusiasm for Mendelssohn's *Midsummer Night's Dream*, we find both in No. 1 and No. 5 features that distinctly mark the developing personality. Especially noticeable is it how the composer begins to find the ordinary tonality too restricted for him; even by this time he had begun to use features from the old ecclesiastical modes to procure stronger contrasts. The Doric alloy in No. 1 and a certain fluctuation between major and minor in No. 5 are the first slight signs of those characteristics which came later to play an essential part in Grieg's artistic make-up.

The same tonal deviations from major and minor are to be found also in several of the songs. "Morgenthau," to words of Chamisso's shows the Doric alloy and in Heine's "Es war ein alter König" the composer, with sure instinct, has used features from the Aeolian mode and so given the music that suggestion of old and far off times which expresses in so characteristic a way the ballad tone of the poem. The two other songs to Heine's words are nearly related to the love songs from the Leipzig period and seem like these to have a deeply tragic background. "Wo sind sie hin?" is a dark, menacing nature impression into which subjective experiences burst with passionate violence, while "Abschied" speaks the quiet, contemplative language of resignation. For completeness, "Die Waise" (Chamisso), in which the short ritornello in particular points the way to the later Grieg, and a fresh and gay "Jägerlied" to words of Uhland must also be named.

It is interesting to note the change Grieg's musical diction undergoes as soon as he begins to occupy himself with Danish lyrics. It is as if the dark, threatening shadows recede and a lighter, clear, more transparent color-tone prevails. The contrast effects are not yet very bold, but the fundamental tone is different. Into the coloring has come a brightness, blue and hopeful. The five songs to words of Christian Winther certainly mark the first meeting with Danish poetry, in spite of the fact that they bear the opus number 10 and were published several years later. They are very simple and stand close to the folk song, both in style and form. As the poetry is unpretentious and simple, so is the music both melodically and harmonically. But they have charming qualities of innocence and naïve grace. This is especially true of "Taksigelse" (Thanksgiving) and "Skovsang" (Forest Song) which, indeed, it is difficult to connect with Grieg, even though the ritornello in the first has a strong resemblance to "Ensom Vandrer" (Lonely Wanderer) which was written many years later when Grieg was himself and no other. In "Blomsternes Tale" (The Flowers Speak) one seems, on the contrary, to glimpse the composer's characteristic face. But this song is spoiled by a stiff and awkward handling of the words, a thing rare with Grieg, who has almost always a very sensitive ear in regard to the treatment of the text in his vocal compositions. In "Sang på Fjeldet" (Song on the Mountains) it is again only in the ritornello that one recognizes the composer's characteristic touch.

The songs, Opus 5, to words by Hans Christian Andersen, which under the name of *Hjertets Melodier* (Melodies of the Heart) first made Grieg's name known in the Scandinavian countries, bear witness to quite another maturity. The manuscript, which is to be found in the Bergen Library, is dated Copenhagen, December 1864, and the collection is dedicated to "Hr. Professor H. C. Andersen with admiration and esteem."

> I lately saw two bright brown eyes,
> In them my home, my whole world lies.

It is the dawn of love that speaks through these songs, stamped with the grace of the Danish landscape. It is worth noting what a large place the feeling for nature occupies even in these early compositions. While before it was German nature impressions, now it is Danish scenery, Danish feeling for nature that frame his spiritual experiences and throw them into relief. "Jeg elsker dig" (I Love Thee) is the one of Grieg's love songs that most quickly made its way in all countries, although few indeed know how to render the purity of feeling and the chaste abandonment breathed out from this youthful confession. "Du fatter ei Bölgernes evige Gang" (Can'st Gather the Speech of the Ocean's Swell) has still something of the Leipzig period's menacing passion over it, but "Min Tanke er et mægtigt Fjeld" (My Mind Is Like a Mountain Steep) both as to melody and harmony keeps to quite a simple style. Yet another song to words of Andersen's was written this year, "Kjærlighed" (Love), which is of no interest except that it shows the transitions of the composer's mood towards the bright and hopeful.

For the first time too Grieg uses this year a Norwegian poem, writing music to Andreas Munch's "Solnedgang" (Sunset). But there is nothing to show either in words or music that we have come home to Norway; we are still in smiling and graceful Denmark.

As a whole, the productions of this year show Grieg approaching his fatherland. It seems to beckon in the distance, and the dream has been so nourished that there may now be hope of its being someday realized.

Grieg had gone to Copenhagen to learn to know "Northern things" but he found these least where he had expected them most, that is with Gade, "who obviously could not satisfy that longing," he writes in a letter. But on the other hand, Gade was not without importance to him in his youthful years. With his sure mastership, his great command of all the technical side of music, Gade was a pillar of strength, a stern controller, whose hard hand made short work of everything that smacked of deviation from purity of style, all that could offend against "the beautiful" as it was apprehended by every faithful disciple of Mendelssohn. But stimulating Gade's influence on Grieg certainly was not, in this period when he was striving to find himself.

It may well have been that his acquaintance with the works of Hartmann was of greater significance to him. Here Grieg found a nature more closely related to his own, here he heard notes directly inspired by Northern saga- and folk-life, here he often heard the voice of his race, clear and pure.

In the summer of 1864 Grieg returned home to Norway to Bergen, where he was much with Ole Bull at Osteröy. They explored the neighborhood together, Ole Bull booming away about his delight in Norway, his enthusiasm over the land and the people, and never tired of preaching to his young friend the enormous possibilities of their country. But when it came to giving shape to his enthusiasms, translating his raptures into actual music, then Ole Bull stuck fast. He had created one fine melody—that to "Sæterjentens Söndag" (The Sæter Girl's Sunday) though he was unable to harmonize it himself, and he was brimming with excitement over Norwegian folk music. But to initiate the process which shapes *art* out of the rich possibilities of a given material—no, that was not Ole Bull's affair.

Grieg and Ole Bull made much music together this summer; they played sonatas—mainly Mozart's. Now and again John Grieg would come out and then they would play trios. For the newer movements in German music Ole Bull had no sympathy. Even Beethoven was almost too much for him, and as for Wagner —the house of correction was, he believed, the place for him!

Edvard Grieg was now twenty-one. He had had from his earliest childhood the best of instruction from his mother, he had continued his education at Leipzig in the best school of the period, and in Denmark he had come into touch with the Northern spirit in music.

But what now? He felt drawn both to German romanticism and to the manifestations of the Northern spirit which he had met with in Denmark, but in neither could he find full satisfaction.

What then was blocking the way, since the disproportion between what he *would* and what he *could* do was still so great?

The trouble was that he could not see clearly before him and this filled him with unrest, with anxiety. Often he felt as though he were groping his way in a fog, afraid at every moment that he might plunge over a precipice.

He was going through, as he puts it himself, a prodigious process of fermentation. It was in this state of mind that he returned to Copenhagen in the autumn and met—his fate. He came upon the man who was to exercise a decisive influence on his whole development, both as man and artist, the man who was to give his personality its enduring stamp. What Grieg had himself sensed dimly, had circled about in thought but had not been able clearly to discern, he now met realized in a form so brilliant, of so sparkling a clarity that, marvelling, he recognized at a glance what it was that had lain hidden for years behind the German mist.

In his own words, "I saw, as Björnson in *Arnljot* puts it, 'Norway in the rising sun.'"

RIKARD NORDRAAK

FOR most people in our country, Rikard Nordraak's fame rests upon the fact that it was he who gave Norway the music for her national anthem. That is well and good enough, for no more beautiful motto than the sonorous "Ja vi elsker dette Landet" (Yes, We Love the Land that Towers) could he have had for his life's work.

By others, by the majority of musicians and many besides, Nordraak is admired first and foremost as the creator of a series of fresh ballads and choruses to words of Björnson's and as the composer of *Mary Stuart* and *Sigurd Slembe*. That also is well and good enough, for what finer epigraph could one wish for than these young, pure stanzas sprung out of a warm and rich nature?

But Nordraak was something much more. He possessed an almost radioactive capacity for stimulation, powers and faculties the potency of which we feel to this day as strongly as his contemporaries felt it, and the influence of which will continue to be felt as long as work on Norwegian music goes on in Norway. His sight was visionary. It pierced far back into the land's grey antiquity, and it shone with dazzling clearness into the future and discerned the path that the art of music in Norway must follow.

Rikard Nordraak was himself a piece of Norway—Norway seen in bird's-eye perspective, a Norway which had lived a thousand years with Hafrsfjord, Hjörungavåg, and Svolder burning in its veins, a Norway with sagas and folk poetry surging in its soul, a Norway with a folk music that embraces everything: the austere, pathetic gravity of ancient ballads, the wild abandon of the dance tunes, comic songs, love songs, pastoral melodies, cradle songs—everything, even to the sobriety and pious devotion of church music; a folk music as rich and luxuriant as the Norwegian scenery. All this combined and fused in one personality—that was Rikard Nordraak.

From this sprang his self-confidence; the proud spirit that made him at barely twenty exclaim with charming naïveté, "Great Rikard Nordraak!" From this arose his violent collisions with his teachers, whose attempts to force upon him the rules of German classicism were so hard to carry out.

Like Wergeland, who felt the necessity of withdrawing from intellectual union with Denmark and did not hesitate to break with the common Danish-Norwegian literature, Nordraak felt the impossibility of finding utterance for Norwegian musical feeling by way of German classicism and romanticism.

While Grieg, when studying at Leipzig, occupied himself only with German music and German literature, we see from Nordraak's letters what was the spiritual food *he* found essential during a sojourn in a foreign land. From Berlin he writes in 1861 to his father begging him to send Snorre Sturlason's, Wergeland's, Björnson's and Ewald's works. "I don't see how I can stand it here without them and I hope you will give heed to my earnest request, since these books are really necessary for my compositions and my development."

In another letter also from Berlin we see how his thoughts are occupied with Norwegian folk music and its possibilities for development. He is even prepared to reform the language and writes in detail on this subject to his cousin Björnson. What heights he would have reached had he lived, no one can guess.

Grieg, in his letters, expresses several times the opinion that he was a visionary of genius, but would never have become a fully developed artist in the widest sense of the word. "Good for him that he went away before reality took him by surprise." Inevitably there was a great disparity between what he had in him and what in his short life he was able to find expression for. He was laden with material, laden to the breaking point, so charged with it that the sparks flew at the least touch. He was the first who from the depths of the people, from the hidden springs, shot up into the light of day and looked around him in astonishment in a world so infinitely unlike that he came from. He was himself the spirit of the people embodied in music. Björnson writes of him: "He was all clarity and strength, a full, round sum of Norwegian melodies and Norwegian national enthusiasm, Norwegian character sketches and anecdotes, Norwegian dreams and fairy stories, a profusion of plans for Norwegian operas and symphonies. A Norwegian tone poem which, like a fountain, sprang up gleaming into the sunlight, only to sink back again a moment later. That radiant fountain was a wonderful harbinger of great glory." Add to this his personal charm. Again let Björnson speak. It was while he lay ill at Aulestad in 1900 that he dictated to Rosenkrantz Johnsen his recollections of Nordraak from which the following has been taken: "I still remember his face when he played: he had large eyes which he kept half shut, his mouth stood half open, his whole face was intent. He had red hair and freckles and an exceptionally delightful smile at once tender and merry, showing his beautiful teeth. I can still hear his voice, so warm and fresh. I can safely say that in company he was the most fascinating young man I ever met. Not only was he beyond comparison the most gifted, full of interest in everything at home and abroad, but his good nature, humor, buoyancy, his playing, his compositions, his plans and his love affairs enveloped one like an unending springtime." Is it to be wondered at that he took Grieg by storm, completely changing his ideas, chasing away all doubt, all caution, all compounding with the "Northern." "We hated indiscriminately everything established and dreamt ourselves into a new Norwegian—Norwegian—Norwegian future," is how Grieg puts it in one of his letters.

GRIEG AND NORDRAAK

O F THE meeting itself Grieg wrote to Aimar Grönvold: "What actually happened at my first meeting with Nordraak was so characteristic—of Nordraak—that I can conjure it up at will as if it were yesterday. It was one evening at Copenhagen's Tivoli that I was introduced by Fru Thoresen to a young man who called himself Nordraak and whose opening words were: 'And so we two great men really meet!'[1] Bearing, gestures, voice, all suggested that here I had a man who felt himself the future Björnson plus Ole Bull. But there was, at the same time, something so touchingly naïve and lovable about him that he took me by storm. I had never, till that moment, considered the possibility of being or becoming a great man. I was a student, nothing more—timid, shy, and delicate. But this assurance of success was just the medicine for me, and from that moment it was as if we had been friends all our lives."

Nordraak went home with Grieg and sat down at the piano where he played and sang his airs from Björnson's peasant stories, his scene from *Sigurd Slembe*, his "Purpose" from *Mary Stuart*, and other things. "I shall never forget the impression he made on me," writes Grieg. "Of a sudden a mist seemed to clear from my eyes and I knew what it was I wanted. It wasn't quite what Nordraak wanted, but I think that for me the way went through him. Now came a happy time of joyful excitement and production. This was in 1864-1865. In daily intercourse at Copenhagen with Nordraak and other youngsters enthusiastic about the North, I wrote in a short time many songs, the Humoresques, Opus 6, sonata Opus 7 and sonata Opus 8. It was touching how we almost fell in love with each other. How he adored my Humoresques! 'Yes,' he cried at the minuet, with a conqueror's assured self-confidence, 'that is as if I had written it myself!' and I—I worshiped his songs no less!" And the letter goes on: "When you ask about Nordraak's influence on me, it is as you suppose that his view of our folk music strengthened my own. But my national enthusiasm had already awakened before I knew him, though it

[1] Grieg and Nordraak were at this time twenty-one and twenty-two years old, respectively.

had not borne fruit in my art. It was the impact of our meeting that caused the productive outburst of this enthusiasm. But who understands the secret laws of influence? I only know that he appeared like a good genius upon my way, that I am eternally grateful to him, and that without him I might have had to struggle, who knows how long, without finding myself. We were completely unlike in spite of our mutual sympathy. And just because of this, we could influence each other fruitfully."

This letter to Grönvold was written in 1881. Much has been said and written since about Nordraak's influence on Grieg and some have thought that it has perhaps been a little exaggerated. To that Grieg answers in a hitherto unpublished letter to Iver Holter of February 9, 1897: "Nordraak's importance for me is *not* exaggerated. It is like this: through him, and through him alone, light came to me. Danish literature can show something comparable. Had Oehlenschläger not met Steffens he would not perhaps have found himself. As Kierkegaard says, the occasion is nothing and the occasion is—everything. What we all know of Björnson applied also in a high degree to Nordraak. His personality was fascinating. He was a dreamer, a seer, without being destined himself to bring his art to the height of his vision. That is to say, in small songs he could do it, but he would hardly have been able to fulfill his promise had he lived."

The letter goes on to say: "I was longing to find expression for the best that was in me—a best that lay a thousand miles from Leipzig and its atmosphere; but that it lay in love of my fatherland and in my feeling for the great, melancholy Westland nature I did not know and would never perhaps have found out if I had not, through Nordraak, been led to self-examination. This had its first result in the Humoresques, Opus 6, dedicated to Nordraak, in which the direction of development is plainly shown. I willingly allow that Nordraak's influence was not entirely musical. But that is exactly what I am grateful to him for, that he opened my eyes to the importance of that in music which is *not* music."

EUTERPE—THE SOCIETY FOR THE ADVANCEMENT OF NORTHERN MUSIC

INEVITABLY—one might almost say—the meeting between Nordraak and Grieg resulted in the formation of a society. Euterpe it was called and amongst the founders, besides Grieg and Nordraak, were the Danish composers, Emil Hornemann and Matthison-Hansen. The object was the performance of Scandinavian works. About this event Nordraak writes to Björnson on March 24, 1865: "But the most important happening is the foundation of Euterpe of which, during my illness, I have been appointed co-director. And I have put my own mark upon it, Northern aims, the Northern spirit; and we have already had results that surpassed our highest expectations. Enclosed I send you our announcement to the musical public, also the newspaper report of our first concert, which was held last Saturday. The press is not, however, so well disposed towards us as the public, which rewarded Euterpe's programme with the very greatest kindness. It was my happy fate to be the hero of the evening. I conducted the choir and orchestra myself. First your ballad 'Brede seil' (Broad Sails) was sung, then came a new setting to 'Bangen' in Ole Vig's book of folk songs. The choir was scraped together in a terrific hurry and there was a great shortage of first tenors, but all went tolerably well, as I had rehearsed everything very conscientiously. The audience seemed to think well of the two compositions, but liked better still the 'Solo with Choir and Orchestra' from *Sigurd Slembe* that followed.

"When the concert was over and I left the hall, I could hardly get away from the astonishingly friendly crowd. Ladies and gentlemen quite unknown to me came to congratulate me and wish the promising young composer luck, and the people pressed curiously around me. The poet, H. C. Andersen, to whom I have never been introduced, recognized me, presumably by my hair. He came hurrying up, the friendly soul, and I was astonished at his sympathetic interest. 'But, my dear young friend, you have a great talent. How glad I am to have heard your beautiful composition, it shows kinship in spirit with Björnson. Do you know him?' 'Yes—

he is my cousin.' 'Is that possible; give him my kindest greetings when you write. And you must promise to come and see me, I should like so much to talk to you and hear some of your things—I am at home from 1 to 4.' And then the dear poet left me.

"Praise and happiness make one conceited, they say. I don't know, but I have never felt so humble as that evening. I was almost upset at the amount of praise I got and the notice taken of me and felt how little I deserved it all. But I was glad for the sake of my cause and vowed that I would make myself worthy of recognition.

"I think you will admit that it has not been lost time for me here in Copenhagen. You can imagine that getting a thing like this put through has been a hard job and as I was feeling weak and nervous, it was often almost more than I could bear. But it is over now and it went well; I've laid the foundations of my future here and thank God for it.

"Kind Fru Thoresen wrote to congratulate me at once. How good people are down here, how they help and support one! When will it be the same with us?"

At the next Euterpe concert, which was given on April 1, Grieg appeared for the first time as conductor, and produced the adagio and intermezzo from his symphony. Though naturally he did not succeed with this somewhat impersonal symphony—which suggests rather the work of a clever student than that of an artist expressing his experience—in awakening the same interest in himself as did Nordraak, Grieg showed that he could make up for it in another direction. It was at this time that he initiated his more personal work with the Humoresques for the piano, Opus 6, and they were followed by an exceptionally fruitful period of production.

THE ARTIST COMES INTO HIS KINGDOM

LOOKING at the works Grieg wrote this spring and summer, one receives an overwhelming impression of an exceptionally felicitous creative faculty at work. It is as though all barriers had suddenly given way. He overcomes technical difficulties with apparent ease; with liberated imagination he creates one work after another. And it is now not only the smaller forms he masters—he subdues the exacting style and form of the sonata with his youthful arrogance, with his glowing faith and enthusiasm.

He makes use also of the ballad in its most exacting form and writes the broadly planned and consistently worked out songs, "Efterårsstormen" (Autumn Storm) and "Udfarten" (Outward Bound).

The Humoresques, Opus 6, are Grieg's first real contribution to the literature of music. Against the background of his earlier compositions this work has an astonishing effect, not only because of the originality of its subject matter, but also because of the splendid mastery of technique it shows, its bold, harmonic style, and the quite individual way in which the instrument is used.

One might imagine that Norwegian spring-dances and flings had been Grieg's models here, but in his notes to Finck, already referred to, he makes it clear that at this time he hardly knew our folk music. "When I wrote the Airs for the piano Opus 3 and more especially, perhaps, Opus 6 (the Humoresques) in which the national element comes up repeatedly, I knew practically nothing of our folk songs."

From a purely artistic point of view this statement is of interest, for it shows how real was Grieg's ability to penetrate to the heart of the spiritual life of the people as it expresses itself in music. But even if Grieg at this time had had an intimate knowledge of our folk music, even if the Humoresques had been built on motives from Norwegian peasant airs, his merit would be no less on that account. For it is the way the material is handled that makes art. If that were not so, Norway with its rich folk music might have had a hundred composers of the same importance as Grieg.

If Nordraak was delighted with the first brilliant results of his work of revival, there was another who opened his eyes wide over these "national" productions, and that was Gade. "When as a young man (1865) I showed him my Humoresques for the piano, he sat turning over my manuscript without at first saying a word. Then he began to give some little grunts, then louder ones till at last he burst out with, 'Tell me, Grieg, is this stuff supposed to be Norwegian?' And I, feeling humble and hurt, 'It's meant to be, Herr Professor'—though that I was a young beginner and he the famous master must always be remembered in these little stories. But he cherished always till the day of his death a strong sympathy for me, sometimes openly expressed, sometimes concealed." Grieg writes thus to Iver Holter in a letter of January 8, 1897.

Grieg wakened Gade's evident interest with his next two works —the piano sonata in E minor, Opus 7, and the first violin sonata, Opus 8. Both were written in the summer of 1865 at Rungsted, near Copenhagen, where Grieg lived with Benjamin Feddersen. In an interview for *The Woman at Home* Grieg says: "Whether it was the enchanting surroundings or the stimulating air that inspired me, I cannot say. Enough that in eleven days I had composed my piano sonata and very soon after my first violin sonata. I took them both to Gade at Klampenborg. He looked them through with pleasure, nodded, patted me on the shoulder and said, 'That seems a good bit of work. Now we'll look into the seams more carefully.' Then we marched up a small steep stair to Gade's workroom, where he sat down at the piano and played with absolute inspiration. I had been told that when Gade was inspired he drank great quantities of water. That day the Professor emptied four large jugs full." And who could wonder at Gade's delight. Both works are full of a fire and inspiration that sweep one off one's feet and make one forget that here already there lurks a secret conflict between material and form. The classical sonata form, with its strictly logical building up, its demand for the development of motives, its closely knit system of modulations, its tendency to keep all musical thought in narrow channels, was obviously ill adapted to hold the wild mountain river with which Grieg's music may best be compared.

Of the two works, the piano sonata keeps nearest the traditional form, and for those who are wont to assert that Grieg "could not" write an ordinary sonata, he proves in the development of the first movement that he understood very well what thematic work should be. The development—precisely the part of the movement that is the touchstone of talent—he masters in a way both interesting and easy. The third and fourth bars of the principal subject form the thematic material. In modified forms they dovetail imitatively with each other and show an amount of detail in the workmanship that is unusual elsewhere with Grieg. After being announced first in the remote A flat minor, a change is made to the primary key. A tremolo organ-point in the dominant for the left hand, against a descending voice in the right, leads up to the repeat, where the principal subject now appears in the transformed shape it has assumed during the development. The coda displays a tremendous outburst of energy. It crackles with sevenths and diminished octaves and the whole movement gives an enchanting impression of young courage and proud self-confidence.

In the andante we get an interesting glimpse into Grieg's principles of form. The gentle pastoral mood that distinguishes the principal motive is soon interrupted by vehement fortissimo outbursts. We expect now to be swept into the maelstrom of passion. But no! surprisingly, an intermezzo is interposed. Lightly—almost casually, it seems—the composer sketches a country scene for us, far away as in a vision. . . . Nearer it comes, and before we are aware we are whirled away in lively dance rhythms. Then with a gradual heightening of intensity we are carried over into the principal theme again which now enters in full power and splendor. The general effect is as of moving rapidly through a Norwegian landscape from one surprise to another, and one is both thrilled and startled.

This principle of form, the chief features of which are precisely surprise, alternation, rapidly changing pictures which yet are held together and comprehended in one general aspect, shows the extreme closeness with which Grieg's art is bound to the scenes and spirit of his homeland, to the mountains and fjords of the Westland.

The minuet is definitely Teutonic music, vigorous, sound, over broad chords. The thematic material here does not lend itself so well to contrast as does that of the andante, it is more subordinated according to accepted tradition to general effect, and this is probably one of the reasons for the popularity of this particular movement in Germany, where it may be heard in all possible and impossible arrangements and transcriptions. The trio shows a wealth of interesting harmonic combinations. Grieg with his intuitive genius has conjured into being not only chords of the seventh and ninth, but also what, in modern manuals of harmony, are known as elevenths and thirteenths.

The finale, though even more tempestuous, is nearly related in character to the first movement, and the second subject with its suggestion of the old church mode provides an effective contrast. The working out is not so masterly as in the first movement—there is a feeling of effort about it. This reef, obviously, it has not been easy to avoid.

The coda is built upon the second subject which winds free and unconstrained and with exuberant energy through a series of keys to end radiantly at last in the major.

In the violin sonata which followed, Grieg gives us one of the most impressive and at the same time charming proofs of his happy genius. This work, too, is systematically conceived in strict sonata form, but it deviates so greatly in character from its classical prototypes that it is difficult to connect it with the sonata as usually conceived. It shows an exuberant fertility of invention hard to match. One delightful fancy follows another before the first has had time fully to unfold; we pass rapidly from one picture to the next, carried away and held captive by the inexhaustible wealth of the composer's imagination. We are not conscious for a moment of the rigid form the artist has chosen as vehicle for his material. There is a surprise for us at the very beginning. The key of the sonata is F major, yet the movement is ushered in with triads in E minor and A minor, only to change over suddenly into the principal key. And this is not the only surprise the movement has in store. The development is introduced in a way as effective as it is unexpected. In the first part, the main theme, the subsidiary theme, and the second theme proper seem to vie with one another in singing of youth and happiness; once or twice driving clouds dim the sun, but suddenly all blows over and we are again under the same enchantment that we know from the andante of the piano sonata, again we have a glimpse into Norwegian nature that astounds and thrills us. In a short interpolated andante we have the principal subject, this time in the minor with rich harmonics which reveal suddenly the deep perspective of the theme. It is as though the composer would say, "See! It was *this* I really meant, here is my essence, the inmost, the most precious thing in my nature—the other was only a disguise." Then, as suddenly as it came, the vision is gone. Instead of a coda in the usual sense, he gives us again the same tone picture—but more concisely—a distant view that slowly fades away and disappears. There are inner connections between these deviations from the basic character of the movement, the introductory minor triads, the startling commencement of the working out, and the equally surprising coda. These are like the understrings on the Hardanger fiddle; they form, as it were, the background from which the abundantly exciting movement springs.

In the second part, allegretto quasi andante, we are right in the heart of Norway. Throughout the whole movement dance rhythm prevails and in the trio we find ourselves in the middle of a whirling spring dance. In the last movement, where many composers suffer from lack of material, how Grieg triumphs! Ideas and fancies crowd so thick on one another that they seem almost to fight for a place, one jubilant motive supersedes another, they stream and stream as from an inexhaustible well.

Altogether delightful is the beginning of the working out. Here the composer tries for once to make use of the knowledge acquired at the Leipzig Conservatory. He begins with a fugato—and we expect an artfully built up development. But no. Hardly has he begun when he suddenly abandons his elaborate style and gives his imagination free rein. The effect is as though a child of nature had stuck his head for a moment into a schoolroom, only to slam the door again and scurry off! The sonata ends in a glorious, brilliant presto.

"Autumn Storm," one of Grieg's most nobly designed songs, was written at the same time as the two sonatas that happy summer at Rungsted. It, too, bears striking witness to his genius. With unerring artistic instinct he has grasped the fundamental mood in Christian Richardt's poem and with that as basis he elaborates the details with an exceptional feeling for character, using strong colors, crude contrasts, but always preserving the unity of the poem as a whole. We follow the poet and the composer through the devastations of autumn storms.

> When Storm on his great horn a loud blast blows,
> Through the thickest of leaf-walls a trembling goes.

Again the storm blows up and the "woods' green hat" changes color. After the third attack the land stands stripped and bare.

> One autumn night is the world laid waste,
> Grim winter's banner is raised in haste
> O'er a desolate land, where his icy breath
> Many a fair tree has doomed to death.

Over short, clipped chords on the piano the voice declaims the saga of transience. Once more the storm waxes, to sink finally into the torpor of winter. But even autumn storms have their mitigating aspects.

> But poor folk rejoice in the wild wind's spoil,
> Bright fires to warm them reward their toil. . . .

Supported by bright major chords the voice recites the comforting stanzas so naturally and simply that one forgets that this part of the text is not perhaps well adapted for setting to music. Winter covers over atoningly "every wound the storm has dealt," and above all it bears in itself the promise that "there comes at last so fair a spring." And now the composer points the way that leads to deliverance—to the unfolding of the spirit of life. A glance is cast back on winter and then he breaks out in jubilation:

> What has the earth more fair to show
> Than first flower blooming in latest snow!

It is his own history Grieg records here, it is his own deliverance he exultantly announces. He too has broken through the winter cold that threatened to freeze him in, he too has felt the blessedness of liberation. It is worth noticing that in "Autumn Storm," which was written after the Humoresques and at the same time as the two sonatas, there is not one thing in the musical diction that is characteristically Norwegian. So extremely sensitive was Grieg, so delicate his mind, that he could adapt himself wholly to the material he was using. Danish lyric poetry, the seas and woods of Denmark he had to treat; his notes adapt themselves exactly to the given material, and yet the composer's personality is preserved. So rich was his mind, so complex, so many-sided.

In the quantity of interesting documents found among Grieg's papers after his death were a number of letters from Rikard Nordraak, hitherto unknown to all except the recipient. They betoken a continuance of the happy companionship in Denmark and they give beautiful expression to the warm sympathy and devotion Nordraak felt for his friend and colleague. But they also deepen the picture of Nordraak as an artist, they afford glimpses into the mind of a young genius who received among his cradle gifts the precious faculty of being able intuitively to understand and to follow the secret laws of nature.

In these letters, from which, for lack of space, we can only quote a few selected fragments, we get also a delightful impression of Nordraak's rich, warm humanity, his faithfulness and sincerity, and they help to explain how it was that he came to have so over-whelming an influence on Grieg. In May, Nordraak had gone to Berlin to continue his studies and it is from there he writes these letters to Grieg. The first is dated Berlin, Grosse Friedrichstr. No. 205, bei Bath, June 12, 1865. Nordraak writes here: "One mustn't lose faith in one's own times—that means losing faith in oneself. And I feel so clearly that now great things in music are approach-ing. How far we young people with our hopes and longings will reach is in the hands of God; but *long* it will not be before we of the North will hear our notes echoed from the rest of the world. And I, who so early felt it would be so, heard the promise in the great 'small melodies.'—I have had to cry it aloud. Forgive me, Grieg, forgive me everyone, if I have often spoken too highly about my-self, please believe me (and all who know my heart will believe me) that it was love of the cause rather than of myself that shone through my often, alas, boastful utterances." In the same letter he goes on to say: "How glad I am to have met *at last* one in whom I put such firm faith and hope. Dear Grieg, you mean more to me than I can say—the more I think about the essential you, the more beautiful it becomes to me. How glorious to hear your last com-positions now that you are beginning, as you say yourself in your dear letter, to realize more and more the greatness of our national ideal which you now embrace with your whole soul. I was so glad when I read this that tears fell on those unforgettable lines. You will see when we two go hand in hand that it will be for the hap-piness of others besides ourselves."

While they were still in Copenhagen, Grieg and Nordraak had arranged to go to Italy together. On August 1, Grieg's father writes to him: "I read in the last *Christiania Aftenblad* that there is talk of Nordraak as conductor of the orchestra there, and what about your tour to the South then? You must not go alone on any account. I won't deny that I should have liked someone else with you on this tour, for from what T. has told me of Nordraak, and what John says of his great conceit, it seems to me he would not be the best possible daily companion for you."

Grieg writes at once to Nordraak to find out if he really is thinking of the position in Christiania. To this Nordraak answers in a letter dated Berlin, September 2: "My dear and excellent friend ——To your questions I answer at once (1) I am not going to Christiania in the winter as conductor of the orchestra in the theater—how could you imagine I would? I shall wait till I feel myself really fit to tackle a thing like that. Real power and superiority are needed with us at home above all, if anything is to be made of crude capacities. I am prudent, I will not prejudice my own great ideal which could too easily be made to seem something smaller than it is if outwardly it did not carry that stamp of maturity which must be manifest before people can understand."

In the same letter he writes: "Thousands and thousands of thanks for your good opinion of me! God grant I may be worthy. And thanks for having started the revolution in the world of musical criticism! That had to be, and we Norwegians who know the fresh, untainted air of the mountains can feel more clearly than most others the lamentable spiritual falsity of the musical production of our time. You put your case well, one can feel the heart of the gifted artist who lets enthusiasm for a great idea guide his pen; but, my friend, calm, calm, and again calm there must be towards those who till now have called themselves critics, however much reason they give for fury. Hold out—*don't let yourself get angry*. I and others will share with you the idiots you have to deal with in the newspapers who understand no more of music than a cat of mustard—folk like that rely on their journalistic routine to help them and try with torrents of words to obscure the issue, to vilify a sensitive man and so provoke him into doing or saying things he will regret afterwards."

NO ONE could wish for a happier time than was Grieg's in the summer of 1865 at Rungsted. Good fortune seemed to seek him out from every quarter. It was not only in his work he was happy—his daily life too was rich in experiences and impressions.

Friends from Copenhagen often came over, they made excursions in "the forest." His brother John came to visit him on his way from Dresden, and one fine day Björnstjerne Björnson himself appeared. As soon as Nordraak heard that Björnson had come to Copenhagen he wrote to Grieg, "You must, of course, seize the opportunity of getting to know this genius." And then to crown everything came his betrothal to Nina Hagerup. They had been secretly betrothed since July 1864. "We played Schumann's B flat major symphony as a duet—and got engaged!" relates Fru Grieg.

It was no simple matter, however, to get the parents' consent. "This foolish betrothal," writes Edvard's father; he cannot understand how Edvard can dream of such a piece of folly. Nor were Nina's parents particularly delighted with the prospect of having a penniless young musician as a son-in-law. Fru Hagerup knew too well from her own experience the insecurity of the artist's life and wished more easy circumstances for her daughter. But the young people would not give each other up. On May 27 his brother John writes to Edvard from Dresden: "For yourself, matters I hope are now righting themselves; I can't but think that father and mother, as things are now, have given their consent to making the betrothal public." And from a letter of July 2 from John to Edvard, it would appear that all parties have at last given in and the betrothal is announced—a very ceremonial affair in those days.

But soon the lovely summer was over, the summer that Grieg in later life always looked back on as the brightest and most beautiful memory of his youth. In September he began to prepare for his tour to the South. The first plan was that he should not go further than Germany. On September 12 his father writes in great detail to him about the money he is sending and says: "When you write from Germany, telling me where you propose to spend the winter, I will write further as to how much you will have to manage on; meantime you have something now to begin the winter with. You are a costly chap!—in every way—there is no doubt about it."

Just before Grieg left Denmark he wrote one of his most beautiful and broadly conceived songs, "Udfarten" (Outward Bound), to lines of Andreas Munch. In the reminiscences already mentioned written to Finck, Grieg states that "my choice of poet is always suggested by what I am experiencing." What strikes one again in this song is the matchless sensitiveness of Grieg's mind through which he comes into a close and intimate relationship to the poet he chooses at the moment. As regards Andreas Munch, it is very possible that in this collaboration it is the composer who ranks highest. But the poet gives him an opportunity to display his best qualities: depth of feeling and the ability to fill the details with character and make them in the best sense pictorial, while still preserving the unity of the poem so that it stands out for us in a glorified form.

The soft, slurred chords and the rocking rhythm in the piano reflect the introductory mood of nature.

> At break of dawn on a summer's night
> A ship at anchor lay fast
> In lee of an island, whose hanging woods
> In the clear sea their image cast.

And there comes a note of painful foreboding with the announcement that "when the first golden spears of day the sky behind the mountains pierce, out must she steer from placid fjord to face the ocean strange and fierce. . . ."

In the music there seems to sound a premonition of the tragic ending. And how vividly has Grieg depicted for us the following:

> And see! on deck athrill with hope.
> My bride sits, young and fair:
> So lovely she—as beautiful
> As dreaming roses are.

We are with her in her happy anticipations now to be fulfilled— together they will journey,

> Far over the ocean to foreign shores,
> To the smiling land of the South.

With warm, living colors the composer paints the whole for us and when we read, "She floated out on her glorious path, like a queen in a poet's dream—" the music rings out like a fanfare of victory.

It is interesting to observe Grieg's thematic treatment, his use of motives. The theme which, enveloped in melting tones, prefaces the song is the same he now employs in its full brilliance. Then follows abruptly and without any phase of transition the tragic ending of the poem. Here too Grieg has helped to give unity to the whole and soften the abrupt transition by his use of motives. The same theme it is which at first conjures up "my sweet young wife" and now, transposed to the minor, recounts:

> May God be praised then that never for her
> Did Fate draw back the veil.
> Beneath the ground soon, soon she lay,
> Quiet and straight and pale.

Over bright sonorities, in which use is made of the church mode, the narration takes on a wonderful gentleness, to sink down finally into the depths enveloped in somber funeral chords. Yet once more the composer softens the heavy blow of fate, bringing in a shining tremolo—like a faint shimmer of starlight over death and the grave. . . .

Grieg could not well have said a more beautiful farewell to his young bride, his friends, and Denmark. Here too, as in "Autumn Storm," it is a Danish nature impression that has inspired him to this pictorial rendering of the text.

One other song dates from this year—the "Vuggesang" (Cradle Song)—also to words of Munch's. And so Grieg set out on his "glorious path" to "the smiling land of the South," to "wander in youthful joy by Arno's, by Old Tiber's strand." And at that moment he could take Munch's words in "Outward Bound" for his own, he felt that life lay before him "so day-long, so rich in beauty."

But little did he guess that the tragic ending of "Outward Bound" would be fulfilled here too, that his companion, the friend nearest his heart, would lie so soon "beneath the ground, quiet and straight and pale. . . ."

NORDRAAK'S DEATH—FIRST VISIT TO ROME

JUST as Grieg arrived at Berlin on his way to Italy, Rikard Nordraak lay down upon the sick bed from which he was never to rise. In the beginning of October he had a violent attack of inflammation of the lungs which developed into galloping consumption.

From Nordraak's diary it appears that Grieg and Edmund Neupert visited him daily. On October 14 Nordraak notes that the Scandinavian Society held its first meeting of the winter session. "Grieg and Neupert were there. Mr. Storjohan made a speech for me and proposed my health."

A letter found among Grieg's papers after his death shows that on November 2 he had been with his sick friend to say good-bye. For now Grieg was to go on a tour to Leipzig where his two sonatas were to be performed at a concert given by the Conservatory in the Gewandhaus. On November 6 Nordraak notes in his diary, "Letter from Grieg in Leipzig." On the 12th there is an entry: "Registered letter arrived from Johannesen[1] to Grieg. When I saw that it contained money I opened it and found a money order for 60 specie dollars. Johannesen's letter I read: it was a letter of thanks to Grieg for his kindness during my illness. In it was enclosed one from father, no doubt in the same strain."

Next day, Grieg telegraphed from Leipzig to ask how his friend was and on the 19th Nordraak had a letter from him telling about his performance in Leipzig. On the 20th Nordraak notes in his diary: "Grieg's letter yesterday describes his performance of his piano sonata and his sonata for piano and violin at the evening entertainment in the Gewandhaus in Leipzig. A tremendous success. Encored. How I am looking forward to his coming."

But now Nordraak begins to be impatient. By November 12 he is writing urgently begging Grieg to come. The letter, which was found among Grieg's papers after his death, is written in pencil and apparently with the greatest difficulty. Part of it shall be quoted here:

[1] One of his father's colleagues.

"Berlin, November 12, 1865.
"Dearest Friend!

"For a short moment I have the strength, as I sit supported by my most excellent landlady, to send you a very few words. Thank you for your letter so dear to me. I can't tell you how much good it did me, especially as I had not then heard a word from home in answer to my telegram. Eight days of waiting, distress and longing definitely aggravated my illness. At last came letters from my father, my sister, and my stepmother, as loving and sympathetic as they could possibly be. And my stepmother sent me father's portrait which delighted me and is now hanging over my bed." The letter ends, "Now you must come, Grieg. Don't delay any longer.—I must have you again. Write immediately when you receive these few lines to say that you are coming at once to your devoted

"Rikard Nordraak."

But Grieg delayed and at last, on November 30, Nordraak received a letter from him saying that he was not coming back to Berlin at all. He had found another companion and was going direct to Italy.

It was only natural that Nordraak, lying sick to death and knowing well how it was with him, should have felt this bitterly. In the letter he sends Grieg that same day he expresses his disappointment and indignation in words at times so strong that they must have wounded Grieg sorely. It is certainly to this that Grieg alludes when, in his letter to Nordraak's father, he writes: "I know what I had to suffer in forsaking him, my best friend, on his sick bed, in seeing love and solicitude misunderstood."

For a long time yet Nordraak lay and fought with death, but though his strength failed and he felt himself grow physically weak, his spirit remained alive and strong to the last. In the preface to the letters he left, published by Wladimir Moe, the editor writes: "On his deathbed he wrote Taylor's Song in *Mary Stuart*, one of his sublimest tone poems. Soon after, on March 26, far from all his dear ones, he closed his eyes. In the Jerusalemer Kirchhof in Berlin he was laid to rest.[2] How sad it is to relate that his death

[2] Nordraak's remains were removed home to Oslo in 1925.

and burial passed so unnoticed that only *one* sympathetic soul followed him to the grave."

Edvard Grieg came six weeks later to Berlin, this time on his homeward way from Italy, and surely it must have been with strange feelings that he now sought his friend—at the Jerusalemer Kirchhof. To Grieg's noble character, to his deep and true feeling for Rikard Nordraak, both as artist and man, the letter he wrote to Rikard's father from Berlin bears witness:

"Berlin, May 7, 1866.
"Hr. Nordraak,
"Christiania.

"It is with a heavy heart that I take up my pen to send you a few lines from this city of sorrow. I could have answered your friendly letter from the South, but I have the conviction that it is best like this; why in the first overwhelming moments of grief pour more gall into the bitter cup you must empty? What I must have written then could only have been an echo of the darkness and desolation that enveloped me. I do not know how the love of a father compares with that of a true friend, I only know that I loved Rikard with all my heart. I know what I had to suffer in leaving him, my best friend, upon a sick bed, in seeing love and solicitude misunderstood, in having to hang about in suspense and anxiety for five long months in the South and then at last, when hope was beginning to stir in me, to receive the hard tidings that our young national art must pale in death since he who sustained it was no more!

"I know what I went through those days in the South when I could not confide in a living soul, since no one understood my grief. Only in music was there sympathy. To the mournful tones that never failed me in the hour of sorrow I turned and found comfort. They whispered to me that Rikard Nordraak's name will live in our Northern art—his great beautiful idea will endure beyond the oblivion of the grave, for it bears the stamp of truth. 'He who has something to live for cannot die,' he said to me once in a happy intimate moment. That is not true, of course, in the ordinary sense, but I now begin to understand fully the deep significance of his words, and perhaps he used them in the assurance of the ultimate triumph of the idea, even though the body fail before its dreams can be fully realized. But it shall come to fruition. For it shall be the task of my life to carry on the work in his spirit. I feel the responsibility, but I feel also the strength, the courage—double now as though he had bequeathed his to me, as if his fresh, youthful lust of battle had flown to me at his departure and taken up its dwelling in my soul. We had hoped to work together for the advancement of our national art; since that has been denied us, all I can do is to hold faithfully to the promise I gave him that his cause should be my cause, his goal mine.

"Do not think that what he yearned after shall be forgotten; it is my great task to make known his few works of genius to the people—to our Norwegian people—to fight for their recognition and build upon their strong foundation.

"What he wanted was still too new to take root in the people, but a time is coming when the national consciousness will be clearer, the desire to cultivate it greater, and the name of every one who in his own way has worked towards that end will be written in indelible letters in our history. And among these, if art has any deep national significance, will be named among the first: Rikard Nordraak! Therefore be comforted—let him rest softly here in this foreign land, his soul will hover over his home where his cause shall live and conquer!

"I beg you not to misunderstand these lines, they come from a heart that has felt for friend and for artist. Both have meant to me more than I can say, and love veiled in sorrow will keep them treasured in my memory.

"And now, goodbye. In the hope that some day, in Christiania, I may learn to know you personally, I sign myself yours faithfully,

"Edvard Grieg.

"The enclosed oak leaf is from Rikard's grave at the Jerusalemer Kirchhof. It lies in an open and beautiful position, looking out to the city."

Of Grieg's first stay in Rome there is little to relate. It seems to have been difficult for him to find peace and power of concentration enough for artistic work. A first visit to Rome offers besides such a profusion of impressions and experiences that they are in themselves enough. Grieg was a diligent frequenter of the Scandinavian club and here he met for the first time Henrik Ibsen, who had not perhaps an altogether stimulating influence on his "national" enthusiasm. A couple of years before, the poet had, with justified bitterness, turned his back on his fatherland. In Grieg's autograph album he wrote the following warning words to the composer who, in spite of all, meant to settle in the homeland and dedicate his powers to the service of Norwegian culture:

Orpheus woke with crystal tones
Souls in brutes; struck fire from stones.

Stones there are in Norway plenty:
Brutes far more than ten or twenty.

Play, so stones spark far and wide!
Play, to pierce the brutes' thick hide!

During his stay in Rome, Grieg made his first trial of the orchestra as an instrument and wrote the overture "I Höst" (In Autumn). The material is taken from "Autumn Storm" and it is clear that the composer felt a need to deepen this romance, already broadly designed, by the employment of the richer resources of the orchestra. What the overture was like in its original shape it is not now easy to find out. The edition now published is the result of a remodeling undertaken by Grieg at the end of the Eighties, when the overture was performed for the first time by an orchestra at a music festival in Birmingham in 1888. The thematic material is almost identical with that of the romance, but the form has been expanded and an introduction and coda have been added. The strength of the work lies, as is so often the case with Grieg, in its nature impressions. There is a charming blending of the melancholy and cheerful reflections on the time of the year that the subject—autumn—gives rise to, and the overture ends very effectively with the joyous song-dance of the harvesters.

There is no doubt that if "In Autumn" has not easily won a footing in the concert hall, it is because of weaknesses of form. It must be admitted that it is a little too spun out. This applies specially to the development, which does not show the material in any new light but confines itself chiefly to repeating the theme, or scraps of it, in different keys, so that when the repeat proper comes, interest has already weakened. Had Grieg shaped a set of short, concise nature pictures out of the given material, his autumn overture, with its inspired subject and its pictorial motives would have won a popularity comparable to the stage scenes of *Peer Gynt*.

Grieg's musical language has quite another strength and intensity in his funeral march for Nordraak. Here he uses the simple form of which he is always master and through which his thoughts and feelings express themselves with perfect freedom. After the beginning, with its muffled chords and its alternation between major and minor, so typical of Grieg, outbursts of pain come with a rending violence.

Grieg himself was very fond of his funeral march and on his tours in later years he always had it with him, orchestrated for a military orchestra. He had early decided that it was to be played at his own funeral. The manuscript, which is to be found in the Bergen library, is dated Rome, April 6, 1866.

The summer brought Grieg again to Denmark, where he took organ lessons from his friend Matthison-Hansen. It was a question of making a living and Grieg had two posts as organist in Christiania in his mind's eye.

On July 9 his father wrote from Bergen: "I wish with all my heart that I could do something to help you to a means of livelihood. There is plenty of time for the posts you mentioned as organist in Christiania, as only one of the churches has been begun and that not so very long ago."

Grieg had also another post in view which would have enabled him to earn a steady income; the position of conductor of the orchestra in the theater at Christiania where Björnson was director. In a letter from Ibsen, found among Grieg's posthumous papers, we get a clear idea of how much Grieg's heart was set on it. This letter, like the Nordraak letters, has not hitherto been known to any but the recipient. It runs as follows:

"Frascati, the 24th of August, '66.

"Dear Grieg,

"I hope you have long since had an answer from Björnson. Your letter was rather old when it reached me out here; but I wrote at once to Björnson and, though I am afraid that my letter would reach him first in Stockholm, he has had time enough now to think. Uncertainty about his own future position with the theater is sure to have been the reason for his silence. But whatever the outcome may be, you have no right to say that it is a question of your whole future. No, dear Grieg, your future is something more and better than the post as conductor of an orchestra; it would be ungrateful of you to estimate the talents given you according to so low a standard, but I know quite well what you mean. Please rest assured that I have put your case briefly but strongly to Björnson and have told him what you are. I expect that the disputes in the theater will soon be settled, and then I hope to hear of your appointment. Bear no grudge against Björnson—I am sure that he is not against you. Write him once more, if necessary, tell him that he *must* let you have the post; make him responsible if he refuses, and if the thing doesn't come off you can show by your musical deeds what a mess they have made of things, and the whole affair will seem like a momentary postponement, nothing more. Only don't be discouraged; you have neither reason nor right to be. Good luck to you; my wife sends many greetings, as does also your devoted

"Henrik Ibsen."

But Grieg did not get the post—fortunately, perhaps we may say. Hennum was appointed soon after.

It goes without saying that during his summer stay in Denmark Grieg called on Gade to show him his new work for orchestra, the overture "In Autumn." Grieg relates in a letter to Iver Holter on January 8, 1897, that the reception this time was anything but encouraging.

"The song 'Autumn Storm,' written at Rungsted in 1865 to words of Richardt's, I used during the winter in Rome as the basis for the overture 'In Autumn.' When I brought it to Copenhagen and showed it to Gade, he said, 'This is trash, Grieg; go home and write something better.' I went home—and with respect be it said, wept. The overture was not well orchestrated—that I remember. So, from sheer want of courage, I let it lie, arranged it as a duet, and played it at home with Nina. In this form I sent it to a competition arranged by the Swedish Academy. The judges were Rietz in Dresden, Söderman in Stockholm, and—Gade in Copenhagen. The overture won the prize, was printed and published as a duet in Stockholm. (Obviously Gade had forgotten all about it.) Such is the way of the world!

"In 1887 I orchestrated the piece again and published the score at Peters'."

With the summer of 1866, Grieg's student days and wander years were over. He proposed now to settle down in his homeland and shape himself a future. Filled with glowing enthusiasm for the national idea called to life by Nordraak and with a faith in the possibility of its realization which he believed to be justified by the results already achieved, he set out in autumn for Norway to make his home in Christiania.

CHRISTIANIA PERIOD
1866-1874

ON THE first page of *Morgenbladet* for September 14, 1866, there is an article entitled "On Norwegian Music and Some Compositions of Edvard Grieg's," which fills several columns. The article is unsigned, but it is obvious at once that the writer is a musician and one with both knowledge and insight and, indeed, with very decided opinions as to how the interests and possibilities of Norwegian music can best be advanced and safeguarded. The main idea in the rather detailed article, which runs through two numbers of the paper, is to point out the possibilities of our folk music as the basis of an independent Norwegian "art" music. The introduction runs as follows: "In a time like ours when nationality in all its relationships plays so prominent a part, the importance of the movement amongst us towards developing the national element in language, poetry, and art will be quickly realized and, by whatever different ways we seek to reach it, we shall all work towards the same end, the independent development and advancement of the nation. In regard to music also, an active striving towards nationalism has for some time manifested itself—in different ways many have been working towards the same end—the lifting up of folk music into the realm of art. A glance at these movements with some suggestions as to the means by which our national music, as one feature of the whole, can be developed into something greater, more universal, may not, therefore, be without profit."

There follows a long discourse on our folk music, in which certain of its special characteristics are pointed out. Then the author goes on to say that "if our folk music, as I believe, has in it the vital force necessary for its development into an original and national musical art, now is the time to try to fill with its spirit the large musical forms which the art of the great cultured nations has fostered." The author outlines also the tremendous difficulties Norwegian music is faced with, since in art music we are without tradition and so are forced from the beginning to appropriate a foreign musical language from which we must later free ourselves. And in this there is no little danger, because in foreign music schools, though we come into contact with a fresher, fuller art life, we find no trace of our native notes.

On the other hand, the author sounds a note of warning against the over-enthusiastic "emotionalists"—necessary, no doubt, to awaken and sustain the national consciousness—who are afraid that learning may stifle the germ of national growth and who insist not only that the national spirit must be sought for among the peasants, but that every form of *expression* also must be taken directly from this source. No—study there must be, the author maintains, a fundamental study of what is established and unshakable. Otherwise there is the risk that the people will be given back practically unchanged the material taken from them, and in that way one gets not a step further.

After mentioning what had already been achieved in Norwegian art music by Waldemar Thrane, Ole Bull, Lindeman, and Kierulf, the author comes to Grieg's compositions, which he discusses very fully. He seems specially enthusiastic over the piano sonata; the violin sonata, he concedes, is no doubt superior in fluidity of style and beauty of form, but with all its advantages of form it does not make the same fresh impression as the piano sonata. "The truth is that the subjects sometimes lack interest and that it suffers from the influence of Gade, which may be very beneficial where form is concerned, but is unsound in regard to ideas. But it is easy to see why Grieg thus drew near to Gade; he imagined, no doubt, that in him he would find a compatriot in art, but it is to be hoped that he has already awakened from this illusion."

Of the Humoresques he goes on to say: "Here he begins to rattle his chains—a sign of a strong spirit which, realizing that it has been fettered by foreign hands, and exasperated beyond bearing, can contain itself no longer." Of the first works, *Four Pieces*, *Poetical Tone Pictures*, and *Heart Melodies*, the author says little, though he admits that they bear witness to an unusual talent, but their relationship is rather to the composer's own development than to Norwegian music. The whole article is written with warmth and enthusiasm and contains ideas and observations that even now are of vital importance, as for example the necessity for the study of fundamentals which he emphasized in opposition to the "emotionalists" who saw in this a danger to nationalism.

It was Otto Winter-Hjelm who in this instructive way raised his voice in support of the works of Edvard Grieg and greeted his colleague and brother in art with a "welcome home."

Not long after the appearance of the article it was announced in the leading Christiania newspaper, that Edvard Grieg was coming to town in the middle of October and would take pupils. Immediately after, Grieg advertised that his first concert would take place on Monday, October 15. Fru Wilhelmine Norman-Neruda and the singer Fröken Nina Hagerup were also to take part. In more than one respect the concert was calculated to arouse attention. It was not only Edvard Grieg's first appearance in the capital after having already made his début both in Copenhagen and Leipzig, but for the first time the programme consisted exclusively of the works of Norwegian composers! The giver of the concert himself played his piano sonata and his Humoresques and, with Fru Norman-Neruda, his violin sonata; in addition he accompanied Nina Hagerup in songs by Kierulf, Nordraak, and himself. Both *Morgenbladet* and *Aftenbladet* praised the concert unreservedly.

Naturally, there were great rejoicings over the event which, besides being an artistic success, helped to fill the coffers. "There was nothing but Norwegian music in that same concert (!) and it brought me in about 150 Specie dollars (!). Above all, this good beginning has given me courage and trust in the future," wrote Grieg to Matthison-Hansen.

His parents and brothers and sisters, who were informed by telegram of the happy result, were delighted and hurried to write letters of congratulation. "You made a great début in Christiania," writes his younger sister Elisabeth. "Had you expected a reception like that? Though I had greater hopes than father, they were by no means so great as not to have been exceeded now. A thousand congratulations, dear Edvard; I cannot tell you how absolutely delighted I am."

His mother, too, who wrote as a rule very seldom, now took up her pen:

"My dear Edvard,

"I must send you a few lines to tell you, no doubt quite superfluously, how deeply happy and thankful I am over your success. A thing like that is exalting: it puts you into the frame of mind that is essential if you are to make the most of yourself in the situation in life you desire to reach. It is of as great importance for you and your spiritual life to feel yourself understood to some extent by the outer world as it is for me, in my walk of life, to feel that my devotion to those near and dear to me and my ways of showing openly my interest in them is not an embarrassment to them but, on the contrary, is *for them also* something necessary to their happiness. Yes—there is one thing certain: the greatest and best things in life derive from the blessing of reciprocity!"—Then she ends by saying: "But Edvard, you wretch, how could you put us off with a telegram? You know so well—all too well—how dear you are to us. Cannot that knowledge wake a kindred feeling, a desire to let us know in some detail as quickly as possible all that concerns you?

"Good-bye, Edvardman!

"Your never changing mother,

"Gesine Grieg."

THE ACADEMY OF MUSIC—CONDUCTOR OF THE
PHILHARMONIC SOCIETY

EVERYTHING looked bright for Grieg now. The musical public of the capital took him up warmly, and he was much sought after as a teacher. The Harmonic Society, which had been at a standstill for a time for want of support, availed themselves of his popularity and appointed him as conductor. And, finally, Winter-Hjelm sought his collaboration in order to make a reality of his dream of founding a Norwegian academy of music. So there were tasks enough and Grieg took hold with the courage and enthusiasm of youth. Of special interest is the attempt he and Winter-Hjelm made to launch a Norwegian academy of music. There were so many significant features in their reasons for thinking a seat of learning necessary that a part of the long prospectus which was published in *Morgenbladet* on December 12, 1866, will be included here. It is clear that it was Nordraak's nationalistic idea that had come to life again. But now Grieg could build upon his own experience—he knew for himself now what it meant to have to work his way into an art alien to him, only to have to attempt afterwards to find a way back to what was originally his own. It was with the strength of personal experience, therefore, that he could express himself in the prospectus as follows:

Though we wish the national element to be respected, we do not, of course, intend by this any narrow desire for isolation. We wish only that the student of music should learn to know also those things which are his own heritage, which lie nearest him and are perhaps best adapted to work fruitfully upon his imagination; then, when he is ushered into the presence of all the power and grandeur of foreign music, he will not be so overwhelmed that the impression of his homeland's music is effaced—as is, alas, so often the case now. Then if the student has thoughts of his own to develop and shape, he will achieve his end much more easily than if, having worked himself with all his strength into foreign music, he has to free his thoughts from it again, since his work has not been grounded in the tunes that have been sung into him from the cradle up. And time will be saved in development if the student keeps his national stamp. He will learn to appreciate what is beautiful and perfect in our melodies and when later he wishes to follow in the footsteps of the great masters, he will not imitate their mannerisms and special peculiarities but their greatness and perfection in the development of their own individual ideas.

These words, alas, are even today sadly applicable to Norwegian music, and everyone working at the creation of music in this land may profitably pin them up on his wall for contemplation and consideration.

On January 9, 1867, the Academy of Music announced: "Since a sufficient number of pupils have sent in their names, the Academy will begin work on Monday, the 14th. Pupils are requested to meet at the house of the undersigned, Grieg, on Thursday, the 10th, at 8 p.m. for a conference."

Grieg now began also his arrangements for the Philharmonic concerts, three of which were planned for the winter season. The principal item in the first concert, which was held on February 2, was Beethoven's Fifth Symphony. The following advance notice in *Morgenbladet* gives a rather comical glimpse into the primitiveness of the musical conditions then existing: "We would request the audience to put their cloaks, coats, and other encumbrances out of their minds during the finale of the symphony (Beethoven's Fifth) and to remain in their seats till the last bar, so that everyone may have the pleasure of hearing this brilliant piece of music to the end." The concert was very well attended and Grieg's conductorship highly praised. "The conductor displayed much self-possession and energy and acquitted himself very well. The only criticism we have to make is that the tempo in the overture to *The Magic Flute* and in the first movement of the symphony was rather slow."

At the second concert on March 23, the adagio, intermezzo, and finale of Grieg's own symphony were performed, besides the first part of Gade's choral work *Korsfarerne* (The Crusaders). Of Grieg's symphony, *Morgenbladet* said that it was received with applause and played with spirit and, considering the small number of rehearsals, very well. The reporter finds also that it requires a good deal of brain-racking on the listeners' part "as the main outlines do not always come out clearly." The critic suggests that this is because the work took shape in the high summer of the romantic movement, when not much weight was laid on beauty of form, if the subject matter showed talent. At the third and last concert on April 13, the principal item was Winter-Hjelm's new symphony in

B minor; ballads of Nordraak's for male voices and his scene from *Sigurd Slembe* were also performed.

To his Danish friend, Emil Hornemann, Grieg wrote: *"Sigurd Slembe* created a tremendous furore here. I have reorchestrated it so that it rings out more powerfully. You should have heard our students' choir. This was something altogether different from the performance in Denmark. It gripped me so strongly as I conducted that a kind of shudder went through me."

Now the first season was over and Grieg seems to have been satisfied. He wrote to Hornemann on May 5 asking to be allowed to resign his directorship of Euterpe. "I am now so sure of my work up here that it is quite likely I may not come back to Denmark, and to keep my name would be an empty form.—You have worked like a horse at Euterpe this winter—though not harder than I at the Philharmonic here. And I have besides the Academy and private teaching. It is not difficult to see what is going to become of the composer. But wait—that will come all right."

MARRIAGE—HALVDAN KIERULF AND JOHAN SVENDSEN

IT WAS of great importance for Grieg that from a purely financial standpoint his prospects now seemed so good that he could, without too much anxiety, lead his young bride to the altar. As early as December, he wrote to Matthison-Hansen: "After a winter brought to a successful conclusion, I am coming back to the green woods happier than I have ever been before. Down there, under the bright arches, I shall meet my little maid, go with her to church, and from there our course will be laid homeward towards the coast of Norway, where I shall live and work. It is a wonderful thought, a wonderful blending of rapture and sadness. It is my enthusiasm for the nationalistic idea that makes me reconcile myself to my fatherland as a dwelling place for an artist, but there are dark moments when the future looks clouded because of the complete isolation and the lack of any artistic influences up here. Still—if I have no individuality, nothing is lost; if I have any, it will certainly carry me through in spite of everything—that is my comfort."

In a letter of May 5, he wrote to Emil Hornemann: "Next month I am coming to Denmark, but only for a short time—three or four days. The fact is that I am getting married. But we must meet somehow."

In the beginning of June Grieg came to Denmark and on June 11, 1867, the wedding took place in Copenhagen. Relations with the parents-in-law were anything but good, and moods at the marriage were subdued. Fru Grieg relates that during the whole period of his betrothal Grieg was never in his father-in-law's house; if he wanted to see Nina they had to arrange meetings in the streets in Copenhagen or out in the woods. In a letter to Matthison-Hansen Grieg writes: "Relations with Nina's parents were, as you know, bad, so don't go there." And when one hears the words with which Fru Hagerup bewailed her future son-in-law, one gets a strong impression that it really was bad. "He *is* nothing, *has* nothing, and writes music no one will listen to." That was not exactly encouraging to a young artist.

The singer, Stenberg, who even then was a warm admirer of Grieg, tried to comfort the mother-in-law. Enthusiastically he exclaimed, "Only be patient, one day he will be world-famous!"

Grieg himself had no intention of letting himself be cowed by the scepticism either of his parents-in-law or of his own parents. Shortly after the wedding he went off with his young bride to Christiania, where in Övre Voldgate 2 iv he had arranged a very plain and modest but comfortable little home. And now for the moment he was on holiday, now he was free from all duties, so now to work!

In three weeks' time, in the month of July, he wrote his second violin sonata in G major. If we regard this sonata as an autobiographical work, as we well may along with most of Grieg's works, we get a very good glimpse into the young artist's indomitable courage and his delight in life. It begins certainly with a lento doloroso, but that only helps to set the rest of the sonata's contents in relief. At once, in the introductory bars on the piano, we meet the typical Grieg combination: octave, seventh, fifth, and when the violin breaks in with a baroque and highly imaginative passage we are not for an instant in doubt as to whom we have before us! Exactly as in the first violin sonata, the composer here too prepares a surprise. Were we to judge from the introduction, we should imagine that it was with highly serious and fateful problems the twenty-four year old composer meant to deal. Instead of which, off he goes into a spring dance! A spring dance as principal subject in the first movement of a sonata in classical form, that was a bold bit of work. Grieg has been abused for it by critics with conservative views. The second subject in elegiac mood forms no very strong contrast, for here too the dance rhythm soon takes the upper hand, and the whole movement shows what a strong impression Grieg had received from Norwegian folk-dance music and with what ability and understanding he could introduce this apparently alien material into the classical sonata form.

The second movement, allegretto tranquillo, goes like the first in three-fourths rhythm and, in spite of its basically elegiac character, here too the folk-dance rhythm is lurking and breaks through again and again. Grieg has never, as is well known, written a sustained adagio movement; his lively Bergen blood makes itself felt even in slow movements, and soon one is swept away in a whirlpool of passion—so it is here. But exactly as in the andante of the

piano sonata he breaks off suddenly and slips in one of his magnificent nature tone-pictures. In this trio movement, Gerhard
Schjelderup sees before him the Hardangerfjord, shining mirror-
like with picturesque farms and blossoming fruit trees; a boat
with bride, bridegroom, and fiddler rows slowly past. Well, each
listener can feel and think what he will, and in the case of this trio
movement all listeners must receive a strong impression of Norwegian nature, whether or not Hardanger be the actual scene
visualized. For some, perhaps, the greatest charm of this movement will be in its pathetic longing for nature. Grieg wrote the
sonata in the middle of summer in Christiania, and at a time, moreover, when he had never even set eyes on Hardanger!

The last movement reverts to the fundamental mood of the first
and is built up exclusively on dance rhythms. It crowns in the most
beautiful way this wonderful youthful work and is like a radiant
hymn to the joy of life, expressed through glowing colors and buoyant rhythms. Speaking broadly, the basic mood of the G major
sonata is the same as in the F major sonata of two years before,
but the ideas are more original, the style bolder and more daring,
while the rhythmic elements play a more prominent part and are
besides better differentiated.

Joy in life, youthful exultation and sense of power the two sonatas have in common, and though the G major sonata shows a
richer alternation between light and shadow, one can very well
understand the German musical writer who says of this sonata
that "one may justly assume that its composer has been a thoroughly happy man." Happy indeed Grieg felt himself this summer,
yes, perhaps even more than that.

At the end of July, just when he was at work on this sonata, his
father wrote in answer to a letter Grieg had sent him: "It seems as
though your success had made you arrogant, and that you know
is the thing I least of all can tolerate."

If for a time now Grieg felt full of mettle, perhaps even over-full,
it stood him in good stead. Soon it began to be evident that the
exuberant interest with which he had been received at first in the
capital did not go very deep. Like many another, Grieg found out
what it meant to work in a society that was almost without cultural qualifications to understand his work. That in itself might
well be hard for an artist, but what certainly wore him down much

*Nina Hagerup Before Her Marriage
to Grieg*

Edvard Grieg in 1868

more was the scepticism with which several of his own colleagues gradually came to regard his work. And, finally, there were the third factors of envy and malice, these two fungous growths that with the inevitability of a law of nature spring up in the shadow of every artist with personality who wants to do anything out of the common.

Just after he had finished the violin sonata, Grieg wrote to Matthison-Hansen that he was looking forward to Svendsen's coming so that he could hear his sonata played: "He is really the only one to whom I dare give it—the other violinists all hate me from envy apparently; with them it is as Andersen says somewhere, they point out only the weaknesses and do not, or will not, see what is good. It must look as though I were fortunate in my new connections and surroundings, but in reality it is not so. Most people hate my compositions, even musicians. For some they are certainly a closed book and such cases are forgivable, but there are those who do understand them and behave towards me as if they admired them but to others say they wouldn't give a penny for them. Kierulf is among them, and that is less than generous."

With regard to Kierulf, the hurt feeling which Grieg gives expression to here was probably of a passing nature. The relationship between the two composers gradually became of the best. But there are many things which suggest that Grieg had grounds for what he said. The explanation is to be found, first and foremost, in Kierulf's attitude towards Norway's nationalistic endeavors in the domain of art and literature as a whole.

When Gerhard Schjelderup in his Grieg biography in 1903 wrote of Kierulf that he was a martyr who was done to death by his miserably straitened circumstances, Grieg thought it necessary to correct this, and wrote to Schjelderup: "It won't do to call Kierulf a martyr. He received much recognition amongst those who understand music and it was only his illness (consumption) that did him to death, if such an expression must be used.—No, Kierulf's was no miserable fate. It interested him to give lessons and he had always more offers than he could undertake. And he was not at all so badly off. Take it all in all, he had a brilliant life on the high places of that period, especially perhaps in the Welhaven circle."

Though this is a matter of a correction only, one cannot avoid noticing the reserved tone which, in spite of all his appreciation and admiration, marks also Grieg's article on Kierulf in *Musika-*

lisches Wochenblatt for 1879 on the occasion of the publication of
the first collected edition of his works. But we must remember that
the contrast between them was great. Kierulf was by this time an
older and certainly a disappointed man, while Grieg was full of
youth's enthusiasm for and faith in his nationalistic ideas. But that
Grieg cherished much affection for Kierulf and that all his life he
was a warm admirer of his best romances, there can be no doubt.
He realized too that Kierulf's work in the service of Norwegian
music fell in a time even more difficult than that in which he himself lived. Shortly after Kierulf's death in 1868, Grieg gave several
concerts to raise funds for the bust that now stands in Kierulf's
Square in Oslo.

A much warmer tone, however, is heard both in Grieg's letters
and articles when he is speaking of Johan Svendsen, who in the
autumn of 1867 came home from Leipzig and gave two concerts
consisting in part of his own compositions. "Today I have been at
the rehearsal for Johan Svendsen's concert and heard his symphony," Grieg writes on October 8 to Matthison-Hansen. "What
good fun! The most sparkling talent, the boldest national tone, and
a really brilliant manner of handling an orchestra. All, all had my
fullest sympathy and took hold of me with irresistible power."

And after the concert, which took place on October 12, there was
in *Aftenbladet* a long enthusiastic notice written by Grieg: "Today
Norwegian art has celebrated one of its triumphs. For a triumph
it must be called when an audience, unenlightened in a musical
sense and consisting only of a few hundreds, is so carried away by
the absolutely new and great that it forgets that the symphony—
'art music,' as it is called—is its hereditary enemy and breaks out
in enthusiastic applause. The concert opened with Svendsen's
symphony in D major—a work that gives a glimpse into an individuality so great that it would be easier to write books than
pages about it. What above all produces so excellent an effect in
this symphony, naturally and unconsciously in the case of the non-
musical listener but resulting for the musician in a refreshing sense
of calm, is the perfect balance between ideas and technique." The
following observation on Svendsen's orchestration is interesting:
"His skill in orchestration may well be compared with that of the
North's foremost master in orchestration, Niels W. Gade, and it is
interesting to observe how his principles in regard to the handling
of the instruments go in precisely the opposite direction. Gade tries

as much as possible to blend the tone colors so that they melt together into one great broad character. Svendsen, on the contrary, deliberately separates groups of instruments that reciprocally answer one another. Hence, the uniformly soft color with Gade and the sharp contrasts with Svendsen."

The long report which describes in detail each item of the programme ends with a complaint about the poor attendance: "In the big Lodge Hall there were assembled yesterday about four hundred persons. Of these, about one-third had bought tickets. That an artist like Johan Svendsen, after such a pecuniary result, should shoulder his knapsack and take his leave rather sooner than later, is very natural. But it will be deplorable if nothing is done to keep him among us. We have only a few men of great talent of our own, but enough perhaps to bring a real art life into being by mutual effort. We are confident that Johan Svendsen would not have deserted us if the reception given him by the public had not forced him to it. It is a dreary thought, but it must be uttered nevertheless, that if the public continues to behave towards the best of our own men as it has done thus far, in no long time Norwegian music at home will be merely a phrase, whilst abroad, and especially in enlightened Germany, it will find the recognition it deserves.

"Svendsen already proposes to leave us next week—apparently for Leipzig."

DIFFICULT TIMES—ALEXANDRA GRIEG

FOR a time Grieg was alone in the struggle and his youthful courage was more than once put to a hard test. On October 14, the Philharmonic Society announced that four concerts were to be given during the winter under the leadership of Edvard Grieg. But only a couple of weeks later the newspapers announced that the Philharmonic had broken up for want of support. "Our musical affairs are in a pretty mess just now," wrote Kierulf to Erslev on October 24. "It looks as though the Philharmonic Society is going to come to grief, which, of course, it has often done, only to begin again and carry on more splendidly than before. But this time things look serious; and then Grieg will probably try what he can do at his own risk."

Sure enough, on October 31 Grieg invited subscriptions to a series of concerts of his own with the same programme as the Philharmonic. "As I anticipate that a not small number of former members of the Philharmonic Society will subscribe, I will take the liberty of sending them tickets which, of course, they will be at liberty to keep or not, as they wish." And indeed so many subscribers joined that Grieg felt justified in going ahead. On December 12 the first concert was launched with the performance of Mozart's G minor symphony, a selection from Beethoven's *Egmont* music with connecting poems from the German recited by Laura Gundersen. Of Norwegian music, the programme contained Grieg's funeral march for Nordraak for a large band of wind instruments, and some romances of Kierulf's, sung by Fru Nina Grieg.

A month before Grieg had himself given a concert at which mainly his own works were performed, amongst them the new violin sonata, which he played with Gudbrand Böhn. The overture, "In Autumn," was arranged for the occasion "for two pianos for eight hands" and opened the very full programme which included also two quartets for male voices, "Björneskytten" (The Bear Hunter) and "Aftenstemning" (Evening Reverie) to poems by Jörgen Moe. Grieg's Gavotte and Minuet for piano and violin were also given. These two numbers appear often at Grieg concerts throughout the years, but since among Grieg's works no gavotte for piano and violin is to be found, it was justifiable to wonder whether this was not merely an "occasional piece" which the composer suppressed later. The work has been found, however, amongst Grieg's posthumous papers and we see that the gavotte is identical with the march "Ved mandjævningen" (The Trial of Strength) from *Sigurd Jorsalfar*, while the minuet is the middle movement of the first violin sonata. To Matthison-Hansen, Grieg wrote of these concerts on December 23, 1867: "They don't bring in a penny, you may be sure of that, but I must have this sort of thing if I'm to keep going; all the rest of my time I spend giving lessons so that my wife and I shan't starve up here."

It was with no little bitterness that Grieg in after life looked back on this period in Christiania when almost all his energy went in instructing young ladies who wished to play the piano, instead of being available for creative work. It was almost only the summer holidays that allowed him the peace and concentration necessary for a creative artist. "I never compose"—he wrote in the already mentioned letter to Matthison-Hansen—"have neither the time nor the desire. I am completely unmusical."

A hitherto unknown letter to the Danish music publisher Emil Erslev gives the impression that he was already beginning to feel the crippling influence of despondency. But far worse times were coming! The letter is dated Christiania, December 29, 1867, and after a few words on matters of business it goes on: "Here I sit in a corner of the world craving to work and to cooperate in the life of art. If you had an organist's post for me I would come at once to Denmark and would gladly write you a song a week. That I am willing on such conditions to forsake Norway you can blame on the state of things up here. I will come to say, like Björnson in *De Nygifte* (The Newly Married Couple): 'Something is dying in me' —if I can't get away. Till summer then, when I hope to greet you in dear, beautiful Denmark. Then I shall compose, and forget all dullness and pettiness. It is not because none are born that Norway has no eminent artists in music, but because all are suffocated in their homes before they can develop and because, as a rule, economic pressure makes it impossible for them to free themselves. A painful truth. But my determination not to be beaten is as great as is my awareness of the danger. If I can get a stipend, I will be off to Leipzig with the hope of settling there."

At Christmas 1867 there was printed a new work by Grieg, *Lyriske Smaastykker* (Lyrical Short Pieces) for the piano, Opus 12. The volume contains eight pieces for the piano and Grieg here, for the first time, breaks the ground he was later to cultivate with so great success. That Schumann had served as his model is not difficult to see in "Arietta" which opens the collection and in which we clearly mark the master's influence, both thematically and in the handling of the instrument. The following waltz is very much more independent, though both in it and in the "Album-blad" (Album Leaf) Chopin's influences can be felt. "Vækter-sang" (The Watchman's Song), composed after a performance of Shakespeare's *Macbeth*, is a deeply impressive lyrical, emotional picture. In the intermezzo, where we hear the voice of the ghosts in the night and the watchman's shout, we observe how Grieg with the simplest materials contrives to stimulate the imagination. "Alfedans" (Dance of the Elves) too shows genuine inspiration, subtle in its pictorial effect. "Folk-song" and "Norwegian" reveal in different ways the composer's intimate relationship with Nor-wegian nature and peasant life. The collection ends with "Fædre-landssang" (Song of the Fatherland), a powerful, pathetic com-position in the usual quartet style. This it was—we shall shortly hear more of it—which so aroused Björnson's enthusiasm that he immediately wrote words for it. It is now best known in Norway as a song for a male choir to Björnson's text.

We swing into the year 1868, which to begin with did not pro-duce any great changes in Grieg's daily life. He went on with his piano lessons and his teaching at the Academy of Music; he con-ducted the rehearsals for his subscription concerts and in the few leisure moments left he wrote a cantata for the unveiling of the Christie[1] monument. The manuscript, which is dated April 27, 1868, is to be found in Bergen's Public Library and shows that the rather dull and commonplace text has given birth to similarly commonplace and uninteresting music. The cantata for large choir and orchestra was performed on May 17 in Bergen, once only.

On February 18 the second subscription concert took place. At the third concert, the very young pianist Agathe Backer took part as soloist in Beethoven's E flat major concerto and on

---

[1] President of the first Storting, 1814.

April 4 the last concert of the season was given with the performance of Mendelssohn's symphony No. 3 in A minor and Gade's
choral work *The Crusaders*. Now there was only the Academy and
private pupils again and the joyful holiday time was drawing near
—the holiday which was the only time that allowed the *composer*
facilities for work! It sounds like a paradox, but it was so in all the
precious years of Grieg's youth, and musical history shows that he
was not the only one who came to look upon holidays in this light.

But shortly before the longed-for holidays, an event occurred
this spring which was perhaps equally longed for in the simple
artist home in Övre Voldgate. On April 10 a little daughter came
into the world, and was baptized Alexandra after her grandfather.
The family letters show with what touching tenderness the event
was regarded by all Grieg's nearest of kin. There was no lack of
good advice and admonishment to the young, unpractical artist
pair, but everything went well and before long Edvard Grieg could
hold a little daughter in his arms and meet a pair of eyes that in
the most beautiful way mirrored his own deep blue child eyes. It
was perhaps apropos of this event that Grieg for the first time made
use of a poem by Ibsen as subject for musical composition. In
"Margrethe's Cradle Song" from *The Pretenders* he found a text
which allowed him to give expression to the feelings animating him
at such a moment:

> To the blue, starry vault
> Open the roof's arched beams,
> And little Haakon flies
> Upon the wings of dreams.
>
> Between the earth and heaven
> See! a steep ladder stands
> And little Haakon climbs
> Holding an angel's hand.
>
> God's little angels guard
> The cradle child in sleep.
> God bless thee, Haakon small,
> Watch too thy mother keeps!

The song, in all its simplicity, is so deeply felt and experienced that
involuntarily Grieg's words to Finck come to our minds: "My
choice of text is always dictated by my experiences." Although it
is only a cradle song he is here dealing with, the composer does not

neglect the opportunity for contrasting color effects. The bright, pure harmonies with which the piano follows the lines of the middle verse form a perfect contrast to the soft coloring indicative of the basic mood, strengthen the effect, and show the picture-making quality of Grieg's imagination. Like a golden streak of sky above the horizon the picture rises before us. And like an under-string which vibrates gently in sympathy, immortal longings find expression.

SÖLLERÖD

BUT NOW summer was drawing near, the glorious holiday time that gave opportunity for work. This time too they went to Denmark, where friends were eagerly waiting. In the beginning of June, Grieg with his wife and little daughter arrived at Copenhagen. The child was put in charge of the grandparents and Grieg and his wife went out to Sölleröd, a little country town an hour's journey from Copenhagen. Here Emil Hornemann and Edmund Neupert had rented for Grieg a gardener's house with two small rooms, and now he was to work! Only in the evenings the friends were to meet in the one inn of the little town for a glass and a chat.

That was a delightful summer, Fru Grieg relates. Edvard was in a fever of eagerness for work and, as always in such periods, in great spirits. Did he get up early in the morning? Far from it. He took things easily, felt that he needed much rest, ate his breakfast, smoked a cigarette, and enjoyed life. No depressing problems, whether of art or life, troubled him. But if once he got to work, it was impossible to get him away from the piano.

It is a well known fact that Grieg, like many others, not only conceived, but worked out his ideas sitting at the piano. In a letter to his parents he happens to make some remarks that give a good insight into his methods of work. In this letter, written from Rome, he says: "I might not perhaps have got as far as writing today, either because I was deep in work, that is I was thumping the piano like a madman so as to forget everything around me—only in that way can I get into the mood—but fate willed that I should hear my neighbors in the next room come home—they are Scandinavians—and that was enough: the mere thought of being criticized in my workroom sends all my ideas flying. I may just as well stop at once. I envy lucky painters, sculptors, and poets who haven't this to battle against."

This excessive sensitiveness about being overheard while at work, which could drive even a Beethoven almost mad, was certainly a great trouble to Grieg and often a direct hindrance to his work. In later years especially, when he travelled much but was able sometimes to remain for a few months in Christiania, Copen-

hagen, or Leipzig, it was an obstacle that he tried in vain to overcome. And here, I dare say, we have the reason why Grieg wrote
many of his best things in small, isolated huts which he sometimes
had built for himself. Even in his early youth his mother arranged
a workroom for him at Landås, a storehouse where Edvard could
give himself up to his work of composition entirely undisturbed, a
workroom he always used when he visited his parents in summer.
When later the family had to sell Landås, the brewer Rolfsen's
pavilion out at Sandviken, near Bergen, was lent to Edvard. Here,
among other things, the fragment of opera, *Olav Trygvason*, and
most of the *Peer Gynt* music came into being. At Lofthus he had a
little hut built so far away from the farm that no one could hear
him. Even when he got his own villa, Troldhaugen, he built a hut
to work in down by the fjord, where he could feel quite safe from
listeners and interruptions. And out at Sölleröd in the summer of
1868 he was safe too; it was arranged among the friends that they
would not disturb one another. Only at rare intervals would
Neupert come to Grieg's house, knock on the window with his long
stick, and say to Fru Grieg, "Shall we go to Höibjerg and leave
Grieg in peace?"

So in this happy summer there came into being the work which,
with *Peer Gynt*, was to do most to make Grieg's name known the
world over and gain him entrance to all concert halls—the piano
concerto in A minor, Opus 16. Divine inspiration can never surely
have translated itself more freely and directly into substance!
Seldom have we felt the freshness and spontaneity of a young
composer's rich and vigorous nature more strongly in music—and
above all never before have nature impressions found a more beautiful and graceful expression within the strict boundaries of the
classical sonata form. It is perhaps this last that gives Grieg's A
minor concerto its incomparable charm and its special assured
place amongst the piano concertos of the whole world.

It is easy then to understand why Gerhard Schjelderup was so
overwhelmed by these nature impressions that he seemed to see
all Norway in its infinite variety and strong magnificent unity before his eyes. And one readily agrees with the enthusiastic author
when he compares the adagio to a lonely mountain tarn girt
around with mountains, which lies dreaming of infinity. . . .

The orchestral introduction is here in itself of an incomparable
beauty and has so great a depth of feeling that it produces the

effect of a revelation rather than of "written" or "composed" music. The last movement crowns in the most beautiful way this work written by a young genius. But from a purely technical point of view also, the young, twenty-five-year old master shows an astounding maturity. The sonata form is handled easily and without constraint and does not seem to put any obstacles in the way of inspiration's flow and free unfolding. As regards form merely, we can see that Schumann's piano concerto has served as pattern, especially in the first movement, which so far as the construction is concerned, runs exactly parallel with the Schumann concerto. But in subject matter Grieg's concerto is wholly original and as regards richness of material stands even above its German twin brother. In melody, rhythm, and not least in the handling of the instrument, Grieg here takes his place beside the greatest masters.

One would have thought now that the world would welcome eagerly this fresh, full spring, this welling up of a new, unknown music. But no, to begin with it was not by any means easy for Grieg's concerto to make its way, especially in Germany, thanks to a narrow-minded and conservative music criticism. Today, when Grieg's piano concerto is found in the repertory of every pianist the world over, it may be of interest to see how a couple of the leading German journalistic writers received the work when in February 1872 it was performed for the first time in Germany at a concert in the Gewandhaus in Leipzig with Fröken Erika Lie[1] in the solo part.

The *Signale's* critic wrote: "Kürzer als über die Suite haben wir uns über die beiden anderen Novitäten zu fassen. Sie wurden mehr oder minder von der Hörerschaft abgelehnt, und leider sind wir nicht in diesem Falle gegen dieses Verhalten Einspruch zu erheben. Es sind eben Produktionen, die wir als in glücklicher Stunde geschaffen nicht bezeichnen können—weder das Grieg'sche Conzert mit seiner setzenhaften Factur und seinem mit Schumann und Chopin durchsetzen und verquickten Skandinavismus.[2] . . ." And the notice ends: "Nun bleibt uns noch zu sagen übrig, dass Frl. Lie in dem unglücklichen und undankbaren Grieg'schen Stück und in den beiden Chopins sich wieder als treffliche Pianistin zeigte."

[1] Later Fru Erika Nissen.
[2] The rest concerns a work of Rubinstein's.

The *Neue Zeitschrift für Musik* wrote in its notice: "Viel Colorit, jedoch etwas wenig Gedanken, originelle Detailwendungen, nordische Farben, reizvolle Mischungen von Dur und Moll, von Gade, Mendelssohn, und Willmers mit etwas Weber und viel Liszt."

Here a rather too eager resemblance hunter has been at work. To discover that Grieg's piano concerto has been brought to birth with the help of five other composers is a little too much of a good thing! Johan Svendsen, who was present at the production, is clearly of a different opinion from the German critics. In a letter of May 5, he wrote to Grieg: "Last winter I at last made acquaintance with your piano concerto. It has, if such is possible, increased the respect and admiration with which I always think of you. It is all so plastically clear, so full of originality, and so magnificently orchestrated that I greet your work as a great step forward in your development."

"That our mutual friend, Bernsdorf,[3] did not let such an occasion pass without showing his endearing qualities was to be expected. Why are you original?—why are you beautiful? . . ."

It goes without saying that there were those at home who saw to it that *Signale's* criticism and no other should appear in the Christiania newspapers.

But there was one who from the very first hailed the new work with warmth and enthusiasm, and that was Edmund Neupert. As a matter of fact, he had watched the concerto as it gradually made its way and followed its forward steps with both anxiety and rapture. It was he also who presented the concerto for baptism, since he played it for the first time in Copenhagen on April 3, 1869.

In a letter dated Copenhagen, April 6, he gives an account of the event: "On Saturday your divine concerto resounded in the great hall of the Casino. The triumph I achieved was tremendous. Even as early as the cadenza in the first part the public broke into a real storm. The three dangerous critics, Gade, Rubinstein, and Hartmann, sat in the stalls and applauded with all their might. I am to send you greetings from Rubinstein and say that he is astounded to have heard a composition of such genius; he would like to make your acquaintance. He expressed himself very warmly about my playing of the piano. I was recalled twice and to finish up was accorded musical honors by the orchestra."

[3] *Signale's* critic.

INTRIGUES—AN APPLICATION FOR A STIPEND AND
A LETTER FROM LISZT

THE period now beginning for Grieg in that precious Norwegian capital was to teach him in sober earnest what it meant for a man of genius to work in narrow circumstances. *Great* sufferings an artist can and must go through and these he can bear even though they leave behind them sore and ugly scars. But malice, venom, intrigues, pettiness, the instinctive attempt of the whole pack to pull down a great personality—all that he cannot bear because it is so crippling. That winter Grieg would certainly have received an injury he would never have got over if help had not come when the need was greatest—from abroad!

In September Grieg with his family was again installed at Övre Voldgate, where he began once more his daily giving of lessons. The Academy of Music was beginning to show the first sign of that decline which before long led to the breaking up of the institution. When Grieg went abroad next year, the whole affair collapsed and with it disappeared the dream of a Norwegian academy—disappeared, never to be revived again. Though we acknowledge gratefully the devoted attempts that have since been made to establish an academy of music in Norway's capital city—such an academy as Ole Bull, Nordraak, and Grieg had dreamed of—the country and the people have not achieved it and there is today little sign that Norway is within measurable distance of achieving it. And yet music is named as Norway's national art above all others. . . .

In the beginning of November Grieg announced as usual four subscription concerts. At the same time he sent an application to the town council for a reduction in the rent of the Lodge Hall. But how dared he do a thing like that? Whom did he presume himself to be? Was it not enough that he had gained for himself an incontestable reputation as an artist? Some indeed in those days called him Mozart—a nickname which held a mixture of fear and admiration. But what was he thinking of now? Did he really mean to use his musical abilities to make money for himself? No—there must be limits. In *Morgenbladet* there popped up a person—anonymous, it goes without saying—who "found it only reasonable that the town council should not grant this application, especially as the concerts which originally were given by a long-established musical society, indifferent as to profit, were now being carried on as the private enterprise of a single man." On November 19 Grieg announced that "the subscription concerts could not, on account of unexpected circumstances, be given as advertised."

It was altogether a mistake, however, to imagine that a stop had been put to Grieg's activities. When three of the first violins demanded an honorarium which exceeded what was possible to pay with the scanty resources at his disposal it certainly meant that Grieg had to forego his orchestra! But that wasn't going to stop him. "Energy is the main thing, and I shall work though my back breaks." These words of his mother's must certainly have run in Edvard's mind at this time. And so he announced subscription concerts without orchestra.

In a letter to Matthison-Hansen Grieg writes on April 10, 1869: "Just imagine, this whole winter I have heard no music except what I have had to do with myself. I have come into collision with the orchestra; some of the first violins demanded 5 dollars each for a concert with three rehearsals. The result of which was that I did without an orchestra, as I didn't want to be arrested for debt on that account. These gentlemen give chamber music evenings, so it is easy to see why they would gladly have my concerts go to the dogs. But—their trick failed. I was determined not to let myself be cheated of my job, changed, or rather gave up, the beautiful programme I had sketched out in Denmark in the summer—and which had cost money enough, since in the summer also I had had the scores written out by the Musical Society in Copenhagen—and prepared a new one consisting of choral works for choir and piano, etc. N.B.: no arrangements, so that the whole had an artistic justification, though not, of course, the same satisfaction for me as works for choir and orchestra. But I was determined now to push my concerts through in some form or other, no matter what—and they went."

Yet Grieg realized that the time had come when he must see to getting away and the sooner the better, even if it were only for a time. Accordingly, he wrote to Gade and Hartmann and to his master at the Conservatory, Ignaz Moscheles, asking them to support an application for a travelling stipend which he intended to send to the government. In addition to letters from those three, he received quite unexpectedly a letter that not only cheered him greatly, but proved to be of the highest importance for his prestige as an artist.

Grieg writes of it to Aimar Grönvold: "It was indeed a distinction of great importance for me that one day in December 1868, just as the darkness seemed thickest in Christiania, I received a letter from Liszt which brought sunlight into my universe. There was at that time no one at home who cared anything at all about me as a creative artist. I had expressed my despondent feelings in a letter to a Roman friend; he had spoken of it to Liszt, who he knew was warmly interested in me, and it shows a very noble trait in Liszt that he sat down immediately at his writing table, conscious of the good he could thereby accomplish. I had thought it worth while to apply for a travelling stipend but had little hope of getting one, since I was in the black books of our conservative musicians and the rest of the ruling music dilettantes. But Liszt's letter worked wonders."

The letter read as follows:

"Monsieur! Il m'est fort agréable de vous dire le sincère plaisir, que m'a causé la lecture de votre sonata (oeuvre 8). Elle témoigne d'un talent de composition vigoureux, réfléchi, inventif, d'excellente étoffe—lequel n'a qu'à suivre sa voie naturelle pour monter à un haut rang. Je me plais à croire, que vous trouvez dans vôtre pays les succès et encouragements que vous méritez: ils ne vous manqueront pas ailleurs non plus: et si vous venez en Allemagne cet hiver, je vous invite cordialement à vous arrêter un peu à Weimar, pour que nous fassions tout à fait bonne connaissance. Veuillez bien recevoir, Monsieur, l'assurance de mes sentiments d'estime et de considération très distingués.

"29 Decbr. 68. Rome.

"F. Liszt."

This letter Grieg enclosed in his application for a stipend and now the unbelievable happened, not only did he get his sti-

pend, but the general feeling completely changed and when in
the spring of 1869 he was leaving Christiania, he was the "recipient of a rain of undeserved compliments from all sides, utterly
mal à propos, in other words, only a result of the compliments imported from Rome." So Grieg expressed himself in a letter to
Grönvold.

In his application for a stipend he explained that since autumn
1866 he had lived uninterruptedly in Christiania, where he had
worked in the service of the national art of music, in part as a
creative and directing artist, in part as a teacher. "This latter
activity has, unfortunately, in a high degree enervated my spirit,"
he wrote, "but I have had to devote myself to it to support myself
and my family. (I have been married since June 1867.) It is therefore my highest hope to win with a sojourn abroad time and peace
for creative activity as well as the opportunity, through intercourse with art and artists, to refresh my mind and widen my
outlook on the ideal which, under the conditions in which I now
live, cannot but be narrowed."

In a letter to Matthison-Hansen on April 10 we find: "I write
you on what is a festival day for me. My little daughter is having
her first birthday. It is delightful to see the happiness round me.
Yesterday too was not less a festival though in another respect, I
received five different letters from dear Denmark speaking of art
and friendship there. Among them was yours. Such an understanding greeting is like a ray of sunshine in my lonely home. Since I
lack anything like it at home and you know well that the ideal life
is conditioned by such things."

After having given a very successful concert for the benefit of a
memorial to Halvdan Kierulf, Grieg went with his family to Bergen to spend the summer with his parents at Landås.

Almost immediately after their arrival at Bergen little Alexandra died, barely thirteen months old. It was a painful blow for
the young parents, and Grieg for many years could not get over his
sorrow at the thought of his child's short life.

Now too it was music that brought him comfort and lightened
his darkness. His song to Kristofer Janson's poem "Millom rosor"
(Among Roses), which was first published many years later, was
written in 1869.

In a garden a mother sat, babe on her knee
    Among roses,
Day long she fondled him, laughing with glee
    Among roses,
On his eyes, on his cheeks her warm kisses she pressed,
Oh, could I but know that through life you would rest
    Among roses, among roses.

The garden lay leafless, no longer they played
    Among roses,
The boy, cold and pale, in his coffin was laid
    Among roses,
Sore weeping the mother bound flowers for his bier,
Now would she see always his resting place here
    Among roses, among roses.

THESE hard times in Christiania, which Grieg thought of later only with bitterness, had one gleam of brightness and that was Björnson. Big and powerful, young, strong, and full of the joy of battle, he stood there and time after time chased doubt and despondency from the door with his unshakeable belief in the future of Norwegian art.

"I must not forget to mention a man who, in the musically empty Christiania years, 1868-1872, filled me with his mighty personality—that was Björnson," wrote Grieg in 1881 to Grönvold. "He was a true friend to me in those years, and it was to him I owe it that I kept up. Although he did not understand music, he believed in me and that put courage in me."

If we look at the list of works composed in these years, we see that it was not only through his powerful personality that Björnson exercised his stimulating effect on Grieg, but even more through his poetry, which provided the material for most of the works that mark these youthful years. Typically enough, the majority of these works are the result of a definite commission from Björnson. Often they were "occasional works" on the part of both.

The first collaboration between the two artists came about in the rather unusual way, that the poet wrote the text to the composer's music and not the other way round. Grieg describes it in the book of commemorative addresses to Björnson on the occasion of his seventieth birthday, in a way that gives a vivid glimpse of their life: "It was Christmas Eve, 1868, at the Björnson's in Christiania. They lived at that time in Rosenkrantzgaden. My wife and I were, so far as I remember, the only guests. The children were wild with joy and excitement. In the middle of the floor there stood in state a huge Christmas tree in the full glory of all its lights. In came all the servants, and Björnson made a little speech, warm and beautiful, as he can do it. 'Now you must play the hymn, Grieg,' he said and though I had a momentary qualm at the thought of officiating at the organ, I, of course, obeyed without a murmur. It was a hymn of Grundtvig, 32—two and thirty—verses long. I accepted my fate with the greatest composure. In the beginning I kept up gallantly, but the endless repetition acted soporifically. Little by little I went into a sort of trance, like a medium. When at last we had wound our way through all the verses, Björnson said: 'Isn't it beautiful? Now I shall read it for you!' And we had all the 32 verses over again. I was completely awed.

"Among the Christmas presents there was a book for me from Björnson, his *Short Pieces*. On the title page he had written, 'Thanks for your *Short Pieces*. Here are some of mine in exchange.' I had that same day presented him with the first part of my newly published *Lyrical Short Pieces*. Among these there was one with the title, 'Song of the Fatherland.' I played this for Björnson who liked it so much that he felt moved to write words for it. Glad was I. Though afterwards I said to myself: Liking is all very well. He has other things to think of. But the very next day I met him to my surprise in the full joy of creation: 'It's going splendidly! It will be a song for all the youth of Norway. But there is something at the beginning I haven't got hold of yet. A particular turn of expression. I feel that the melody requires it and I shan't give in. It will come all right.' So we parted. Next morning, as I sat up in my attic at Övre Voldgate, giving a piano lesson to a young lady, I heard a ring at the door that threatened to bring down the bell, wires and all. Then a rumbling as of wild hordes invading and a bellow: 'Forward! Forward! Hurrah! Now I have it! Forward!' My pupil shook like an aspen leaf. My wife in the next room was frightened out of her wits. But when the door flew open and Björnson stood there beaming like the sun with delight, then there was jubilation! And then we heard that beautiful, just completed poem:

> Forward! was our fathers' battle cry,
> Forward! we, their sons, too shout on high!

The song was sung for the first time by the students at their Welhaven procession in 1868."

On the same occasion too the serenade to Welhaven was produced. This song is not one of Grieg's most important, the text not being very inspiring, and purely technically Grieg seems here, for the first and only time, to adopt the quartet style often used by Kierulf. Grieg is probably right when he says in a letter to Grönvold: "I am not conscious of having been much influenced by Kierulf, in spite of my warm admiration for many of his songs."

It was not always so easy, however, for Grieg, always delicately adjusted, to be ready on the instant with music to fit the multifarious demands made by Björnson. They touched on everything between heaven and earth. Now it was a regatta meeting in Stavanger in 1868 for which "Den Norske Sjömand" (The Norwegian Sailor) had to be set to music, now a political election song, now a cantata for the twenty-fifth anniversary of the Brothers Hals' piano factory in which untuned, old, and overstrained pianos were to find voice! Another time, music had to be written in a hurry for a whole evening's performance of *Sigurd Jorsalfar*. Soon after a bazaar was to be held at the fortress to collect money for the restoration of Trondheim cathedral. That too called for a song and "Landkjending" (Landsighting) resulted. In addition there were the plans for an opera which Björnson hoped now at last to realize! It was not the first time Björnson had had a scheme for an opera in his head. He had before approached Kierulf with the suggestion of musical-dramatic collaboration, and Nordraak's early death had, without doubt, been a sore blow to the optimistic poet in this connection too. Now here was Grieg ready to take hold. A little trial was made with *Arnljot Gelline*, and then a fragment of *Olav Trygvason* came into being. Add to all this, works like *Foran Sydens Kloster* (At a Southern Convent's Gate), "Bergliot," the songs from *Fiskerjenten* (The Fishermaid), "Prinsessen" (The Princess), "Dulgt kjærlighet" (Hidden Love), and "Fra Monte Pincio," which were all composed in these years, and it is clear that for a time Grieg's music was wholly bound up with Björnson. Though it is understandable that Grieg now and again felt as if he were "the passing barrel organ," as he himself expresses it, yet the meeting between him and Björnson was productive of a series of works which so illuminate Norwegian national character, Norwegian landscape and history as to be indispensable to a full and complete picture of our land in the fruitful years of conflict in the latter part of the nineteenth century.

To his last days Grieg treasured the vivid impression made on him in his youthful years by Björnson's overwhelming personality. Nor did he ever forget that it was to Björnson before all others he owed it that he did not in these dark years lose all hope in himself and in the future of Norwegian music.

As late as May 16, 1907, only a few months before his death, he wrote to the friend and spiritual patron of his youth: "Yes, dear

Björnson, I can truly say that the thanks I send you today are more heartfelt than ever before. From the gratitude of youthful emotion has developed the gratitude of comprehension, of conviction. The years have ripened my thankfulness, deepened it, made it richer. May you feel that all I have of good in me is gathered up in that Thank you!"

The summer of 1869, which was passed with his parents at Landås, was the first for many years that Grieg had not been in Denmark, in Danish scenery and among Danish friends. Perhaps it was his longing for life in Denmark that made him occupy himself almost exclusively at this time with Danish poems. Of seven songs dating from this summer, six are written to words of Hans Christian Andersen, while one, "Ungbirken" (The Young Birch) is to the Norwegian poem by Jörgen Moe.

The most important is "Vandring i skoven" (Wandering in the Wood). This gay and charming love song has the fresh and spontaneous emotion of the days of betrothal, and the whole is in the most lovely way framed by the nature impressions which Grieg can always in the clearest and most graceful manner interweave with his personal experiences and moods. "Hun er så hvid" (So White Is She), which Andersen has adapted from the Russian, is matchlessly delicate and pure in feeling and is characterized by a certain reaching out towards the alien and unknown. More reflective is "En dikters sidste sang" (A Poet's Last Song) and "Poesien" (The Poem), while "Hytten" (The Hut) and "Rosenknoppen" (The Rosebud) have charm and naturalness without coming into the first rank of Grieg's important songs. The same may be said of "The Young Birch."

Of much greater interest and much greater importance when one is tracing Grieg's development as an artist is the fact that at Landås this summer for the first time he came into contact with the source that was to supply him with such rich material for future tone poems, Lindeman's collection *Ældre og nyere fjeldmelodier* (Old and New Mountain Melodies). This is the first time Grieg used folk music directly as the basis for his art, and one cannot but notice that his treatment of it is marked by a certain caution. If we compare these Norwegian songs and dances with some of Grieg's earlier original compositions, the Humoresques for example, which have quite another boldness, we can see how mistaken is the view, which some have tried to uphold, that Grieg

owed his Norwegianism and his originality first and foremost to
the circumstance that he used Norwegian folk music as the material for his compositions.

But this collection of twenty-five dances and songs, Opus 17,
which naturally was dedicated to Ole Bull, shows, however, many
interesting features, both as regards harmony and rhythm. If we
compare them with Lindeman's treatment of the same material,
the result is astounding. Folk music is limited to the life from
which it springs. It is completely wrong to imagine that it can be
transplanted, just as it is, to art. Many have tried it with the most
magnificent material, but have fallen miserably short, because
they have not had the ability to infuse the original material with
their own personality. It is here that Grieg succeeds so well, and
thus a great part of our folk-dance music and very many of Norway's most characterful folk songs have been, through Grieg's
treatment, reborn in a form which renders them accessible and
understandable to every music lover the world over.

In the autumn of 1869 Grieg and his wife went on their "stipendium" journey to Italy. In Copenhagen they stayed some little
time and gave two concerts in the hall of the Casino. At the first
concert his last violin sonata, some piano pieces and romances
were performed. At the second, Neupert played the piano concerto,
the composer himself conducting, while the Students' Choral
Society took part with, among other things, "The Serenade to
Welhaven" and "Björneskytten" (The Bear Hunter), to words by
Jörgen Moe.

The rest of the journey and the eventful meeting with Liszt in
Rome Grieg has himself described in his report to the government,
and, especially, in two letters to his parents, so vividly and amusingly, that both letters shall be given here:

"Rome, Feb. 17, 1870.

"Dear Parents!

"This morning we were to have gone out with several Scandinavians to Tivoli for a few days, but what do you think happened? Yesterday afternoon, as I was sitting in the Scandinavian
Club playing whist, in came Sgambati—a very fine pianist,
I think I have spoken of him—bringing a message from Liszt that
he would like to see me at his house the next morning at 11 o'clock.
Though I had been looking forward very much to the Tivoli tour,

this came first, naturally, and the plan was changed. This wasn't, however, my first meeting with Liszt—as you shall now hear. He has, since the beginning of the Council (he can't bear either it or its principles) gone back to Tivoli, where he resides in the Villa d'Este. Very rarely he comes to town and on one such occasion I got to know that he was here, went right away to see him, did not meet him, and left my card. A couple of days later he went away, but just then I met Ravnkilde, the Danish musician, who lives here; he told me that he had just had a note from a German painter whom Liszt had asked to find me out through Ravnkilde. He was to tell me that Liszt was extremely sorry that he had not had time to look me up and to ask if I would come to see him the next morning at 10. He was in town and expecting me. I rushed out to him. He lives close to the Titus Triumphal Arch and the old Roman Forum, in a monastery. But Ravnkilde had told me that Liszt likes people to bring something with them and, alas! my best compositions have been either at home or in Germany for some time now. I had to rush up to Winding to whom I had presented earlier a copy of my last violin sonata and play 'Giver-giver—taker back.' Winding kept the envelope, I took the contents, wrote on the outside 'To Dr. F. Liszt with admiration'—took besides under my arm my funeral march for Nordraak and a booklet of songs (the one with 'Outward Bound' in it) and hurried down the street, with a little qualm at my stomach I won't deny, but that I could have spared myself; for a more lovable man than Liszt it would hardly be possible to find.

"He came smilingly towards me and said in the most genial way, 'Nicht wahr, wir haben ein bischen korrespondiert?' I told him that I had his letter to thank for being where I was, which drew from him a roar of laughter like that of Ole Bull. All the while his eyes, with a certain ravenous expression in them, were fixed on the packet I had under my arm. Ha, ha, I thought, Ravnkilde was right. And his long, spider-like fingers approached to such an alarming degree that I thought it wisest to set about opening the packet at once. He began now to turn over the leaves, that is to say, he read the first part of the sonata through cursorily, and that there was no humbug about the reading was shown by the significant nod, 'Bravo' or 'Sehr schön!' with which he marked the best bits. My spirits began to soar; but when he now asked me to play the sonata my courage altogether failed me. I had never before tried to put the whole thing together for the piano and I would gladly have escaped having to sit and make a mess of it before him. But there was no help for it.

"So I began on his beautiful American grand piano (Chickering). Right at the beginning, where the violin breaks in with a little baroque but national passage, he broke out, 'Ei, wie keck! Nun hören Sie mal, das gefällt mir. Noch einmal bitte!' And when the violin the second time slips into the adagio, he played the violin part higher up on the piano in octaves with such beautiful expression, so remarkably true and singing that I smiled inwardly. These were the first notes I heard from Liszt. And now we went dashing into the allegro, he the violin, I the piano. I got more and more into form, I was so happy over his applause, which in truth flowed so copiously that I felt the most singular thankfulness streaming through me. When the first part was over, I asked him if I might play something for the piano alone and chose the Minuet from the Humoresques, which you no doubt remember.

"When I had played the first eight bars and repeated them he sang the melody with me and did it with an air of heroic power in his bearing that I entirely understood. I saw very well that it was its national character that appealed to him. I had guessed it would be so and had therefore taken things with me in which I had attempted to pluck the national string. When the Minuet was over I felt that, if there was to be any question of getting Liszt to play, it must be now when he was obviously in great spirits. I asked him and he shrugged his shoulders slightly; but when I said that he couldn't surely intend to let me leave the South without having heard a note from him, he mumbled, with a little flourish, 'Nun, ich spiele, was Sie wollen, ich bin nicht so!' and in a second he had out a score which he had just completed, a kind of ecclesiastical processional march to Tasso's grave, a supplement to his famous symphonic poem for orchestra *Tasso, Lamento e triumpho*. Then down he sat and set the keys in motion. I assure you that he belched out, if I may use so unbeautiful an expression, one mass of fire and fervor and vivid thought after another. It sounded as if he were invoking Tasso's spirit. He paints in garish colors, but a subject like this is just for him; to portray tragic greatness is his strength. I did not know which to admire most, the composer or the pianist; for his playing was magnificent. He doesn't exactly play—one forgets that he is a musician, he becomes a prophet who announces the day of judgment, so that all the spirits of the universe quiver under his fingers. He invades the most secret places of the soul and delves into one's innermost being with a demoniac power.

"When that was over, Liszt said quite casually, 'Jetzt wollen wir mal weiter gehen in der Sonate!' and I, naturally, 'No, thanks very much, after that I shouldn't like to.' But now comes the best. Says Liszt, 'Nun warum nicht, geben Sie mal her, dann werde ich es tun.' Now remember, first he didn't know the sonata, had never heard or seen it before, and second, it was a violin sonata with a violin part that develops independently of the piano, now above, now below. And what did Liszt do? He played the whole affair, lock, stock and barrel, violin, piano, nay more, for he played with more fullness and breadth. The violin was given its due right in the middle of the piano part, he was literally all over the whole piano at the same time, without a note being missed. And how, then, did he play? With majesty, beauty, genius beyond compare in interpretation. I believe I laughed, laughed like an idiot. And when I stammered some words of admiration he mumbled, 'Nun das werden Sie mir doch zutrauen, etwas von Blatt zu spielen, ich bin ja ein alter gewandter Musiker.'—Wasn't it all gracious and kind from first to last? No other big man I have met among them has been like him. Then finally I played the funeral march, which also was to his taste, then I talked a little with him about all sorts of things—told him among other things that my father had heard him in London in 1824, which pleased him. ('Ja, ja, ich habe in der Welt viel herumgespielt, zu viel,' he said.) Then I took my leave and made my way home, wonderfully hot in the head but conscious that I had spent two of the most interesting hours of my life. And now I am asked to go to him again tomorrow, and naturally I am delighted.

"The day after the visit I have just described for you, the Italians Sgambati and Pinelli (pupils of Joachim) played my first violin sonata at a matinee where the whole fashionable world was present. Liszt came in the middle of the concert, just before my sonata, and that was well. For I do not put down the applause the sonata received to my own account. The thing is that when Liszt claps they all clap—each louder than the other."

"Dear Parents,

"This time I can say in earnest: where shall I begin or end! All my impressions and experiences swarm together in my brain in one stupendous chaos. The best thing will be to give a biographical sketch of the weeks just passed. First I must give you an account of my second visit to Liszt, which took place soon after I had sent my previous letter and was in no way behind the first in interest. Fortunately I had just received from Leipzig the manuscript of my piano concerto and this I took with me. Besides me there were present Winding, Sgambati, and a German Lisztian, unknown to me, who carries plagiarism so far as to wear the dress of an abbé, then there was a Chevalier de Concilium and a few young ladies of the kind that would like to eat Liszt up, with hair and hide. Their admiration is simply comic. They competed for the honor of standing by his side, of touching a corner of his long abbé's robe, making occasion to press his hand—even ignoring with complete want of consideration the space every player requires for the movements of his arms. These ladies crowded round him at the piano when he played later, their greedy eyes fixed upon his fingers as though they might be expected to disappear at any moment into the already gaping mouths of the little beasts of prey.

"Winding and I were very anxious to see if he would really play my concerto at sight. For my part I thought it an impossibility. Liszt, however, thought otherwise. He said, 'Wollen Sie spielen?' I excused myself with a 'No—I cannot' (I have never so far practised it). So Liszt took the manuscript, went to the piano, and said with his own particular smile addressed to all present, 'Nun, dann werde ich Ihnen zeigen, dass ich auch nicht kann.' Then he began. I admit that he took the first part of the concerto rather too quickly and the beginning lost a little by it, but later, when I made an opportunity to indicate the time myself, he played as only he and none other can play. It is characteristic that the cadenza, which is technically extremely difficult, he played perfectly. His dramatic gestures are beyond words. He does not rest content with playing only, no, he talks and criticizes at the same time. He flings brilliant remarks now to one, now to another in the company, deals out significant nods to right and left, most when something pleases him especially. In the adagio and even more in the finale he reached his culminating point both in regard to execution and to the praise he gave.—I must not forget a really divine episode. Towards the end of the finale the second theme is repeated, as you will remember, in a grand fortissimo. In the preceding bars, where the first note of the theme's first triplets, G sharp, changes to G in the orchestra, while the piano in a tremendous scale figure traverses all its range of the keys, he stopped suddenly, rose to his full height, left the piano and paced with stalwart, theatrical step and arm uplifted through the great hall of the monastery while he fairly bellowed the theme. At the G I have spoken of, he stretched out his arm commandingly like an emperor and shouted, 'G, G, not G sharp! Famos! das ist so echt schwedisches Banko!' and then, as if in parenthesis, almost pianissimo, 'Der Smetana hat mir neulich etwas davon geschickt.' Then he went back to the piano, repeated the whole strophe, and finished off. At the end he said with a singularly cordial accent as he handed me the book, 'Fahren Sie fort, ich sage Ihnen, Sie haben das Zeug dazu, und—lassen Sie sich nicht abschrecken!' This last has infinite importance for me. There is something I will call consecrated in it. Often, when disappointment and bitterness come, I will think of his words, and that the remembrance of this moment will have a wonderful power to sustain me in days of adversity, I firmly believe."

In his long report to the government on his tour, Grieg writes among other things: "But the thing that has been for me personally of the greatest importance is my acquaintance and association with Franz Liszt, who was at that time resident in Rome. I have learned to know in him not only the most talented of all pianists, but what is more—a phenomenon of spirit and greatness, with no limits in the domain of art. I brought him several of my compositions, he played them and it was of the greatest interest to me to observe how it was the national element in them that first startled —then roused him to enthusiasm. Such a triumph for my endeavors and my nationalist outlook is of itself worth the journey.

"In May 1870, after having seen a southern spring in the neighborhood of Naples, I travelled back to Denmark to find peace to work. On the journey itself and during my sojourn in Italy impressions were so many and so overwhelming that one, so to speak, counteracted the other—for the moment. Therefore, I have noted down a series of sketches and written various lyrical small things, but have not had peace to immerse myself in the great forms. But I have material in my memory in full measure and that must be admitted to be the main thing. If now I am fortunate enough to implant here at home a little of that confidence and belief in the future of our art that my travels have revived in me, I am convinced that the honorable department will see with me the importance of my journey for me and, through me, for the art of my fatherland."

THE SUMMER of 1870 found Grieg again at Landås with
his parents, where he was occupied not only with composition but also with a problem not unimportant for a young
composer, the finding of a publisher. Hitherto his works had been
brought out by widely different publishing houses. The first violin
sonata and a couple of booklets of piano pieces and songs had been
published for him by Peters in Leipzig, the second violin sonata
and the piano sonata by Breitkopf and Härtel. Songs and small
lyrical pieces were published by different publishers in Copenhagen, the overture "In Autumn" in Stockholm, and the Norwegian dances and folk-songs, Opus 17, in Bergen by Carl Rabe.

That it is not altogether of no consequence to a composer by
which firm his work is sent out, Grieg, like every other composer,
soon found out. Of one of the volumes of piano pieces, now perhaps
among the most popular and sold in hundreds of thousands the
world over, two copies only were sold outside Norway during the
three first years after their public performance—according to
Rabe's own statement to the composer.

Now the question arose of getting the piano concerto printed.
On his way through Copenhagen, Grieg had met a music dealer,
Hagen, who had taken over Hornemann and Erslevs' publishing
business, and to him he now turned. "Will you strike a vigorous
blow and publish my piano concerto? For I shall have no small
things out till Christmas time and the concerto must and shall appear now." He goes on to suggest modestly: "I would be glad if you
would be kind enough to decide upon the honorarium yourself. It
is difficult for me to say much about this venture, but considering
the numerous enquiries I and my people in Norway have had, and
the way in which the public in Denmark received the concerto, I
cannot but think that it would pay before long." But no, Hagen
would not embark upon so daring an enterprise as the printing of
Grieg's piano concerto. In a letter on December 8, 1871, Grieg
wrote to Hagen: "I have always understood from you that you

only publish conditionally and in that case, naturally, I also will only pledge myself to you conditionally. It would be another matter if you would take my future works, great and small. It might be an advantage to have everything collected in one place, and to that I should be delighted to agree after a suitable honorarium had been arranged; but apparently this is not your intention—you refused even my piano concerto. In any event, however, I am willing to submit my smaller things to you and have them printed by you if you do not pay me less than others. It is tiresome to have to discuss these things, but you should know how poorly I am placed and how I long for artistic freedom. I often feel a wonderful longing to create, but I am busy all the time with practical matters and have to resign myself."

It was Svendsen who had helped Grieg to get his second violin sonata published and now again it was this noble colleague and friend who helped him to get the piano concerto printed. In a letter of July 14, 1871, Svendsen wrote from Leipzig: "I have spoken at length with Fritsch[1] about your piano concerto—without knowing it myself—and made his mouth water, and I feel pretty certain that he will print it. Taking everything into consideration, I advise you to write to him yourself. He is an honorable man of the rarest kind and will dare all for anything he believes to have a future." Fritsch both believed and dared; he published the concerto in 1872 and continued to take others of Grieg's larger works. It was not till long after, when Grieg had become a famous composer, that all his works went over to the world-famous publishing house of Peters in Leipzig.

Since it was so difficult to get the works out, it was only to be expected that the payment should be in proportion. A glance at the sums Grieg received at this time for his works shows them to be throughout so low that it might well be thought they were set down for form's sake, so that it might appear that the works were bought and paid for by the publisher and not simply placed at his disposal gratis by the composer.

Now there would be nothing to say about that if the composer had been entitled to a share of the profits in the event of the works really coming to be commercially valuable. But there obtained at this time the immoral arrangement between publisher and com-

[1] Svendsen's publisher in Leipzig.

poser that the works became the publisher's own property, as a rule for all countries, for all time and with all rights. Thus the publisher had all the chances—the composer none! An arrangement, moreover, that has continued right up to our own days.

What good did it do a composer if he became popular—if his works were performed the world over? No material benefit accrued to him from that. Indeed, even so late as the end of the Eighties, we find Grieg applying for a stipend to help him out. He is in financial difficulties in spite of being by this time a well known and highly appreciated composer—and not in Scandinavia only. His name had now rung round the musical world and his works had risen to being coveted securities in the world's exchange. Not till he had found refuge in "Father Abraham's arms," that is to say, when the enterprising and generous Dr. Max Abraham, lessee of the world-famous Peters in Leipzig, undertook the publication of Grieg's collected works, was he enabled to work under wholly secure financial conditions. But by that time his genius had already passed the height of noon. . . .

In September 1870 Grieg was again in Christiania and had taken up his daily work. He began by giving a concert, the programme of which consisted for the most part of his own and Nordraak's compositions. Now, as before, both with his own and with the subscription concerts, he had invaluable support from his wife, who sang the new songs that had come into existence in the intervening time. He also announced, as before, four subscription concerts, with orchestra. But the most important event of this period was the planning and founding of the Musical Society. As early as September, Grieg had written on the subject to the members of the orchestra of the Christiania Theater and he took up work amongst those interested in the town. But a year was to pass before the plan could be realized, and it was not till October 1871 that the public proposal for its establishment was sent out. The press looked approvingly on the new enterprise and it also won the support of the public. With the founding of the Musical Society, orchestral music in Christiania—thanks to Grieg's initiative and tireless energy— had taken a more permanent form and, in spite of changing times and many difficulties, it is the Musical Society that has been the foundation of Norway's musical life. It is upon this foundation that the present-day Philharmonic Society is built.

In the first two seasons four concerts were arranged, but with Svendsen's homecoming in 1873 there was a great increase of interest, and the directors sent out invitations for sixteen concerts for the coming season under the leadership of Grieg and Svendsen. Even though the number had to be reduced to eleven, it was still something hitherto unknown in the musical life of the capital.

Now our two young chieftains stood at the head of the musical life of the country and shared work and honor in brotherly fashion. Of course there were those who tried to stir up trouble between them, which seemed likely to be an easy task, inasmuch as Svendsen was undoubtedly superior as a leader of the orchestra. But a split between our two composers, as noble-minded as they were gifted, could not be brought about either then or later.

"All the more I am drawn to Svendsen's art," wrote Grieg in 1881 to Grönvold, "though nothing could be more different than our artistic natural endowments. He has taught me to believe in myself and in the power and authority of individuality. There was a time in Christiania when to be individual was the same as to be a criminal. But then Svendsen came and he too was individual, and so the miracle happened that from then on I too was tolerated. There are few artists, therefore, to whom I owe more than to Svendsen. When he came home in 1872 there were a number of people who were very anxious to have us enemies. But—thanks to mutual sympathy for our art—the plan was a complete failure."

If Grieg cherished a warm and affectionate feeling for Svendsen, numerous letters show that the sympathy was no less on the other side. Some extracts may be quoted here to illuminate the relationship between these colleagues, unique in Norwegian music. We have already heard how eagerly Svendsen worked to find Grieg a publisher. It appears from the letters that Svendsen took every opportunity too to spread knowledge of Grieg's music. In a letter of 1871 Svendsen writes: "You wouldn't believe how happy and proud I am over every mark of friendship that comes from you, you excellent, open-minded genius of a friend. Your words of praise about my violin concerto I value so much the more because I am convinced of your unshakeable honesty and sincerity. It is a matter for regret to me, perhaps to us both, that we are so far from each other; how stimulating, and therefore fruitful, companionship with you would be! I don't know what you think, but I feel at times an intense desire to busy myself with you and your productions." And the following enquiry from Svendsen in a letter of September 22, 1870, testifies to a friendship rather exceptional and unselfish among artists: "For a long time I have been thinking much about writing music to Björnson's *Halte-Hulda* and *Sigurd Slembe*. I should not like, though, to thwart you in an enterprise of this kind and ask you, therefore, to let me know if you perhaps have similar plans, in which case I will set myself to the solving of other problems."

As a beautiful ending to this eventful season, when the two colleagues worked side by side for musical culture, came the government's grant of a composer's honorarium[2] to them both on June 1, 1874. With this, Grieg felt himself freed from his chains of slavery, he gave up his residence in Christiania and, except for the winter 1876-1877, never lived there again. Therewith began a new chapter in his life.

Before going further, however, we must look a little at the circumstances which mainly conduced to fill Grieg with the bitterness towards the capital which he never could overcome, and we must examine more closely also the works which date from this time.

---

[2] The most prominent artists of Norway are granted a yearly honorarium from the government.

LIKE a red thread through all letters during Grieg's eight years' residence in Christiania there runs complaint over the poorness of his circumstances.

"My long residence in Christiania I prefer to pass over," he wrote to Grönvold in 1881. "To write my biography from these years would be to write mainly a life of art in Christiania, and that was a poor affair, God knows. I stood alone; Kierulf, who to begin with had supported me warmly, fell away in 1868 and I can only say that in the following years, until Svendsen at his homecoming won hearts, I can look back only with bitterness to the indifference, even contempt and hate, that was shown towards Norwegian music. I could tell things about that time which sound almost unbelievable. But there was also a total want of what is called artistic morality."

In a letter to the music dealer Hagen, January 15, 1871, he says: "Remember how a real breath of spirit may affect me up here in my dull loneliness." And the next year the same complaint is heard, also in a letter to Hagen. "Björnson said in ending his work for *Folkebladet* last year, 'One thing is wanting up here and that is spirit.' And he is right. It will certainly come, but it is a heavy job for the representatives of the spirit to live among the dry 'food and railway interests' up here. Send me a breath of air from down there and if you see any criticisms of my things be sure to send them too. I want folks here to know that intellect is appreciated amongst you people. You understand, I must myself, through my friends, compel the newspapers here to publish foreign criticisms. I am much too unimportant for criticisms at home—it's only real swells like Fru Emma,[1] etc., etc., who are worthy of such favors. The thing is, the philistines who control the artistic press here have unanimously made up their minds to do me down by silence. But they won't manage it. So certainly as I write only from the bottom of my heart, so certainly my work will struggle through. And I see the best sign of that in the fact that my appreciative friends are as enthusiastic as my enemies are bitter. That is always a sure be-

[1] The composer Emma Dahl, wife of the bookseller Johan Dahl, famous from the Wergeland-Welhaven conflict.

ginning. For without enemies on the one side and friends on the other one can never win through."

Six years later, in 1877, he wrote to August Winding: "Much as I love my fatherland, I can't help longing to get away from here, since there is no understanding whatsoever of my art in my own home and that is hard to bear, as you can imagine. If it weren't for a lively breeze from abroad, the outlook would often be pretty desperate."

In his article on Grieg in *Norsk Folkeblad*, April 10, 1869, Björnson wrote: "Grieg did not get much encouragement as a composer here at home; and in other ways also he met many and various obstructions. But a spanking breeze reached him from abroad; not only in Germany and especially in Denmark was he looked upon as the coming man, but recently when he was collecting testimonials from the most renowned composers in Europe to send with his application for a stipend, he received the highest possible words of praise. Moscheles, Rubinstein, Hartmann, Gade, Liszt, and others increased the joy of work for him."

It seemed essential, on the whole, for recognition to come first from *outside*, otherwise it was hardly possible to believe in the value of an art that laid claim to being anything so extremely odd as "Norwegian."

After having played his first violin sonata with Wieniawski, who in the spring of 1877 gave a series of concerts in Christiania, Grieg wrote: "I assisted by playing my first violin sonata with him, and such is the public that, while usually they sit and yawn over my music, this time they nearly brought the house down with one recall after another."

The following bitter observations in a letter to John Paulsen give an impression of what Grieg felt about the city in which he offered up the best of his youthful vigor: "If you come to the capital, you will meet at first a courtesy and friendliness that will astonish you so much that you will say, 'There can never be anything but straight dealings here!' But—the old fox is at work. What am I talking about? That can only be hinted at. Go after your own ideals and you will bruise yourself against the ogres of prejudice, of indecision, of slackness, of egoism, of hate, envy, yes, even of brutishness, of low thraldom, sooner or later. How to deal with it only your own good genius will be able to tell you, but a warning from one who wishes you well may be of service."

At this time, conditions in Christiania in a purely musical sense were very primitive. In a letter to Matthison-Hansen of March 18, 1868, Grieg describes the orchestra as simply disgraceful. Furthermore, the members of the orchestra, had very little discipline and it happened more than once that a single instrumentalist threatened the ruin of the whole enterprise.

When Grieg complains over the pitiable state of things, over want of understanding, over intrigues and malice, one can well understand that all this put his courage and his talents to a hard test. Naturally it was bitter to experience that amateurishness was so highly rated, that when, for example, Grieg and his wife along with Björnson gave in 1872 an evening entertainment at the Students' Society for the benefit of the Danes who had suffered through the flood, about fifty people came, while an amateur concert in the Lodge Hall for the same object had an audience of over a thousand.

It was still more bitter to find that the music both to *Sigurd Jorsalfar* and *Peer Gynt* waked such interest that the public did not care to hear it at all! In *Morgenbladet*, April 14, 1872, this is sharply complained of in an article on "Music in the Theater" on the occasion of the production of *Sigurd Jorsalfar*, and the paper remarks: "Although we do not particularly admire Herr Grieg's music to the above-mentioned play, we do think that most people would like to hear it undisturbed, so as to be able at least to form an opinion about it one way or the other."

Four years later, when *Peer Gynt* was performed for the first time, the conditions were the same. On March 26, Christian Cappelen wrote to Grieg, who by this time was living in Bergen, after first having described the defective make-up of the orchestra: "And the audience, good Lord! they jabber and chatter and laugh and make a noise and don't vouchsafe the music a particle of interest, so that any poor creature who would really like to hear might just as well not be there if he went to listen to the music."

In the midst of all the difficulties attendant upon getting the Musical Society's concerts firmly on their feet, a new and unexpected obstacle suddenly made its appearance. On account of the engagements of the various musicians in cafés and similar establishments round about, Grieg and Svendsen in the 1873-1874 season had to give matinees at midday on Sundays. But then the Christians fell upon them. On January 18, 1874, *Morgenbladet* had an article, "To the Police Authorities and the Directors of the Musical Society," which said: "Many opinions have been expressed regarding the impropriety of holding concerts at midday on Sunday and we desire in the interest of the development of music in our town to say a word in this matter. When we speak of the 'impropriety' of holding musical matinees on Sunday, it is on the ground that such a condition of things cannot be regarded as right from the Christian point of view." The article continues: "The Musical Society is an all too precious treasure for us calmly to see it carrying an unchristian device upon its spotless shield." And it ends with the following appeal: "So let the directors of the Musical Society and our zealous chief of police take heed to this matter—it is certainly worth consideration."

Aimar Grönvold, who followed musical events closely in those years, writes: "It is amazing to those who experienced Grieg's first appearance on the scene to see him as a figure in musical celebrations. When Christiania from 1866-1874 had him in its midst the city's cold calm was not for a single day disturbed on his account. It took very coolly all the beautiful music that came into being in a little room up in Voldgaten or in other more modest quarters of the town to which Grieg, as the years went on, removed with his piano."

But it was not these difficulties, almost inevitable for every young and unknown artist, that hit Grieg hardest during the long years in Christiania. Things happened—things that place our cultural life in an exceptional position, things that struck deeper, that went beyond the wounding of an individual.

Edvard Grieg came to Christiania full of Nordraak's idea of creating a national art based on folk music. He looked up to the capital of the country as to a center for all movements stirring in the people, especially those concerned with the renewal of intellectual and spiritual life. But whom did he meet and what did he meet? He met the destiny of the country, or, more rightly, the adverse destiny of the country so purely and completely crystallized in precisely the "leading circles" in the capital that suddenly he got a harrowing glimpse into the pitiable state of the national culture.

And who were these leaders, these heads who believed themselves to represent the highest strata of society? Simply a parvenu class whose cultural sense was so shallow that instinctively it felt its position menaced by every sign of life from Norway's own culture, every manifestation of independent Norwegian thought and will. This it was that led to violent reaction, whether in art or social and political life. Here Grieg had to share the fate of Wergeland and Björnson, Aasen and Vinje, Garborg and Aukrust—to name only a few of the prominent figures in the tragic battles Norwegians have fought to reconquer their land and make Christiania the capital of the country in more than name. It stands like a sorrowful symbol of the whole cultural and political demoralization in the very capital of the country, the place where all threads should be entwined, the capital which should give expression to all that is best, noblest, most characteristic of Norwegian talent, will, and power, but all together raised to a higher level— precisely there opposition was most stubborn each time the spirit of the Norwegian people put forth new, fresh, and magnificent flowers.

The conceptions signified by "Norwegian" art, by "Norwegian" culture, these could be met only with contempt and derision. And what were these conceptions exactly—what was the reality they implied? Yes, what were they? That was just the question, because all were ignorant of the foundations of this culture—namely the whole of Norway's rich and comprehensive peasant art. A few knew it superficially as a kind of curiosity, as a kind of remote, romantic idea, above all as something that had to do only with the past.

In August 1887, Grieg wrote to Winding: "Norway is a funny country. Because, while the country folk delight in their own ways and count as their highest happiness to be able to live a wholly sound national life, in the towns and especially in the capital the exact opposite is the case. The more imported the better!"

Avowing oneself to be a "Norwegian" artist, fighting the cause of Norwegian music, brought its own punishment, and it was not until the acclamations of Europe were behind him that Edvard Grieg bore down all opposition. Even then he could not help observing the same when others were in question. Thus as late as 1901 he writes: "Christiania affects me this time, as always, as uncomfortably cold. And the Northern spirit—even with regard to things peculiarly Norwegian—has a home in Denmark for those capable of seeing and feeling it." Even in his speech on his sixtieth birthday he broke out violently against the capital. Grieg's old friend, Director Johan Bögh, relates that he had begged him as nicely as he could not to mention Christiania in his speech, since gifts and a great address of gratitude had come from that city. Grieg promised he would not, but in the excitement of his speech he forgot himself, his old and ever fresh bitterness welled up in him, and he made accusations in phrases which were not exactly well considered. Then friends had to fly round to the members of the press who were present and beg them for Grieg's sake to leave out these strong expressions in their reports. And so it was arranged.

We all know how Wergeland fought for Norwegianism and how the opposition he encountered in Christiania evinced itself! We all know how Björnson fought for the same ideas, the same end, we all know the political battles of the Eighties and how they were fought out in the capital. We all know how our two great poets and sages, Aasen and Vinje, went about almost like two pariahs in the capital of the country. And why? Because they saw it as their life work to preach the gospel of nature and truth to a sick and mis-guided people and to point out to them the means by which they could win through to freedom and salvation. They had the very curious idea that its language, its speech—the living word—was a people's dearest possession; if that should be suppressed, if the people should lose that, then it was all up with it as a nation. If the people should fall so far into decay as to give up its instinctive claim here, its instinctive right, then all was over with Norwegian culture, with Norwegian spirit and will.

Let us take an example from our own time. About thirty years ago, the Norwegian Theater was opened in Christiania. One of the objects of this theater was to provide a stage for the living Nor-wegian language in the capital of the country, a place where it could find expression and prove its possibilities as a language of culture. How was this received by the inhabitants of the capital, especially its young people? With howls and shrieks, with demon-strations night after night, until large reinforcements of police had to be called in to keep order among the embittered elements.

What was Edvard Grieg's attitude towards "this so inevitable historical movement" which the capital looked down on from so elevated a standpoint? In letters to Hulda and Arne Garborg he expresses his opinion in a way that admits of no doubt.

To Fru Garborg he writes in a letter dated Troldhaugen, August 18, 1898: "If I did not feel so strongly how glorious it is to belong to this half-wild land laden with substance precisely now when it is on the verge of forming itself anew—I could wish to have lived some generations later, only to have joined in speaking that Norwegian tongue which I love with the strength of instinct, and in its poetry especially, as it has found expression in works like *Haugtussa*. What a deepening in the spirit of the language and—what a world of unborn music!"

In a letter to Garborg from Stockholm, November 8, 1899, Grieg wrote: "It is not many weeks since I had a dispute with Björnson on the language question. Unfortunately, we are altogether at variance. It's the devil and all that we do not have B.B. with all his driving power on our side." Then follows a strong reservation on the subject of "fanatics" who may take note of Björnson's opposition. And the letter goes on: "But two things which I think of the greatest significance B.B. and those who agree with him have not mentioned. (1) Our Danish speech is forced upon us through school and church. Justice requires that what is now merely the language of the peasants should be given the same right. That must in a few generations (perhaps even in one) be forced on us. I am not afraid of the peasant culture. It offers rich material and will blend in a higher unity with town culture. And from their union will derive that language of the future in which I believe. (2) B.B. does not mention that four-fifths of the nation use the peasant speech. That for me is decisive.

"I had to be allowed to say all this since you spoke of the matter in your letter. Hurrah for the future!"

Statements could be multiplied. They would all only show that there was consistency in Grieg's national tendencies and that he had the ability to separate essential from unessential. If Grieg and many with him reacted so violently towards the Christiania of their time that we sometimes find their expressions exaggerated, we must remember that at the core of this feeling there was, nevertheless, something positive. If Norway ever gets so far that the capital, both in its inner and outer manifestations, gives expression to what is best in the Norwegian spirit and will, and in all truth stands as a symbol of Norwegian national culture, then Edvard Grieg is among those who will have helped most to bring this about, not only through his art but as much by his healthy capacity for reaction and, most of all perhaps, by the incorruptibility and reliability of his character.

COMPOSITION INSPIRED BY BJÖRNSON

THERE was little opportunity for creative work during the busy winter session in these years. In a letter to the music dealer Hagen, Grieg wrote on January 15, 1871: "Thoughts keep whispering in me, and whenever I am not too much taken up with concerts, I am delivered of some of them. But it is also a fact that all creative power is used up in the discharge of one's duties towards art when performances with choir and orchestra have to be set going."

So now, as before, it was holiday time that gave the composer opportunity for work. Six songs were published in 1870, so unlike in character and design that one might believe them to have been written in different periods of the composer's production. But what they show is now, as before, how Grieg's imagination and the world of his ideas willingly lent themselves to the elucidation of the most widely differing subjects. "From Monte Pincio" (Björnson) paints a vivid and richly colored picture of Italian nature and peasant life. In "Odalisken synger" (The Odalisque Sings) (Carl Brun) we are carried away to regions still more remote, to the land of the Sultan—the Bosphorus. Long before exotic music made its entry into Europe with impressionism, Grieg wrote this song which shows the ability and accuracy of his characterization. It is not amongst his most important songs, but neither does it deserve the treatment it has received from earlier biographers. It may be regarded as a slight and sketchy study in color and, as such, is both of interest and has its value. In "Langelandsk folkemelodi" (Danish Country Air) (Hans Christian Andersen) we are taken over to Denmark to be brought back finally—in the two Björnson songs, "God morgen" (Good-morning) and "Det förste möte" (The First Meeting)—to Norway and home. With the remaining songs to Björnson poems from these years, "Prinsessen" (The Princess) (1871), "Jeg giver mit dikt til våren" (I Give My Poem to Spring) and "Tak for dit råd" (Thanks for Your Advice) both from 1872, they are of special interest because here for the first time in Grieg's vocal productions we meet a feeling for *Norwegian* scenery. While the instrumental works, piano pieces, sonatas, the piano concerto and the rest have been strongly marked by Norwegian nature impressions, the words chosen have entailed that in his songs he has wandered for the most part in foreign lands. With the Björnson songs Norwegian nature makes its entry into his vocal works also and it is probably largely because of this that his personality unfolds more freely here, that his originality, his fresh lyrical vein flows more richly and purely than in earlier works. And yet we stand only at the beginning, we near the land, as it were, from the outside, we are still out on the coast, have not yet made our way far into wonderland. Like a shining glimpse of spring, like an anticipation, a hint of coming riches, these Björnson songs take their place among Grieg's vocal compositions. It was reserved for other poets to lead him deeper in, to guide his sensitive and receptive mind into the mystic, secret kingdom of nature, to the very nerve of life in the land. But the way there was still long. . . .

"Modersorg" (A Mother's Grief) to words of Chr. Richardt (1870) and "Ved en ung hustrus baare" (At a Young Wife's Bier) to words by O. P. Monrad (1873) are both inspired and deeply felt songs arousing reflections on the transient nature of life in a way that is both moving and elevating. Björnson's poem "Dulgt kjærlighet" (Hidden Love), on the other hand, does not seem to have inspired Grieg specially. That the song is not composed as a unit, combined with the constantly repeated sequences, weakens the effect. The same can be said of Grieg's first attempt to write a rather larger vocal composition, *Foran sydens kloster* (At a Southern Cloister's Gate), the words for which are taken from Björnson's *Arnljot Gelline*. Even in the prelude the orchestral accompaniment, impressive in itself, suffers from too great a use of sequences, and when the alto and soprano solos come in and through four verses repeat the same sequences, into which only the modulation brings a touch of variety, an impression of monotony cannot be avoided. It is felt rather as a deliverance when the choir of nuns at last breaks in with its melodious, even though slightly commonplace, final hymn. That a work like *At a Southern Cloister's Gate* has won great favor in certain circles and remains a favorite to this day is due partly to the nature of the subject and the lyrical-sentimental character of the music which, moreover, whether in orchestral, choral, or solo parts, presents no great difficulties. The composition is dedicated to Liszt. Grieg says of this in a letter of October 13 to Hagen: "There is rather a joke about the dedication. As a matter of fact I had at first inscribed the last piece to Hartmann when I got a letter from him saying that he had just composed a setting for the same words. As the dedication in these circumstances might lead to misunderstanding, it fell through, naturally. I think too that there is a good deal to be said for dedicating this particular piece to Liszt." The arrangement for piano, which is to be found in the Bergen library, is dated August 11, 1871.

How altogether different is the flash of Grieg's genius in the other Björnson work which dates from the same year, "Bergliot," in which Björnson's poem is declaimed to the music of Grieg. Here the vivid quality and richness of Grieg's dramatic gifts are very apparent. In spite of the host of small characterful details with which the poem is illuminated, and in spite of the fact that the form in itself might very well invite only to the construction of a series of excellently drawn dramatic pictures without inner cohesion, the whole is held together with a strength and integrity of vision that lift it up to the level of great art.

The prelude itself, in all its brevity, gives us the spirit of the saga, its pure air, its strong and simple lines. It provides, too, a stage for the drama that is to unroll before us, and from now on we follow the development of the work in suspense and excitement. We follow Bergliot, daughter of Håkon of Hjörungavåg, in her anxious forebodings, in her anguish, her tenderness, her bitterness and wrath and, above all, in her deep, august sorrow. And everywhere the rich, amazing gamut of emotional nuances is conjured up against a background of scenic and dramatic pictures which show the events in singularly effective relief. "How the sand drifts down the road, and a clamor rises!"—with a few strokes we are in the world of enchantment and we feel not only the first stirring of anticipatory alarm, we experience also the landscape. "The open fjord and the low hills. I remember the town of my childhood: hither the wind hounds the wild dogs."

And the scene where Bergliot tries to incite the peasants to fight, the provocative fifths in the horns and the explosive strength of the outbursts, "Up, up, peasants, he is fallen; but he who struck him down lives!" or "Shoot out dragon ships from the land! Einar's nine dragon ships lie here, let them bear vengeance on Harald!"—a passage which has not only the character of a call to arms, but conjures up besides that wild and many colored life with impressionistic richness. Or the funeral march at the end, to name only one or two detached scenes, the funeral march which could as well be inscribed: *marcia funébre e triomphale*. The march that from deep, sublime sorrow in the remembrance of the fallen hero rises suddenly with the words "nor ever Einar's step in the porch calling on all to arise, for now the chieftain is coming!"—to take on a triumphant character and then sink back again to its original mood—in which finally one only distinguishes steps, the creaking of wheels as the procession slowly passes on and disappears. . . .

Seldom have poetry and music so completely fused and been merged in a higher unity. In thinking of this work we first begin to realize what a loss it is that Grieg did not confer upon us a dramatic work on the grand scale. Though "Bergliot" was composed by 1871, it was not instrumented for orchestra till 1885, when it was first performed in Christiania, declaimed by Laura Gundersen, to whom it is dedicated.

Nearly related to "Bergliot" but without the concentrated strength of that work is the music to *Sigurd Jorsalfar* (Sigurd the Crusader). In a congratulatory article on the occasion of Björnson's seventieth birthday, Grieg relates that he had only eight days to compose and orchestrate the music. That is not strictly correct. *Sigurd Jorsalfar* was performed for the first time on April 10, 1872, but as early as January Björnson wrote to Gotfred Rode: "Meantime Grieg is setting the piece to music." And in a letter on February 2 to Margrethe Rode, Björnson refers to Grieg's music again. It is, of course, immaterial how it was exactly, but it is further evidence that Grieg is not always strictly accurate as regards dates and his own experiences. The year of its first performance Grieg also gives wrongly as 1870, long before Björnson had even begun to think of writing his national drama!

The music to *Sigurd Jorsalfar* consists of two marches, a rather melodramatic introduction, and two songs for solo baritone, male voice choir and orchestra. The introduction to the first act, "Borghild's Dream," Björnson had imagined as being continued, so that the whole of Borghild's long monologue would be declaimed to music. Grieg has stopped precisely at the moment the monologue begins. But otherwise he has followed the poet's instructions and has created an inspired and stirring piece of music which in the most beautiful way fulfils Björnson's desire: "Before the curtain goes up, quiet music begins, and as the curtain rises, it depicts Borghild's restless sleep till it gathers itself into a great dread."

This music, too, closely allied as it is to "Bergliot," shows the intensity of Grieg's dramatic powers.

The introduction to the second act, the march "Ved mand-jævningen" (The Trial of Strength) had been composed, as already mentioned, in 1869 for piano and violin and, under the name of Gavotte, played several times at concerts, by Grieg's mother among others. But the music is so Northern in spirit that it could be fitted admirably into Björnson's play. Indeed, it could very well be taken—as it actually was—for an attempt to portray the two royal brothers, the proud, virile principal theme signifying King Sigurd and the mild, weaker, but still dignified, theme of the middle movement, King Öistein.

In the "Triumphal March," Grieg has created one of his most inspired tone poems. It would be difficult to find a festival march of such high artistic value. At the very beginning Grieg offers us something unusual. The grave, solemn principal theme is introduced almost piano and is played by a quartet of cellos! The theme is taken up by the violins and carried on by the horns and wood-winds. Not till the place where Björnson has noted: "Here the halberdiers enter in pairs and place themselves on both sides of the steps," does the music suddenly change in character. In a gigantic leap of the seventh, the tuba and the bassoon take the lead while the whole orchestra, little by little, joins in and a working up section develops at the moment when the two kings come in hand in hand, followed by Sigurd Raneson and Ivar Ingemundson. But the composer has still a trump card in reserve: after the brilliantly built up climax, the principal theme of the march now is brought in fortissimo and in augmented notes! The effect is overwhelming. Kretzschmar has hit it exactly when he says that it has the effect of an immense crowd breaking out into spontaneous jubilation.

In 1892 Grieg published the three orchestral selections of the music to *Sigurd Jorsalfar* as a suite and in partially revised form. The "Triumphal March" has been much expanded and it cannot be denied that it has lost thereby something of its strong, pregnant character. The added trio is musically of value, but the many repetitions tend to weaken the form. The short, effective fanfare that Grieg has inserted before the theme of the march itself has certainly the effect of an assembly call, but it deprives the composition of something of its nobleness and dignity. In its original shape the *Sigurd Jorsalfar* music can only be found now in Wilhelm Hansen's edition for two- and four-handed piano. The two songs, "Norrönafolket" (The Northerners) and "Kongekvadet" (Song of the Kings) show how by the simplest means Grieg is able to catch the color and atmosphere of the times with absolute precision. It is folk music, sound to the core, permeated with the spirit of the saga.

While the great popularity which has long been attained by Björnson's drama in Norway is due in large part to Grieg's music, the suite from *Sigurd Jorsalfar* has had great difficulty in finding its way into concert halls both at home and abroad.

In his birthday address to Björnson, Grieg describes its performance in the Christiania Theater very amusingly: "The piece was to come up for hearing in the Christiania Theater at such short notice that I had only eight days to write and orchestrate the music. But I had the elasticity of youth and got through. The performance took place as arranged but—without Björnson.

"So dawned May 17, 1870,[1] the day appointed for the performance. I persuaded Björnson to witness it. Good-natured, as always, he came, and so it happened that we sat side by side that evening in the first row of the stalls. Although it was commonly said that the Christiania Theater was a place for those who sought solitude, that was assuredly not the case on May 17. It was crammed from floor to ceiling." After having described the acting, which was not precisely such as to gratify the poet, Grieg goes on: "But now came my turn to be nervous, yes, even to forget where I was. It was not always pleasurable for the composer to listen to the rendering of his music given on the boards. No doubt Hammer was a talented actor. Here he had to be a singer too. He did his best. But when it came to the Song of the Kings I had a strong feeling of discomfort, which increased till the pains in my ears were such that I longed to hide myself away, and instinctively bent over more and more. Finally, I had sunk so low in my seat that, supporting myself on my elbow, I could hold my hand before my face. I tell this to illustrate how alive Björnson now was as to what the situation demanded of us. For suddenly he gave me a none too gentle thump and whispered, 'Sit up properly!' I hurriedly straightened up as if a wasp had stung me and sat from then on in blameless immobility to be gaped at right to the end. But then the May 17 jubilation

---

[1] Should be 1872. May 17 is the Norwegian independence day.

broke loose in earnest. The applause, which had been warm before, now became uproarious. There were calls upon calls and at last the shouts for Björnson and myself were so prolonged that we had to show ourselves upon the stage. Then I drove home with Björnson to his house in Piperviken where we shared a noble old cheese in the big bright kitchen which was arranged as a dining-room. There, like happy children, we enjoyed our triumph, which culminated when all the little ones with Björn at their head came bursting in: 'Just think, we were up in the gallery and saw father and Grieg come on to the stage.'

"Yes—that was a great time! Thanks for it, Björnson!"

That selfsame May 17th yet another Björnson-Grieg work was brought out in Christiania—and that for the first time. At the Fortress a bazaar was being held to collect funds for the restoration of Trondheim cathedral. Björnson was asked to write a song and, of course, Grieg must set it to music. The poem is to be found on the front page of *Aftenbladet* for May 17, 1872. It was called "Landkænning" (Landsighting).

If Grieg had had scant time to write the music for *Sigurd Jorsalfar*, "Landsighting"[2] seems to have been produced at even shorter notice. This is indicated, not only by the fact that the composition does not deal with the poem as a unit, and the first verses are set to one and the same melodic stanza, but the orchestral accompaniment which, in spite of the stanza form, could have illumined the progression of the words begins only with the solo part. And in this form "Landsighting" was produced for years. Even today the work can be heard as an *a capella* song in which only the solo part and the concluding stanzas are supported by the harmonium or organ.

The year after, Grieg wrote to Björnson that he had now changed the recitative and was pleased with the piece, and when "Landsighting" in 1881 was brought out by the Peters publishing house as Opus 31, the work had been completely revised and was now arranged for male voice choir and baritone solo with accompaniment by a large orchestra. The stanza form is held to, but

---

[2] Usually in this book the English titles given for such of the songs as have already been published in English translation are those under which they are known in the Peters edition. In the case of "Landkænning," however, the American translation, "Landsighting," is given in order to avoid the somewhat cumbersome title "Recognition of Land" which it bears in the Peters edition.—*Translator*.

what we do not get in the choral part the composer gives us in the orchestral, which, in spite of its simplicity, is worked out in such a way that it illumines and elucidates the text in the closest possible manner. The characteristic small interlude, which both deepens and leads up to the simple stanzas of the chorus, contributes not a little to this result.

Thus it was that we came into possession of the well known, well loved choral work "Landsighting," which with its Northern spirit, its fresh natural lyricism, and noble final apotheosis has become a constant feature in national festivals and is known and loved by all singers, not only in the North, but the world over.

Barely a week later, on May 22, the young pianist, Agathe Backer, gave a concert also for the benefit of the Trondheim cathedral, and on this occasion too a new work of Grieg's took a prominent place on the programme. It was his *Pictures from Folklife*, Opus 19, "Fjeldslåt" (Mountain Dance), "Brudefölget drar forbi (The Bridal Procession Passes) and "Fra Karnevalet" (From the Carnival) which were played for the first time. The pieces were composed in the years 1870-1871. Sketches and rough drafts had been made already during the stay in Rome, but the work was completed at Landås in the summer of 1871.

"Mountain Dance" is an effective character piece, but it does not show Grieg from the most interesting side. He is experimenting here with thematic work. The theme of the middle movement is treated canonically and when after a crescendo it reenters, the principal motive, the mountain air itself, forms the counterpointing part. But it is not by such means that Grieg can make the most of his powers. On the contrary, they seem here rather to have restricted than furthered his creative ability.

This is best seen when "Mountain Dance" is compared with that other piece in the collection, "The Bridal Procession Passes." Here Grieg is on the heights, here he is on a voyage of discovery in the wonderland of harmony, melody, and rhythm. Here he conjures up unguessed and unknown values. Harmonically above all this piece provides a series of surprises which show Grieg's rare and subtle feeling for color. No wonder that the French impressionists regarded Grieg with special interest and that his music has left clear traces in their productions. Color, movement, rhythm, dynamic contrast, all these combined are precisely the means the impressionists fondly availed themselves of when, twenty years later, they began to make themselves felt in European art music. Even such a prominent representative of modern French music as Maurice Ravel said during his visit to Norway in 1926, when the talk turned on this point: "I have never till this day written a work that was not influenced by Grieg!" And though we may put down part of this exaggerated statement to courtesy, it is clear, nevertheless, that both Ravel and Debussy studied Grieg's harmony with profit and found values there which released coincidently much of what was most significant in their own genius.

The last piece, "From the Carnival," is not upon the same level as "The Bridal Procession." It gives musical impressions of carnival time in Rome, depicted with liveliness but yet a little stagnant and poor in respect to harmony. And when at the end of the piece the composer tries to bind the three pictures together by bringing in motives from the first two, no unity is achieved because there is no inner coherence.

IT IS not surprising that Björnson, hearing all the magnificent music that his poetry gave occasion for, became anxious to collaborate with Grieg in a big work and to realize the plan in which both Nordraak and Kierulf had failed him, namely to write a Norwegian opera. It is said to be the music to *At a Southern Cloister's Gate* in especial which gave Björnson the feeling that the time had come. Nor was the idea new to Grieg. In a letter to August Winding, January 3, he wrote that he had conceived *At a Southern Cloister's Gate* as a scene in an opera. It would appear that Björnson and Grieg were soon agreed about the plan, for by January 23 the poet was writing in a letter to Gotfred Rode: "In summer Caroline and I and the whole household will be off to the mountains; we shall live in Valdres all the summer in the wonderful mountain air up there. Grieg and his wife are coming with us. I shall rewrite *Arnljot* for an opera for him up there, which will be soon done; the whole plan, scene by scene, is prepared."

And Björnson kept his word. Quick on the trigger, rapid in work, not prone to hesitation, as was his nature, he wrote *Arnljot Gelline* as a text for an opera. But Grieg got no further with the subject than to "smell at it," as he expresses it. Among his posthumous papers Björnson's manuscript was found and a few loose sketches for the music. Among these is a rough draft for "Bjarkemål" which has a strong and individual saga tone. That the *Arnljot* plan was not merely the outcome of a passing mood is shown by the fact that Grieg, three years later, on May 14, 1875, wrote to Björnson: "Do you know that in these last few days I have read through both the first acts (of *Olav* and *Arnljot*) and have come to the conclusion that my musical-dramatic interests incline towards the latter? . . . It is a good thing that *Arnljot* has lain awhile; I have become abler, have a better eye for drama, and I have a decided feeling that it will come to something. Don't please imagine that I have gone quite mad. Though I know it is dangerous to have two subjects at the same time on one's chest."

But alas, nothing came of *Arnljot Gelline* either then or later and, what perhaps we have more reason to deplore, nothing more came of the other subject either, of *Olav Trygvason*, than what was already done.

Which of the two, poet or composer, was really to blame that the collaboration so successfully begun was not continued has been much discussed and written of. Both stoutly disavow all "guilt," if such an expression may be used, and it may be of interest, therefore, to see how matters really did develop.

Björnson had long cherished the idea of writing a drama about Olav Trygvason. As early as July 13, 1871, he speaks of the drama in a letter to Gotfred and Margrethe Rode in connection with the mention of *Sigurd Jorsalfar*. On May 30, 1872, he wrote to Dikka Möller that he was working on his opera text and that his reading for the time being was Northern mythology. On November 23, in a letter to the same address, he says: "Now read my *Sigurd Jorsalfar* and my new story and wait for *Olav Trygvason!*" On November 30 of the same year, he writes to S. A. Hedlund: "Next Sunday (December 8) I shall be forty. I hope that *Olav Trygvason*, which I have now begun, may be my good deed in the new decade I am now beginning!"

Björnson prepared himself thoroughly and put much work into his opera text and not till July 10, 1873, did he send Grieg the three first scenes, accompanied by the following characteristic note:

"Dear Grieg,

"I have finished this part, so I am sending it to you. The rest will very soon follow. The piece should be ready by October and may bring you some money. The music must go at a devilish rate. I am not joking. You must steam ahead. Things grow steadily worse and worse. A hell of an uproar is coming now over the miracle, and then more miracle, wild obsessions, dance, delirium, hu, ha!—

"Greet your sweet one and her sister and your brother and his— from your

"Björn."

It is not to be wondered at that Grieg felt he must make Björnson understand that it took ten times as long to write an opera as to write a drama. But now, as before, he let himself be carried away by Björnson's powerful personality and the imaginative might of his poetry. A week later Grieg writes from Bergen: "Thanks for what you sent. There is a matchless mysticism about it and I am eager to get to work. I have had a summer-house lent me by Rolfsen in Sandvigen and there I shall let myself go! But I should have liked to know a little more. Is this the last night's sacrificing before Olav's coming? And what sort of contrast is there to be after? Reading it through, it struck me that much of it should be handled as declamation to music, and in this respect you must give me a free hand. I have learnt much now that will be useful here. But above all, send the next as soon as you possibly can."

But no more of the text came from Björnson, who went abroad soon after. Then came the autumn and with it Grieg's duties in Christiania, concerts, pupils. . . . So his hopes had to be placed on next summer, next "holidays."

But it was a fatal delay—fatal both for poet and composer. By next summer Björnson had moved on very far—both in his thought and his writing. On June 26 he wrote to Grieg: "I have worked much! Amongst other things, two modern pieces (one printed, the other being printed), each to fill out an evening's performance." He says also that he is busy with a third modern play which he hopes to have ready in the autumn.

And Grieg, where was he—what was he busy with? That we learn from his reply to Björnson, dated Bergen, July 5, 1874, in which he says that when he did not then answer (it was a question of the composer's honorarium) it was because he was in a rage with Björnson (probably because he had not sent the continuation of *Olav Trygvason*). "And you ask why?" writes Grieg. "Because now I am sitting here composing music for *Peer Gynt* instead of for *Olav Trygvason.*—There you have the reason."

But that was a dangerous explanation and with it arose the first ill-humor between the two. Nor was Björnson slow in giving expression to it. What irritated him specially was that he thought it was an *opera* Grieg was writing to *Peer Gynt*. On July 14, he answers from Schwatz in Tyrol: "For those who are busy with other writings it is a great loss of time and money to write opera texts. All the same, I had volunteered to begin at once as soon as you came. But unless you are there my text will be written in uncertainty, not as you would like it *from the first*, and so perhaps alteration on alteration— and for that I simply haven't the time. Even in Bergen it was arranged that you should follow us. And for that I got money for you through Behrens. On that account I supported your application for a stipend. Who has broken faith? You or I? Who has been prepared to make sacrifices—you or I? My offer was repeated when summer came and with it time for work for you. Again with no result. Now you are at *Peer Gynt*. Much good may it do you! It has *some* parts for poetic music but as a whole it is a flight away from it, often through comic, dry places that you won't be able to do anything with. Again, you are wasting both your time and your powers. I cannot forbear sending you this warning, even though it hurts."

Grieg, however, was by no means willing to allow that *he* was to blame that *Olav Trygvason* was not gone on with. He wrote to Björnson September 12, 1874, from Christiansand, on his way to Denmark: "Your last letter was certainly extremely strange. Do you imagine that I forbore to come last winter of my own free will? If you had a share in the 300 specie dollars from Bergen, I thank you with all my heart, but could I and my wife go out into the world on a sum like that to do nothing but compose?"

As regards *Olav Trygvason* he says straight out: "The fact is that if I had actually had your text I should have said No to Ibsen and fought shy of *Peer Gynt* with its many rocks." He explains at the same time that it is only a matter of some fragments here and there and that he hopes to have finished them soon.

Björnson answers this, obviously relieved that at least it is not an opera Grieg is writing to *Peer Gynt*. But he continues: "So then, you deny that it is any fault of yours that *Olav* has not been gone on with. Well, blame anyone you like so long as it isn't me; for that would be an abject lie. But I stick to my word: till you are with me, you shall hear nothing from me. I dare not. My time must not be wasted. But, on the other hand, I should be delighted to begin."

Now began an interchange of letters between the two. Meetings were discussed, but what suited the one was not convenient for the other, at least it seemed extremely difficult for Grieg to make up his mind. If we look for the real reason for this, it is to be found in *Peer Gynt*. It runs like a red thread through all Grieg's letters that he dared not take on other tasks before *Peer Gynt* was off his hands, and that was going to take much longer than he had thought.

On September 12, 1874, he writes: "I hope to have finished with this work by autumn (it is only a question of little bits here and there) and will be ready and eager then for *Olav Trygvason*."

On October 1 he says: "I won't have finished with the work I am at now until about Christmas time: it is a promise that the score shall be given in then, therefore I must work here, both for the sake of the work itself and to make money enough to get away." And the letter goes on: "The thing hangs like a nightmare over me, if it were off my hands a word would get me away."

On January 2, 1875, he writes: "With *Peer Gynt* it goes on as you predicted, it hangs like a nightmare over me and I don't believe I'll get it off my hands before the spring." On February 21 he writes that he will work like a horse and hopes to get the score off his hands by April 1. But on March 17 he announces that he has been informed that *Peer Gynt* is not to be produced that season—"to my great delight, for now I can get my job done quietly here before I start for the South."

On April 21 he says: "Thanks for your letter from Sorrento. But your coming home earlier than was first decided plays havoc with my plans. I had expected to have got my work done while I was waiting for you at Munich or to have met you in the Tyrol after it was finished."

At one moment it does still look as though they were going to meet and resume work. On May 8, Grieg writes from Leipzig: "That will suit splendidly. I shall be here till the last days of the month (on the 15th I have to be in Weimar, but shall be back the same night) so welcome whenever you like to the second act. I shall find a room all right, there are several quiet, cheap hotels quite near me. I very much need an outline of the whole plot, but more of that when we see each other."

But no; only six days later he is writing: "Dear Björnson, These lines in great haste to let you know that if I said in my last letter I should be here till the end of the month I was talking nonsense, and you must not on any account delay starting. I shall be leaving in the last week of May, the 22nd, 23rd, or 24th." In the same letter he explains that the rooms in Fredensborg in Denmark, where he had been invited by August Winding to stay, would be ready for occupation from the end of May till the end of July—"so you see I must make use of every day."

And what was it that made time so precious that every day must be used? It was, of course, *Peer Gynt* which, even now, was not finished. It was not till he was staying in Fredensborg that Grieg completed the orchestration of the *Peer Gynt* music and it was

September before he could tear himself away from the score and send it in to the Christiania Theater. The production took place on February 24, 1876, and on May 2 Grieg turned again to Björnson urging that the work on *Olav Trygvason* should be resumed. "I come to you claiming your understanding and I long to hear from your own mouth that you do understand. If it is so, don't refuse me what I now beg for: Give me an outline of the plot of *Olav Trygvason*—but soon, at once. Good God, while I write this the longing to buckle down at last grows to active passion. And it is well that all this time has passed, for I have become another man and see differently and better. Dear man, do what I ask."

But it was now too late. Björnson had lost patience and the estrangement between Grieg and Björnson lasted for a long time.

Fourteen years after, when Grieg took out again the three finished scenes to orchestrate them for performance in the concert hall, he tried to get into touch again with Björnson. About this the poet wrote to his daughter Bergliot in January 1889: "Yesterday I had a letter from Frants Beyer, Grieg's best friend and neighbor, begging me most earnestly to finish *Olav Trygvason* for him. That's how it goes—they all want to use me, all, all."

That nothing came of this is clear from a letter Grieg wrote to Iver Holter, September 24, 1889, shortly before the production of *Olav Trygvason* in the concert hall: "To put you straight about the piece itself I need only tell you that the sketch dates from 1873! I have developed very much since then and cannot exactly say that it is bone of my bone and flesh of my flesh as I am at the present day. But on the other hand I felt there were things here that might well be rescued from oblivion in the waste-paper basket. On the stage I feel sure it would go; about the concert hall I am a little doubtful, but I have hope. The chief reason that the piece was not then gone on with was that it didn't please Björnson to send me more text. That was characteristic of him and his stage of development at that time. Naturally, nothing more will ever come of it, nor should there. It could only be continued now at the expense of unity of style, both as regards his part and mine. This is strictly private to you as friend and artist."

As a conclusion to the interchange of letters between Grieg and Björnson about *Olav Trygvason* there may be quoted the letter Grieg sent Björnson in which he again stretches out to his old friend the hand of peace and reconciliation. The letter was sent from Christiania on October 6, 1889, shortly before *Olav Trygvason* was performed for the first time at the Musical Society, and it led to a reconciliation between the two. It reads:

"Dear Björnson,

"When I ask you to allow me to dedicate to you the music to the completed scenes of *Olav Trygvason* (which is shortly to be performed here at the Musical Society under my leadership) I should like you to see in it a proof that ever since we parted I have always loved you and what you fight for—and a heartfelt desire that this work, which was the cause of our losing each other, may also be that which brings us together again! And so: Wipe out all the smallness and let these dramatic sketches, which come from a full heart, find their way to yours, that great heart which I loved in the old days and love still in the assurance that it is still to be found in the same place as of old! Warmest greetings to you and your wife from both Nina and

"Yours

"Edvard Grieg."

So ended the saga of *Olav Trygvason* and even though it did not run so tragic a course as that of the battle of Svolder, it was serious enough in all conscience. Not only because the loss we suffered was great, but because it was irreparable. The way was clear for the creation of our national, historical opera. It was not only that we had the men who, both in poetry and music, were equal to the task, it was, even more, the fruitful adjustment of the times to the material. What a stimulating factor such a work might have been in Norway's cultural life, what an integrating power it might have had among the people, can perhaps best be felt today when intellectualism with negativism in its train has laid its clammy hand also over Norwegian historical researches.

OLAV TRYGVASON

INSTEAD of spending too much time in contemplating what we might have had, let us rather look more closely at what Grieg and Björnson gave us in this draft—these short scenes of musical drama about Olav Trygvason. If in my examination of the work I come to estimate it rather differently from most of Grieg's previous biographers, it is because I hold that we must look at and judge Norwegian art starting from our own premises and not from those of others. Above all, it will not do to set up Wagner's works as the norm for all that goes by the name of music drama. If kinship for Grieg's opera fragment is to be sought, it will be found rather in French and Russian music than in German. A comparison with Mussorgsky's opera in particular might offer much of interest, as it would show that contemporaneously in European musical life there were creative spirits who set themselves other aims and used other means to guide dramatic music into new paths than those which, through Wagner, were the only accepted ones in Germany. Significantly enough, the two works, the Norwegian *Olav Trygvason* and the Russian *Boris Godunow*, were written at the same time. Mussorgsky's work was performed for the first time in 1874. But it did not become known outside of Russia till after Grieg's death.

That Grieg reacted against one of the fundamental features in Wagner's ideas of reform, the treatment of the singing voice, is not only shown by his music, we have his own word for it as well. In the summer of 1876 he was present at the Bayreuth music festival and wrote from there a series of articles to *Bergensposten* in which he deals with the Wagnerian reforms. In his discussion of *Die Walküre* Grieg writes: "In the second act there is again one of these long dialogues of which one easily grows tired. Unfortunately, the situation is not in itself interesting enough independently of the orchestra to captivate the listener. These dialogues are a principle with Wagner. He defends them passionately. And to tell the truth they need an advocate of genius, for they by no means speak for themselves, not even in a musical sense, and when he tries, with an ardor that altogether overrates the capacity of music, to characterize individual words in notes, formlessness results."

In his notice of *Götterdämmerung* Grieg writes: "When I examine the musical part I am brought to a stand in the very beginning by 'The Song of the Norns.' The somber color over this piece is remarkable. The monotonous figures sound utterly dreary against the harmonies so full of foreboding. The orchestra spins the thread of life fully as well as the Norns, who really only supply an accompaniment of mezzo voices. I have heard this scene under Wagner's own direction at a concert in Berlin. He had no Norns then, he simply let the orchestra play alone and hummed along with it himself. I mention this because it strengthens my argument, when I urge that the singing voices in the whole work do not stand in relation to the orchestra, but often function simply as an appendix. The orchestra is utilized to the full, why not the singing voices also? Because the words would be lost? But to that my answer is that for the most part they are lost in any case, unless they are in the hands of unusually talented interpreters or unless one has made oneself very familiar beforehand with the script. Either the voice should be allowed in at least the same degree as the orchestra to express the deepest things that move in the human breast or it should not be there. But then we have declamation to music. Such a transitional style of song and not song has no future, cannot, broadly speaking, become alive to people, even though defended in a whole literature of brochures. It is the feeling of untenability in Wagner's theories about the treatment of the voice that checks the spontaneous enjoyment a great work of art should give. It is a not too pleasant duty to throw so much cold water as I have now done. But I must say what I think."

That Grieg was a great admirer of Wagner's genius need not be emphasized. He has many times expressed his admiration. But he was no blind and uncritical admirer. The remarks cited show his sound reaction and his instinctive anticipation of things that were to come to pass. Later developments have shown that he was right in the reservations he made about Wagner. We have seen how programme music, precisely because of the support of Wagner's overestimation of the pictorial power of music, has led to formlessness and often deteriorated into a kind of caricature, and on the other hand we have seen how his treatment of the voice led, in his followers, to a gradual desiccation of the melodic line so that finally all that was left was the so-called "Sprechgesang," a bastard which is neither speech nor song, but which nevertheless attempts to be both. But now the whole musical world is in flight from these ideas which threatened to lead the art of music to dissolution. In dramatic music the "Spielopera" stands at the door and in instrumental art absolute music is again making its entry.

Having made this necessary digression, let us go back to *Olav Trygvason*.

The action takes place in an old Norwegian sacrificial temple in Tröndelagen just before the coming of Olav. Besides the chorus, to which is entrusted the largest share of the task, only three persons appear: a sacrificial priest, a woman, and the Volva (wise woman). The work begins with the priest invoking the old gods in a somber threatening recitative. As an effective contrast follows the woman's solo marked by gentleness and pure longing. Here already we feel Grieg's remarkable sense for strong color contrasts; the contrasting colors are set up directly side by side. The chorus supports both parts with its constantly repeated "Hear us! hear us!" The recitative and the solo grow in strength, rise higher, take on a steadily more threatening and always more intense character until the combined chorus succeeds them in a *molto piu animato*: "Other gods have come, strong gods, victorious gods!" Pride and confidence begin to be heard in the music. The pious mood that broods over the beginning of the following passage, "You, who from out the well of the Norns pour vital force over the world," is only of a transient nature; it is the assurance of victory and the joy of battle which here already characterize the music.

The second scene is altogether dominated by the Volva who, with her enchantments, her conjurings, and her wild incantations, sends the music soaring and brings speed and movement into the dramatic development. After having taken auguries and received a sign that it is in the temple the gods will meet Olav, the mood of the chorus too becomes more and more arrogant. It is infected and carried away by the Volva's wild hate of "the evil man, he who comes from the South," and of the gods who follow his train. Derisively the chorus repeats the Volva's reply, "Comes he out unscathed, we shall believe him!" And in the choral passage that now develops, assurance of victory and joy of battle more and more take the upper hand. After the priest has consecrated the drinking horn in a solemn song, comes the final scene in which the gods receive homage and honor with dancing and sacred games. This part consists of a broadly designed dance scene, a round dance, and a

sword dance round the holy fires, a scene that ends in a wild, whirling presto.

The musical construction of these three scenes is in itself masterly in every respect and shows Grieg's sure sense of form, even
when dealing with large dimensions. From the sacrificial priest's
somber and threatening opening recitative, the pure longing of the
woman's solo, the mounting joy of battle in the chorus, the wild
incantations of the Volva, and finally the working out of the dance
scene to the wild conclusion in a furious presto—through the whole
there runs one line, a steadily ascending line which, with unde-
viating consistency, goes on to its goal. As of a mighty flood which
has gathered into itself all the brooks and tributaries and now with
resistless force rushes towards its goal, such is the effect of these
cult-scenes, when our old mythical Asa faith gathered all its
strength to meet the new unknown god who threatened it from
without.

Now all is well set so that the contrast may find effective expression. Darkness lies over us—now there should be light. And from
the few hints that are available as to how the continuation of the
drama had been conceived, it would seem that this was precisely
what was intended. In an interview in *Verdens Gang* before the
performance of *Olav Trygvason* at the National Theater in 1908,
Fru Nina Grieg says: "I could have wished that at least the closing
scene of the act had been completed. The plan was that this act
should finish with the remaining behind of the priest's daughter in
the temple after the others had gone. When she is about to shut the
door, there stands Olav suddenly in gleaming armour that shines in
the sunlight. Overwhelmed and transported, she falls to her knees
before him. With that, the act was to finish."

From Björnson himself we learn how he had imagined the ending. In a letter to Grieg he says that he has discussed his drama
with Dr. Gehring, docent in mathematics in Vienna and one of
Germany's most profound connoisseurs of music. "When we came
to the final tableau," writes Björnson, "Olav on the stone steps
before the burnt-down temple, with bishop and people disposed
about the steps singing God's praise, and from the heights and
woods all round is heard the demand for baptism from the white-
clad multitude arrayed in baptismal robes, white men, white
women who come singing from all sides, white music, white sun on
land and faces. all gathering behind him, over him, round him,

close, close, close; white, white, white; he felt the sketch such an apotheosis of Christianity that he considered it would have the most extraordinary effect. And when I described to him Olav in amongst the gods who talked to him, waxing in power, while the music waxes with them, of the miracles, the battle, the dismay, the fire—and that we left him in the midst of all that to turn back to the anxiously listening troop outside before whom at last the temple door bursts open and everything behind him who is emerging is in flames—howling, terror, triumph, sudden attack—and then the mute stillness of fear, fear of what would follow on Olav's murder of Jærnskægge, storming up against him as against a phantom, fear amongst Olav's men and the pagans—fear, fear, the stillness of fear—and then *her* coming! Well, you can imagine he opened his eyes wide!"

As we can see, it was precisely great effects of contrast that the text called for. But alas! We were to have only one side of the picture. We might have had a work that made use especially of broad surface effects, a special decorative music far from Wagner's differentiation and over-luxuriant shades of color. We might have had a work that in a purely musical sense used the same means of expression that we find in our old tapestries, in Munthe's decorative works, or in Munch's paintings in the University hall. To use Wagner as a standard for Grieg's opera fragment is about as reasonable as to take one of the Renaissance masterpieces and use it as standard and basis in the judgment of our old decorative art. What Grieg was about here was the knitting together in a genuine manner of past and future—in a way such as might have been of far-reaching importance in the development of Norwegian music. That certain foreign music critics have not understood this is natural enough, but Grieg's own countrymen should not accept and associate themselves with complete misjudgment, even though it comes from abroad. That there were some among the German students of music who felt and understood the significance of Grieg's work is shown by Professor H. Kretzschmar's comments which stand in happy contrast to all the misjudgment this opera fragment has had to contend against both abroad and at home. Of *Olav Trygvason* Professor Kretzschmar writes: "Es zeigt ihn als einen Dramatiker, der an Sicherheit des Stils und an Gehalt der Erfindung dem ganzen Wagnerischen Nachwuchs unendlich weit voraus ist."

What strikes one in listening to this music is how magnificently Grieg has caught the color of the period. Purely musically we feel ourselves directly transported to an old Norwegian temple at the end of the tenth century. And if we try to understand how the composer has managed to do this, we find that it is in large part due to the employment of our antique modes, Lydian, Doric, Phrygian, and mixo-Lydian. The priest's opening recitative makes from the start a singular impression through the use of the Lydian mode, the extremely effective heightened fourth, an expedient we find again in the Volva's part and in the chorus. And what a gust of the Norwegian spirit, what an atmosphere of far-off times the composer has evoked by the employment of the Phrygian mode, where, in her wild incantations, the Volva says, "Seek your goal in the North!" And what a heightened impression of austerity and gravity is achieved by the mixo-Lydian mode in the first entry of the chorus, "Other gods are come, strong gods, victorious gods!"

Nor is it only through these purely tonal relationships that the impression of old and far-off times is produced—it is also through the form Grieg has adopted for the delineation of the melody, a distinctive, angular line-drawing, in harmony with Werenskiold's and Munthe's illustrations for Snorre, and far from the soft and undulating lines of romanticism.

But here, as when he uses our old modes, Grieg has arrived at this form for the delineation of the melody by the way of instinct. This is best shown by the want of consistency with which he employs it. He might perhaps be blamed for this, and no doubt consistency would have given the style a purer, stronger character, but on the other hand, the effect achieved has now the direct charm which pertains to anything that is the outcome of intuitive experience and not of sober calculation.

He had yet another resource at his command for local and period color, and that was the orchestra. Here too it is plain that he was striving after something, though in a much more modest way. The beginning in especial is striking with its characteristic theme in the basses over the sustained note in the horns and the tremolo of the strings, also the horn quartet supporting the baritone solo, "Now the drinking horn is raised, the horn of Odin, father of armies," and the use of the shrill, passionate piccolo during the incantations of the Volva.

But the vital point is that the work is genuinely inspired and experienced from the first to the last note. In no other of Grieg's works have the critics been so busy finding reminiscences of other composers as in *Olav Trygvason*. Some resemblances can be shown, but they are all entirely external. To show the value of some of the objections that have been raised, I shall only mention that one German critic considered that the passage "Three nights we prayed" was taken from Meyerbeer's opera *The Prophet*, while another says that the same passage is identical with a song not unknown in Germany called "Deutschland, Deutschland über Alles." Weighty indeed seems the objection of the critic whose opinion it is that Grieg has become infatuated with the gypsy airs in *Carmen*! But this objection loses much of its weight when we know that Grieg wrote his temple dance two years before Bizet's opera saw the light of day!

In the concert hall, where *Olav Trygvason* now has its secure place as a feature of the permanent repertory, the work usually has a run of several performances every time it is given. Always it is greeted with enthusiasm. On the stage its effect is said to have been very much greater. All the papers emphasized this when in 1908 *Olav Trygvason* was given as an opera at the National Theater.

We may perhaps conclude this saga of Olav Trygvason with the words used by Björnson when in 1906 he unveiled the monolith on Rikard Nordraak's grave in Berlin, words he may well have used with Norwegian opera in his mind: "That which does not come at the right time never comes."

BERGEN AND LOFTHUS
1874-1885

COLLABORATION WITH IBSEN

IN THE eight years Grieg lived in Christiania he was so occupied with practical pursuits that it was only the summer
holidays that gave him the opportunity to devote himself
wholly to the work of composition. But thanks to his government
grant as a composer—and 1600 kroner had a much greater value
in the Seventies than today—he was able to resign his position as
director and escape from the exhausting piano lessons.

If, however, he had hoped that the time of struggle was over, he
was grievously mistaken. The period on which he now entered was
above all a period of struggle. But it took place on other fronts, it
was of a much more serious nature, and penetrated much more
deeply both into his art and into his life.

When at the end of May 1874 Grieg left Christiania to spend the
summer at home in Bergen, he had undertaken a piece of work
which he thought he could finish, with his usual expeditiousness,
in a month or two. As a matter of fact, it came to occupy all his
time and thoughts for almost two years.

On January 23, 1874, Henrik Ibsen wrote from Dresden a long
letter to Grieg in which he explained that he proposed to adapt
Peer Gynt—a third edition of which was shortly to appear—for
performance on the stage. He asked accordingly if Grieg would undertake to compose the necessary music for it. In the letter Ibsen
mentions the places where he thought music might play its part
and he indicates also what he thought the character of the music
might be. In the second act the scene between the three sæter girls
might be treated as the composer thought best, but devilry there
must be in it! writes Ibsen.

From the letter it appears that the poet has had the singular
idea of doing away with the fourth act. He writes of this to Grieg:
"Almost the whole of the fourth act will be left out for the performance. In its place I had thought of a big tone painting which
would suggest Peer Gynt's wanderings in the wide world. American, English, and French melodies might run as motives through it,
alternating and disappearing. The chorus of Anitra and the girls,
pp. 144-145, should be heard behind the curtain in conjunction
with the orchestral music. While this is going on the curtain should

rise to show, as in a far dream picture, the tableau on p. 164, where Solveig as a middle-aged woman sits singing in the sunshine by the door of her house. After her song the curtain comes slowly down, the music continues in the orchestra, and changes in character to depict the storm at sea with which the fifth act begins."

Ibsen ends the letter by stating that he intends to stipulate for 400 specie dollars as an honorarium for the performance, to be shared equally between poet and composer, and he thinks that one can certainly count on the piece being performed both in Stockholm and Copenhagen.

From Ibsen's next letter, dated Dresden, February 8, it appears that Grieg has agreed to the proposal. Ibsen thanks him and adds that how much music he will write, and to which scenes, will naturally be left entirely to himself. "A composer must have a completely free hand in such a matter," writes Ibsen. He says also that there is no reason why the work should not be postponed till the summer, as the piece will not come up for performance till the following season.

This time too Grieg set to work in Rolfsen's pavilion out in Sandviken. Beautiful Landås, which had hitherto been the Grieg family summer residence, had, alas, been sold and they were living then out in Sandviken to get away from the town a little in the summer. The elder Grieg's financial position had been steadily deteriorating for some years past and in his letters to his son he complains about this. It was on this account that he had had to give up Landås.

In a letter to Björnson, Grieg calls *Peer Gynt* "the most unmusical of all subjects," and to Frants Beyer he writes in a letter dated The Pavilion, August 27, 1874: "With *Peer Gynt* it goes very slowly and there is no possibility of being finished by autumn. It is a frightfully intractable subject, with the exception of one or two parts, as for example where Solveig sings—all of which I have done. And I have done something for the hall of the troll-king in Dovre which literally I can't bear to hear, it reeks so of cow-turds, ultra Norwegianism, and to-one's-self-enoughness! But I am hoping that the irony will be able to make itself felt. Especially when Peer Gynt later, against his will, finds himself forced to say, 'Both dancing and playing were, scratch me, jolly fine.' "

The day after he writes to Ludvig Josephson, who was then the chief of the Christiania Theater: "I was glad to learn from your letter that it is decided that the first performance of *Peer Gynt* will not take place till 1875, because it would have been impossible for me to have had the music ready for the earlier date. The task is much greater than I had thought and in some of the passages I come up against difficulties that bring me to a standstill. But I hope by the end of the year to have finished it." In the same letter he says: "I see to my sorrow how slowly I am working at present." And he goes on: "I hope you understand that I am writing this in a rather dispirited mood. Tomorrow I shall probably regret bitterly what I have written, but that is just my nature."

A short time after these letters were written Grieg went, in the beginning of September, to Denmark, where he remained in Copenhagen till the end of the year. About New Year he continued his journey to Leipzig. In the end of May he was again in Denmark, this time in Fredensborg, near Copenhagen, where he had been invited to stay in the house of his friend and colleague, August Winding, for the summer, and finally, in autumn, he is once more in Bergen. All the time it is the work on *Peer Gynt* with which he is engrossed and from which he cannot tear himself away. In the discussion about *Olav Trygvason* we have seen how the work dragged on and on. At first Grieg had hoped to finish it during the summer, then it was to be during the autumn, then at Christmas, then by April 1, then in summer again, but it was not till the autumn of 1875 that he could cut himself adrift from his score and send it in to the Christiania Theater. But that he does not yet feel finished with his music and that there are many things about which he is in doubt the long and detailed letter he sends from Bergen on December 14 to Kapellmeister Hennum shows. It is not only the interpretation he is nervous about and in regard to which he gives detailed instructions, even in the orchestration itself he suggests a number of changes and improvements.

On February 24, 1876, *Peer Gynt* appeared for the first time on the stage of the Christiania Theater. The performance was a great success both for poet and composer, and the piece was performed thirty-six times in the same season. Neither Ibsen nor Grieg was present at the first performance. The papers spoke in the most laudatory terms of Grieg's music.

It was not till September of the same year that Grieg had the opportunity of being present at a performance of *Peer Gynt*. He says, writing of it to his German publisher, Dr. Abraham, that he had the honor, both in the middle of the play (after Solveig's song) and at the end, of being greeted with storms of applause. At the end of the play he had to leave his place and show himself upon the stage.

But Grieg was not entirely satisfied with the music in the shape in which it first appeared. To his American biographer, Finck, he wrote that he had not himself the opportunity of witnessing the first performance but that as regards sonority the effect was mediocre. This idea is strengthened by the fact that Grieg later undertook radical changes in the orchestration, both when a part of the music was published in the form of suites and when *Peer Gynt* was performed in Copenhagen ten years later. He wrote of this to Frants Beyer on January 5, 1886, from Copenhagen: "You can imagine I am a busy man these days. I am hard at it with *Peer Gynt*, which I am re-orchestrating, many parts entirely. But now I am at the last, thank goodness, for it is high time. In the café I am bombarded by music copiers and music directors who snatch the score from me sheet by sheet as soon as I have them ready. Then we try them over bit by bit. I was much pleased with two parts at the first rehearsal. These were the introduction to the second act and the scene with the sæter girls. The latter you wouldn't recognize. At the time I conceived it I felt something but now I *know* something, that is the difference. Life, color, and devilry have come into it, which certainly were not there before, so defective was the orchestration."

The performance in Copenhagen was also a great success and Grieg wrote to his publisher, Dr. Abraham, on February 3, that *Peer Gynt* had had a brilliant reception, almost every evening the house was sold out. To Dr. Abraham's enquiry about the publication of the music, Grieg replied that it went without saying that it would be an honor for him to have the score published by Peters and that he would come back to the matter later. The great thing was, of course, he continued, to prepare an edition for concert use. He had little belief that *Peer Gynt* was ever likely to be performed in Germany. For Ibsen's poetry is just as "national" as it is profound and full of genius—the letter goes on to say. Even as late as 1904, when Grieg, along with Hinrichsen, was present at a performance of *Peer Gynt* at the National Theater in Oslo, he expressed the same opinion and added that both Ibsen and he were prepared for *Peer Gynt's* never being performed outside Scandinavia.

If only Grieg had lived ten years longer! He would then have experienced, precisely in Germany, such a success with *Peer Gynt* as neither he nor Ibsen could have imagined possible.

The first performance in Berlin took place in February 1913. Fru Nina Grieg was present, invited as the guest of Kaiser Wilhelm. *Peer Gynt* was played in two theaters in Berlin at the same time and always to full houses. Altogether *Peer Gynt* ran in Berlin alone for over a thousand nights, according to the statement of Herr Hinrichsen, owner of Peters' publishing house. Thence it went on its victorious way over Germany and was performed altogether in more than fifty German theaters. In Paris, too, it had a great success and was performed over a hundred times.

How much of the credit for *Peer Gynt's* victorious progress on the stage is due to Grieg it is difficult to say, but it does not seem at all unreasonable that people who knew Grieg's music were anxious to get to know Solveig, Ingrid, Åse and the Hall of the Trolls more intimately.

It is sad also that Grieg did not live to see the publication of a complete edition of the *Peer Gynt* music. After his fame began to grow, and especially after the *Peer Gynt* suite made his name known to all the world, enquiries were made about the rest of the music. In a letter to Finck he laments that there is no complete edition of *Peer Gynt* in print, but he finds it natural, inasmuch as the drama had not gone beyond the Scandinavian stage, and as all that could be performed in a concert hall was already to be found in two suites.

It was not till 1908, after Grieg's death, that Peters in Leipzig published the complete score with Norwegian and German text, comprising in all twenty-two numbers.

THE PEER GYNT MUSIC

THE prelude to the first act bears the title of "I bryllups-gården" (At the Wedding) and is an exceptionally vivid picture of peasant life. The principal theme, which is intended to characterize the young Peer Gynt, is tense and glowing with life and strength. Excellent are the effects produced by the sudden introduction of abbreviations of the thematic material. They give the music a rhythmic, springy quality so that one actually sees the untamed, unbridled Peer Gynt living always wholly and completely in his life of the imagination. As always with Grieg, the form here too is extremely concise. Just as we seem about to get a grasp of the figure, there is a sudden break, a single note on the horn is prolonged as if in anxious expectation, mild harp chords waft us magically into a wholly different world and Solveig's form glides before our inward eye. This is the first time we hear in the piece the now so dear and familiar notes and they could hardly appear upon a more well adapted background, delivered as they are by the clarinet and oboe alternately, to the accompaniment of harp and strings. Now follows a passage where we hear behind the scenes a solo viola play a "halling" (fling) and a spring dance. In between, Solveig's motive appears in the orchestra and at the end of the spring dance rises to a fervency and strength of expression that give the originally clear and simple motive a stamp of greatness, power, and pathos! So vivid is the music that we see clearly before us the scene at the wedding at Hægstad, when Peer Gynt meets Solveig for the first time at the wedding-feast where she dawns upon him like a revelation of purity, fineness, and delicate charm. In the repeat the material is expanded and receives an all-round elucidation through modulations and thematic work. The short coda which finishes with a constantly repeated motive in semi-quavers forms a perfect introduction to the scolding scene between Peer Gynt and Ase, with which the drama begins.

In later years Grieg inserted his piano piece "The Bridal Procession Passes" into the *Peer Gynt* music; it is played before the wedding scene at Hægstad. But in spite of the richly colored music which has been very finely orchestrated by Johan Halvorsen, one has a feeling that it blurs a little the strong impression which the prelude has given of this scene in particular.

Of other music, the first act contains a fling and a spring dance, which are played by a solo violin at the wedding at Hægstad, as Ibsen suggested in his letter.

The prelude to the second act Grieg has called "Bruderovet og Ingrids klage" (Abduction of the Bride and Ingrid's Lament). Again we meet the principal motive from the prelude, this time in the minor key and delivered allegro furioso. Twice this reappears and each time is answered by heavy chords in the brasses. Then follows Ingrid's lament, a broadly designed elegy that ranks amongst the most beautiful of Grieg's inspirations. He writes himself of this piece in a letter to Hennum: "Special weight must be laid here upon the contrasts, for through them different characters are suggested: andante, Ingrid lamenting, towards the end almost beseechingly, even threateningly, and allegro furioso, Peer Gynt telling her to go to the devil! The horn passage in the andante suggests the demoniac element which appears later in the song of the sæter girls."

About the scene with the sæter girls, Grieg has felt uneasy, as is shown by the long and very minute instructions he wrote to Hennum: "This is a dangerous bit, which will produce either a very poor or a magnificent effect, wild and devilish and sensual, entirely according to how the actors and musicians sing and play. This is just one of the places where I think the music ceases to be music. The sæter girls must shriek the first 'Trond i Valfjeldet!' speaking all at the same time, they must not turn to the audience but only to the mountains around them. Later they must simply declaim the words clearly, that is the important thing, and they must not stand still for an instant but circle around Peer Gynt in wild desire, first a little, then more and more. It will naturally be difficult, when the players are so occupied on the stage, to keep their attention on the conductor's baton *without the situation suffering from it*. Before Peer Gynt's reply, 'Where are the lads then?' the last 'Lacking the lads one dallies with trolls,' must be worked out with special attention to ritardando, clear enunciation of the words, and precision; and the last word 'trolls,' in especial must be worked up both with the bowing in the strings and the ring of the voices, so that the sforzando which follows shall be wild and rough. Then comes the laughter which must have a purely witch-like ring and be supported by music and gesture, still more the second time, and most the third time. Then I suggest that Peer Gynt should come right forward to the footlights and the sæter girls after him so that all they have to tell him can be caught by the audience. But not till the allegro vivace in three-eighths should Peer Gynt with a leap stand right in the middle of them. At the end, quasi presto, the orchestra has its work cut out for it, and if the passage is given its due I think it should sound really devilish. Regarding this scene as a whole I beg of you, urge Josephson to do, along with you, the best he possibly can. You will, of course, have a rough time with the singers, for prima donnas, ex professo, think it beneath their dignity to sing this sort of thing because they reap no laurels from it, and among the actresses there are probably not enough with singing voices. If only life is put into it! That is the main thing."

We see also how, when ten years later he orchestrated the work for performance in Copenhagen, this was the piece that chiefly occupied his thoughts. And we can easily understand his anxiety. It is difficult for the music alone to produce much effect. The whole stands or falls with the life that can be conjured up on the stage and only in connection with this does the music too have interest.

The end of the scene with "the woman clad in green" is drawn with few strokes and gets its character through the use of the mixo-Lydian mode. In a letter to Hennum, Grieg writes of this little sketch that "there is nothing to do but keep at it and make a good diminuendo to indicate that the actors are moving away."

But the composer makes up for it in the next scene in the hall of the Dovre-King. Here he has created music which shows us the full strength and originality of his imagination, and we are led into domains hardly touched before by the art of music. At the same time there is a technical mastership in the handling of the orchestra rarely met with. And the powerful effect is achieved by the use of one motive only! Deep down in the basses and cellos it comes creeping forth, quite pianissimo, the bassoons take it up, the violins, pizzicato, carry it further, answered by the clarinets and oboes, and little by little the whole orchestra wakes into activity, while at the same time the tempo increases. As the curtain goes up for that swarming life in the hall of the trolls a chorus of trolls in unison joins in the ensemble. Song and dance are accompanied by threatening movements towards Peer Gynt, while the chorus sings:

"Kill him! the son of a Christian who has seduced the Dovre-King's fairest maiden." The music and dancing express steadily increasing wildness and frenzy, little by little the trolls come threateningly nearer to Peer Gynt and are just on the point of throwing themselves upon him, but suddenly fall back at the word of the Dovre-King, "Ice in the blood!"

The scene makes an unforgettably grotesque impression. Outside the theater too this is the number that has done most to make Grieg's name known and esteemed all over the world. Even the most recalcitrant of Grieg's critics among the professional musicians here take their hats off to the master. The dance of the Dovre-King's daughter takes its character from the Lydian mode. Grieg writes of it to Hennum: "The music must be absolute parody so that the audience will perceive it. Only then will the effect be comic. Cowbells, of course, can be replaced by the triangle. The piece must begin piano and grow steadily louder."

In the next following declamation "Peer Gynt jages av trolde" (Peer Gynt is chased by the Trolls) the same thematic material is used as in the hall of the Dovre-King. Here we are at one of the weak points in the musical illustration of Ibsen's poem. At the place marked "The trolls fly hurly-burly, howling and shrieking. The hall crashes in, everything disappears," the composer has contented himself with cheap chromatics and purely superficial effects of strength. One can well understand why in his letter to the conductor he writes that the main thing is to go at it hammer and tongs so that there is not a moment's pause(!).

We pass over now straight to the scene with the "Böig." In a letter to Hennum Grieg writes of this: "Naturally there is no question here of music but only that the chords sound as hollow and heavy as possible." And one must agree with the composer: of music there is little. Tremolo in the strings and the coming in of an augmented fourth in the horns and bassoons—that is all. And when the chorus in unison joins in, the same interval is kept up persistently, though with each verse it is moved a semitone up. A composer could hardly have tried in a more primitive way to illustrate this scene so full of character that one might well have imagined really valuable thematic material in connection with it. But declamation to music is a dangerous form of composition; this thought strikes one not only here but also in other parts of *Peer Gynt*.

The rather short introduction to the third act, "Dybt inde i barskogen" (Deep in the Pinewood) was not in the original *Peer Gynt* music but was composed for it later. It is in design a nature impression, full of atmosphere, but its effect is more that of a detached sketch than a mature composition and as a prelude to the act it is rather unsatisfactory.

"Åses död" (Åse's Death) according to the composer's instructions should be played twice. First before the scene in Åse's hut and the second time almost pianissimo from far away, beginning with Peer Gynt's words "Gee-up, get on Blackie!" and ending with the words "Leave off your majestic airs; for mother Åse shall enter free!"

Here by the simplest methods—he uses only the string orchestra—Grieg has created one of his deepest and most inspired tone poems, equally fine whether we regard it as absolute music or as melodrama. Not least moving is this andante doloroso when coupled with Peer Gynt's wild, far-flying fantasies at mother Åse's death bed, to which, in its inevitability, it forms an eerie contrast. It is like a last flaming up of life and a slow sinking down—a last deep breath drawn before the coming of the great peace.

The fourth act, which takes place in Africa, is fresh evidence of the extreme sensitiveness of Grieg's mind. His imagination yields itself willingly to the material and unfolds itself as freely and as easily under the southern sun as under the northern sky. Already in "Morgenstemning" (Morning Mood) which was originally composed for the fifth scene of the act, "early morning," we observe the change of musical diction. The atmosphere of the music has changed, a certain cool peace and pastoral balance leave Norway with its problems, its fantastic nature, its intense emotional life and motley portrait gallery of humans and trolls far, far behind us. In a letter to Hennum we read: "This piece is to be treated simply as music, everything lies in the execution. It is a morning mood in which I imagine the sun breaking through the clouds at the first forte." Included in the *Peer Gynt* suite this piece also has gone on its victorious way all the world over.

Of the little scene with the thief and the receiver, Grieg writes that the tempo must be very rapid and the whole thing must sound mysterious. "It is important that the words should be clearly heard. It is with this in my mind that I have kept the music so simple that anyone can sing it, but to play it is what everyone can *not* do. Peer Gynt does not come upon the stage until the piece is over."

In the Arabian dance with a chorus of women, we see best how freely and naturally the composer moves under a foreign sky. The music has a typically oriental character, yet all the time we feel Grieg's strong personality, particularly in the elegiac interlude in A minor, which is sung and danced by Anitra alone. The feeling of foreignness is strengthened by a piquant and colorful orchestration and the whole becomes a graceful ballet scene, poles apart from the grotesque scene in the hall of the trolls, impressive evidence of the reach and many-sidedness of Grieg's genius. He is fully justified in writing to Hennum: "It is a piece I think should make a great effect. I hope each of the dancing girls will have her own tambourine, that will be the only way to get the sound I wanted. I heard something of the kind last winter that sounded splendid. You must see that the beats fall exactly together. I will be delighted if Fru Juul sings Anitra—greet her from me and tell her that. Peer Gynt's speech towards the end of the piece begins, I think, a little too soon; he shouldn't begin before the flutes have played their last notes, while Peer Gynt follows the receding dancers with his eyes. The deep bassoons and the big drum must sound thoroughly Turkish."

Of Anitra's dance Grieg writes that "it is a soft little dance which I am very anxious should sound delicate and beautiful, on no account must it be danced by more than a few. In order that Peer Gynt's speeches during the dance may be heard by the audience, it is orchestrated in such a way that if necessary it can be kept all the time *ppp*. Do please treat it like a pet child."

It is easy to understand Grieg's tenderness towards this piece, which certainly lay very near his heart. In spite of the graceful, airy character of the dance, there is no lack of passionate moments. It is precisely that dualism so often found in Grieg's music which finds expression here in an exceptionally fascinating way.

With Peer Gynt's serenade the Eastern part of the music comes to an end. To a not over-grateful text Grieg has written music which is both characteristic for the situation and genuinely felt and experienced.

Like a sparklingly clear and fine little star-flower in the wood shines Solveig's song, in the midst of all the Eastern luxuriance. "The actress who takes the part must do the very best she can with this song, as it characterizes Solveig," wrote Grieg to Hennum. "Once in a weak moment I noted in the score that if the actress was not able to manage the humming part, a solo clarinet might do it and Solveig spin as long as it lasted. But I've quite given up that idea, first and foremost because it will not do for her to spin in three-fourths time, secondly because it is not in the character of the song, and lastly because the whole originality of the effect goes by the board. You must be sure, therefore, to practice the humming with the actress. Technically it is not difficult and it can be sung quietly. The whole song should be kept in the tone of a folk tune."

The fifth act opens with a magnificent piece of tone painting, "Stormfuld aften på havet" (A Stormy Night at Sea), a powerfully drawn marine picture in which Grieg shows with what mastery he could handle also a great orchestra. It is very probable that Grieg, himself a native of the Westland, felt a special satisfaction in dealing with a subject so familiar and homelike as storm and shipwreck. The fury of the elements, the terrific squalls of wind, the mournful whining of the storm in the rigging of the ship—all are depicted with naturalistic strength and distinctness. What distinguishes this music from the many tone paintings with which the cultivators of programme music have blessed the world is that the musical material is in itself so valuable and is so deeply rooted in rich and vigorous emotional life that it can well bear its profuse embellishments. Both thematically and in the use of the orchestra there is a resemblance to Wagner's overture to *The Flying Dutchman*, but the likeness is purely external and by no means belittling to Grieg, whose strong personality makes itself plainly felt here also. What is said about the piece in the letter to Hennum shows that it has been revised. Grieg says: "The aim of this piece of music is to characterize a night of storm at sea. All the crescendos and diminuendos must therefore be brought out strongly and the tempo must be very fluid. No. 22. This depicts the going down of the ship. The crashes are denoted by the big drums, kettledrums, and the basses' tremolo, which accordingly must make a terrific noise. The wailing notes in the trebles from the 27th bar must begin each time very softly and afterwards play in a loud crescendo. The tempo a little quieter until the next two-fourths allegro marcato. The presto and the shriek must break in terrifyingly and the kettledrum solo that follows suggest the apprehensive stillness."

One difficult problem still remained to be solved, the scene where the voices of conscience begin to be heard and accuse Peer Gynt: balls of yarn that roll along the ground, withered leaves that fly before the wind, a soughing in the air, dewdrops that drip from the branches, broken straws, and finally, from far away, mother Åse's voice—all make their accusations with steadily growing insistence. Here with combined forces a scene strong and original in its effect might have been created. But Grieg, alas, stopped at the design. The working out clearly occasioned great difficulties and so he was brought to a standstill and could get no further. Once again tremolo and chromatics are to compensate us for the lack of imaginative ideas. Even the same motive is repeated unchanged no less than six times with only differences in scale and increase of tempo and degree of loudness to indicate the progress of the action. Ibsen must therefore be accorded the greater part of the credit when this scene, nevertheless, makes an impression in the theater.

As with the other weak parts of the *Peer Gynt* music, Grieg here too is extremely careful in his instructions as to how it should be performed. He writes to Hennum: "This part, where the music expresses Peer Gynt's qualms of conscience and the growing vehemence with which his deeds accuse him till the last 'Så får du nok,' depends very much on how it is interpreted. Where the woodwinds begin behind the scenes they must make the loudest possible crescendo. In the same way, the strings in the orchestra that come in soon after with a tremolo must begin *pp* and each time make a great crescendo and diminuendo. I expect the device here of having the wind instruments behind the scenes and the strings in the orchestra should have a very good effect. But most important, you must be sure to drill the wind instruments and chorus behind the scenes so that there is no dragging. The effect should be like this: First faint and far off, then all the time growing gradually very loud. The chorus in unison must sound more and more menacing and there should be a suggestion of stretto as the singing progresses."

A hymn which the church folk sing on the path through the wood carries us over to the end, Solveig's cradle song.

"Here I hope for a poetic effect through a combination of expedients," writes Grieg to Hennum. "During the prelude I have

imagined Peer Gynt lying as if hidden in Solveig's arms while the
horizon foreshadows the breaking through of the morning sun,
which must take place at the point I have marked so that Ibsen's
words, 'She sings higher in the splendor of the morning,' get their
due. I hope that the strings here will play evenly, quietly, and
gracefully. I hope that the actress will sing quietly and fervently,
and towards the end higher and with a fuller voice. In order that
the song shall not sound long drawn out, I suggest that where the
three horns break in with the words, 'The boy has rested on his
mother's breast,' Solveig should sing un poco animato and then at
'the livelong day' again tranquillo. In the same way at 'the boy has
lain close to my heart' un poco animato and at 'the livelong day'
again tranquillo. Where the change over into D minor takes place,
the playing and singing must be from the heart and the repeated
'sleep!' must be full of feeling. Always more and more softly and
always so that the notes of the horn and the voice's 'sleep!' come in
in contrast to each other. Then the strings must always accentuate
the beginning of the bars and change immediately to *pp* so that the
whole gives a dreamlike effect, especially where organ and voice
far off and softly are heard coming in behind the scenes. From the
place where I want the sun to break through completely, the orchestra should, little by little, broaden out and the expression
marks be accurately followed. In the same way, Solveig's last verse
very broad and full of feeling. The curtain must fall very slowly
while Solveig remains sitting, bowed over Peer Gynt."

As is apparent from the letter, it is not only the orchestration
that deviates from the now familiar version. Originally Grieg had
finished the song with the entry of chorus and organ behind the
scenes.

Solveig's cradle song gives the *Peer Gynt* music a sublime ending.
It shows us Grieg when he plumbs the depths of the poet's world
of thought and ideas. It is as if all the threads twine together in
this tone poem, monumental in all its simplicity, which gives expression to the power of pure, simple, and faithful love. It is not
for nothing that Ibsen has let the sun rise over this scene and
Grieg, too, has had a purpose when he lets the sunrise be reflected
in the music, which in the end gathers into itself all the motley
scenes and episodes of the work and raises them up into a light of
transfiguration.

As was to be expected, opposing voices have been raised against this—from a naturalistic point of view—rather remarkable ending. A cradle song which ends with the words: "Sleep and dream, dear boy of mine" should end softly and dreamily and not as Grieg ends it in a splendid forte. Just as the critics in the case of "Åse's Death" insisted that the music should reflect what specifically was transpiring at her death bed—that is to say, Peer Gynt's far flying fantasies!

But here, as always, we see that instinct is the artist's surest guide. Where reason and sober-minded consideration often lead to results which endure only for a season, which in twenty years time, perhaps, are faded and withered, instinct points the way to the values that endure for ever.

It is with this feeling of liberation that one leaves Grieg's musical elucidation of *Peer Gynt*.

THE BALLAD AND THE IBSEN SONGS

AT THE end of the long *Peer Gynt* letter Grieg writes to Hennum: "How gladly would I come to Christiania if I had not been living through such sad experiences that I feel quietness is the only thing in which I may hope to find myself again."

The sad experiences that had befallen him were that both his parents had died that autumn. On September 18 he followed his father's coffin to the grave and a short time after, October 28, Fru Gesine Grieg was carried to her last resting place. To the director of the theater, Josephson, Grieg wrote in a letter dated Bergen, September 28, 1875: "I send you these lines in a mood of despondency. A few days ago I followed my father to the grave and my mother lies so dangerously ill that we expect her death at any moment."

After the passing of his parents Grieg and his wife moved back to his childhood's home in Strandgaten, where with his brother John and his family they lived through the winter. Grieg had a workroom in the town and was only with his family at mealtimes. What he was working at no one knew, but from his letters it would appear that it was at this time he wrote his great Ballad in the form of variations on a Norwegian folk tune, Opus 24.

As often in sad and difficult times, Grieg turned now also to the source of Norwegian music, to the fountain, to the rich treasure of Norwegian folk music. In Lindeman's collection he found material for that work which even today towers up alone in Scandinavian piano music.

The Ballad is built on a folk song from Valdres, "Den nordlandske bondestand" (The Northern Folk), the text of which too is so characteristic that it could stand as a motto over Grieg's whole life work and artistic endeavors.

> Many a bonny song I know
> Of lands under warmer skies;
> But never yet have I heard the song
> Of what at our doorstep lies.

So now I'll try if I cannot make
A song that will let folk see
How fine it is in that North country,
The South treats so scornfully.

Grieg's treatment of folk music is always of great interest. Whether he contents himself with treating it harmonically or, as in the Ballad, uses it as material for a great tone poem, we obtain in either case a deep insight into his own individuality and into his greatness as an artist.

Folk songs never go beyond voices in unison, they do not command "art" music's rich trelliswork of voices and that is perhaps the reason for the extreme intensity and concentrated strength that can lie in a simple melodic line. It is as if the whole thought and emotional life of the race is forced to utterance through the one melodic line, the deep perspective of which it requires an artist's mind of extreme sensitiveness fully to understand and grasp. It is of this Grieg in the Ballad gives us living evidence.

Even of itself, the harmonic treatment of the theme shows how, from an apparently simple melody, he makes a whole world to grow. And in spite of the harmonic luxuriance, an impression of monumental peace is conserved because the whole is bound to and rests upon a strictly drawn line. In the first variations the theme is almost concealed in the harmonic web, only now and again it shows through and disappears again. In the following variations it is conducted through a wonderfully rich range of shades of feeling, now in a quiet, contemplative adagio, now hidden under the mask of humor, then reappearing once more in a recitative heavy with reflective thought. Or he uses a little piece of the theme as building material and sets it out, through the medium of chords, as a grotesque scherzando, or, imitatively treated, in a hurrying chase of semiquavers. Next, over broad chords, the melody follows in a devotional lento and after an intermezzo in which Schumann's influence is seen, the great building up begins. While hitherto the material has been illumined from the most varied angles so that gleams of light reveal the depths of its perspective, the next variations show integrating tendencies. The dotted quavers motive in which, in a burlesque allegro, the theme first appears, becomes from now on its fidus Achates. After having fought its way through a series of modulations, steadily supported by the dotted motive, the melody, over broad chords, breaks out again in the major, radiantly, like a hymn of victory, the dotted motive now too bearing it up like the arches in a Gothic cathedral. And in an instant we are over into the coda, an allegro furioso over broken chords, which conjures up still another surprising harmonic richness and which plunges into a spring dance in wild presto. But just at the moment when everything seems worked up to the utmost limit of its capacity, suddenly it breaks off! A note struck violently deep down in the bass is held long, long, before it finally glides down and finds rest in the dominant. And again we have the theme in its original form, quiet, contemplative, resigned.

The Ballad bears witness to harrowing inner experiences. It gives us an insight into the spiritual struggles of a great artist, his aspirations after light and liberation, his battle against the powers of darkness, a battle which strains his powers to their utmost capacity but which ends, nevertheless, in quiet resignation.

The treatment of the piano is in itself more interesting, richer and more versatile than in any other of Grieg's works. The possibilities of the instrument are exploited in a masterly way and harmonies are elicited, from the most intimate and delicate to those giving the effect of a full toned orchestra.

It is worth noting that the Ballad is never to be found on Grieg's concert programmes. It is as though he shrank from betraying to the public what had most deeply moved him when he wrote this work. Even in the letters, the Ballad is very rarely mentioned, and that in spite of its being his principal work for the piano. It is and will always be a work for the very few and it is a rare experience to hear it authentically rendered in the concert hall.

To Herr Hinrichsen of Peters' publishing house Grieg wrote from Troldhaugen on July 21, 1904: "Ich erinnere noch, dass ich vor vielen Jahren sehr unglücklich war, als ich Dr. Abraham meine Ballade Op. 24 vorspielen musste, weil ich davon überzeugt war, dass dieselbe nicht gefallen könnte. Als ich geendet hatte, sagte er aber zu meinem Erstaunen: 'Ein grosses ernstes Werk, welches ich mich freue erwerben zu können, denn es wird Ihrem Namen einen noch grösseren Klang geben.' So ungefähr waren seine Worte. Und, die Zeit hat gelehrt, dass er recht hatte. Es ist überhaupt mit dem sogenannten Erfolg, besonders mit dem 'künstlerischen' sonderbar bestellt. Bisweilen fällt sogar ein Werk im Anfang durch, und der Erfolg ist doch da, NB für den, der einen weiten Horizont hat. . . .'"

Iver Holter relates that Grieg played the Ballad for him in

Leipzig not long after it had been composed, probably in the summer of 1876. It made an unforgettable impression, says Holter. Grieg put his whole soul into the rendering and when he had finished, he was so exhausted bodily as to be bathed in sweat, and so moved and shaken that for a long time he could not say a word.

It is natural that this work should be followed by a series of Grieg's deepest and most inspired songs. In the spring of 1876 in Bergen he wrote six songs to Ibsen poems and from the same time date some of the best songs he composed to poems of John Paulsen. The first of the Ibsen songs, "Spillemænd" (The Minstrel's Song) begins with the typical Grieg leitmotif, octave, seventh, fifth. In the wider sequence-like development it is the treatment of the piano that holds our interest most, while the voice only sustains a recitative. Not till towards the end, after a tremendous crescendo, do we have the motive again, now accompanied by deep, devotional chords. The song is an ungrateful one for those vocalists whose principal thought is to show off their voices, but sung by a really fine artist it makes a deep impression. It is, therefore, not much to the credit of our singers that "The Minstrel's Song" is practically never heard in the concert hall. The same fate has overtaken another of the Ibsen songs, "Stambogsrim" (Albumlines) and for the same reason. Here again there is no opportunity for the *bel canto* singer, but—what a moving effect an intelligent interpreter could achieve with this intimate combination of poetry and music! Yet another of the Ibsen songs is undeservedly neglected and that is "Borte" (Departed), which shows so beautifully Grieg's ability to give expression to spiritual emotions framed in an arresting nature impression. When one thinks of these songs— seldom or never heard—one can well understand Grieg when he writes to his American biographer, Finck, that he has often marvelled at the way in which Mother Nature deals out singing voices to just those people who do not possess either the intelligence or the depth of feeling to use their voices to serve a higher purpose.

"En Svane" (A Swan), in spite of the great demands it makes, both artistic and vocal, is among the most often sung of Grieg's songs. The cryptic text, so charged with meaning, has been clothed in music of corresponding genius. Grieg has aptly indicated that it should be sung "slowly and with reserve" and that is its basic mood. But all the time an undercurrent of passion can be felt that suddenly flares out at the words

> But last meeting,
> When oaths and eyes
> Were secret lies,
> At last thou sangest!

In his letter to Finck Grieg writes that a Belgian singer, Grimand, sang "A Swan" with orchestra at a concert in Paris, under his own conductorship, very dramatically and with great beauty. No Norwegian would dare to render such a poem with the musical expression that answers to the power of the tragic subject, writes Grieg. Our natures have to fight here with the shyness peculiar to our nation.

"Med en vandlilje" (With a Water-Lily) Grieg has directed should be sung "quickly and archly." To get the true impression of this song, which is filled with springtime rapture and youthful longing, beneath which there run also deep and dangerous undercurrents, one should have heard it rendered by Nina Grieg with the composer at the piano. A feeling of complete liberation marks the last song in the collection, "En Fuglevise" (Bird Song). It too is filled with an enchanting natural archness and again we must admire the feeling for landscape which places the experience in a so flattering relief:

> Upon a linden swaying
> In summer wind and sun,
> A mother bird sat singing
> To please her little ones.

Like the liberation of spring after a dark and heavy winter, it rings out in its rapture and young joyfulness.

Springtime jubilation and rapture mark also the first of the Paulsen songs, "Et Håb" (Hope). Here there is no undercurrent of longing or aspiration, here we deal with fulfilment, and the joy of life finds free and unhindered expression. "Jeg reiste en deilig Sommerkvæld" (A Lovely Evening in Summer 'Twas) has its charm in the fine nature impression with which Grieg has enriched the simple text. It is the same with "Med en Primula veris" (The First Primrose), in which the composer by very simple means produces effects the listener can never forget. "På Skogstien" (Wood Wanderings) touches deeper chords; we meet again the wealth of chromatics and the violent flaming up that are such typical characteristics of Grieg's passionate musical speech. "Den ærgjerrige" (The Aspiring) is not altogether convincing. It is marked allegro agitato and certainly there is much agitato about it, but, taken as a whole, this song makes its mark rather by external effects than by inner experiences.

It is not only the general impression made by his compositions which suggests that Grieg at this time slowly worked his way out from heavily burdened darkness to liberating light and spring in his inmost mind. His letters too show that there was an intimate connection between his personal experiences and his art. To Björnson on May 2, 1876, in the letter in which he begged—in vain, alas!—for the renewal of collaboration on *Olav Trygvason*, he wrote as follows: "Yes, I really am alive still—though only now in these lovely days of early spring wakened from a long, long torpor. Since last you heard from me heavy billows have gone over my head; you may have heard perhaps that in the autumn both my parents were suddenly called away and I came to spend the winter here. It has been a dark and heavy one and I have lived locked up in reflections of the most varied kinds. What I have written during this time bears the mark of it."

And in a letter to John Paulsen of June 27, 1876, we read: "In you I see much of myself in my younger days. And so I say to you: 'Get steel into you, steel, steel!' And if you ask: 'How can I get it?' there is only one terrible answer: 'Buy it with your heart's blood.' God knows that I speak from experience. Believe me, my friend, I don't know that I'd ask steel for you—it costs so much! God strengthen you!"

IN THE same letter Grieg says that he is going to leave Bergen in the middle of July and will be in Copenhagen a week later. He asks Paulsen to greet the ever-faithful Feddersen, tell him to have house room for him and also to make ready to go south. It was to Bayreuth Grieg went this summer, where he was present at the first performance of Wagner's *Der Ring des Niebelungen*. To *Bergensposten* he wrote six travel letters in which he reviewed in great detail Wagner's gigantic work and stated what impressions he had received in the holy place of the Wagner worshipers.

From the beginning Grieg's power of vivid description is evident. "This place so swarms with musicians, poets, painters from all the corners of the earth that one stumbles over them wherever one goes. From the whole of Europe the best names are assembled—they have come streaming even from America. In the long run, the flood of artists would be unendurable. I do not stay in an hotel but in a private house and imagined that at home I could be by myself. But no, in corridors, on stairs one meets the famous. Next to me lives a renowned composer of opera, on the other side of the corridor a famous singer, below a famous court bandmaster, and above a celebrated critic. As I sit here I hear Wagner motives being hummed, sung, yodelled, and bellowed from the garden. I go to the window and see Walkyrs and Rhine daughters, gods and humans strolling about in the shady alleys."

In the description of *Olav Trygvason* some of the, at times, strong objections Grieg found he must raise against the Wagnerian ideas of reform have been quoted. The general impression gathered from the Bayreuth letters is that he was certainly impressed, sometimes indeed strongly impressed, by the power and vigor of the gigantic work, but carried away and enraptured he was not. His description of *Rheingold* gives us an insight into the oddly reluctant manner in which he does honor to Wagner: "On the poetry itself I shall not, of course, pass decisive judgment, but it is obvious that the whole of this so-called Vorspiel has been forced into a dramatic frame that is not suited for it, since it is basically epic and as such this material has always been treated previously. One does not feel with these mermaids, giants, gods, and goddesses; one looks at them and admires them upon the stage, but where, as here, they do not come into opposition to human beings so as to stir our human feelings, one gets tired of them. It is characteristic of Wagner that he depicts giants and gnomes with far greater truth than gods. He has not the exalted serenity, the noble simplicity with which Wotan must be drawn."

Grieg finishes his report by saying: "I go home and say to myself that in spite of all that may be objected to the restless, bustling way in which the gods are depicted, to the many chromatic transitions, the incessant changes of harmony that little by little reduce one to a state of nervous irritability and leave one finally utterly limp, in spite of the excessive filigree work, the complete lack of resting points, in spite of the fact that the whole thing stands at the extreme margin of beauty, in spite of everything, this music drama is the work of a giant, equalled perhaps in the history of art only by Michael Angelo."

As we have seen, it is a rather qualified homage Grieg brings to the Bayreuth master and though in later years he many times expressed his admiration for Wagner, the two masters differed too widely in disposition for Grieg to feel that near spiritual kinship which is essential for whole-hearted devotion and enthusiasm. When we consider, for example, the extreme concentration of form in Grieg's work, it is easy to understand that it was difficult for him to tolerate the excessive breadth of Wagner's designs. In a summing up of his position to Finck, Grieg touches upon the Norseman's tendency and ability to express himself in a concentrated way and, in connection with his reaction to the luxuriance in all the external apparatus of Wagner's work, it may be of interest to repeat Grieg's words here. This letter, like all his foreign correspondence, was written in German. "Wer die ältere Edda liest, wird bald die wunderbare Kraft und Knappheit des Ausdrucks, die Eigenthümlichkeit, in wenigen Worten viel zu sagen, wahrnehmen. Er wird die einfache, plastische Gliederung des Satzes bewundern. Dasselbe gilt von den norwegischen Königssagen, besonders denen von Snorre Sturlason. Je tiefer die Regungen des Herzens, je verschlossener, räthselhafter ist der Ausdruck. Die Sprache bleibt immer herb, ernst und würdevoll. Das stürmische Ocean der Leidenschaften ahnt man mehr als man es erblickt. Es galt für brutal, seine besten Gefühle zu zeigen. Gerade für diese ist deshalb der Ausdruck ebenso knapp wie keusch. Diese Sagenliteratur ist der Basis, auf welchem Björnson und Ibsen gebaut haben. Man kann sagen, dass in derselben Weise das Volkslied das innere Seelenleben des Volkes musikalisch wiederspiegelt. Was die Dichter in dieser Beziehung erreichten ist es, was ich in der Musik erstrebte, vielleicht vor Allem in den Liedern zu den tiefsinnigen Gedichten der Volksdichter Vinje und Garborg. Das überschwengliche, reiche des äusseren Apparats, wie es den Deutschen eigen ist, lag nicht in der Natur des Nordländers."

It is natural that with such a conception of style and form it was difficult for Grieg to feel in sympathy with an artist who seemed to base his treatment of his subjects upon such entirely opposite presuppositions. And it has happened to many listeners to find, as Grieg did, that at a Wagner opera lasting four, five, or perhaps even six hours they were reduced first to a state of nervous irritability and finally left completely limp—to use Grieg's words once more.

On his way through Leipzig, Grieg played his Ballad for Dr. Abraham who at once acquired it for Peters, which published it the same autumn. While in Copenhagen too, on his way home, Grieg did some "business" getting the music to *Sigurd Jorsalfar* and the most of the *Peer Gynt* music published for piano solo and duet. On September 2 we find the usual announcement in the Christiania newspapers: "Edvard Grieg will begin his music teaching in the second half of September. In the meantime applications will be received at Warmuth's music shop."

The winter Grieg now passed in Christiania must have been an anxious and difficult time in more than one respect. At all events, in spite of his being able to devote himself almost exclusively to composition, it was a surprisingly unfruitful one. And the two years he had been away do not seem to have changed his feeling for the capital. To John Paulsen he wrote on November 15, 1876: "It was a difficult transition to come back here again from the South —more difficult than I have ever felt it before. I was received with icy coldness on all sides and it would not have taken much to send me on my way again. But now—what happiness—I feel, as a not unknown poet says, 'every symptom of fossilization.' " A letter to August Winding of December 29 shows the same despondent mood: "I have little, far too little, to do and yet I am composing nothing, as I have no room of my own. The choir rehearsals begin soon though, and then I shall have something to take an interest in."

In the beginning of December Grieg and his wife gave concerts in Stockholm and Upsala "to earn some cash," he writes to Winding. "We didn't attain our end. But in all other respects it was a wonderful tour." In a letter of April 23, 1877, also to Winding, he tells what exactly he has been doing in the way of composition: "In my free time lately I have been busy composing 'piano secondo' to the Mozart piano sonatas and have just tried it over with Fru Lie-Nissen. Much of it sounded very fine—so fine that I have grounds for hoping that Mozart will not 'turn in his grave.'" And to his publisher Dr. Abraham he wrote on May 27: "Ich habe im Winter eine Arbeit vorgehabt, was mich interessierte; nämlich ein freies, zweites Piano zu mehreren Sonaten von Mozart hinzukomponiert. Die Arbeit war zunächst für den Unterricht bestimmt, kam aber zufälligerweise in den Konzertsaal und die Geschichte klang überraschend gut."

Grieg has been criticized for his "manipulation" of Mozart and, from a strictly artistic point of view, criticism is justified. The best one can say of manipulations of this sort is that they are unnecessary. And to provide work so sparklingly clear and so full of delicate feelings as Mozart's with needless duplications and paddings is a dangerous thing to do. But from his letter to Dr. Abraham, it would appear that it was with teaching in his mind that Grieg began the work. Nor would he ever have intended that this "opus" should come to be reckoned among his works, as has actually happened owing to the way in which it was sold and dealt with by the publishers. But there came a time when everything with Grieg's name on it had acquired an undreamt-of sales value.

After having played his first violin sonata on June 2 with Henri Wieniawski, who gave a long series of concerts to tremendous audiences in Christiania, Grieg and his wife went westward as usual in the summer. In a letter to Winding he wrote about his summer plans: "I shall probably settle on some little farm or other. I am considering Hardanger."

There are many things which suggest that Grieg had begun to wonder not a little whether the so much longed for freedom was altogether good for him from the purely artistic point of view. The last winter in Christiania he had been practically free from chores, he had conducted one concert and given a few lessons, that was all. Yet the artistic result was no more than second piano to some Mozart sonatas! And that in his thirty-third year, the best years of his manhood and before illness had begun to impede him in his work! There must then be other and deeper reasons for this strange stagnation of his creative activity. Again the question of technique began to occupy his thoughts and he noted to his dismay that time after time he was held up completely when he set himself to work in real earnest. On October 13 he wrote to Matthison-Hansen: "Something I must do for my art. Day by day I am becoming more dissatisfied with myself. Nothing that I do satisfies me and though it seems to me that I have ideas, they neither soar nor take form when I proceed to the working out of something big. It is enough to make one lose one's wits—and I know well enough what it comes from. It is want of practice and accordingly want of technique, because I've never gone further with it than to compose by fits and starts. But there must be an end to that now. I will fight through the great forms, cost what it may! If I go crazy on the way, you now know the reason. I write this to you because I know and feel you have had a greater degree of sympathy with my art than most."

For the first time doubt begins to invade his mind, doubt of his own talents and power. "I will not have you calling me our first skald in music, do you hear!" he writes to John Paulsen. "I don't want to hear any more of that, because it is not true. I might have become that—but now am not. For the rest, it is my intention to challenge fate to a battle. I have still strength to dare that and we shall see if I win. To which end I am resigning all my labors in Christiania and will probably settle down in this corner of the world for the winter so as to be able to work undisturbed."

On October 17, when he had decided to remain for the winter at Lofthus, he wrote a letter to Matthison-Hansen which shows that, along with the problem of technique, the national question too had cropped up again. "You must not say that because the old masters used national motives only now and again, therefore we should not do it, in other words, that we should not adopt another and closer relationship to the national folk music than they did, because *we do*. I do not believe, as Gade says, that one gets weary of what is specifically national, for if one could it would not be an idea to fight for. But as to myself, I believe that I have come near stagnat-

ing through lack of the technique of composition, routine altogether—and lack of occupying myself with the great forms. But I
can take a hint and you are right: No chasing after nationalism. I
will try to throw reflection to the winds and write from the heart,
whether it turns out to be Norwegian or Chinese. And it is to have
peace for this that I have chosen a place like Ullensvang. In
Leipzig or anywhere down there, I should not get that peace. I
know how, when last I was down there, I was made uncertain of
myself by what I heard round me. I dare not and will not come to
Germany without having something 'in my portfolio'—that is the
thing. I believe that at a certain period in one's life one must regard musical impressions like nature impressions. One lives by
them, but one musn't go out after them in order to create *simul-
taneously* with the receiving of the impressions. For that, I have
felt, doesn't work. Nor is it for the sake of nature impressions that
I want Hardanger. I am longing, not only for peace, but for *concentrated* peace. Even if one doesn't give lessons in a town, there
are parties and entertainments of all sorts that lead to indolent
habits, etc., but you must remember that it is not my intention to
isolate myself always—but only when I stand on dangerous ground
as at present."

Grieg had in truth good reason to feel that he had reached a
point of danger in his development. He found himself at a crisis,
both as artist and man. He felt the net beginning to draw close
around him—it was a question now of "to be or not to be." The
conflict between what he had in him to express and the technical
means at his disposal was becoming steadily sharper. In Norwegian nature, in Norwegian folk poetry and Norwegian folk
music he sought to find a foothold. To this bitter conflict it is that
the coming works give beautiful, but often tragic expression.

HARDANGER

IT WAS about St. John's Day (June 23) 1877, that Grieg and his wife came to Hardanger for the first time. They settled at upper Börve in Ullensvang and remained there throughout the summer. The farm lies high up on a steep hillside and has a wide outlook over the Sörfjord with the Folgefonn glacier directly opposite. In a ravine above it a rapid mountain river plunges down in a fall that sprays freshness and coolness round it even in the hottest summer weather.

As always, Grieg's first thought was to procure a peaceful workroom for himself and this he found in the little school which lay only five minutes' walk from the house and stood empty during the summer months. From his letters we see how well Grieg felt in these surroundings. "You couldn't help feeling well if you were here," he writes to Winding on August 13. "Air so light one feels like a feather or rather—one *could* feel like a feather if one hadn't the weight to bear of the happiest and unhappiest fate on earth— to be an artist." A week later in a letter to John Paulsen he says: "It is a lovely Sunday morning. I am sitting in the schoolhouse in which I have commandeered a workroom and can see the churchgoers rowing past out on the Sörfjord. They are making for Ullensvang. Meantime, I shall go into another church, the great church of memory, and let my thoughts rise up like pillars towards beauty and light."

This summer at Börve he wrote "Langs ei Aa" (By the Riverside) to words of Vinje's, and some of his choruses for male voices based on Norwegian folk songs. In addition, he began work on the string quartet which was to occupy him for nearly a year.

Hardanger suited Grieg exceptionally well, Fru Grieg relates. It was as much the people he learned to know as the beauty of the surroundings that fired his imagination. He was carried away on an overwhelming wave of enthusiasm for the Norwegian peasant—for his manners and customs, his speech, his aristocratic nature, his feeling for art, his home craft, his dress; in short, everything to do with the peasants had something almost holy about it for him and on this subject he could not bear to hear a disparaging word. An enthusiasm flaming up so violently naturally went too far and brought him many disappointments. But in Hardanger he learned also to know people who never changed throughout life's many changing relationships and who came to be numbered amongst his best and dearest friends. Chief among them were his host and hostess, Hans Utne of Lofthus and his wife Brita (née Aga).

When Grieg decided to remain for the winter in Hardanger, he felt that Börve would be too out-of-the-way and difficult of access. He chose, therefore, the neighboring Lofthus where he and his wife lived with the Utnes. But there was difficulty about a workroom— here there was no empty and solitary schoolhouse, and working in a room at the Utnes' was out of the question. There was nothing for it but to build a little hut to work in, far enough from the house for him to feel sure he would not be heard while at work. So in the autumn, while Grieg was in Bergen, where he gave two concerts to make some money for the winter, the hut was put up. From letters to Hans Utne, we see with what care and attention he followed the setting up to get all as he wished.

On September 27, 1877, he writes to Utne: "Brita promised me to ask you to keep an eye on my house—that is to see that the work is well and solidly carried out and, above all, that the building is wind- and water-tight. There is nothing in the contract about the foundation being plastered, but if you think that important for foot warmth, you must get the man to do it.

"The contract provides that outside the double doors there should be a sort of covered-in porch for security against snow-drifts, etc. It was not arranged that this covering was to come down to the ground, but on the advice of several friends I have changed my mind. Will you do me the great service of getting the builder to carry the covered part right down and board it in all round so that it forms a sort of porch, only big enough to allow of one man standing in it—one door, opening outwards, to be at the outer end and the other, opening inwards, at the inner end, giving access to the room itself? A single glass window I should like if possible on one side of the porch. I don't suppose that much timber or work will be needed for the little change I am suggesting, but since the builder's charges, according to various accounts, are high and I have already had to pay a good deal, I shall be very grateful to you if you will make an arrangement with him about these small things so that they do not cost more than is reasonable. Herr Arctander has also promised me to take a look at the work and it would be very kind if you both would go up there in a moment of leisure. According to the contract, payment of 70 specie dollars should be made on October 15, by which time the house should be finished (except for a stove); may I take the liberty then of sending you this money and may I ask you at the same time to advance whatever extra is needed for the alteration until we meet."

On October 26, Grieg came back to Lofthus and stayed there with his wife till late autumn of the following year. They lodged at the Utnes', where Fru Brita was their excellent hostess, and Grieg began his daily journeys to and from the little hut where so much of what today we reckon most precious in Norwegian music came into being. The painter, Wilhelm Peters, was also living in Lofthus this winter and in the *Century Magazine* for November 1907 he has related many things that help us to form a picture of their daily life.

Grieg had built his hut in an out-of-the-way position, Peters says. "Not only was there no road to the house, but from his place at the piano Grieg could see, like Odin from Lidskjalf, whenever anybody tried to approach from afar. I was chosen architect and superintendent of building, an easy enough task, because the house was nothing but a square wooden box big enough for a piano, a fireplace and the master himself." Grieg could not bear to have anyone listening while he was playing or composing. "If he noticed an auditor he immediately shut the piano, and ceased to work. His wife was his inspiration as well as his best interpreter; for no one can sing his songs as she does. I believe that during their long married life—they were both about twenty when they married—they were never a day without each other's company; but even with her in the room he could not work."

An amusement much enjoyed on rainy days was fishing. "We would put on our fishing togs and sit for hours in a small boat, hauling in fish while the mist made fantastic caps and hoods for the mountain peaks, and a musical quiet reigned undisturbed except for the jovial song of a bird or two, while the far-away waterfalls furnished the tuneful undertone."

On stormy days in winter, "when the wind shook our house, rattling doors and windows like spirits playing an immense orchestra, Grieg sat in a corner listening. I have known composers, who, in writing a little song, would use up a cartload of paper. Not so with Grieg: he would use only a single sheet. He wrote his music with a lead pencil, rubbed out, and substituted, and changed again, until he was satisfied. Then he wrote it over in ink, and sent to the publisher the same sheet with which he began." During this winter Grieg wrote several of his quartets for male voices and often the neighboring peasant folk came and sang old folk songs for him.

The little hut was very well placed, but still more than once Grieg was disturbed by inquisitive listeners. He decided, therefore, to move his house down to the fjord in the hope of being at peace there. Grieg has himself given so lively and amusing a description of this removal that it deserves a place in his biography.

The Compost

"In truth a harsh sounding name for an artist's dwelling! But the little room I had set up in my winter lair was christened thus by Hardanger peasant wit. Little and young in years, it has already a history which the publisher of this paper has asked me to relate, since he thought that, told by myself, it might win sympathy among friends of my art.

"It was in the year 1877 that I went to the Sörfjord in Hardanger in order to find peace to work. I stayed for the summer at the farm of Börve and was so impressed with the magnificence of the scenery that I decided to remain there for the following winter. But since Börve was too lacking in comfort, even for a 'native,' I chose the neighboring Lofthus in glorious Ullensvang of which Wergeland has sung. A place had now to be found for my workroom and not then knowing the neighborhood, I chose a secluded hill slope to which there was no visible path, in the hope of being free from intruders. But—ill luck would have it that an old right-of-way footpath, of whose existence I was unaware, led directly to the place. And the country folk weren't long in finding the way— not they. For they wanted to listen. So all winter through I had the pleasure, when the weather was not too impossibly bad, of hearing stealthy footsteps round the hut as I sat at work. And as I rose often from my writing table to try a new-born thought on the piano, more than one tender nursling was smothered at birth by the peasant critics who were listening behind the house to stand godfather to the child.

"The way over the fields through yard-deep snow was often heavy enough for me and, as it turned out, the hut lay so exposed

to the weather that in the tremendous winter storms I often really
thought that I and the house together would fly up into the sky.
One day I could bear it no longer. I decided, like a new Aladdin, to
remove my castle and was so fortunate as to find amongst rocks
and copsewood right down by the fjord a quiet sheltered place,
looking out to the icy slopes of the Folgefonn glaciers. Easter was
already drawing near when I proceeded to carry out my project. I
summoned about fifty peasants—there couldn't have been less—
who had promised with the greatest goodwill to attend. (N.B.
not as paid workmen—nothing would induce them to do that—
but as friends and acquaintances.) Our peasants have still the fine,
ancient custom of helping each other with work for which many
hands are needed, with no return other than free refreshments. . . .

"One beautiful morning on the stroke of 9 the whole stout company assembled, obviously in holiday mood, which was in no way
damped at sight of the numerous preparations in the way of food
and drink I had had the wisdom to lay in. A barrel of Hardanger
ale, of the kind known for its strength, stood ready beside an
adequate supply of genuine Norwegian aqua vitae, with appropriate edible delicacies, such as 'flatbrödlefser,' 'kringler'[1] and so
on. All these national delights were despatched to the new site
where, when the work was over, the actual feast was to take place,
presided over by my worthy and amiable hostess, famed throughout Hardanger for her beauty and intelligence.

"With my countryman, Wilhelm Peters, the painter, who also
was staying in Hardanger for the winter and who functioned with
great success on this occasion as a sort of lieutenant-general, I set
out at the head of my army to the spot in question. Rôles were
assigned, each man ordered to his place, and it will be long before
I forget that glorious moment in the history of the 'Compost'
when, with a mighty tug, he was loosed from his foundations
amidst the tumultuous shouts of applause from the assembled
peasantry, while the pupils from a nearby girls' institute, who had
established themselves outside their school in a body, rent the air
with an enthusiastic hurrah, full of youth and spring, and accompanied by the waving of handkerchiefs. It was as if we were all
electrified by these blithe, gay girl voices and with rejoicing the
house was now borne off—sometimes dragged, sometimes rolled

---

[1] *Flatbrödlefser*—a kind of thin oatcake; *kringler*—a kind of sweet biscuit.

The Work Hut Which Grieg Built at Lofthus in 1877

on the trunks of young trees—to its new home. A rest by the way presented a diverting scene, Messrs. Peters and Grieg going from man to man pouring out drinks right and left, while pithy jests flew round, bearing good witness to the general enjoyment. Then off we went again and, among renewed shouts of hurrah, reached the selected site. When at last the house was lifted on to its new foundation, where, among birches and rowans by the glass-clear fjord, it looked superb, the bowls of ale began to circulate, and they were needed, for many a stout carl could be seen to wipe the sweat from his brow after the exertion. Little groups were formed on the grass and peace descended on them. How genial and hearty the Sörfjorder can be was proved to the full at this stage of the feast. Lively banter, spiced with wit and mischief, flew from mouth to mouth and legends and fairy tales were heard from eloquent lips, related with such primitive power and saga-like conciseness in the noble, sonorous peasant speech that it sounded in my ears like the most beautiful music. But—the work was not yet quite finished, for the piano had still to be brought and put in its place. A detachment of troops was sent off and in a few minutes came galloping madly back, carrying the heavy case as if it were a feather. The remaining section of the guests had applied themselves so diligently meantime to the ale that the general mood was beginning to be suspiciously animated. Already a few were overcome and lying round like dead bodies in the grass.

"The rest of the company now insisted on my playing to them and, of course, I neither could nor wished to refuse. In less than no time the little room was so crammed with listeners that I could hardly move my arms. Those for whom there was no room on the floor stood in the open door or sat in the window, while the rest of the listening crowd stood outside and stretched their necks to see 'the playing.' To the accompaniment of a listener on the left, who kept crowding in on me so that I almost fell off my seat, and another to the right, who made so fiery a speech that he spluttered over the keys of the piano, I played a Norwegian folk dance called 'Stabbe-Låten' (Log-Dance). There was now, I must admit, a moment when all was still, but it was only a moment. The next a hoarse voice was heard from a corner of the room: 'Thank you—

but devil take me, that's enough for today!' A most cheering critic! I didn't let myself be driven away, however, though it was all I could do to play for laughing, but went on until the dance was finished, inspirited by the short shrift given the disturber who was instantly kicked (literally) out of the 'concert hall.' As the last note died away, a sober speaker wished good luck to the house and I replied with thanks to all the partakers in the work and a 'skaal' to the Sörfjorders. Outside the hut the fun began to be fast and furious and stones and clods were flying. The men at first aimed at each other but that soon palled and the brimming bowls of ale passing from hand to hand became the selected target. The clods were aimed with amazing accuracy. Ale and earth showered over the bystanders so heavily that the air seemed darkened and when anyone got a good 'ale bath' the laughter was deafening. It was a grotesque sight!

"While this was happening up at the house, down by the sea lay certain blessed ones on whom the vicinity of the ale keg exercised a magical power of attraction. At last stupor conquered completely, and a poor fellow who was dead drunk and lying stretched out upon the grass was, with demoniac laughter, fairly buried alive under clods. At this stage of the festivities I found it best to disappear unnoticed. But when I visited the place next morning, a sorrowful sight met my eyes. The beautiful greensward had completely disappeared and torn-up clods, tree stumps, branches and stones, sometimes spattered with blood, strewed the field of battle.

"Thus was the house dedicated—and I can truly say that if the dedication cost blood, my sojourn there has done no less. For nowhere else has my heart's blood flowed as in the music that came into being here. It was a glorious time. Here I found peace and quiet, until the summer holidays at least, when tourists saw fit to establish themselves in their boats right under my window. That put an end to my happiness. Later I sold the 'Compost,' which has now been moved to the Ullensvang rectory as—a doll's house!

"Edvard Grieg."

About the heart's blood that flowed inside the hut there can be no doubt, as anyone who will look deep into the works created here can satisfy himself. As to the blood Grieg pictures as flowing outside, it may well be that his imagination has been a little too lively and the incident too dramatically presented. At any rate, the Sörfjorders protested vigorously against the latter part of Grieg's sketch, they would not have the shame of having behaved like that fastened upon them, and it is at the desire of Brita Utne, among others—she was herself present as hostess—that I correct this little inaccuracy in Grieg's account.

THE FATEFUL WINTER AT LOFTHUS

A SEARCH for the cause of the extreme intensity in Grieg's music reveals that the reasons for it were many. As an artist, Grieg was emphatically a lyricist with a strong dramatic strain and he had it in common with the romantic masters that his thoughts sprang direct and spontaneous from his creative brain in the very moment they came into being. His near kinship to folk music explains perhaps something of the freshness and originality, the thrilling sense of nature and folk life that are such essential characteristics of most of his music.

But there is another thing of the highest importance for anyone trying to trace the source of the pregnant strength which characterizes Grieg's musical language and which often makes one feel that there is contained in very small compass embryonic material enough for a whole world of thoughts and feelings. The most, and certainly the best, of Grieg's works took shape against a background of notably unproductive periods in his life, times when it was impossible for him to work, tragical states of incapacity, out of which he tried in vain to tear himself. These periods were filled with ceaseless hurry and fermentation of mind but also with gnawing doubt and, when at last release came, it was with a violence that gave the act of creation itself an almost explosive character.

Grieg tried to find the reason for these strange periods of standstill, the reason why he was never able to compose except "by fits and starts" as he calls it, and he was always imagining that he had discovered it. In the first years of his youth, before he had yet met Nordraak, it was the German school that had prevented his powers and talents from developing. During the Christiania period there was constant complaint in his letters that practical affairs, pupils, conductorship, pot-boilers, etc., hindered him from composing. But when at last, after eight years, he was released from his duties and found himself a comparatively free man, it was soon clear that this explanation would not hold water and it became evident also that the intervals between the spasmodic, fruitful periods were tending to become longer, and he found himself more than once in the position of being unable to work, even though there were no external hindrances to prevent him. But for this too Grieg thought

he had found an explanation; he believed it to lie in his poor education—he lacked technique and the whole blame for this he laid very
naturally upon the shoulders of the Leipzig Conservatory. Time
after time he repeats his complaints about the Leipzig institution.
He wrote to Julius Röntgen from Lofthus in October 1884 saying
how he envied Röntgen a technique which he himself felt the want
of more and more every day, and he added: "Daran bin ich nicht
allein Schuld sondern und hauptsächlich das vermaledeite Leip-
ziger Konservatorium wo ich auch gar nichts gelernt habe!" One
would have thought that Grieg, still in the best years of his youth,
would now have done something to make up for lost time and acquire that knowledge the lack of which he felt so bitterly. But there
is nothing to suggest he ever attempted to do this; and as the years
went on it became little by little his health that was the subject of
complaint. In his poor health he thought he had found the reason
for the scant production of his later years, it was his health that
must be blamed each time the voice of conscience, like the "balls
of yarn" in *Peer Gynt*, grew too loud in its accusations. But if we
compare this with Klaus Hanssen's medical report which affirms
that Grieg's health was good, that he was able to stand frequent
and often very exacting concert tours, and that until three years
before his death he undertook mountain excursions in the Jotunheim each year, it seems possible that it was a purely psychological
depression which affected the physical powers and weakened
physical resistance, and not the converse.

Grieg does not seem to have understood the actual cause, the
true reason for these fatal checks in his production. He does not
seem to have realized that there was always in his works an inner
antagonism—an antagonism which in his early days abundance
and richness of material could cover over, but which nevertheless
was there and was so serious in character that as time went on
there developed from it a tragic situation of conflict.

In following Grieg's development it becomes evident that musical feeling in Norway, though of an abundant richness and
variety, lacks the technical resources, both stylistic and formal,
necessary for expression in the form of "art" music. Grieg shows
how far this unique material can be dealt with by a technique with
which it has indeed some features in common but which in important respects has a restrictive rather than a liberating effect
upon it. The richness and individual character of the material are

such as to demand the methodical labor of generations if a technique is to be evolved which can express it fully.

This is the deep cause of the conflict in which Grieg now found himself involved, a crisis so serious that it might well be called his tragedy as an artist. Should one question the correctness of this view, a study of the works Grieg created this winter of his great self-adjustment in Lofthus will remove all doubt; they speak with a clear and convincing voice. Nor did Grieg stand alone in this; he was in the most intimate contact with the problem overshadowing all cultural life in Norway—the problem of how to create a vehicle of expression for the fettered powers struggling for liberty in a people who for hundreds of years had been without a culture genuinely their own and common to the whole people.

The work that occupied most of Grieg's time this winter in Lofthus was the string quartet in G minor, Opus 27. It had been begun in the summer of 1877 at Börve, but not till a year later, in July 1878, could Grieg write to Dr. Abraham that at last he had got the work out of his hands, the final step having been taken after a long and voluminous correspondence on technical details with the violinist Robert Heckmann.

It was to be expected that Grieg should meet great difficulties in the creation of a string quartet, the most exacting form of chamber music. After having completed the quartet, he writes to Matthison-Hansen: "You have no idea what a job I have had with the modelling—but that is because I had been near stagnation and that again was the result partly of many 'occasional' works (*Peer Gynt, Sigurd Jorsalfar*, and other such stupidities), partly of too much popular stuff. To that I mean to say 'Farewell my shadow,' if it can be done."

Here, more than in the preceding sonatas, it becomes evident that the material of which he was possessed could not be forced into the customary mould of classical chamber music. His quartet in G minor betokens a break with tradition so serious that it has set its mark even on the music of other lands. There can be no doubt that Debussy, when he wrote his own string quartet ten years later, sought support from Grieg. No composer hitherto had so completely abandoned the polyphonic style in a string quartet, making almost exclusive use in its stead of a strict melodic-harmonic technique and yet succeeding in the creation of a work that takes its place among the best of its kind.

The singular intensity Grieg can achieve through melody which has a quality of inevitability in it, the highly characteristic relief he gives through the ingenuity—amounting to genius—of his harmony and the way in which the whole is further strengthened by the stirring dramatic quality of the style and the animation of the rhythm are proof of the justice of this claim. In this work too, the impressionistic treatment of nature makes its first appearance in the classical forms, the subjective experiences stand out against a background depicting Norwegian landscape and peasant life. There are things which suggest that the string quartet should be regarded as autobiographical to an exceptional degree, a work which, besides reflecting the serious crisis Grieg passed through as an artist, gives also a glimpse into grave personal experiences. Our attention is sharply roused from the very outset. Again we meet the theme from "The Minstrel's Song," the setting to Ibsen's fateful poem. Is there perhaps something of a programme concealed in this? Do the exceptionally dramatic diction, the passionate musical language, the essentially tragic stamp of the whole work hint at correspondingly dramatic and tragic experiences in the artist's own life? This question cannot yet be answered—the time is not yet come for a complete clearing up, but when all the material bearing on this part of Grieg's life is at last available, it may show that here too there was the most intimate connection between his life and his art. However that may be, the way in which Grieg uses this motive has resulted in giving the work exceptional unity. The quartet shows besides a grasp of thematic composition and a technique in the use of motives that are both interesting and original, and seldom found elsewhere in Grieg.

The motive not only frames the work like two great pillars but puts its stamp also on the individual movements. In the first and last part it forms both the introduction and the coda and appears also as the subsidiary theme in the principal movement, where it forms an effective contrast to the dramatic first theme. In the second part, which Grieg has called "Romance," the rôles are changed. Here it is the leading motive that represents the dramatic element and breaks disturbingly, time after time, into the idyllic mood pervading the main theme, displacing and dissipating it so completely that it can only with great difficulty be brought back into the movement again. Three times the dramatic leading motive strikes perturbingly in before the idyll brings the movement at last to a triumphant close. The third part, "Intermezzo," has a principal theme derived from the leading motive. This movement is bursting with rude energy and has a racy humor that makes it one of Grieg's most typical productions, not least in regard to the elements, strongly contrasting in both character and dynamics, that are here set abruptly side by side. The trio is nearly related to folk music and paints an animated scene.

In the last part we have the leading motive again as introduction in a broad lento, from which the movement breaks suddenly into a passionate *presto al saltarello*, a wild and long movement in which dance rhythms play the characteristic part. It seems to have been written, almost without stopping to draw breath, in one great wave of inspiration, growing wilder and wilder, more and more intense until at last the leading motive reappears over broad chords in the major like a conqueror's triumphant announcement of victory.

In the letter to Matthison-Hansen already mentioned, Grieg himself writes of this work: "I have lately completed a string quartet which, however, I have not heard yet. It is in G minor and is not planned to be meat for small minds! It aims at breadth, vigor, flight of imagination and, above all, fulness of tone for the instruments for which it is written." This last hits the nail on the head with special accuracy, for Grieg's quartet is indeed full-toned, so much so sometimes that one can imagine oneself listening to an orchestral suite played as a string quartet; which is to say that the intimacy which is the soul of chamber music, and which only the polyphonic style can make possible, is sometimes lacking.

From his letter to Matthison-Hansen, it would appear that Grieg regarded the string quartet chiefly as a preliminary study for coming works. "I needed to do it as a study. Now I shall make a start with another piece of chamber music. I believe I shall find myself again this way." It was, however, to be his only quartet.

The other work he completed this winter, the *Album for Mandssang*, Opus 30 (Album of Songs for Male Voices), Grieg describes in the letter already mentioned as written mainly for relaxation and rest. None the less, these songs for a choir stand out as finished masterpieces. They are twelve folk songs and dances from Lindeman's collection, freely treated for a solo voice and chorus.

Here the composer goes deeply and directly down into our folk music, stamps it with his own strong personality, and lifts it up into the realm of the world's immortal music. It is just in these songs and dances that the composer finds expression for what is most individual in his own nature. He sees himself as in a mirror. His composite, divided nature streaming through these highly concentrated tone poems, swinging from gay humor to the agonizing pain of love and to religious devotion, is like light broken up in passing through a prism. Most of the songs are written for baritone solo with double quartet or a small chorus; they aim rather at the intimate contemplative emotions than at brilliant mass effects.

The sounds Grieg succeeds in eliciting from a male voice choir and the effects he achieves within the strictly limited framework are altogether staggering. They are such that several of the melodies seem to reveal their true nature, their inner power and intensity for the first time through Grieg's harmonic treatment. This is especially so with the well known melody to "Jeg lagde mig så sildig" (So Late I Went to Sleep), in which Grieg's harmonies give us an insight for the first time into the deep perspective of the melody. The same can be said of "Han Ole," the ballad of Ole Vellan, in which the treatment brings out a typical feature of our people's musical, intellectual, and emotional life—outwardly unpretentious, simple, and confiding, inwardly so full of thrilling life as to embrace the whole universe.

In "Torö liti" (Little Torö) we see best how delicately Grieg proceeds in his delineation of the progression of the plot and how he is yet able within sharply defined limits to present an entire drama in miniature. Noteworthy is the stirring effect attained by the choir's steady repetition of "Å höyr du Torö liti," while the soloist declaims his message: "Oh hear, thou little Torö, I speak to thee, All's in God's hands. Wilt thou not fly from the country with me? Our Lord send us his mercy." It sounds like a mysterious choir of spirits which in steady crescendo at last assumes a character of impending terror. And then again in the major, lightly and with a touch of warmth, through which is caught a glimpse of hope: "Wilt thou not fly? Oh hear, thou little Torö." After a pause comes the question yet once more, but now quite pianissimo and in the minor, like an anguished foreshadowing of the soloist's answer: "How then could I follow and fly with thee? All's in God's hands. The king's son of England is wooer to me. Our Lord send us his mercy."

The same technique and method of treatment are used in "Dæ æ den störste Dårlehet" (It Is the Greatest Wickedness), a song of love disdained in which from simple words and melody a moving work has been created. All the compositions named here are love songs, but their emotional content verges on the religious; there is a strong intermingling of religious feeling in them which penetrates deeply and helps to give them a stamp of nobility and loftiness.

On the other hand, in one of the religious songs, "Deiligste blandt kvinder" (Loveliest Among Women), a hymn to the Virgin Mary, we find earthly love side by side with the religious adoration of God's mother. It is written for five solo voices or a small choir and shows an attempt at a polyphonic style which one may regret Grieg did not try to utilize to a greater extent.

"Den store, hvide Flok" (The Great White Host) expresses religious emotion, pure and simple. Here is seen best what treasures otherwise lost in darkness and forgetfulness this artist of genius has been able to bring into the light. There can be no doubt that it is due to Grieg when this melody has become a possession of the whole nation. This composition shows also what material we have at our disposal when it comes to laying the foundations for a future Norwegian church music.

Humor fills a large place in the collection, both the grotesque kind, bursting with energy, such as we meet in two *hallings* (flings) and in the spring dance, "Går e ut ein Kveld" (If I Go Out of an Evening), and the more meditative, half melancholy, as in "Fantegutten" (The Gypsy Lad) and the priceless "Bådn-Låt" (Lullaby) to the special popularity of which the mewing of a cat sandwiched into the second tenor part has, no doubt, contributed. Grieg shows in these songs that he possesses what is essential for all sound, genuine humor—fellow feeling, secret sympathy, that precious quality which is far more fruitful and of far greater value than sterile wit.

Only one of the songs, "Rötnams-Knut" (Rotman's Hill), is written for a large choir. It forms a magnificent termination to the collection and shows the close connection between vocal and instrumental elements in our folk music.

Yet a third work is bound up with the sojourn in Lofthus that winter, a work modest enough in size and externals, but which for inward strength betokens perhaps the highest point in Grieg's production. It is "Den Bergtekne" (Taken into the Mountains) for baritone solo, string orchestra, and two horns. The text Grieg found among the old verses in Landstad's *Norwegian Folk Songs*. It runs thus:

I sped wildly through the wood
　　The river rocks among,
The troll's daughter stole my wits
　　And to my home I never won.

I sped wildly through the wood
　　Where swift the river flowed,
The troll's daughter witchèd me
　　I never found my road.

I have been where the troll lives;
　　The troll ran after me,
The young maids said I lured them on
　　Though they were hid from me.

I have been where the troll lives;
　　The great troll followed me,
The young maids said I ravished them
　　Though ne'er I did them see.

The fishes in the bonny burns,
　　The herring seek the sea—
Many greet their sons-in-law
　　And wot not who they be.

The fishes from the bonny burns,
　　The squirrel in the tree,
Each has its mate—for me alone
　　Mate shall there never be.

I sped wildly through the wood
　　The river rocks among,
The troll's daughter witchèd me
　　And to my home I never won.

From a letter to Gerhard Schjelderup it appears to have been Grieg's intention to compose a large work for choir and full orchestra, but he could not find the text he wanted. The letter, which is dated Bergen, September 18, 1903, says: "I knew well that you would be able to appreciate 'Taken into the Mountains.' Among the mountains of the Sörfjord in their winter mood, when I wrote it and much of the best I have done (the string quartet for example) I got hold of Landstad's Folk Songs. I searched for more poetry of the same vintage as that I have called 'Taken into the Mountains.' Then I would have used also chorus and full orchestra. But I did not find the right words and so it remained only a fragment. That was in the years 1877-1878. That was a period of great importance in my life, rich in events and spiritual shocks."

"Taken into the Mountains" is then only a fragment and surely there is something symbolic in that as in the work itself. It is as if the fate of Norwegian music was here portrayed. And more closely even than in the sonatas, the piano concerto, and the string quartet, the forces of nature are woven into this strange picture, unique in the literature of music. If it can be said that here Grieg touched the highest point in his creative activity, that is because no other work of his shows such a concentrated power or points towards such a multitude of possibilities as does "Taken into the Mountains."

In his reminiscences to his American biographer, Finck, Grieg discusses "Taken into the Mountains" in this particular connection: "Ich habe hier die gedrungene Knappheit des Styls welche in der altnorwegischen Poesie erschütternd zum Ausdruck gelangt auch in der Musik erstrebt, und was ich darunter verstehe, ist es mir vielleicht in diesem kleinen Stück am besten zu zeigen gelungen."

Rich indeed is "Taken into the Mountains," that is certain. It has the warmth and abandonment of lyric poetry, it contains dramatic kindling material enough for a whole opera, it shows to an exceptional degree the power of Norwegian music to express a feeling for nature more varied in its elements and more remarkable than that of any other nation. Most important of all, it sounds the depths of the artist's own nature and gives a harrowing glimpse into his spiritual combat, reaching in at the same time to what is central in the fight of the nation itself for cultural emancipation.

Who then is this man "taken into the mountains?" In a landscape veiled in mist and darkness we find him, in a niggard land, crushed in between mountains, borne down by cold and want of understanding, overwhelmed by mysterious forces of nature. It is the tragedy of the great artist, his loneliness, his pining for sun and warmth that have here found expression as moving as it is possible to achieve through music.

The way in which Grieg himself speaks of "Taken into the Mountains" shows how near this work lay to his heart—how much it had cost him. In the letter in which he tells Matthison-Hansen that he means to dedicate this work to him, he writes: "I knew of no one better to whom to dedicate it. I knew yours was one of these frightful natures that demand blood; and a nature like yours will not look long before finding spots and stains here and there of sheer, pure heart's blood. But who has the feeling for such things?" And after a performance in Christiania, he wrote to Frants Beyer: "It is a glorious thought to be able to say here with Björnson, 'God knows that it is written with religious devotion!' I feel as if in this piece I have done one of the few good deeds of my life."

But though "Taken into the Mountains" was one of the works Grieg himself puts highest and constantly turned back to with affection, it has had great difficulty, nevertheless, in winning its way to popular favor both here and in other countries. The manuscript, which is to be found in the Bergen public library, is dated April 1878.

Grieg finished some minor piano pieces also during this stay at Lofthus. They were *Improvisations on Norwegian Folk Songs*, Opus 29, and the last of the four *Albumblade* (Album Leaves), Opus 28. The *Album Leaves* belong to widely different periods of the artist's life. The first was composed as early as 1864 and gives us a charming impression of the young Grieg, before he had come to know Nordraak. It is graceful, lovable music without very much individuality. Nor is the second, written in 1874, of special interest. With the exception of one or two turns in the cadenza-like development, in genuine Grieg style, it breathes throughout the spirit and style of Schumann. In the third, composed in 1876, Grieg's personality begins to show more clearly, but not till the fourth, the product of Lofthus, do we meet the real Grieg. It is not for nothing that it is headed andante serioso; it is a wonderful, deeply felt elegy which shows us the composer at his best, both as maker of melody and harmony. And, as always, when Grieg has something of special value to impart to us, it is fitted into a framework of nature and folk life.

Grieg told Julius Röntgen that as he was sitting at work in his little hut composing this *Album* piece, he suddenly heard soft music out on the water. It came from some fiddlers rowing on the fjord and the music from the water fitted so wonderfully with his mood that it inspired him to that extremely effective middle part in D flat major, where almost pianissimo, as though from far away, we hear folk-dance music.

The two *Improvisations on Norwegian Folk Songs*, Opus 29, it is not easy to connect in one's thoughts with the works of this year from Lofthus. They were written to order and were a gift from the composer to the fund for the Holberg monument in Bergen. They are occasional pieces, then, and show clear traces of it. They are easy to play, well-sounding entertainment music, and bring to mind Liszt's Hungarian rhapsodies, though without their pomp and brilliance and versatility in the treatment of the piano.

When Grieg went to stay at Lofthus it was, as we have heard, to challenge fate to battle. He would fight his way through, cost what it might, he would acquire a technique that would allow the rich material he was possessed of free expression and development. Above all, he would be done with these wretched periods of incapacity, with being able to compose only "by fits and starts" as he called it: now his artistic work should go on steadily.

What then was the result? For us and for Norwegian music it is suggested in what has just been said about the works that date from this year. But what was the result for himself? That may be gathered from his own comments on these works. The string quartet it appears he regarded mainly as a necessary preliminary study for future works. He had also begun another piece of chamber music—most probably he had thought of a piano trio—but no more than a single movement was sketched out. Among his posthumous papers there has been found an andante for violin, cello, and piano, dated June 17, 1878. This was published by Julius Röntgen in *Die Musik* for 1907.

The *Album of Songs for Male Voices* is said to have been written principally for rest and recreation after his strenuous work with the quartet. "Taken into the Mountains," which had originally been conceived as a large work with full orchestra and choir, remained merely a fragment.

As we have seen, he looked upon all he had done as preparatory, he had not yet got down to the real task. There can be no doubt that it had been his secret desire to open up a way not only for himself but for Norwegian music in general; to wake to life the spirit from Hafrsfjord, fit together heterogeneous elements, and lay the foundations of a new kingdom of music in Norway. It was a beautiful dream and a proud thought, and if the dream was not realized it was because it had originated in and been maintained by instinct rather than by clear, sober calculation. And both are necessary. In spiritual battles too one must forge weapons for oneself. Grieg possessed a leader's best qualifications; he had faith in his task, he had courage and the will to sacrifice and, above all, he had a heart of gold and a mind without guile. But a leader must have weapons, or he falls at the first onset.

We shall hear later how Björnson in his great speech on Grieg's sixtieth birthday touches on precisely this fatal difficulty, that Norwegians have rich talents but do not know how best to use them—are too poorly equipped, do not set themselves the far goal.

It is noteworthy that Björnson, even on Grieg's festival day, returns to this problem of such grave importance in Norwegian music. Can it be imagined that Björnson was himself so well versed in things musical—or did he get it from Grieg?

That Grieg was very deeply affected by the issue of the Hardanger conflict, we have now good grounds for asserting. Let us look first at the effect these preparatory works had upon his further productions.

After the Ballad and the Ibsen and Paulsen songs were finished, a whole year passed in which he accomplished practically nothing, in spite of there being no outward impediments to hinder him. What now of the steady creative activity? In spite of the most careful investigation, nothing can be found to show that Grieg was seriously occupied with composition from July 1878, when he finished the string quartet, until the beginning of 1880, when he wrote his Vinje songs—a period that is to say of almost two years. That looks very much as though the outcome of the conflict had been a partial paralysis of his creative powers. And from remarks in his letters it appears that, in part at least, he was well aware of it. Not yet thirty-eight years old, he wrote to John Paulsen, speaking of the latter's active productivity: "My productive time was so short; I have waited, am always waiting still for it to come again. But the fine web of relationships must be properly adjusted before that happens." And hand in hand with the crisis he was going through at this time as an artist, there came personal experiences which seem to have affected deeply the whole tenor of his life.

On September 8, 1879, he writes to John Paulsen, speaking of lost illusions: "As for myself, I cannot speak of one lost illusion at a time, no, with me they have showered down in hundreds like rotten fruit in the wind. I have indeed been out in the storm—perhaps a little of the good fruit has gone too—alas—but something I have left and that of the best, of the kind that does not fall to the ground in stormy weather."

In the same letter we find the following bitter remark which seems to have behind it the strength of personal experience: "Remember: women *will play* and then that is the end of it! That sounds hard and material, but there is something true in it all the same. Women have never comprehended and never learn to comprehend the something great, wild, and boundless in a man's—an artist's—love. And if I am right in this, it follows that an artist should not marry. I cannot pretend that it was this I set out to prove, but so it came to my pen."

It looks as if now also there was the closest relationship between life and art. In his purely personal confidences we are aware of the same central idea, the same emotional content that infuse the Ballad, the Ibsen songs, "Taken into the Mountains," and the string quartet.

But fortunately he had—as he expresses it himself—something of the best in reserve, something of the kind that does not fall to the ground in stormy weather. This is most beautifully demonstrated in his next work, which is called *Twelve Melodies to Poems of A. O. Vinje*, Opus 33, which marks the highest point in his song production and which can first be wholly and completely understood when the background of tragedy both for artist and man against which the songs are set, is also understood.

But before going on to discuss these noble songs of Norwegian romance we shall first follow Grieg further on his way through life.

CONCERTS ABROAD AND AT HOME

ON JULY 22, 1878, Grieg wrote to Dr. Abraham that he was as happy as a child because he had obtained the royal stipend for which he had applied before in vain, and now he was rejoicing in the thought of coming out into the world and being again in the company of musicians. In the autumn he went to Germany, first to Cologne, where Robert Heckmann, at his first chamber music recital of October 29, was to produce the string quartet for the first time. The concert was given as an entire Grieg evening and, in addition to the string quartet, piano pieces, songs, and the second violin sonata were performed, with Grieg himself taking part at the piano.

That the concert went off successfully appears from the letter Grieg sent soon after to his hosts at Lofthus, Hans and Brita Utne. The letter is dated Leipzig, November 18, 1878, and gives a glimpse of Grieg in gay and cheerful mood. It bears witness also to his warm feelings for Hardanger and the people he had learned to know and value there:

"My dear friends, Hans and Brita,

"Please let me call you that, for the way in which my heart turns back constantly to Hardanger and the joy I have in the thought of seeing you again show me how much you mean to me. Furthermore, I now for the first time realize that the time I lived amongst you was not spent in vain. If only I could be left at peace for my work, no summer should pass that did not see me among you. From Nina I hear that all goes well with you and I can say the same of myself. I have had some lovely days by the Rhine in Cologne and Bonn, especially in Cologne, which I was visiting for the first time, a memorable town, not only because of its great cathedral, its beautiful situation, and the famous 'Eau de Cologne,' not to speak of the Rhenish wine which flows everywhere, but chiefly because of the heartiness, naturalness, and hospitality that distinguish the residents. In the course of five days I had to play four times in public. You, Brita, I must tell that 'The Bridal Procession' (you remember it) waked such enthusiasm that after I'd played it once I was recalled four times and had in the end to play

it over again. Tell me one thing: Who wrote that bit about me in
Hardangeren? Was it perhaps Lars Kinservik? At least I think it
might be he. If I am right, tell him with my hearty greetings that
it pleased me more than twenty newspaper articles from foreign
towns or countries."

Grieg ends by saying: "If you think that I am writing this letter
without expecting anything in return, you are making a mistake!
I am a great egotist and am only sending these few lines to have the
pleasure of hearing from you. So write soon—to the above address!
Kind greetings to everyone, but first and last to yourselves and the
children!

> "Your affectionate
> "Edvard Grieg."

Warm and hearty as was the reception in Cologne, it was to be
regarded, nevertheless, as an affair of outposts. Not till judgment
had been given in Leipzig itself, the metropolis of music, could a
success be of real significance for the composer. It is not unlikely
that this time Grieg had no great expectations when he set out for
Leipzig to present in the Gewandhaus itself a series of his most
representative productions. After the treatment his piano concerto
had received there six years earlier from the ruling powers of
Signale, he had good ground for expecting the worst. And his forebodings were justified. The reception given by one portion of the
press to the string quartet in particular led—according to Grieg's
own statement—to its lying paralyzed for years. Such was the
importance of what the professional press wrote about a new work.
And there were other consequences. From Grieg's correspondence
with Dr. Abraham it appears that his publisher too, who otherwise
had become a warm admirer of Grieg's works, now joined the ranks
of the sceptics with regard to the string quartet. That this should
be a blow to Grieg is only natural and there is a touch of hurt pride
in the warmth with which he defends his work against the objections Dr. Abraham had brought forward. But this time, too, as six
years before with the piano concerto, the string quartet was published, not by Peters but by Fritsch, Svendsen's friend and publisher. On the whole, it seems that Dr. Abraham was exceptionally
cautious in regard to Grieg's greater works. He had before declined
to print the piano sonata, the second violin sonata and the piano
concerto, and now the same happened with the string quartet. It

is rather remarkable, therefore, that several of Grieg's earlier biographers emphasize precisely his *boldness* in acquiring and circulating Grieg's works. That later, when Grieg became popular all over the world, he bought up everything that came from his hands, besides the greater works which formerly he had refused to publish, can certainly not be regarded as boldness; it should be called rather by its proper name, good business sense.

Reading today *Signale's* review of the Grieg concert which took place in the Gewandhaus on November 30, it is difficult to understand how a music reviewer, to whom moreover was entrusted the responsible task of expressing his opinions in the most influential professional journal of the day, could be so utterly unable to perceive the values which found expression in Grieg's tone poem. Nor was the review of this concert by any means an isolated phenomenon. Quite the contrary! Every time Grieg appeared in Leipzig with a new work, the comments from that quarter were much the same—right up to his last year. This explains something of the bitterness with which Grieg in the last year of his life used to speak of the German professional press. Reading *Signale's* reviews, we realize that he had good reason to feel himself unjustly treated. The article written by E. Bernsdorf, the paper's regular reviewer, is to be found on page 1046 for the year 1878 and runs as follows:

Das R. Heckmann'sche Quartett aus Cöln—bestehend aus den Herren Chormeister Rob. Heckmann, Otto Forberg (Violinen), Theodor Alekotte (Viola) und Richard Bellmann (Violoncell)—hat sich am 30. Nov. in einem im Gewandhaus gegebenen Concerte producirt, nicht etwa, um, gleich anderer Quartettgesellschaften, durch die Vorführung von Kammermusikwerken verschiedener Meister aus älterer oder neuerer Zeit ihre executivisches Vermögen darzuthun, sondern nur, um einen Tonsetzer modernster Datum—Herrn Eduard Grieg aus Christiania—Terrain gewinnen zu helfen. Es war also ein rein propagandistisches Concert welches der Cölner Verein uns vorsetzte, und Herr Grieg hat alle Ursache, Herrn Heckmann und seine Genossen dankbar zu sein für diesen Act der Unterstützung und Hebung. Könnten wir für unseren Theil den Cölner Herren nur eben so dankbar sein, wie Herr Grieg! Aber leider können wir's nicht, ja wir müssen sogar den Umstand, uns einen ganzen Abend lang mit lauter Grieg'schen Erzeugnissen tractiren lassen zu müssen, als eine Zumuthung sehr starker Art bezeichnen. Denn Freude und Vergnügen hat uns keine der gebotenen Grieg'schen Productionen gemacht—weder die Sonate in G-moll für klavier und Violine (Op. 13) noch das bis dato unedierte Streichquartett (ebenfalls

in G-moll) weder die Reihe von Liedern, noch die von kleineren Clavier-
stücken aus Op. 6, 19 u. 28; im Gegentheil nur Mishagen und Wider-
willen haben wir empfunden gegenüber den Scurrilitäten und Absurd-
itäten, die unter dem Deckmantel des national-norwegischen Charak-
ters angesammelt sind, gegenüber der nur mühsam hinter eben jenem
norwegisch zugeschnittenen und gefärbten Aufputz (den ohnedies
der Nicht-Norweger nur auf Treue und Glauben hinnehmen muss) sich
verbergenden Unbedeutendheit der Erfindung und gegenüber endlich
dem Mangel jegichen Gestaltungs-und Entwicklungsvermögens, jeg-
licher Fähigkeit, den Rahmen eines ausgeführten Satzes (wie hier
speciell in der Sonate und dem Quartett) gehörig, d.h.mühe- und
lückenlos, ohne blosse Flickarbeit, anszufüllen.—Herr Grieg persönlich,
war an dem Concert auch executirend betheiligt, indem er bei allen
obengenannten Sachen (auser dem Streichquartett natürlich) das
Pianistische gegenüber besorgte. Herrn Heckmann kennen wir von
früher her, als tüchtigen Geiger; um ihn und seine Genossen als Quar-
tettisten zu beurtheilen, müssen wir nothgedrungen eine andere und
bessere Folie als das Grieg'sche Quartett abwarten. Die Lieder wurden
von Fraülein Minna Sciubro, Concertsängerin aus Neapel, vorgetragen,
welche aber weder durch Stimme noch Expression uns für sich ein-
zunehmen vermocht hat. Schliesslich wollen wir noch des Umstandes
gedenken dass—so merkwürdig auch die Sache von unserm Standpuncte
aus uns vorkommen musste—Personen und Sachen in den Concerte
fast ausnahmslos durch Beifall ausgezeichnet wurden, ja dass sogar
Herr Grieg das Stück "Norwegischer Brautzug im Vorüberziehen"
wiederholen musste.

This was undeniably a powerful volley for a young composer
who wanted to strike a blow for his art in the very cosmopolis of
music, as Leipzig was at that time. And Grieg was to experience
that it influenced the way in which his art was judged in other
places. On his way home in spring, on April 30, 1879, he gave a
concert in Copenhagen, having first appeared at a Concert Society
evening on April 5, where he conducted the first performance of
Den Bergtekne and also the piano concerto with Neupert in the solo
part. From a letter to Dr. Abraham, it appears that his own concert in Copenhagen had been in all respects a great success. "Everything went splendidly," he wrote, "the house was sold out, the
King and Queen were present, there was great enthusiasm and
many recalls." But he notes from the newspaper reviews that the
critics, at all events, have read *Signale*.

Nevertheless, his position seems steadily to have become stronger, more and more secure—even in Leipzig. This is suggested by the fact that soon after the murderous attack in *Signale* he is again to be found amongst the performers at the Gewandhaus, this time taking part in a recital of chamber music on March 29, at which he played the piano part in his first violin sonata. Naturally, *Signale* is more than peevish in its account of the sonata and adds that the applause with which the work was received can only be described as exaggerated. But a powerful and original talent cannot be so easily downed, even by the press, and before Grieg left Leipzig that winter he had accepted an engagement to play his piano concerto at one of the great subscription concerts at the Gewandhaus! That was a triumph, besides being the best answer he could give to an adverse and uncomprehending critic.

The summer of 1879 he spent again in Lofthus, where many of his friends came to visit him. Fru Sara Bull in her biography of Ole Bull writes as follows: "The summer of 1879 was one of the happiest ever spent by the artist in Norway. One memorable day was when a party of friends went down to the little hamlet of Lofthus, in the Hardanger, to be immortalized, as Ole Bull told the peasants, because the composer Grieg had chosen to stay there for months and to write some of his best works. They had now come to celebrate his birthday. No spot could be more enchanting, so wonderfully blended were the beautiful and the sublime in nature. The little study of one room, erected by the composer for perfect retirement, was perched halfway up a rock and near the fjord. In the field above, the apple trees were in bloom about an old farmhouse, where the guests assembled. From the summit of the beetling cliffs not far away fell a beautiful waterfall, while the opposite mountain shore of the broad fjord, clothed with heavy forests of pine above and the feathery birch below, presented range after range of lofty peaks and domes crowned by the great Folgefond with its eternal snow. The day was as perfect as friendship, music, and lovely surroundings could make it."

On his way to Germany, Grieg gave concerts in Bergen on October 2 and 7, at which he played his piano concerto, among other things. On October 30 he appeared with this work at the fourth subscription concert at the Gewandhaus in Leipzig. The concert, as nearly always happened, was a great popular success for Grieg and the critics were also friendly, some indeed very ap-

preciative, except, of course, *Signale* which referred to its earlier
comments on Grieg's piano concerto and went on to say that the
composer had not even sufficient technical accomplishment to
enable him to present his work at all effectively. The reviewer
ended by remarking that though many, perhaps, might be unable
to see the necessity for Herr Grieg's appearance at the Gewandhaus, the concert nevertheless—"allerdings mit einigen Ach und
Krach"—was a success!

The American composer and conductor, Frank van der Stucken,
has described in Finck's Grieg biography some traits of Grieg,
whom he met on this occasion in Leipzig for the first time. "As a
stranger in a strange country," says van der Stucken, "my only
method to get some recognition was to send complimentary copies
to the musical periodicals and to the prominent musicians who
lived in Leipzig at that time. One morning, after breakfast, I was
sitting in my lonesome den in the Post-strasse at work on a new
song, when a rap at the door announced my first visitor: and
presently a little gentleman, with flowing blonde locks, with
friendly and bright blue eyes, walked towards me and introduced
himself as the Norwegian composer Grieg who wanted to make the
acquaintance of the young musician, whose first compositions he
had received and read with great interest. Ever since that hour our
friendship was sealed, and scarcely a day passed during Grieg's
stay in Leipzig that we were not found together, either at dinner,
supper, or some musical or dramatic performance. Through him I
was introduced to the artistic life of Leipzig, and more especially
to his Scandinavian friends, Sinding, Kajanus, Holter, Olsen, and
others. Grieg was fond of cards, and after lunch we used to spend
one hour at the Café Français playing whist. He was a very lively
comrade in good company, and liked to tell and to hear a good
square jest; but when we were alone, the keynote of his character
was a gentle melancholy resignation, tempered by witty satire and
weird phantasy. He was rather a 'gourmet,' and even a 'gourmand.'
A fine portion of oysters, caviare, or Norwegian snow-hen, with a
glass of good old wine, could excite and cheer him up wonderfully.
One day we lingered before the shop window of a renowned
delicatessen store, when he—armed with his inseparable gloves,
umbrella, and galoshes—exclaimed, enthusiastically: 'What an
ideal symphony! How perfect in all its details, in form, contents,
and instrumentation!' His favorite modern composers were, then,

Chopin, Schumann, and Wagner. He also spoke in the highest terms about his countrymen, the composers Svendsen and Nordraak, and the celebrated authors, Ibsen and Björnson, the friends of his youth and manhood, who had such a decisive influence on his career. In music as in literature, Grieg also had a great penchant for the French masters, because they express so clearly whatever they have to say. He always was a Republican at heart, and spoke about Norway's absolute independence as long as I knew him—citing Björnson as sharing his opinions."

Later in the winter, Grieg left Leipzig and, as usual, wended his way to Copenhagen, where on February 4, 1880, he gave a specially successful concert with the help of his wife, Edmund Neupert, and the Students' Choral Society. In the review in *Fædrelandet* we can read that the concert was given to "so packed a house that it was barely comfortable to be in the small hall of the Casino." The reviewer finishes by saying that "the audience, the whole evening through, showed the liveliest appreciation, was unusually liberal with encores, and was obviously delighted when Herr Grieg received a handsome laurel wreath."

Barely a week later, on February 11, Grieg and Fru Nina were again in the limelight, this time as guests of the Musical Society, where Grieg, with Kapellmeister Schjörring, played his second sonata for piano and violin, Opus 13, while Nina sang songs of Schumann's and Grieg's.

Some weeks later we find them in Christiania, where a great plan was about to be realized. Grieg sent out invitations for not less than four chamber music matinees or "private matinees" as they were called, at the piano warehouse of the brothers Hals. In *Nordisk Musik-Tidende*, which Carl Warmuth had just begun to bring out, we read that "the subscription list to these matinees, which was circulated in private, was rapidly filled up, which is happy witness to the fact that the musical public knows how to value the deep imagination and originality that mark this artist's works and make them among the best our musical literature has produced."

Immediately after these concerts, which were a great success both artistically and financially, Grieg went home to Bergen and at last—after a pause of almost two years—took up again his work as a creative artist.

"In the year 1880 I came home to Bergen in May and wrote, at my brother's in Strandgaten (up in an attic room of the house) all the Vinje songs," he said in a letter to Iver Holter. To Finck he relates that he was completely swept off his feet when, in the spring of 1880, he learned to know Vinje's poetry, so filled with deep life wisdom, and that he composed in the course of eight or ten days not only the songs published together in Book 4 but others also to poems by the same author, which even yet have not been published.

THE VINJE SONGS

W E HAVE seen the results as regards his art of Grieg's battle with fate at Lofthus. The works he wrote that winter he regarded merely as preparation for the real tasks he meant ultimately to take in hand; and the techinque he had hoped to acquire in order to make continuous artistic work possible seemed, like the call of a decoy, further off than before. Those tormenting periods of incapacity which were to have been made an end of appeared now in a graver, more threatening, and deeply gripping form than ever before. So long a period of incapacity (to use his own words) as that he had lived through these two years had never before occurred in his life; and this was from his thirty-fifth to his thirty-seventh year, before we hear any talk of poor health and with no outward obstacles blocking the path of creative activity. It is the tragic outcome of this fight, this reckoning he had had with himself, which casts the dark shadow of conflict over the Vinje songs. Here we find the spiritual reflection of the state of mind in which he found himself when *doubt* began to gnaw at him, when in his self-knowledge he felt that he was facing the worst unhappiness that can overtake an artist: to receive the first warning signs that soon all will be over, that soon he will be finished, that he is moving towards spiritual death—a state of things that for an artist is tenfold worse than any form whatsoever of adversity, struggle, need, or misery.

So dearly bought was the capacity to write these songs; so low he had to bow down in order fully to understand and feel what moved in the depths of the people's soul, and to clothe Vinje's words in music wholly worthy of them.

Now with the strength of conviction he could sing with Vinje in "The Youth" which begins the collection:

> You've wandered far; for weariness
> Your footsteps halt,
> Oft has your pillow in the night
> With tears been salt.
> But bitter salt washed out in tears
> You change again
> To the sharp, caustic lye that cleanses life
> From soil and stain.

Now know you what it means
    Dreams to forget,
To die to hopes, to all on which
    Your heart is set.
The green you gathered withered fast
    As flowers to hay;
That was the least; your young love too, alas!
    Withered away.

But had you not so often met
    Deceit and wrong
Then love you never could have sung
    With the true song;
Whole first when on your ruined life
    Erect you stand
And from the height thus gained, amazed,
    Survey far lands.

Grieg's music to these words forms a very beautiful introduction to the whole collection. In short, concise stanzas, expressively declaimed and firm as if cut in stone, the melodic line rises to the highest pitch of pathos and pain.

One can imagine that, were our Edda poems to be expressed in music, they would require melodic treatment of just this kind—pregnant with meaning, concentrated, chiselled. The use of the stanza form, here as in most of the other Vinje songs, serves to heighten the effect and, above all, to preserve the unity of the style.

In "Spring" the poet and the composer have given us a work that has no parallel in literature. It stands, like "Taken into the Mountains," almost alone in Grieg's compositions, and shares with that work the fate that only the few, those truly akin in spirit, know how to give expression to so intimate a confidence. Even "great" and famous prima donnas fall short here as a rule.

Again the composer has searched out the very life-nerve of his people's cultural struggle. Again one is struck by the awareness, the sensitiveness and vision that are born of suffering. But for that, Grieg could not possibly have clothed Vinje's poem in music such as he has given it. The darkly bright shining of this song acts like the dawning of a ray of hope—a ray of hope for the release of a people's spirit in spite of all. This spirit lay chained and fettered as Grieg felt his own genius did; like him it lacked language in which

to express itself fully and completely. As with a compelling voice
from the dim founders of his race the soul of his people spoke to
Grieg in Vinje's words:

> All that Spring bears to me in her fair train,
>   Flowers waked from sleeping,
> Our forefathers' spirits meseem, come again,
>   Dancing and weeping.
> Therefore I found 'mong the birches and pine
>   Spring's secrets hide,
> And in the flute that I cut and made mine
>   Woke sorrow and cried.

Note carefully the melodic and harmonic devices Grieg employs
to give vivid life to the poet's words when in the first verse he says:

> Yet once again it is given me to watch
>   The ice sea-ward making,
> See the snow melting, the down-crashing fall,
>   Hissing, foaming and breaking.

One feels clearly how far this music is from all that is tangible
and material, how far from the direct speech and graphic pictures
of naturalism. It is because the song goes beyond the expression
of the purely personal, the subjective, to deal with the common
fate of a people—the universal destiny—that words and music are
here so affecting in the fervor of their emotion, in the depth of their
pain.

In this song too the composer keeps to the stanza form—it is not
composed as a unit, and for this he has been blamed both at
home and abroad. We need only answer that this reproach is
levelled at Grieg by a German critic and biographer on the strength
of a translation in which Vinje's poem is entirely remodelled!
Similarly the Norwegian biographer, whose criticism, on this point
especially, is even harsher, uses to support his case a Danish para-
phrase of Vinje's poem which not only robs it of all beauty and
poetry but even of meaning! If these things are borne in mind the
apparently well grounded criticisms lose much of their weight.

Grieg's sure instinct here, as before, has plainly led him aright
in choosing the stanza form. His music reaches down so deep and
takes so firm a hold on the fundamental meaning of the poet, and
in its highly concentrated form it is so instinct with feeling, that to

have taken the whole poem as unit would have seemed like an infraction of style.

The composer's work shows here a close relationship to the ancient ballads, which have the property of being able through one and the same melody to illuminate the progression of the plot and bring out the richness of the detail. That Grieg himself was aware of this kinship with the old ballad is evident from an article he wrote in a congratulatory address to Thorvald and Molly Lammers on their silver wedding. After having thanked Lammers heartily for having in the Eighties introduced many of his Vinje songs, he goes on to say: "You have found in these songs an element akin to yourself—which brought up into the light of day something of what was still lying latent in you. As the songs are in a way the child of the folk song, so your interpretation of them has been infused with its spirit."

The next song in the collection, "Den særde" (Wounded), both as regards theme and in its depth of feeling, stands in close relationship to "The Youth" and "Spring," outwardly simple and full of character, but vibrant, nevertheless, with fullness of life. In this song too the stanza form is kept, and here too Grieg has had to meet criticism, as unjustified in my opinion as in the case of the other songs.

The mood in "Tyttebæret" (The Berry) is more pastoral and the colors are brighter, but here too pain runs like an undercurrent until it breaks out in flaming passion.

"Langs ei Aa" (By a Riverside) was written, as has already been said, at Börve in the summer of 1877. The manuscript is dated Sunday, July 8. Again a deep and arresting song, in which the thoughts and ideas of the poet are reflected in the music as only an artist of genius can do it. One is almost astounded at the epic calm and bright tone that mark the beginning of this song, pregnant with fate; only little by little does it work up to the outburst of pain which gives liberation to the fundamental emotion of the poem. Not least worthy of admiration is the rhythmic movement in the piano accompaniment, those sighing quavers so typical of Grieg, which help to emphasize the song's character.

"Eit Syn" (A Vision), within the framework of an ecstatically moving dance, paints a vivid picture of a woman. In the middle movement the composer pauses in a still rapture, but only for a moment. Immediately after, he returns again to the passionate

basic mood and at once the vision has disappeared. The dance
rhythm continues for a couple of bars after the song is finished,
then breaks off suddenly, and a somber minor chord hangs on the
air like a sad memory.

"Gamle mor" (The Old Mother) was already written in 1873
and, according to Grieg's own statement, arose out of the thought
of his own mother who "with unrelenting energy and sense of duty
slaved and toiled till she dropped." It has that intensity of feeling
which admits both the tragic and the heroic.

"Det fyrste" (The First Thing) is akin in design to "By a
Riverside." Here too the tragic subject is concealed under the light
pastoral tone of the beginning and the song works up little by little
to a high pitch of pathos.

On the background of these gloomy, and in some cases tragic,
songs it is cheering and stimulating to come upon the pure feeling
for nature with which "Ved Rundarne" (On the Way Home) is
infused. Like the lost paradise of youth, this landscape picture
stands before one, given depth and greater beauty by the struggles
and sufferings which lie between the unreflecting, spontaneous joy
of early experiences and retrospective, pain-blended emotion. This
song, with "The Old Mother," is among the best known and loved
of Grieg's songs and in Norway has for long been a treasured national possession.

"Et Vennestykke" (Friendship) seems to move in the land of
shades. Gloomy, somber chords accompany the mild, resigned
melodic line which, both in design and character stands rather
apart from the rest of the Vinje songs. This applies also to the next
song in the collection, "Trudom" (Faith). The composer seems to
have designed his music on the basis of the first stanza, "God's
kingdom is a place of peace" and on this foundation he has written
a devotional song in the manner of a chorale.

Like a crown upon the whole collection comes next the magnificent "Fyremål" (My Goal). In its strong, virile melody, in its
bold harmony and rhythmic firmness, in the graphic quality of its
nature sketches, it has the effect of a fresh and cheerful salute to
the future.

The Vinje songs stand on a level of excellence with the best
Grieg has produced. It is seldom that his musical language possesses such intensity and fulness of life as here, and yet he had to
experience that there were but very few who could fully under-

stand these songs, which in all truth he could say were written with his heart's blood. That the Vinje songs are still amongst the least known abroad of Grieg's works is due very largely to poor translations, which make it impossible fully to understand and apprehend them.

What difficulties Grieg had to battle with in the matter of translations we get some idea of in the autobiographical notes he sent to Finck. He says here that if his songs—as compared with the rest of his works—have as yet found little recognition abroad, while in the North they have found favor everywhere, it is undoubtedly the result of the difficulties attendant on translation. "When I write songs," he goes on to say, "it is not chiefly a question of composing music, but above all of helping to give expression to what the poet has felt and meant most deeply and intensely. To let the poem stand out with enhanced potency, that was my problem. If that problem is solved, the music is successful. Otherwise not, though it were ever so heavenly beautiful. But when the Norwegian poet's words, which foreigners can neither understand nor sing, are ruined in translation, it is not only the poet who suffers from this devastation, but the composer also. Unfortunately in my struggles to secure good translations I have often had very bad luck. It is true that the task requires a versatility one seldom finds, as the translator must be at the same time poet, linguist, and conversant with music. And to this must be added the melancholy fact that most publishers are far less likely to appreciate a good translation than—a cheap one! My Leipzig publisher, C. F. Peters, has certainly tried hard to procure good translations. But the result has been that even in favorable cases the relation of words to music has produced a forced and unnatural effect."

This is perhaps one of the reasons why Grieg transcribed two of the Vinje songs, "Spring" and "Wounded," for string orchestra. In this form, where both the language problem and the difficulties of translation are eliminated, Vinje's and Grieg's poems have won favor and understanding over the whole of the musical world. That there were many who puzzled over Grieg's musical elucidation of a subject so well known and so frequently treated as "Spring," is not to be wondered at, especially when the poem was not at the same time available.

From Bergen on December 8, 1881, Grieg wrote to Angul Hammerich, after the latter had reviewed the two songs which had been published for string orchestra under the title *Two Elegiac Melodies*, Opus 34: "I must express my delight that you have been clear-sighted enough to think of the possibility of another interpretation of 'Spring' than the prevailing one. I grant that it is a mistake that a broad outline of the contents of the poem has not been given and you will do me a great service if you will rectify this mistake if your position gives you an opportunity to treat these things as news in any of the papers. I have asked Hansen to send you my songs to Vinje's poems. You will find enclosed the two in question, which have been adapted for string orchestra. Both poems are, in my opinion, so wonderful, each in its different way, that they well deserve publication. In a paper here I see it quoted from the *Berlingske Tidënde* that after Gade's 'Fantasy on Spring,' 'Spring' is disappointing. When you have read the poem you will be in a position to tell all whom it may concern that that is simply nonsense."

Speaking of the two elegiac melodies for string orchestra in his notes to Finck, he says that the deep sadness of the poems explains the grave sonorities of the music and induced him, in adapting them for string orchestra where the poems are not at hand, to try to indicate their contents by means of expressive titles. Therefore, they are called "Letzter Frühling" (Last Spring) and "Herzwunden" (Heart's Wound).

CONDUCTOR OF THE HARMONIC SOCIETY

IN *Nordisk Musik-Tidende* for July 1880, there is to be found an announcement that the post of conductor of the Bergen Harmonic Society will be vacant from "October next. Five to six Symphony Concerts in the season (October to April), Honorarium 800 kroner. Practice in leading an orchestra and mixed choir essential. Applications with the requisite testimonials to be sent in before July 31 to the directors of the Harmonic Society."

Soon after, by August 6, *Bergensposten* could give the music-loving public the joyful news that the directors of the Society had been fortunate enough to induce Edvard Grieg to accept the post of musical instructor to the Society for the coming season. The paper felt certain that this appointment would be epoch-making, not only in a narrow sense for the development of the Society to the service of which the artist would dedicate his eminent talents, but for the musical life of Bergen as a whole, since the mere fact of Edvard Greig's residing in the town a whole winter through would give musical interests there a natural center and a strong support which could not be without influence in wider circles.

It may be of interest to note here that at the same time that Grieg was appointed conductor of the Harmonic Society, Johan Svendsen, after three years' absence, resumed his connection with the Musical Society in Christiania, a position he continued to hold till in 1883 he was appointed Kapellmeister at the Royal Theater in Copenhagen.

Before entering on his conductorship, Grieg gave a great vocal and instrumental concert in Bergen with a Norwegian programme. Svendsen's "Norwegian Rhapsody," Grieg's "At a Southern Cloister's Gate," and "Landsighting" were among the items, and as novelties, "Spring" and "Wounded" for string orchestra. In addition, Ole Bull's "Sæterjentens söndag" (The Sætergirl's Sunday) was played in memoriam. Ole Bull had just died. Sick and suffering, he had come home in summer from America for one last sight of Norway and on August 17 had died at his country house near Bergen. The funeral took place on August 23 and *Bergensposten* describes it as one great mourning ceremony, all the town taking part. Both Björnson and Grieg walked in the huge procession, the latter carrying the gold laurel wreath which had been given Ole Bull in San Francisco. Both made speeches at the grave. Björnson's expressed his sense of how important Ole Bull had been in awakening and strengthening our national feeling and giving us self-confidence, the greatest thing that at that time could have been given us, and Grieg, in the name of the art of music in Norway, said farewell and with the following words laid a wreath of remembrance on the coffin: "Because beyond all others you were an honor to your country—because you raised our people up with you towards the shining peaks of art as no one else has done—because you were beyond all others a pioneer for our young national music, faithful, warm-hearted and a conqueror of every heart as no one, no one else—because you have planted a seed which will grow in the future and for which the coming generations will bless you— with a gratitude that knows no bounds, for all this, in the name of Norwegian music, I lay this laurel wreath upon your coffin. Peace be with you!"

There are many things which suggest that Grieg at this period of his life gave up creative work for a time—and that of his own free will! There is nothing to show that there were any outer circumstances which constrained him to undertake the post of director in the Harmonic Society. Sensitive as he was, he was certainly well aware that concert work would tax his strength so heavily that there would be no opportunity for composition, and indeed this proved to be the case. In the two years he acted as conductor to the Harmonic Society, he wrote only one work, the Norwegian dances for piano (four handed), Opus 35. Yet the season lasted only from October to April, only half the year. Another thing which suggests that he was making no preparation for creative work in the near future is that he sold his little work hut at Lofthus, the little work hut that he had built for himself with such solicitude in order to have a peaceful place where he could give himself up to his music, wholly undisturbed—this he sold three years after having built it.

To Utne he wrote from Bergen on November 7, 1880: "I am willing to sell the house for 160 kroner cash and the sale can take place any time and the house be occupied, if you will be so kind as to send the piano by the first boat." On December 2 he wrote: "Money and piano both received safely—and thanks for the trouble you have taken about both. So that finishes my Hardanger residence for the present. It was a lucky thing for me that I sold the house, as the doctors say that being in it has not done me good."

From an artistic point of view the work in the Harmonic Society does not seem to have been very satisfactory to Grieg, as many remarks in his letters suggest. But neither was it altogether without importance. It is natural to suppose that the close contact with an orchestra had a stimulating and developing effect on his talents as an orchestrator, and very likely it was this which occasioned him in the following year to undertake a critical examination and revision of a series of his earlier works.

Grieg wrote in 1902 to Gerhard Schjelderup: "From the autumn of '80 to the spring of '82, I, as you know, conducted the Harmonic Society in Bergen. What a contrast to life in Lofthus! How unideal in comparison—but how it developed one! But my players, especially the winds, were simply awful, and after two years I could stand it no longer. Yet I wished you could have heard our phrasing in Schubert's C major symphony and Handel's anthems. I really made something of the choir. But, of course, I came into collision with the directors, who either could not or would not understand me, and I waded in trouble, anonymous mud-slinging, and all that goes with that sort of thing."

But let us look a little at his work in the service of the Harmonic Society. It appears both from the newspapers and from Johan Petersen's book on the Society that Grieg's assumption of the conductorship was received with enthusiasm by his townsmen, indeed it was looked upon as the beginning of a new epoch in the history of the society.

The first concert was given on October 22, 1880, with Erika Nissen as soloist. The programme consisted of Svendsen's Norwegian Rhapsody (Opus 21), Mozart's "Vesper Song" for choir and string orchestra, Haydn's Symphony in D major and Beethoven's Fantasy for piano, choir, and orchestra. In addition, Fru Nissen played Bach's Fantasy and Fugue in G minor. The concert began with great ceremony. Ole Bull was commemorated by the playing, before the programme was begun, of "The Sætergirl's Sunday." The whole audience rose spontaneously and listened to the beautiful melody standing. *Bergensposten* writes that evidently a new spirit had been infused into the Harmonic Society and all its forces were working under an energetic and excellent leadership. Never before had a choir which sang so exactly together been heard in the Harmonic Society, and the orchestra played with a precision and displayed a capacity for bringing out nuances and giving expression to changing thoughts and moods such as had never before been observed in any orchestra in the town. The paper notes also that not for many years had the Harmonic Society had so many members.

The second concert, November 18, was given as a Schumann evening and consisted of chamber music and songs. Here Grieg was assisted by Fru Nina Grieg, John Grieg, August Fries, an amateur singer, and a string quartet. Grieg himself took all the piano parts.

At the third concert, on December 9, both orchestra and choir again took part and there were performed Schubert's C major symphony, the first movement of Beethoven's violin concerto, with Fries as soloist, then two choral works, Handel's "Coronation Hymn" and Gade's "Agnethe and the Mermaidens," with Nina Grieg as soloist. The discipline Grieg asked for in order to attain the best possible results was not relished by all and, to judge from an episode before the general rehearsal for the third concert, it would seem that the young ladies found it difficult to submit to the new conditions. In *Bergens Tidende* for December 11, 1880, there is an article with the heading: "That art and good judgement do not always function in unison the following episode seems to establish." It runs:

"A public ball was arranged, and not till later did the members of the Harmonic Society discover that the general rehearsal at the Harmonic was to take place on the same night. Several ladies in the choir had already put down their names and ordered their ball dresses. Who could blame the young ladies for looking forward to the ball with delight and animation?—and that they could not assist at the general rehearsal was a necessary consequence."

The article goes on to say that Grieg insisted on the attendance of the ladies and those who failed to appear received a note from Grieg in which he "dispenses with their future participation in the concerts." The contributor asks: "Whence does Herr Grieg derive his power and authority to promulgate new laws *stante pede* and send out new rules to members, and can he simply ignore the fact that there is a committee of management?"

Grieg's behavior towards the ladies was the common talk of the town and there were many hard words whispered about his despotism. The ladies in question thought that they had been very unfairly treated, in spite of the fact that it was they themselves who had broken an agreement. And all their good friends, male and female, thought the same, and their fathers and mothers and uncles and aunts also, not to speak of gallant cavaliers. But that was not all: *there must be revenge.* So anonymous letters were written to the conductor—in a word, the conductor was made the subject of slanderous gossip and denunciation. But it was not long before opinion veered round in Grieg's favor and several contributors to the newspapers gave him full support, saying that if Grieg was to be abused for having fulfilled his duty and accomplished his task with all the energy, zeal, and punctuality expected of his distinguished name and position, it was time that a very decided protest should be made. It became evident that Grieg's firm stand on this occasion had been well advised and the result of the combat was increased respect both for him and for his art. There was no more going on strike. On the contrary, a ball was gladly given up to sing under the baton of the master.

At the last concert of the season, which was given on March 31, Handel's concerto in G minor for string orchestra and Mozart's Requiem were performed. On this occasion, too, something occurred which excited general attention and annoyed Grieg not a little. The Society had wished to hold this concert in the New Church, but the application, to the astonishment of everyone, was refused by the church authorities. In *Bergens Tidende* for April 1 there is an article with the heading "A public matter which requires public explanation." The article asks on what grounds the refusal is based. "Our ecclesiastical authorities in later years have regularly permitted the holding of concerts in the churches," it goes on, "and here a work was suggested which is unsurpassed in the literature of music. The request was made by a musical society which works only for the promotion of idealistic and artistic aims and, finally, in Edvard Grieg's personality there was a guarantee that the performance, so far as was possible, would satisfy the austere demands of art."

In *Bergensposten* for April 2, "Several" addressed themselves to Bergen's bishop on the same subject and urged "the right reverend gentleman kindly to enlighten them as to the rights and wrongs of the case." But no information could be obtained either from the bishop or any other of the church people. It was not till April 20 that there came an answer signed —e—, in which attention was drawn to the fact that the churches are dedicated to and set apart for the service of God and that concerts of a religious nature, in the strict meaning of the word, have no place in them, because they have no significance as acts of worship but as presentations of art, which, however regarded, could only indirectly be worship of the most High. Further, the writer wished to point out also that in the case under consideration the fact that Mozart's Requiem was a Catholic mass might weigh down the scales. It might, with reason, be said that the concert, considered in regard to its subject matter and not exclusively as an artistic enjoyment, should not on this account take place in a church of the Evangelical Lutheran persuasion.

It may be gathered from the criticisms that there was disappointment that the concert could not be given in the church as had been intended. *Bergens Aftenblad* wrote as follows: "We should like to remark that, in our opinion, Mozart's grand music would have made a very much greater impression under the vault of a large church than in the premises of the Worker's Union, which are too cramped and confining for such an occasion."

Otherwise the performance appears to have been very successful and Grieg is highly praised for "the exceptional sacrifice of time and strength which have enabled him to produce a work like this, a work which we up here in the far North could otherwise know only by hearsay." The concert was a triumph for Grieg. When he came on to the platform, the whole orchestra greeted him with fanfares, while afterwards the audience paid him homage in storms of applause and recalls. As a proof that he came out of the first season an undoubted victor in every respect, it may be related that on his return home from the concert he found a beautiful silver wine tankard from—the ladies' choir! with the following inscription: "Herr Edvard Grieg from the Ladies' Choir of the Harmonic Society—March 31, 1881."

The concert was repeated on April 11 for the benefit of the poor and therewith the season was over and Grieg could feel himself a free man for almost half a year.

What his mood really was after this first Harmonic Society season we see clearly enough in his letters. "Now I have 3-4 months of a life of drudgery behind me," he writes on April 29 to Matthison-Hansen. "Since New Year, 10 concerts:—3 Harmonic concerts, 2 repeat concerts, 3 chamber music evenings, and the rest extra ditto for various charitable purposes. For up here an artist is employed to procure the money which it should be every big merchant's bounden duty to fork out." It appears also from his letters that, speaking broadly, he was well pleased with the artistic results and he must admit that the public had been very amiable and kind. "But *I* cannot go on with it any longer," he writes. "Someone else must carry on now. I have not given a lesson this winter nor composed a note, so you can draw your own conclusions as to the rest." In this last fact now, as so often before, one finds the reason for his dissatisfaction. He goes on to say that he now has a little attic and there he will try to work.

Soon after, however, we find him in Carlsbad, from where, on June 3, 1881, he writes in a letter to John Paulsen: "For a long time my stomach has been troubling me and now the doctor has ordered me off and I had to obey, though it fell heavily on me to see my only work time, looked forward to with so much longing, spoiled." On the 17th of the same month he writes with grim humor to Matthison-Hansen: "Yes, my friend, a poor stomach is a poor lot. I have chronic catarrh of the stomach, blown up intestines, enlarged liver, and what the devil do you call it. I have always been a devotee of enlargement—in the direction of intervals N.B. But now I think I will go over to the side of diminution, for a little while, that is to say. And so I will come to anchor among the pure triads." He goes on to say that he expects to go home in a fortnight to take a so-called after-cure in the country. At last, in the month of July, he is at home and can begin the much longed for composition.

As so often before in similar circumstances, now too it is Norwegian folk music which stimulates his mind, wakens his slumbering powers, and gives him courage again.

In Lindeman's Mountain Melodies he found the material for his *Norwegian Dances. Duets for piano*, Opus 35. Seeing the stimulating and life-giving effect on him of this deliverance, one feels strengthened in the supposition already mentioned that it was rather the periods of spiritual depression that affected his bodily health adversely than his health that acted restrictively upon his creative activity. In other words, the primary cause was mental depression, it was this that brought him down in the purely physical sense also.

After having completed the four Norwegian dances, he wrote in high spirits to Dr. Abraham that he found to his surprise that it was very good for him to compose and that he thought if anyone would pay him 1000 thaler a year in advance, his conscience would give him no peace until he had made ready the quantum agreed upon. He complained further that he could not now continue his composition, though he was feeling so much in the vein for it, because he had again undertaken the conductorship of next season's concerts and must shortly begin his preparations. The answer he got to this letter surprised and astounded him not a little. Dr. Abraham takes him at his word, says that he will gladly agree to his proposition, sends him 3000 marks, and asks to have within a year a piano concerto, some piano pieces, a concert overture, or other works.

Much that was good and positive, therefore, came out of the very short work time he had that summer. Grieg answered Dr. Abraham that he really had not meant what he said so seriously, but if the publisher was willing to venture it, he too would accept the proposal. As he was bound to the Harmonic for the winter, he asked to have his time extended to a year and a half, he would then regard it as a point of honor to make good his obligations.

The motives for the Norwegian dances are all taken from Lindeman's Mountain Melodies. The first, in D minor, is built up over the splendid Sinclair March from Vågå. What Grieg has got out of it is simply astounding in all its naturalness. He seems to have sounded the depths of the very soul of folk music and to have brought up to the light of day its many hidden and only half guessed at powers and faculties, and he seems to reach right back to the very origin of folk and dance music as part and parcel of a religious cult. One feels this specially in the beautiful middle movement in which religious awe and a sublime peace are so impressively united—to swing over straightway into the lively movement and inspiriting rhythms of the dance.

No. 2, which is a "halling" (fling dance) from Åmot, one should really have heard Grieg play himself. The infinite delicacy and grace with which he rendered the principal movement no one who heard it can ever forget. This dance in particular, rightly performed, is a wonderful proof of the high level our folk music had reached and of the refinement of the culture which it reflects. I need only recall the matchless gentleness, the almost caressing tenderness with which Grieg played the three little grace-notes—the charm and delicacy with which he depicted the aristocratic dance scene to which the violent agitation of the middle movement forms so dramatic and effective a contrast. As a rule, one hears this dance played with a kind of perfunctory boldness and an insensitive, distinctly emphasized rhythm which are doubtless intended to be "Norwegian," but which are far from the—in a good sense—subtle conception Grieg has clearly expressed in his treatment here.

No. 3 is also a fling, but of a rather more simple and sturdy character; it is therefore easier, both to apprehend and to perform. Here too one notes the beautiful, enchanting middle part, where the motive in prolongation returns again in the minor, intensified by a harmonic richness which only Grieg can achieve.

The last of the dances is in form the most broadly planned. From a slow introduction, the motive of which is found again in the middle movement, we swing over into a lively dance scene which, with its fresh character and its rhythmic subtleties, provides a series of colorful surprises. The middle movement, which is not in this case built on folk-music motives, forms, in its elegiac mood and tranquillity of line, an effective contrast to the lively rhythms and bustle of the principal movement. Here too, as in the analogous parts of Nos. 1 and 3, one feels the close relationship of the dance and the religious cult. These parts one could well imagine danced in an old Norwegian temple as part of the religious ritual. Comparing these movements with Grieg's own temple dance in *Olav Trygvason*, which treats musically just such a scene, one is struck by the closeness of the relationship. So far back into the source and origin of the material Grieg reaches with his matchlessly sensitive mind and his genuine feeling for the Norwegian spirit.

Not least to be admired in the dance duets is the technical treatment of the piano, how well Grieg understood how to apportion the task between the two players, each of whom is given an opportunity to assert his independence in subjects which are musically significant as well as technically interesting.

It does not seem as though Grieg had begun his second season with the Harmonic with any great pleasure. To John Paulsen he wrote on September 16, 1881: "There is nothing very joyful to report about my affairs. I am moored head and stern here again for the winter, but may the devil put in a strong pickle those who have done it (as Ole Bull said of the directors of the theater in Bergen)." And even after he is in full swing with the work, his mood does not seem to be any brighter. In a letter to Matthison-Hansen on November 18, 1881, he says: "For my part I pay my full tribute to the twenty-four hours and blush for it, but if one has said A, one has to say B also. I am conducting the Harmonic concerts and am fretting myself sick over it. I think I shall turn Catholic. I've got the tonsure already."

After a concert open to the general public had been given on October 4, the real Harmonic concerts were begun on November 1. The principal item at the first concert was Beethoven's Seventh Symphony. In addition, works by Weber, Cherubini, and Max Bruch were performed.

On December 1, the Harmonic celebrated a twenty-five year jubilee—the Society having assumed that name on December 1, 1856. A notable programme was arranged. The chief items were two works which even today rank among the first in our musical literature, Svendsen's B major symphony and Grieg's piano concerto. To finish there was "The Arrival of the Guests at Wartburg" from *Tannhäuser* for full choir and orchestra. That there was great enthusiasm, with an ovation, laurel wreaths, speeches, and a festival prologue it is needless to say.

At the concert on January 26, Saint-Saëns's *Danse macabre* was performed for the first time and seems to have made a deep impression. Between the big symphony concerts there were concerts of chamber music, as in the previous season, and this season also ended with the performance of a great choral work, Mendelssohn's *Elijah*. Among the soloists, as when Mozart's Requiem was performed the year before, was Fru Nina Grieg.

This concert too, which was Grieg's farewell to the Harmonic, was especially successful and Grieg received the warmest acknowledgment of his self-sacrificing work. One paper said: "He has displayed amazing, never failing patience and extreme accuracy in all detail work, combined with an enthusiasm which completely electrifies his co-workers. He believes in his art and is not afraid to take risks for it. This, in conjunction with his brilliant musical gifts, his full mind, his geniality—gives his personality a fascinating power. The festival given for him and his wife by the choir and orchestra of the Harmonic on the occasion of his retiring from its leadership and the ovations he has received from the public show how highly he is valued."

Now Grieg was again a free man and never again in his life did he accept a fixed appointment or take upon him obligations of any kind. From this time on he lived exclusively for his work of composition, but the duties this imposed upon him and the difficulties he had to overcome were of a far more serious nature than those arising from the outwardly rather cramping conditions in which he worked during the two years he was director of the Harmonic. Oddly enough, he had hardly had time to draw a sigh of relief over being free at last from all task work before a new position was offered him, this time as director of the newly established conservatory in Helsingfors, which was to begin its activities in autumn. But, as was to be expected, he declined the offer.

This summer, too, he spent some time in Carlsbad for his health's sake and afterwards went back home to Bergen. He must try to find himself again, he is seeking peace and therefore would be at home, he writes. He wants to be free of all sorts of external impressions of importance and he hopes next autumn—in 1883— to make for the South in good earnest—"And then! Well, we'll think about that when the time comes!"

IT WAS not easy for Grieg to take up his work of composition again. The thread had been completely broken by his journeys and his work with the Harmonic. Since the fateful winter of 1877-1878 in Lofthus, he had, as we have heard, during the course of eight or ten days in May, written the Vinje songs and, during a short holiday in Lofthus in the summer of 1881, the Norwegian dance duets had been created. So in a period of more than four years he had written a book of songs and the dance duets. The fits of inspiration had become more infrequent than ever before! But now he must take hold again—now he really must settle down to steady work once more. There was nothing now to stand in his way, he had time, money too, he had indeed taken an honorarium in advance for the works he was to create.

As was so often the case with Grieg, the result of this winter's work in Bergen was not at all what he had imagined it would be. He encountered obstacles of a kind that not the best outward circumstances, in conjunction with his iron will, were strong enough to overcome. Dr. Abraham had asked for a piano concerto and there can be no doubt Grieg would dearly have liked to give his famous A minor concerto a twin brother!

He began work on this second piano concerto, but he soon realized that he could no longer solve his problems in the same way and by the same methods as when he had written the A minor concerto fourteen years earlier, as the sketches for this concerto found among his posthumous papers show. They consist of a rather short orchestral introduction to the allegro of the first movement and a motive in folk-dance rhythm which was meant, presumably, to be the principal theme of the finale.

This failure of his purpose had naturally a rather discouraging effect upon him and helped to increase his doubt and despondency, and this is clearly expressed in his letters.

As so often before and after, he confided in Matthison-Hansen, to whom of his Danish friends and colleagues he felt himself nearest. In a letter dated Bergen, December 29, 1882, he wrote: "To all appearances I am living a more peaceful life than ever before, but in reality it is a life full of inward struggle. I have no outward activities. I give a few lessons, that is all. Yet I am both spiritually and bodily unwell and decide every other day not to compose another note, because I satisfy myself less and less. When one has to struggle for technique, as I must do—and strangely enough the fight becomes always more difficult—to bring anything to birth becomes so hard at last that all one's strength is exhausted."

He wrote also to Dr. Abraham on May 23, 1883, in a kind of gay self-irony: "And now for a word about Pegasus. He has certainly been here but 'presto' I could not exactly call him—nor could I call him 'allegro'; if I were to christen him his name would have to be 'andante, quasi lento.'" In the same letter he says that he really had made a beginning with the piano concerto Dr. Abraham had asked for, but Pegasus wouldn't move an inch and so he had given it up. A month later he writes that the three promised works are now ready, they are a sonata for piano and cello, a book of duets, *Waltz Caprices*, and a book of small lyrical pieces for the piano. This was the fruit of his winter's toil and struggle—different indeed from what he had hoped and expected.

To Gerhard Schjelderup, in a letter in which he discusses Schjelderup's Grieg biography of 1903, he wrote: "Among my larger works I think you are too kind to my violoncello sonata, which I do not myself rate very highly, because it does not betoken any forward step in my development."

It often happens that when an artist tries to disparage one of his works one entirely disagrees with him. For some unaccountable reason, certain things, perhaps among the very best he has created, stand in the shade, so to speak, in his consciousness. For example, we have heard Grieg refer to *Peer Gynt* and *Sigurd Jorsalfar* as occasional pieces, and other "stupidities" of which there must be no more. But as regards his cello sonata, we must admit he was right. As he says himself, it does not betoken any forward step in his development. If we are to assume that an artist never stands still, that he goes either forward or back, it is plain enough that his cello sonata, especially if compared with his earlier chamber music, the violin sonata and the string quartet, shows a backward step. The thing which is specially striking, and which draws a line between the cello sonata and the other works named, is that it has not the richness of material of the earlier works. Nor do we find here the harmonic differentiation and exuberance that are so captivating and so characteristic of Grieg. The work seems rather to aim frankly at a surface effect—with long drawn lines, a kind of simplification which, had it been supported by glowing, never-failing inspiration as, for example, in the last violin sonata in C minor, might have been very effective, and even have pointed towards possibilities for a real development and revival in Grieg's productions. But it cannot be denied that in the cello sonata one observes for the first time a tendency towards mannerism; that is to say towards the use of devices which have not the vitalizing breath of genuine experience in them, but are employed because they have been mastered, are there to hand and easy to fall back on at a pinch. Yet there is much beautiful music in this work; it is extremely sonorous and shows, as regards the cello especially, a versatility in the use of this instrument that is very striking and effective. We do not find in the cello sonata the strong contrast between the first and second theme usually present in Grieg's sonata movements. Nor is there here, as elsewhere, a secondary motive put in between the first and second themes. But in this very simplicity of outline of the movement, both thematically and harmonically, lie possibilities for a very full utilization of the material in the development, and in the cello sonata this has achieved greater breadth than in the earlier sonatas. Very adroit is the way in which, through a broadly spun out cadenza in the cello, Grieg comes over to the repeat again. The coda offers us familiar material, as it finishes prestissimo, with a free remodelling of the coda in the piano concerto.

In the andante also we meet familiar notes. Its principal motive is almost identical with the theme of "The Triumphal March" in *Sigurd Jorsalfar* and, as in the first movement, we are surprised by a rather broadly designed development. The last movement shows again a close relationship to the finale of the piano concerto without having by any means its richness and freshness. The thematic unity is very obvious as the composer quite simply uses the principal theme, in the major and in augmentation, as secondary motive.

That the cello sonata shows so much skill and versatility in the employment of the instrument and has come to be regarded, therefore, as a very rewarding programme number is probably connected with the fact that the sonata is dedicated to his brother John, whose instrument was the cello. When Grieg was conductor of the Harmonic the brothers played together in recitals of chamber music and often gave concerts both in Bergen and other Norwegian towns.

In the two *Waltz-Caprices* piano duets, Opus 37, we meet Grieg again as the sensitive man of culture, spiritually related to Chopin and, like the Polish master, using the salon and aristocratic social life as a frame for his thoughts and feelings. The two pieces are both graceful, pleasantly sounding music in which one does not at first recognize Grieg, the second indeed has even a suggestion of the Viennese waltz about it.

Grieg's personality comes out much more clearly in the *Lyrical Pieces*, Opus 38. Especially is this so in the famous "Berceuse," which opens the collection. Within the limits of this very simple frame the composer displays such depth and variety of emotion as to show that in the small form especially he now tends to reveal himself with the greatest richness and sincerity. On the background of the grace and charm of the principal movement, in which we actually see before us carefully drawn child faces, appears the more restless and somber middle movement in which subjective experiences and emotions seem to take their color from painful recollections. Involuntarily one thinks of Grieg's own daughter, the little Alexandra, who had so short a life and whom Grieg always held in remembrance with a pathos tinged with pain. The "Berceuse" is one of the most perfect things Grieg has created in small form and is one of the best witnesses to what he was capable of giving expression to in a genre which came later to occupy so large a place in his production.

"Folkevisen" (Folk Tune) is vigorous and full of character but has not the harmonic charm Grieg usually displays in the treatment of a subject like this. Both "Melodi" and "Elegie" are good concert pieces which in mood and subject matter show a leaning towards German romanticism. "Halling" (Fling Dance) and "Springdans" (Spring Dance), on the contrary, are pure Norwegian and pure Grieg, full of rhythmic life and in all their simplicity vigorous and full of character. After a fine little waltz, which whirls past in fiery haste, Grieg ends with a canon. This is the first time his school learning from Leipzig makes an appearance in his compositions but, in spite of the straitjacket he has voluntarily chosen to assume, his personality comes out clearly. It is true that we see his face rather as if behind the bars of a prison window than openly and with unhindered gaze piercing into the future.

Grieg finished yet another little composition this spring, "Sangerhilsen" (A Greeting to Singers) to words of Sigvald Skavlan, so famous in the North. It was written for the great festival of song in Trondheim in the summer of 1883 and is both an impressive and an effective composition, but it does not seem to have set the deeper strings of his soul or temperament in motion— nor did the words invite to this.

He had found time also to give two concerts of his own compositions in Bergen on February 6 and 11. At these the Norwegian dance duets, Opus 35, were played publicly for the first time.

CONCERTS IN GERMANY AND HOLLAND
BUILDING PLANS

THE artistic results of this winter in Bergen do not seem to have satisfied Grieg. And now, just as before, there came periods in which he was a prey to the deepest depression, to gnawing doubt and restlessness from which he knew only work could free him. To get into new conditions, receive new impressions, and especially to learn to know better a musical culture with which hitherto he had had but slight contact, he decided to go to Paris for the winter. For this purpose he applied for a State travelling scholarship—and did not get it!

But let us follow events as they occurred. In the summer of 1883 he went to Bayreuth to be present at the performance of *Parsifal* and stayed afterwards for two months in the little country town of Rudolstadt in Thüringen. His daily companion here was Frank van der Stucken, whom he had met five years earlier in Leipzig. He filled in his time practising on the piano—"laughable," he writes—and taking lessons in French from van der Stucken. As was his way with everything, he took his French lessons very seriously and among his posthumous papers are to be found two French exercise books from this summer in Rudolstadt.

But his letters, especially the many he wrote to Frants Beyer, give us a good idea of the real state of his mind. Grieg and Beyer had met each other in early youth when Grieg was conductor of the Musical Society in Christiania, where both Beyer and his wife sang under Grieg's baton. As the years went on the acquaintance-ship ripened to a warm friendship which lasted to the end of Grieg's life. Beyer was the friend to whom Grieg felt himself most closely attached, the one in whom, especially in difficult situations and in moments of depression, he could confide with complete confidence, a sort of spiritual adviser to whom he more than once opened and relieved his heart. In 1883, then, Grieg wrote to Beyer: "I can only tell you that you are my best friend and that you will mean to me something no one else can mean so long as my heart shall beat." And Beyer would do anything for his friend. He was constantly trying to strengthen him, to give him fresh courage, and help him over difficult times of crisis. A telegraphed greeting just before a concert, a warm friendly letter with fresh, breezy sketches of the dear Westland, a suggestion for a tour in the mountains—all these were things he knew could often have a wonderful influence on Grieg, could assist in drawing him out of periods of paralyzing depression and help him back to health, both bodily and spiritual. As a rule, Beyer's prescription was "nature and work" or "liberation through work."

But this summer, down in Thüringen, Grieg answered that though he looked upon mountain life with Beyer as an invigorating, soul-strengthening bath, yet his solitude down there was of greater importance to him. He ended by saying: "I repeat that to come home now would be a misfortune for me—it would interrupt the course of my development, the fermentation I can only undergo down here."

Grieg's plan was to go to Paris and it was for this he applied for the travelling scholarship already mentioned. "I did not get it, was furious, and swore to get hold of money in some other way," he wrote in a letter. He flung himself, therefore, into restless concert giving, which used up not only all his time but his strength also.

A beginning was made in Weimar, where on October 16 he appeared at the first subscription concert with the piano concerto, "Spring" and "Heart's Wound" for string orchestra. "It was a brilliant beginning and for that I must thank Liszt first and foremost. Ah, how wonderful he was to me." To Beyer he wrote of this concert: "You really should have heard 'Våren' and 'Den særde' last night. It was simply delightful to hear how they played them. Lovely crescendos, pianissimos such as you can hardly imagine, and fortissimos like a whole world of sound. And the Germans were carried away! Besides the applause of the audience I heard from the orchestra: Bravo, bravo! at the best bits and from the box to my left (I was conducting on the stage) I heard Liszt's grunt— the well known sound that is only elicited by something he thinks highly of. You can imagine that Dr. Abraham, who had come from Leipzig in the afternoon, enjoyed the situation. Liszt by the way had become unbelievably old since I spoke with him in Rome. It was sad to see him again."

After this first concert, Grieg went next to Dresden, where in the Tonkünstlerverein on October 22 he played with Grützmacher the cello sonata, its first performance. On the 27th he played the same work with Julius Klengel in the Gewandhaus in Leipzig and had a great success. But, of course, *Signale* was on the spot and gave the cello sonata a review which was worse, if possible, than those Grieg had had five years before. This review, too, is quoted here because it shows how stubborn and persistent was the opposition Grieg met from the most influential center of criticism in Germany. The article runs as follows:

27 Oktober 1883, Gewandhaus: Ihr Program lautete: Str. Quintett in C-dur von Mozart, Sonate für Pianoforte und Violoncell in A-moll (Op. 36) von Edvard Grieg (zum ersten Male) und Streichquartett in C-dur Op. 59 von Beethoven. Je weniger wir gegen die Wahl der ersteren köstlichen und ditto letzteren Programm-Nummer etwas einzuwenden haben, desto mehr gegen die mittlere. Bereits öfter sind wir in der Lage gewesen, den compositorischen Bestrebungen des Herrn Grieg unsere Zustimmung versagen zu müssen; leider können wir auch in gegenwärtigen Falle nicht anders verfahren, ja wir müssen sogar sagen, dass die in Rede stehende Sonate (wohl das neueste Erzeugniss des Herrn Grieg?) uns einen noch stärkeren Wiederwillen eingeflösst hat als die früheren Arbeiten des norwegischen Componisten. Dass derselbe sich in sofern wiederholt, als er ganz dieselben scan- divisirenden Mätzchen macht wie schon immer, das ginge zur Noth noch; dass er aber noch erfindungsdürftiger sich zeigt und seine des- falligen Blössen mit allerhand bunten Lappen und Läppchen zu verstecken strebt, dass er noch phrasenhaft-hohler und gespreizter sich geberdet und in Allem, was Form und thematische Arbeit heisst, fast noch mehr Ungewandtheit documentiert—das Alles können wir ihm nicht verzeihen. Dieses allerdings etwas hartes, aber nach bester Ueberzeugung abgegebenes Urtheil stimmt nun freilich nicht zusammen mit der enthusiastischen Aufnahme, welche dem Werke seitens einer ziemlich starken Publicums-Fraction zutheil geworden ist. Aber Herr Grieg hat merkwürdigerweise nun einmal das Glück, hier in Leipzig eine zahlreiche Anhängerschaft zu besitzen, die sich namentlich aus jüngeren Musikbeflissenen recrutiert, und eben diese Leutchen—welche doch wahrscheinlich nach ganz andere Verehrungs-Objeckte aufzusuchen hätten als Grieg'sche Compositionen—waren es zumeist, welche die von ihren Verfasser und Herrn Julius Klengel vorgeführte Sonate in fast demonstrativer Weise *alle stelle* gehen liess.

So Grieg's hearers were carried away with enthusiasm for this work, in spite of its having been declared by so competent an au- thority to be of no value whatsoever.

After Leipzig he went to Meiningen where he appeared both in orchestral and in chamber music concerts on November 11 and 12. "Here I was as in clover, for Bülow was kindness itself and his patron, the Grand Duke, also. Indeed, he decorated me finally with the inevitable 'Order of the Household, First Class.'"

Then came Breslau with two performances, November 27 and 29. Here the conductor was Max Bruch, "a frightful bore," Grieg remarks. Next Cologne on December 4 and Frankfort on the 14th and after a last concert in Carlsruhe, Grieg went to Holland where he appeared in Arnheim, The Hague, and Rotterdam, finishing his tour at last in Amsterdam.

"After the concert in Amsterdam was over, I actually found myself in possession of 3000 kroner in cash, but what was the use of that now? I was worn out and had to put off both Colonne in Paris and the Philharmonic Society in London. So I stayed over Christmas in Amsterdam with my talented young friend Julius Röntgen and after having rested there for four weeks I telegraphed to Nina, who met me in Leipzig and went with me to Rome, where I spent the winter and early spring."

While living in Rome, Grieg and his wife gave a concert which was a great success. "Think of sitting in the Capitol on a sunshiny afternoon making Norwegian music to the enthusiastic delight of an audience of all nationalities," he writes to Beyer. During this period in Rome too he met Ibsen and had the opportunity with Nina of producing his songs to Ibsen's poems. "Last night we were at a party at the Ross's with Ibsen," he tells Beyer in a letter. "Nina sang a lot of things, among others almost all my songs to Ibsen's poems, and imagine, after little Haakon and especially after 'Jeg kaldte Dig mit Lykkebud' (I Called Thee my Messenger of Joy) and 'The Swan,' the ice crust melted and he came with tears in his eyes to the piano where we were, pressed our hands, hardly able to say a word. He mumbled something about this being real understanding. . . ."

Grieg had, besides, the happiness of hearing his own string quartet played by an Italian quartet ensemble and witnessing the tremendous success it had. "One's own inner spiritual life given utterance to in Hardanger nature—and finding its way straight to Italian hearts—that is a unique experience!" he writes to Beyer.

But after the concerts were well over, and after the intoxication of enthusiasm had died down, it seemed as if the voice of conscience made itself heard with increasing strength. A little of the same bad conscience seems to speak in the following confession to Beyer: "Happy! Why should I be? In my art I ought to be completely happy, but am not, because I have not gone straight forward and so have not achieved what I was called to achieve."

Stimulated by Beyer's building just at this time a house near Bergen, Grieg began to think that perhaps a home would be his salvation. "Lucky beggar! to have hung the wreath upon your house!" he writes to Beyer, "What wouldn't I give for a wreath like that! 10,000 laurel wreaths!"

In another letter we read: "There are many possibilities in this world, especially for an artist, but however that may be, there is something that cries out in me for a house, a home! Only with that can I accomplish anything and it is high time!"

At the same time, the longing for his native land of Norway began more and more to beset him. Never, as now had he felt the truth of the old saying about the plant's dependence on its soil. "So far as some plants are concerned, at any rate," he puts it. "And I, as you know, belong to just that group of plants. I shall simply devour the mountains this summer." He is sitting in an old monastery in Italy but in his thoughts he is up on the Landås hillsides at home. He understands now the enormous advantage the Norwegian artist has in that "no one else can feel as he can that atmosphere of the wonderful and fantastic which lies in contrast."

On his journey northward, he stops in May at Lake Maggiore and is touched to tears by the sight of lake and mountains "for which my heart had cried out so long." The sight has so stimulating an effect on him that he believes he may win back his youthful strength and elasticity. "I can't find any other reason for my well-being than the mountain air and mountain scenery with the fresh, cool water.—It reminds me faintly of the Sörfjord."

At last they make homeward on the wings of longing—a short stay in Leipzig at the end of May—a short stay in Bergen at the beginning of June—and then he is in dear Lofthus again, where friends and acquaintances have made everything ready to receive him. He had written from Rome to the Utnes and arranged everything: "Naturally, we should board with you as in the old days." But as he had heard that Dr. Andersen had left Lofthus, he asked if he might rent his house for the summer. There he would live and work.

In the middle of July the Griegs had a visit from the two Dutch artists, the pianist and composer, Julius Röntgen, and the singer, Johannes Messchaert, whom Grieg had come to know during his concert tour in Holland. They had won his heart at once and both remained his friends for life. Grieg was looking forward with great pleasure to showing them beautiful Lofthus with all its wonderful scenery and he had planned also a tour to Vöringsfoss and only hoped that they were good walkers. During the stay in Lofthus, they enjoyed themselves in every way, went walking in the surrounding country, but did not neglect music either. Almost every forenoon they made music to their heart's content at Grieg's lodgings, where Nina and Messchaert vied with each other in singing and the Hardanger ale went round to the great enjoyment of the visitors. When they left it was in the hope of meeting again soon and they made great plans about bringing Brahms and Herzogenberg, both good friends of Röntgen's, to Norway on their next holiday visit.

At last, at the end of July, Grieg could seriously take up his work of composition again, this time after more than fourteen months' intermission. Fate blessed him again with one of those fruitful working spasms which it seemed impossible to transform into steady working periods. He had to take them as they came and look upon them as the blessing they were, the short and precious moments when he really lived and felt his true value as an artist.

THE HOLBERG JUBILEE

ON December 3, 1884, it was two hundred years since Ludvig Holberg had been born. Bergen was to honor the memory of her great son by erecting a statue of him, the work of the Swedish sculptor, Börjeson, and at the unveiling a cantata to words of Nordahl Rolfsen was to be sung. Grieg was proposed as the proper person to write the music, but we may well agree with him that it is not exactly a grateful task to write ceremonial pieces of this kind. When he was asked in 1906 to write a cantata for the coronation at Trondheim and had refused, he said in a letter to his publisher: "What is a cantata of this kind, which has cost much time and work, *afterwards*? Answer: Waste paper (that is to say, when one isn't a Handel)." Grieg had, of course, tried his hand at this sort of work before. He had written cantatas for the unveiling of the Christie monument in Bergen and the Kierulf statue in Christiania, so he knew what it meant and what he was letting himself in for. "I am bored with writing a male voice chorus for the Holberg festival. But if I am writing poor music, I am making up for it by catching good fish," he writes from Lofthus on October 3. In a letter of October 30 to Röntgen, he draws a picture for him in advance of the whole situation in respect to the unveiling ceremony. "For the rest, so far as music is concerned, I have had a wearisome time, as I have had to busy myself with a cantata for male voices a capella. This affair I have to conduct on December 3 (Holberg's 200th anniversary) on the market place in Bergen, where the monument is to be unveiled. I can see it all before me: snow, hail, storm and every kind of foul weather, huge male choir with open mouths, the rain streaming into them, myself conducting with waterproof cape, winter coat, galoshes, and umbrella! And a cold afterwards, of course, or goodness knows what kind of illness! Oh well, it's one way of dying for one's country!"

When Röntgen some time after asked to see the cantata, Grieg replied: "The Holberg cantata you will never be allowed to see. It is sleeping the eternal sleep, and a good thing too. It is not going to be printed nor to be translated, it is going to be—destroyed." This last is not strictly correct; it is printed both full score and vocal parts. But Grieg has not provided it with an opus number, nor did he include it in the list of his works; so he in a way disowned it. It is a well written and well sounding composition for a male choir, but it does not betray in any way that its begetter was an artist with so individual and original a personality as Edvard Grieg.

All the more real and genuinely experienced is the other work, which arose out of the Holberg jubilee, the suite *Fra Holbergs Tid* (From Holberg's Time). To explain how, psychologically, it was possible for so independent and individual an artist as Grieg to assume the style and form of the rococo period and yet create wholly personal and original music, it is useful to consider the question in connection with the difficulties he had to contend with in those days, particularly in the finding of technical methods to express the ideas with which he was inwardly burning. One can well imagine that it was simply a relief to him to throw off for a moment all doubts and reflections, all painful striving to achieve the necessary balance between material and technique, and simply stroll right in to the firmly constructed and securely founded style and form of a time long past. Considering the artistic result, one is tempted to believe that it was almost a necessary way out for Grieg just then, a curious way, certainly, but nevertheless one by which he could come again to true and genuine expression. He assumes the garments of the rococo period, but he is and remains Edvard Grieg. In the sedate prelude, the sometimes sentimental, sometimes mildly elegiac Sarabande, the gay Gavotte with the roguish Musette, the Air, marked by deep feeling and gravity and last, but not least, in the sparklingly fresh Rigaudon—in everything it is Edvard Grieg's own touch we clearly recognize. He has simply placed himself in the same milieu in which the great satirist lived and worked. He looks at the present through the spectacles of the past—that is all.

From letters to Röntgen it appears that the Holberg suite was originally written for the piano. So early as August 26, 1884, Grieg wrote from Lofthus that he had finished it and on December 7 he gave a concert in Bergen at which both the cantata and the suite were performed, he himself playing the suite. Finally he told Röntgen in a letter of February 1, 1885, that he was busy orchestrating the Holberg suite for string orchestra and hoped that in this form too it would sound well. He even discussed various technical details of his plan. So much the more surprising is it to see that both to his publisher, Dr. Abraham, and to Matthison-Hansen he asserts that the Holberg suite was originally written for string orchestra. On March 12 he gave a concert at Bergen and produced the suite for string orchestra. In sending the programme to Dr. Abraham he wrote: "Dass die Suite *Aus Holbergs Zeit* eigentlich für Orchester geschrieben ist, werden Sie daraus erfahren. Ich war sehr gespannt, das Perrückenstück zu hören, und wie gross war meine Freude, dass es so gut gelang, dass ich das Konzert einige Tage nachher wiederholen musste." And to Matthison-Hansen he said: "You see from this that the Holberg suite is a piece for string orchestra."

Thus, as we have seen before, Grieg is not always to be relied upon as a source of information regarding himself or his works. But in the last sentence in the letter to Dr. Abraham we find perhaps the explanation of this apparently inexplicable duplicity. He writes as follows: "Wenn Sie das Werk in dieser Form drucken wollen, steht es mit Vergnügen zu Ihrer Disposition." He knew well how extremely cautious Dr. Abraham had been hitherto in regard to orchestral works or works for chamber music; he much preferred to have piano pieces. It was best, therefore, not to reveal that the Holberg suite, strictly speaking, was a work for the piano which had afterwards been orchestrated.

At Lofthus during the summer Grieg had made ready also a book of songs, his Opus 39. Only two of these were new, "I lien höit deroppe" (On the High Hillsides) to words of Jonas Lie, and "Hörer jeg sangen klinge" (Whenever I Hear the Ditty) to a poem of Heine's, which had been translated by Nordahl Rolfsen. The rest had been written early in the Seventies.

It must be mentioned also that this winter, at the request of his publisher, Grieg wrote a number of arrangements for the piano of his own songs. It was probably the translation difficulty that induced Grieg to agree to such a proposal, and as regards the publisher, it was no doubt the desire to have as much piano music as possible from Grieg that suggested the idea. Naturally it is of interest to piano players to be able to make use of Grieg's songs, but as piano music these arrangements offer little of interest. It is singular that Grieg, who elsewhere captivates us in his piano works with precisely his individual and marvellously versatile use of the instrument, has here slipped into an impersonal, often purely "drawing-room" treatment of the piano. One can well understand, therefore, why his French biographer, Ernest Closson, was not exactly edified by these piano pieces on his own songs of which Grieg produced in all five books apportioned between two works, Opus 41 and Opus 52.

But there were other matters also, both pleasant and important, occupying Grieg's thoughts at this time. He was building his house! He was about to make a reality of that house he had always dreamt of. In June 1884, when on his way to Bergen he visited Beyer in his new house at Næsset on Nordåsvannet, seven miles from Bergen, the decision was made. He bought the nearest promontory as a site for his house. His cousin, the architect Schack Bull, drew the plans and was in charge of the work of building and by the end of August the first blast of dynamite boomed out on the site. Grieg begged Schack Bull to see to it that in the levelling and the rest of the work on the grounds not one tree more than was absolutely necessary should be sacrificed. He asked also whether in the case of small trees they could not be transplanted rather than cut down.

On December 15, he reported that now the first story has begun to peep up above the ground and in March he was so absorbed in the building operations that he went up every day to see how things were getting on. He told Dr. Abraham in a letter of March 24 that for the time being he does not know whether he is a musician or a master builder. Every day he goes up and down by train to the villa. Up there all his ideas are spent, unborn works are devoured wholesale by the soil itself. "When you come here one day," he writes, "you will only have to dig, and Norwegian choral, orchestral, and piano works will gush out from the ground."

In April he moved into his new house, which he named Trold-haugen (The Hill of the Trolls). He has achieved his aim, he has got the house he has so long been yearning after, he has found a place which is his own and no one else's, and to which he feels he belongs. Now it remains to be seen whether the home fulfils what it promised, whether it gives him the one thing needful, the thing in which happiness lies, the ability and the desire to work.

This and much else will be told in the next chapter.

TROLDHAUGEN

1885-1900

OUTWARD triumphs, inward resignation—that is the main impression gathered from the remaining years in Edvard Grieg's life. He was now only forty-two years old and had twenty-two years still to live.

The knowledge and appreciation of his works were steadily increasing and they were winning their way everywhere into homes and concert halls, especially after the Peters publishing house acquired in 1889 publishing rights to them all. His name and reputation as an artist was steadily going up, he was a known and highly valued composer, not only in the Northern countries and Germany; in England, France, Holland, Belgium, Italy, Czechoslovakia, Poland, and Russia as well he had attained a popularity such as few artists have experienced.

Above all, whenever he appeared, as pianist, conductor, or taking part in chamber music, even, indeed, as accompanist to his songs, he was greeted with extraordinary enthusiasm and homage. Often it was so overwhelming that he could hardly understand it himself, but thought that it must be sympathy for Norway manifesting itself in this way. "I feel so grateful and happy and do not really understand why such good fortune should come just to me," he writes in 1888, and after his first appearance in England the same year, he says: "When I stood and conducted 'Spring' and it rang out as though all nature at home would gather me into her embrace, then I was indeed proud and glad to be a Norwegian. I really think that the sympathy of the English for my art must come from their sympathy for Norway—in no other way can I explain the ovations of yesterday. It reminded me of the old days when Ole Bull appeared with his fiddle before the people in Bergen. Only it lasted much longer here."

Fifteen years later he wrote after a concert in Prague in 1903: "It is unbelievable. I cannot understand it. So many creative spirits far more important than I do not get the sympathy I meet everywhere. One thing is certain. I feel myself so wonderfully small with all this and could wish for a whole lifetime of work only to make myself worthy of some little of all this appreciation."

Vinje's words, "More I got than I had deserved," run like a refrain in his letters when he describes his triumphs out in the world —again and again he repeats them and in the last years he adds mournfully the last sentence: "And everything must come to an end." But his letters show that he was not merely filled with gratitude for the warmth and friendliness which met him everywhere. He was warmed and stimulated, and something returned to him of the strength, faith, and enthusiasm of his youth, which put reflection out at the door. He lived again the precious, ever blessed moments when inspiration took hold of him, when his works came into being. He was again the medium controlled by secret forces, he felt himself again the interpreter and deliverer of the soul of a people.

But only for a short while, only for a moment. No sooner have "the tumult and the shouting died" and everyday life must again be tackled, than reaction sets in with double strength—he becomes a prey to the blackest depression, constant restlessness and constant dissatisfaction. If he is at home at Troldhaugen, he longs to get away and if he is away, he is tormented by a devouring longing for home, for the hills and fjords of his own country, the surroundings he then feels to be essential for the unfolding of his creative powers. "There are times when it seems to me the finest thing in the world to be just a *Norwegian* artist. But other times, today for example, I feel it nothing but a curse. And envy stirs in me when I think that there you sit, you lucky beggar, in a land where you can bathe in beautiful impressions of all kinds. No—a happy Norwegian artist (N.B. one who really loves his fatherland) will never be found till all can strap on their wings and make off like the birds in presto time wherever they feel inclined." This outburst we find in a letter to John Paulsen on April 30, 1885, almost as soon as he had moved into his long-coveted new home!

Some piece of devilry, he goes on to say, he must contrive in order to get out into the world in autumn. In fact, no sooner has he put his legs beneath his own table and arranged things to his own liking within his own four walls, than he begins to speculate as to how in all the world he will get away, get out to wider horizons, out to art and people. And he goes out, not only that autumn but so many autumns, goes out to wider horizons, to art and people, but the same restlessness follows him there. It is in the letters to Frants Beyer that we can best see his constant longing after

Norway and the Norwegian scene and, above all, his constant long-ing after work, the work of *creation*, which stood for him as the only real work. Indeed, if one agrees that it is only in his work an artist is truly happy, it would seem that in spite of all outward glory and success, in spite of all the honors so profusely heaped upon him, happiness was very seldom the guest of Edvard Grieg in these years. Still only fifty-one years old, he seems almost to have settled his account, to have come to an understanding of the situa-tion. He writes to Beyer: "You see, the feeling that my life's work in all important respects should be at an end, I have not till now been able to believe in. It seems to me there is so much I ought to do, so much I feel both the power and the craving to do—in the few good moments. But now I begin to feel that I must try to get the position clear, resign myself, and rejoice over all the good Mother Nature has meted out to me. In other words, I must say to myself, 'Be at peace and be thankful.'"

Again he says: "The music I think of the one day, I pluck out of my heart the next because it is not genuine. My thoughts are bloodless, like myself, and I lose faith in myself. Against that fact it signifies little when Dr. Abraham writes that my works, for ex-ample the *Peer Gynt* suite, are performed in Europe, Asia, Africa, America, and Australia. And so to the mountains, to the moun-tains! Only there is the remedy."

In 1900 he writes with a melancholy self-knowledge what it may well have cost something to confess, even to his nearest friend: "This not being able to satisfy oneself is so distressing that I could wish I had the courage I admire in Alexander Kielland."

In such moments of discouragement, time and time again, it is the thought of Norwegian nature that holds him up and helps him over. In the midst of all the enthusiasm and homage there is an inner voice which says Home! home! and makes it plain to him that he cannot give of his best, travelling about playing to people. "I feel this more and more and it shall not happen again." He was clear about that, even in 1888. But he continued his concert tours year after year.

"I live—and live upon my longing for Norway! The same old song again—but a lovely song without which I should not care to exist," he writes in 1894. About the same time he says: "More than ever I look for salvation in the scenes of my homeland. For there is something locked up in me that no one understands." When he gets a letter from a friend with sketches of home surroundings or some photographs of places known and dear to him, he is stimulated, feels stronger, gets new courage. "When I got home your letter with Troldhaugen and Næsset was lying on the table! It was just as if I filled my lungs again with fresh mountain and sea air." Even the Swiss Alps, so admired of all tourists, are not able to still his nature longing. On the contrary! In Geneva he lived in a hotel looking right over to Mont Blanc. "But the effect is not, in Geneva, particularly impressive," he wrote in a letter of 1894, "and the scenery altogether is so astonishingly outwardly sensational that it impresses me rather as theatrical than really great. No—the home of wildness, of mystery— I know very well where that is to be found."

When the first message of spring reached him in a foreign land, then his longing would grow and grow till it mounted to such a passion that he could hardly wait till the day and the hour came when he could begin the journey north again. Time after time, he gives expression to this in his letters. One only need be quoted as an example. "Now when the spring begins to waken, the longing for nature wakens too with renewed strength, a craving more powerful than ever. And when I think that you are up there, my dear old friend, longing for the same things as I, I feel as though I could embrace the whole world for thankfulness that it is so and not otherwise, as if I could not wait for the happy moment that shall send us out together among the mountains and the fjords." He realized too that only in nature and work was there salvation for him as a creative artist. He agreed, therefore, with his friend who proposed "a little mousehole to hide himself away in, or—a solitary sæter up in the mountains," but added: "I will go a little further and say: 'Life in the Norwegian (Westland) mountains anywhere.' And so long as you feel as I do in this, a balm falls on my soul whenever in a dark moment I can conjure up this happy consciousness. How strange it is, though, that in this respect nature stands above mankind. For human beings—even those we care for infinitely—may disappoint. Nature, never. To her bosom one never turns in vain, no matter what happens. The thought of Norway, that is what I live on when I am abroad—and when I am at home."

He fully admitted the rightness of his friend's constantly repeated precept, "nature and work"; only there was salvation to

be found, but he could not come to a decision. He admitted and
was filled with a deep gratitude for the understanding and sympathy shown him, though it forced him more than once to a difficult self-knowledge. On November 24, 1893, he wrote to Beyer:
"The softness in me, which I usually keep within bounds, is of such
a nature today—I don't know why—that it absolutely will out,
and after having read such a letter, God help me, I sit up here in
my lonely lodging and—weep. If you knew how much good the
tears do me, you would forgive this *con molto sentimento*. And it is
only you, Frants, who can call them out. I feel the truth in every
word you say, the glorious truth which can never make me unhappy, however much I may have to fight against within and without me, that you for me are what you are and that this is and always will be so, in spite of all life's changes. How many are as
lucky? Not one, I think, in 20,000!"

Only very seldom in these years did inspiration flame up again
with an all-conquering intensity and fervor, when, for example,
he wrote his third and last violin sonata, or when he came across
fine poetry which in depth and richness of color approached
Vinje's, such as Garborg's *Haugtussa*. In many of the lyrical
pieces for the piano also, of which, during this period, he gave out
eight sets in all, he found in the small form expression for thoughts
and feelings which may have been working in him for years. They
show a movement towards greater richness of color and a more
subtle harmony which come near to impressionistic methods of expression.

Yet if we are to follow Grieg's real development as an artist—
and he never ceased to develop—we must follow him on the narrow
path which leads always deeper and deeper into the forest, always
further and further into the wonderland of romance, the path
which he finds and points out to us every time he comes into relationship with Norwegian folk music. The symphonic dances, Opus
64, the folk songs, Opus 66, the folk dances, Opus 72, and finally
the chorales for mixed choir, Opus 74, mark this line of development.

It seems as if all the creative power with which he was endowed
but to which he could not, through the unkindness of fate, give
expression in the great forms, crystallizes in these small masterpieces, which, in regard to harmony in particular, look far beyond

his own times. Once more it is Norwegian folk music which is at once the wellspring and the means by which he can come to expression, he, who in the last twenty years of his life, felt himself completely locked up. From the earliest works of his youth, the Humoresques, Opus 6, transcriptions of folk songs, Opus 17, through the Norwegian dances, Opus 35, there runs a direct line to the transcriptions of folk songs, Opus 66, and the folk dances, Opus 72 and also from the choruses for male voices based on folk songs, which he wrote in Lofthus, to the chorales for mixed choir written on a basis of old religious folk tunes. In those works where he creates directly out of folk music without any impediments of style and formula, with no thought of tradition or school, he shows himself at his best; even as a technician, displaying a harmonic and rhythmic subtlety in his treatment of the material, the influence of which has been felt the world over, especially by the French impressionists, and which as regards technique is modern to this day. But the great works he had dreamed of creating—they did not materialize. He tried to write a Peace oratorio for which Björnson, when asked, at once supplied words. Grieg never got further than "smelling at it." He tried to write a string quartet No. 2. Two movements were composed and then he got no further. He tried to write yet another piece of chamber music, a piano quintet, but only a sketch of the beginning came into being.

So he shaped his great works out of compositions written long ago! He began with "Bergliot." It had been completed in 1871 and was orchestrated and produced in 1885. Next he took the overture, "In Autumn," which was composed in 1865 and two years later published as a piano duet. It was revised and reorchestrated in 1887. Then he reorchestrated the *Peer Gynt* music, composed in 1874-1875, and in two suites prepared it for concert use in 1888 and 1891. Then we have the *Olav Trygvason* fragment. It was composed in 1873 and in 1889 orchestrated and performed as a choral work in the concert hall. Finally, there is the music to *Sigurd Jorsalfar*. This was composed in 1872 and in 1892 revised, reorchestrated and performed as a suite at concerts.

ROMANTICISM AND REALISM

ONE of the reasons why Grieg at this time—the Eighties and Nineties—was finding it so difficult to adjust himself, both when abroad and when at home, was probably that he felt himself to stand, if not outside certain intellectual currents of the time, at least in opposition to them. Realism and naturalism had just made their entrance into literature and art. What was Grieg's attitude towards these new ideas? He understood them, he realized their justification, and when it was a question of getting in a blow at official hypocrisy, they had his full sympathy. This is shown by his comment on Christian Krohg's *Albertine*, of which he writes: "It is genuine art because behind it all lurks deep feeling. But that a muddled society does not know what to do with such a book is understandable. However that may be, Krohg is today the most popular man in Norway—if not in the whole North. And for that he can thank the Norwegian government. Because, in spite of its outspokenness and the challenging nature of its theme, the book would not have aroused so much sympathy but for the official morality now sitting at the helm, which to me is worse than if the whole of Christiania consisted only of——."

Also, when Jonas Lie, apropos of the building of the Bergen railway, expressed in a letter his fear lest "the country may lose in sentiment and genius what it gains in flatness and communications," and further, "that we have been such a fairy-and troll-ridden land, with all sorts of fascinating corners and side valleys, snowy hollows and baking sunny slopes—if we become *too* lucid it may be that all the various spirits of the unconscious, which flourish in mysticism's creative obscurity, will fly away," Grieg answered him: "I feel warmly about your beautiful words as to what we may lose in sentiment and genius with the proposed communications. They touch me especially with my Westland store of pent-up longings which seek an outlet in music. But it can't be helped; all fences must go down, and the genius that can't get on without fences must fall with them. For it has not the capacity for a long life."

Sympathy he had indeed for the seeking after truth which the new ideas brought with them, both in life and art, but his heart, his disposition, the whole of his spiritual make-up appertained to and would always appertain to romance.

When, in 1875, through Björnson, he had the first warning of the new forces that were stirring, he replied: "To paint Norway, Norwegian folk life, Norwegian history and Norwegian folk poetry in music stands for me as the province in which I think I might accomplish something—and what you speak of has also certainly my full sympathy, but—I am not the man, not at least in this period of my life. Romance beckons me, for the present, in all its fullness!"

Twelve years later he holds fast to the same standpoint in a letter of January 21, 1887, to John Paulsen: "I think it is the time you live in that gives you its whack. It incites you to imagine that you belong to it. But neither you nor I do that, my friend! We are romantics both, and if for the moment our times seem to have no use for romance in poetry, it would be weak or cowardly to disown it on that account. That brings its own severe punishment, since one makes a muddle of one's own nature that way. Romance will come back sooner than any one suspects."

Only once, in his description of his relationship to the tendencies of the period, does he make observations which, if they do not actually express anxiety, hint at least at a certain doubt which has almost the stamp of self-knowledge. This is in a letter to Beyer four years later, in 1891: "I will not say that I am afraid either of life or death, but there is one thing I am afraid of: to perceive in myself that I am growing old—to realize that youth is sailing out on expeditions the meaning of which I do not understand. In a word, I fear the possibility of not being able to feel what is true and great in the intellectual advanced posts which are pushing out gradually as we grow older. Therefore I have an instinctive craving to know all the subtle changes that are stirring in the intellectual world, now more than at any time. If one lets anything of importance slip by now, without giving it full attention—before one knows, a power has come into being which one does not understand because one has not kept up with what is new from its first breath. To be left lying half-forgotten by the wayside while time marches on over my sinful cadaver, that seems to me the most wretched fate that can befall a man. And to what countless numbers does it not happen? Probably to most. But they do not know it and so do not care. It is otherwise with the artist. When he is on the side of reaction he is done."

Above: Grieg's Home, Troldhaugen Near Bergen

Below: Björnson and Grieg at Troldhaugen in 1903

Even now it is the outcome of the fateful winter in Lofthus that is casting its dark shadow over his universe and calling up reflections like this. It is an instinctive feeling of disagreement between material and technique, a feeling that "there is something locked up that no one understands," as he puts it himself—it is all this that fills him with despondency and often with such a crushing feeling of anxiety that more than once he decides to break off—finish—say "Stop."

Where could he look for help in solving this problem which he sensed instinctively rather than really understood?—this tragedy, that he possessed and was possessed by material for the release of which a technique was needed which it required the work of generations to build up. Where should he—if not find direct help—at least get impulses, be stimulated to take up work in all seriousness?

Had Grieg in these, for him, so fateful years been in more intimate touch with Russian and French music, not the official kind known to all the world, but the real, had he known of the battles that were being fought out on the *inner* frontiers in the musical life of those two countries, he would have learned to his astonishment that several artists there were consciously working at the solution of the problem with which Richard Nordraak in his day had charged him in the case of Norwegian music. Had he made acquaintance with Mussorgsky, Balakirev, and Rimsky-Korsakov in Russia and Debussy in France, he would have learned to know artists who, in violent opposition to the German school, understood the one thing necessary, that the fettered forces could only come to expression through laws dictated by the nature of the material itself, and not through a form and style forced on them from without. He would have found men with the same wide vision, with the same capacity to see relationships between things which in his youth he had admired so intensely in Nordraak and which had so fruitfully roused his enthusiasm. But Russia for Grieg was Tschaikovsky, and France synonymous with Gounod and Saint-Saëns. In other words, Gade over again, only more varied, more gifted, deeper. But actually it was the same spirit that, after his meeting with Nordraak, he had sworn in such proud words to oppose.

So it is understandable that Grieg, in the perplexity that often marked him in these years, should turn his eyes again towards Germany and should come under the influence of the great master

of romance whose works at this time set their mark everywhere—
Richard Wagner. That this influence was not fruitful and did not
help in releasing what lay deepest in Grieg's own nature is only
what might have been expected, and Gerhard Schjelderup was undoubtedly right when he said that "the Wagner sun in Bayreuth
had a disturbing effect for a time on the orbit of Grieg's star."

Had Grieg followed the inner voice which said to him, "Into the
mountains, into the mountains, there only is salvation"—or had
he listened to his friend's advice on "nature and work"—that is to
say, had he in these years tried to acquire for himself a technical
equipment able to deal with the rich material he possessed, the
last twenty years of his life would perhaps have shaped themselves differently and, above all, Norwegian music would certainly
today have been something very different from what it is. So far-
reaching was the dark shadow of the winter of combat at Lofthus.

If we look now at Debussy's article on Grieg, written after the
famous Paris concert in the Châtelet Theater in 1903, we must not
see only Debussy's hard and seemingly heartless words in connection with Grieg's behavior in the Dreyfus affair. Naturally, it was
this that made Debussy speak so ironically and maliciously of an
artist whom he admired and to whom he felt himself closely
allied, one who had obviously not been without importance to
his own works. But there is a passage also which expresses disappointment, disappointment that one of the very few artists whom
he felt to be both an ally and support in the struggle to cast off the
German yoke in the music of his own country should have broken
faith. Debussy's comments in regard to "the affair" which had led
him into a purely personal assault on Grieg do not concern us here,
but one passage is of interest because it comes from a contemporary
master in music who was at the same time a keen observer. Debussy writes:

One may lament that Herr Grieg's sojourn in Paris has not taught
us anything new about his art; he remains a fine musician when he
takes as his province the folk music of his homeland, though he does not
make nearly such good use of it as Balakirev and Rimsky-Korsakov do
in their employment of Russian folk music. Subtract that, and he is
nothing more than a clever musician who aims more at effect than at
real art. It would seem that his real leader and good genius was a young
man of about his own age, a born genius who had given promise of being
a great musician when he died at twenty-four, Richard Nordraak. His

death is doubly to be deplored because it deprived Norway of a great
honor and Grieg of the influence of a friend who would certainly have
prevented him from straying into a wrong path. Or does Grieg aspire,
like The Master-builder Solnes, towards "building mankind a house in
which they can feel at home and be happy?" I found no trace of this
charming picture in what Grieg let us hear yesterday. Do we know
anything of his latest works? Perhaps they are the "happy homes" of
which Ibsen speaks! In any case, Grieg did not give us the pleasure of
walking in. The triumphant reception he received last night must be his
reward for having been at the trouble to visit France. Let it be our
sincerest wish that in the future he will find us worthy to feel ourselves,
if not "at home," at least happy in his music.

Debussy refers in this last passage to some remarks of Grieg's
in an interview in *Signale*, where he says that "artists like Bach
and Beethoven have built churches and temples on the heights.
I would like, as Ibsen expresses it in his drama, to build dwelling
places for my fellow men in which they can feel themselves at
home and be happy. In other words: I have recorded my country's
folk music. In style and form I am a German romantic of the
Schumann school, but at the same time I have drawn from my
country's rich treasure of folk tunes, and from this hitherto un-
explored wellspring of the Norwegian national soul I have tried
to create a national art."
    Now it is plain that at this time Debussy did not know the best
of Grieg's later works. If he had known only the adapted folk songs,
Opus 66, not to speak of the folk dances, Opus 72, his words would
certainly not have struck as hard as they did.
    There was another thing Debussy should have understood and
taken into account, and that was that Grieg in this struggle was in
a much more difficult position than either himself or the Russians.
The latter were at least a small band, a company of five in all, who
stood leagued together in the fight; and though Debussy at first
stood alone, he had support in the old musical culture of France
with such masters as Rameau and Couperin at his back. Grieg, on
the contrary, stood entirely alone—not only in Norway, but in the
North, alone in a land without tradition in art music. If Debussy
had reflected on that, he would have understood that it both explained and excused much. What we have reason to deplore is that
the contact between Norway and these two countries was not more

intimate and that in the extremity in which he actually found himself, Grieg had to turn again to German music.

Gerhard Schjelderup expresses it thus: "Grieg's genuis stood for a moment uncertain with eyes turned now towards the North, now towards Germany where Wagner blazed in glory. Seldom has German influence been so plainly visible in his development as here and it cannot be denied that this influence seems for a time to have had a paralyzing effect on his creative power."

One of our objects, therefore, in following Grieg in the coming years very closely and in great detail will be to show what an amazingly small proportion of his time was given up to creative activity and that his life as an artist in the last twenty years—in spite of all outward success—was, in a word, deeply tragic.

THE summer of 1885 brought Grieg, as usual, to Lofthus. In August he went with Frants Beyer for a fortnight's mountain tour in the Jotunheim. Of composition we hear nothing at this time but, so far as can be judged, it must have been now that he orchestrated "Bergliot" which had been composed in 1871. It was with this and the Holberg suite as novelties in his trunk that he left Troldhaugen on one of the first days of October for Christiania and Copenhagen, where a series of concerts awaited him. In Christiania he gave two concerts of his own, took part in a Musical Society's concert and also in a concert at the Christiania Theater. It was five years since he had last appeared in the capital and "the way in which at his first concert Grieg was received as he appeared upon the platform, which was richly decorated with flags and flowers, finely expressed recognition of his great importance as a composer and musician," wrote *Nordisk Musik-Tidende*. "Enthusiastic and prolonged cheers greeted the composer, flowers and laurel wreaths rained down and the audience—the hall was packed—rose to join in a 'Long live Grieg' followed by resounding hurrahs."

At his own concerts, which were given on October 17 and 21, he played with his brother John the cello sonata and with Erika Nissen the Norwegian dance duets, while Nina Grieg and Thorvald Lammers sang a number of his best ballads. In addition, he himself played a generous selection of his piano pieces.

At the concert of the Musical Society, which was given on the 24th, he conducted the Holberg suite and "Åse's Death" and "Anitra's Dance" from *Peer Gynt*—both works for the first time. Lammers sang "Taken into the Mountains," "which with its wild, passionate and daemonic character had a powerful effect," wrote *Nordisk Musik-Tidende*. The concert ended with "Landsighting," which with Lammers in the solo part and a choir of about one hundred fifty in conjunction with an ample orchestra was magnificently rendered.

Finally came his fourth and last appearance, this time at the Christiania Theater, where in addition to repeating the Holberg suite and the two pieces from *Peer Gynt* he conducted the first performance of "Bergliot" which was recited by Laura Gundersen.

It seems as if Grieg had brought the inhabitants of the capital absolutely to his feet, for this time too his entrance was greeted with storms of cheering, his conductor's desk was decorated with a laurel wreath tied with ribbon in the national colors, and the applause increased after each number, reaching its culmination after "Bergliot." "Both the composer and Fru Gundersen, whose splendid sonorous voice and inspired artistic rendering contributed substantially to the concert's brilliant success, received enthusiastic ovations," wrote *Nordisk Musik-Tidende*. Of the work itself the paper wrote: "Grieg has here produced a deeply moving tone poem: the melodramatic form, against which objections can often be raised, he has used in a masterly way; the splendid poem stands out with double clarity and beauty against a background of richly colored and characteristic music. The composition may be ranked as one of Grieg's most magnificent and interesting works; a product of his genuinely Norwegian artistic nature and genius, which in Björnson's poem has found a rich theme for its original creative art."

Immediately after this concert Grieg and his wife went to Copenhagen where, on November 14, they took part in the Concert Society's concert. On November 23 and 27 Grieg gave concerts of his own and on December 10 he conducted in the Musical Society and finally he assisted the Students' Society with their concert on December 18.

The programmes, to put it briefly, were much the same as at the concerts in Christiania and in his letters Grieg relates his experiences and impressions, often in great detail. After having played his piano concerto under Svendsen's baton, he wrote: "And now a few words about the grand Philharmonic concert. Yes— grand is the word, for Svendsen appeared with the ribbon of his Order, the Queen was at the final rehearsal, and all the royal family at the concert. Everything went well and the whole was a huge success. You can imagine how 'Åse's Death' sounded played by that enormous string orchestra. And it was no small thing to sit there and play with Svendsen conducting. I have a feeling that Svendsen will come to anchor in Christiania again, for he longs to go there and he would like to have me there also."

Grieg goes on to say that, "after the concerts, as you can imagine, we have a good time. We gather in the Vienna Café in the hotel where we live, with musicians, painters, poets, and other friends and make speeches and are merry often till far on in the night. Then we pay dearly for it the next day."

Among the artists with whom Grieg struck up a close friendship this winter was the poet Holger Drachmann. After an evening at his house with Lange-Müller, Grieg wrote: "They are splendid, warm-hearted men whom I am glad to have got to know. They are coming sometime to Troldhaugen, so you can begin looking forward to it."

But after two months Grieg was already feeling his strength begin to fail him; he felt his foundations shaken, his hands and feet were always cold, and a leaden feeling of palsy in arms and legs threatened to make his musical existence impossible, he says in a letter. "All bodily and spiritual energy has been washed out of me," he complains. He decides eventually to consult a doctor, who tells him it is anaemia that is the root of his trouble, but that his nerves too are weak. The doctor advises him to live in the country and do a lot of bathing. "I can scarcely believe that the man now sitting here writing is the same who trotted about the Jotunheim with you in summer!" he writes to Beyer. "If only it were spring—I would turn homeward at once."

It was reaction now again proclaiming itself—reaction after so great a using up of both bodily and spiritual strength. He does all he can to get well and strong again. He walks and walks, eats ham and eggs and eggs and ham, and does everything that could possibly be done. "The result is not first rate, but still, yesterday and today, I can say, provisionally, to the undersigned, Stop your whining! and that is always something."

He has begun already to dream of summer! "Never have I looked forward to it so much as now!" He thanks God that there is still something that reconciles one to existence—the longing to lose oneself in nature. As spring advances, this longing mounts and grows. By the beginning of April his longing to go home is intense. "I cannot feel at peace down here any longer and every day that passes is only so much time wasted." But he has heard that spring is late at home, and it won't do to be imprudent. Besides, he has been reckless enough to promise Nina that she shall see the

Danish beeches in leaf. "It looks now as if that is going to be very late and then I really don't know if the promise will hold."

By the end of April he has both spring and bird song in full measure down in Denmark, and yet it seems to him as if he had no part in it, he writes. Spring for him is only spring in Norway, in the Westland—and even though he is surrounded by bird song, spring, and friends, it seems as if all swam in a mist for him and faded away and he dreams himself home, to a quiet morning in the boat out among the rocks and reefs. So filled is he with this longing that it shapes itself into a gentle song of gratitude. "There is nothing new in it," he writes to Beyer, "but it is genuine and though in reality it is no more than a letter to you, let it stand here." Then he wrote down the little piano piece "In der Heimat" in the letter, and continued: "Had the surroundings of Næsset and Troldhaugen been grander, the tone would have been different. But I like them as they are and it was the feeling of quiet happiness that all is as it is up there which formed itself into music."

At last, on May 12, the journey back from Copenhagen was begun after a final series of festivities and farewell parties for Grieg and his wife. On May 17 they were home in Bergen again. A month's stay at Troldhaugen, and they were off to Lofthus, to the glorious summer time among the mountains and fjords of Norway and to that which was perhaps more glorious still—to work!

WORK ONCE MORE

AGAIN almost two years had passed since Grieg had last been engaged in the work of composition. From the end of August 1884, when he finished the Holberg suite and, soon after, the Holberg cantata, nothing new had come from his hand. He had orchestrated the Holberg suite and "Bergliot" and arranged many of his songs for the piano, but had done no genuinely creative work in all that time. But now, by July 25, he can announce to his publisher, Dr. Abraham, in a letter from Lofthus that he has just completed a new collection of lyrical pieces for the piano, the third volume, Opus 43.

"Summer! Summer! Never have I looked forward to it so much as now!" he wrote in February to Beyer. Involuntarily we think of this outburst when we listen to "Sommerfugl" (Butterfly), the first of the piano pieces. It seems to have been written in a single spasm of ecstasy over the creation which is, in especial, the certain sign of summer. Gleaming in a wonderful glory of color it flies before our inner eye—we follow its graceful curvings and fluttering movements, so vivid is Grieg's music.

"Ensom vandrer" (Solitary Traveller) is full of the longing that constantly possessed Grieg when he was out in a foreign land, the longing to lose himself in nature. It reveals one of the most intimate aspects of Grieg's being and is in all its simplicity a most moving piece.

The next, "In My Native Country," was composed, as we have already heard, as a song of gratitude to Beyer—one of the very few with whom Grieg could share his joy in nature. "The colors are the soft, Westland ones, but the heart in it beat for you, old friend, when I wrote it down," Grieg told Beyer in a letter. How vexatious that he couldn't be at home now that spring was here, he wrote in the same letter. "Just for the bird houses that I had forgotten about. It is provoking, for now it is too late. If only some of the little folk would come and set up their dwellings among us!"

In "Liten fugl" (Little Bird) he paints the most delightful picture of these "little folk." Here Grieg draws near to strongly impressionist methods of expression, impressionism, whose messenger he was along with the young Russians. Though the French impressionists in the treatment of similar themes may have surpassed him in refinements of color, Grieg, on the other hand, captivates us by the depth of feeling to which he gives expression in conjunction with his brilliant capacity for characterization.

"Erotik" (Eroticon) is marked by the same purity of feeling we know from the famous song of his youth, "I Love You." It is filled with the same tender longing that spring now, as then, wakes to life.

The last number, "Til våren" (To Spring), might stand as motto over the whole collection. It is spring apprehended against the background of a dark, cold, and crushing winter. Hence the release is rendered with the intensity and joyful emotion which might be expected from one who felt himself indeed a son of spring—"the children of the month of May, of opening leaves, of rising life," as Drachmann had expressed it in his poem to Nina and Edvard Grieg on their departure from Copenhagen.

Soon after he had finished these piano pieces, Grieg set out for Troldhaugen to meet Holger Drachmann, who was coming on a visit. The two had arranged to make a tour together in the Jotunheim. Drachmann was to write verses and Grieg to set them to music. In a letter to Winding, Grieg wrote of Drachmann's visit: "I made a tour in the Westland with him which ended in the high mountains and was exactly the kind of thing to provide me with new energy for both body and soul. He wrote poems and I the music to them; it was, for once, life as it should be. He is a wonderful personality, your Drachmann, there is something of the troubadour or 'minnesinger' or what shall I call it, about him and he stands out so comically against the sickly realism of our times, it seems to me. In the poems he wrote for me I made him be brief, which as you know, he isn't always."

From various observations, we see that Grieg came back home exhilarated and strengthened after his tour with Drachmann, which had clearly been both pleasant and entertaining. If the artistic results were not up to expectations, the main reason lies in the fact that Drachmann's poetry seldom rose above what might be called more or less successful "tourist poetry," to use a popular expression. And what is it that the poet sings about during this tour in the heart of the Norwegian mountains? Why, four young peasant girls the travellers meet on their way, with whom the impressionable lyricist naturally falls in love. Johanne, Ragnhild,

Ingebjörg, and Ragna are the names of the four lucky ones who have been immortalized by the two lyrical tourists.

It is clear that it cannot have been easy for Grieg to act the poetic journeyman along with Drachmann; and except for "Ragnhild," which is a genuinely fresh, vivid, and colorful song, the result, even so far as Grieg is concerned, was nothing more than light verse set to music which must be rated amongst his weakest things.

One of the most surprising things about these *Reiseminder fra Fjeld og Fjord* (Travel Memories from Mountain and Fjord) is the tone of the prologue and epilogue, which make a frame for the collection. The first has, as subtitle, "På Skineggen, ind mod Jotunheimen" (On Skineggen towards the Jotunheim). Here we might have expected a series of nature impressions, an expression for the rapt absorption and delight in nature we so often admire in Grieg's music. That we are put off instead with Italian opera style and false Wagnerian pathos must be blamed mainly on the poet, he could not but have had a chilling effect on Grieg.

We come to think also of something else, to remember some words of Grieg's own, where he says, speaking of nature impressions, that "one must not go after them with the idea of creating *at the time one receives the impression.* For I have found that does not work." The truth of these, his own words, he proved more clearly now than ever before, and if we require further evidence of the justness of this observation, we have only to remember that the second violin sonata was written in the heat of the summer at Övre Voldgate in Christiania, the piano concerto came into being in Sölleröd down in Denmark, far from the Norwegian scene, and the Vinje songs—they, as we have heard, were written in a room looking into a yard in Strandgaten in Bergen.

Though the artistic result of this journey with Drachmann was so meager, it is clear all the same that Grieg felt cheered and stimulated by the mere fact of having got to work again. He took a brighter view of everything, and he knew a peace and balance such as were seldom vouchsafed him. It was with the highest hopes of a continued period of work that he decided to remain at home for the winter. Peace for work he had that autumn and, what is better, he was blessed again with one of these creative periods which are, he says in a letter to Gerhard Schjelderup, in spite of all the suffering that comes with them, the most beautiful in an artist's life; so long as a period like this endures, one is lifted over all, absolutely all, life's sorrows.

For the last time he took up the struggle with the classical sonata form and wrote his third violin sonata, in C minor, Opus 45. "I will fight my way through the great forms, cost what it may"— these words uttered before the winter in Lofthus might stand as a motto over this work. As Beethoven has his Symphony of Fate, so the C minor sonata might be called for Grieg the Sonata of Fate. It has also been called the *tragic* one amongst Grieg's sonatas and that is true enough. Its fundamental mood is tragic and the brighter episodes in the work serve only to deepen and strengthen the main impression. Because it was a question here of a struggle for life or death, this work in especial perhaps shows us the artist in a pure, noble, and chastened form, in a monumental simplicity such as is only possible when one has gone through the cleansing fires of suffering. The mere arrangement of the work shows us a simplification unique with Grieg. The plan of the cello sonata certainly indicated an attempt in this direction which did not, however, quite succeed. In the C minor sonata, he goes over to an austere simplification of form, a precision in the leading of tonal lines and a unity in the development of motives in marked contrast to his other works, which are characterized especially by their exuberance and luxuriance, both materially and in a purely coloristic sense.

Look, for example, at the first movement of the C minor sonata. Here Grieg works with three principal elements, three principal colors, which he contrasts one against the other: the threatening darkness of the principal theme which, in strongly accentuated movements in the deepest range of the violin supported by the heavy beat of chords on the piano, rises in hurrying chase to the highest degree of expressiveness. Then, as it were in a sort of half light, follows the subsidiary theme which, with its tranquilly flowing voice-leadings, is able for a moment to subdue the tumultuous billows. Then comes the development in which the principal theme is presented in augmented notes in the major and thrown up in a brilliant beam of light, while round it billow harplike chords on the piano, like the music of the spheres.

Even the purely coloristic impression made by the movement shows how the earlier exuberance and luxuriance give place here to a monumental simplicity. A comparison with the first violin sonata, for example, shows the difference plainly. Grieg had been told more than once by the critics that in his greatest works he was too short-winded. When the C minor sonata appeared, it was remarked at once, therefore, how sharply separated it was in regard to form from his earlier works. After a performance in Salle Pleyell in Paris on January 4, 1890, the critic of *Le Matin* wrote as follows: "This brilliant composition seems to dispose completely of the reproach that has been levelled against Grieg, that he is not the man for works that require a long breath (*de longue haleine*).

The second movement—the romance—shows also a breadth in design unique with Grieg, a noble melody introduced by the piano which, after the violin has sung it out in a wonderful mezza voce, is suddenly interrupted by the vehement agitation of the middle movement. The two instruments take the lead alternately in this part, which is only with difficulty led back to the mood of the principal movement, to sing out finally in chords of ethereal brightness.

Involuntarily we think, when we hear this movement, of Grieg's words a short time before: "If things could continue like this, what then? It would be absolute happiness and that seems an impossible idea in the case of this particular person."

The third movement shows indeed how impossible it was. Once again we are in the fundamentally tragic mood of the work. The rhythmically hammering principal theme reminds us in its inexorable persistence of Ibsen's "Blow upon blow till life's last day." Here too the broad melody is supported by a characteristically syncopated secondary motive on the piano, which helps to continue the restless beat of its pulse. Not until the repeat does the subsidiary motive seem to be able to sing its song out freely and fully. Freed, it rises like a bird in the air, high over the agitated billows of the piano accompaniment, and leads us over into the distracted presto which succeeds, however, in spite of all, in fighting its way through to the bright life-affirmatory major key in which the sonata ends.

On January 21, Grieg says in a letter to John Paulsen that he has finished the C minor sonata, but he must wait till the autumn to hear it, for he cannot get abroad till then.

There is much to testify that this sonata worked on Grieg like a liberation and that he felt it perhaps something of a compensation for the many public and private defeats he had suffered in his art during these last years.

Hear his optimistic tone in a letter to Beyer from Carlsbad on his way to Leipzig, where soon after his sonata was to be performed for the first time. "It is a long time since life has looked so bright and good to me as now. I am well, better than I have ever been here in Carlsbad; and many friendly letters, full of kindness and understanding, make it easier for me than it has been for a long time to look the future in the face. Yes, Norway! Norway! Let Ibsen say a hundred times that it is best to belong to a great nation. I can perhaps go with him so far as practical affairs are concerned, but not a step further. For, from the ideal point of view, I wouldn't belong to any other nation in the world! I feel the older I grow that I love Norway just because she is so poor, just because we are such damned idiots in practical respects. Good God, a nation can always become rich and practical, but full of ideas, no, and contemplative, no! And it is precisely these two qualities which determine the future for our people."

On December 10, the first performance of the sonata took place in the Gewandhaus in Leipzig with Adolf Brodsky in the violin part and Grieg himself at the piano. The performance was a great success and in a short time the sonata had achieved an almost incredible reputation all over Europe. It was twenty years since Grieg had last produced a violin sonata and it was not to be wondered at that his many admirers were waiting in eager expectation for the new work.

As was to be expected, Bernsdorf sat in *Signale* and saw to it that the sonata received the requisite rough treatment. For fifteen years now this gentleman, on every possible occasion, had used Germany's most influential professional journal to decry Grieg and his art and he contrived to do so to the end of his days. To show how stubborn and persistent was the opposition Grieg met with in the highest places, Bernsdorf's criticism of the C minor sonata will also be given here. It runs as follows:

Letzgenanntes Stück kam hier in Leipzig zum ersten Male öffentlich zu Gehör und fand, bei Executierung durch den Componisten selbst und namentlich Herrn Brodsky, eine Aufnahme, die an Wärme nichts zu wünschen übrig liess. Darüber wundern wir uns eigentlich nicht; denn erstens befinden sich augenblicklich zahlreiche Skandinaver hier in Leipzig, die ihren Landesmann Grieg doch nicht fallen lassen können, und dann wird ja der Welt fortwährend vor-und eingeredet, dass Grieg ein bedeutender, hochoriginaler Tonsetzer sei. Diese Ansicht zu theilen, sind wir unsertheils—wie den Lesern dieses Blattes bekannt wird—nicht in der Lage, und auch die in Rede stehende Sonate hat eine Bekehrung bei uns nicht zu bewirken vermocht. Denn ganz dieselben Misstände, die wir von jeher an den Grieg'schen Erzeugnissen auszusetzen hatten—Mangel an organischer Entwicklung, durch allerhand Gesuchtheiten (namentlich in harmonischer Beziehung) nur mühsam verdeckte Talent- und Erfindungsschwäche, unter dem Deckmantel der norwegischen Nationalität begangene Geschmacklosigkeiten und Faxen—dies Alles (und noch viel mehr) hat uns in der Sonate wieder unangenehm berührt und unsere Sympathie einen unübersteiglichen Damm entgegengesetzt.

But when Bernsdorf blames Grieg for failure in the organic development of his material in the case of the C minor sonata, he goes a little too far; the C minor sonata, which in precisely this respect can challenge comparison with the best classical models and come out triumphant! And, as usual when an art critic has an instinctive feeling that he is fighting against invincible spiritual powers which render him impotent whatever he may do, Bernsdorf attempts to help himself out with malice. For that there should be in Leipzig precisely at that time so many Scandinavians as to secure for Grieg, this, according to Bernsdorf, unmerited success, out of a kind of local patriotism, is hardly credible. Certainly there were two Norwegian musicians present at the concert, and they were Christian Sinding and Johan Halvorsen. Report does not say with certainty that they applauded much more loudly than the rest of the audience, but even if that were so, it can hardly have been due to them alone that the first performance of the C minor sonata was so great a success for Grieg.

Moreover, Grieg's position was now so secure that Bernsdorf's abuse was not of such moment to him as in earlier days. He could now say with Ibsen: "It is not very dangerous—I have Europe behind me." In *Nordisk Musik-Tidende* for October 1887, it may be read that Grieg's sonatas, Opus 7 and Opus 13, which had formerly belonged to Breitkopf and Härtel, had now gone over to Peters. As a matter of fact this publishing house began to buy up works which it had formerly refused!—a certain sign that Grieg's star was very much in the ascendent. This was further emphasized by Peters's taking over, two years later, the whole of Grieg's works, including those which had been published earlier by various Danish publishing houses.

Grieg remained through the winter in Leipzig, where he cemented a close friendship with his Norwegian colleagues, Sinding
and Halvorsen. For both he was full of admiration. When Sinding
had played the first movement of his D minor symphony for him,
he wrote to Beyer: "He played the first movement of a symphony
for me the other day, which was magnificent. There was the spirit
of the first movement of the Ninth Symphony in it and yet it was
Sinding and not Beethoven."

When in the month of March 1888, Grieg was ready for the road
after the winter's sojourn in Leipzig, he wrote in high spirits to
Beyer: "The spring sun is shining in on me so warm and bright
that I am full of *wanderlust*. What Dr. Abraham has been to us
you can hardly imagine. I assure you he has been absolutely like a
father. When I think too of how lucky I have been in my asso-
ciates this winter, in addition to Dr. Abraham, I can say with good
reason that my journey was worth while, and that is saying something."

This fund of strength, both spiritual and physical, of which he
felt himself possessed was to stand him in good stead now that he
had a series of strenuous and nerve-racking concerts in the great
cities of Europe before h m, with London, Berlin, and Paris heading the list.

FIRST APPEARANCE IN LONDON, BERLIN, AND PARIS

ON ONE of the first days of April, Grieg arrived in London where he was engaged to take part in a Philharmonic Society concert on May 3. That he was by no means unknown in London he was well aware; from early in the Seventies his works had been constantly performed both in London and in other English towns. But that his art was so highly valued and that he had attained so great and wide a popularity as he now discovered, came as a complete surprise to him. The moment he showed himself at the door opening into the orchestra, a storm of applause broke out, so intense and so persistent that for several moments he could only stand there, bowing in all directions, quite overcome. At last there was silence and he could go to the piano to take, himself, the piano part in his C minor concerto. Of his own rendering of the concerto he wrote that it was good enough but was far from satisfying him. Physical strength was lacking. Even when he was practising in Leipzig for the English tour, he wrote that chamber music and small pieces did not trouble him, he could manage these easily enough, but when grandeur of effect was needed from the piano, he never achieved what he wanted and only exhausted himself. But he made up for it all the more when he stood at the head of a string orchestra, sixty strong, conducting "Wounded" and "Spring." Everything was rehearsed with the most minute exactitude, each vied with the other to do his best, and the effect thrilled even Grieg himself. "There were things in it to bring the tears to one's eyes—they sounded so fine," he wrote to Beyer. "There were *ff* and *pp*, accents and soarings, it was like a song of harmonies on ethereal heights such as you know we music-folk long to get up to—but so seldom reach."

If Grieg had a warm and enthusiastic reception from the English public, he had every reason to be pleased also at the way the press welcomed and greeted him. The day after the concert all the London newspapers published long and elaborate reviews and it strikes one, in reading these detailed notices of Grieg and his music, that the representatives of art and literature are by no means the least in value where it is a question of spreading knowledge regarding a country and its people. It is doubtful whether any statesman or political ambassador could have pleaded Norway's cause better than Edvard Grieg did in London both on this occasion and many times later. The *Daily Telegraph* wrote as follows:

Following Tschaikovsky and Widor at the concerts of this society came, on Thursday evening, the composer Edward Grieg, to whom as pianist and composer the first part of the programme was almost entirely given up. We recognize a certain propriety in the sequence of the Russian and the Norwegian. Both artists are strictly representative of their respective countries, both are champions of nationality in art and both, in a large manner, devote their powers to the development of the higher forms of music on the basis of that which is peculiar to the people from whom they have sprung. This may perhaps be said more emphatically of Grieg than of his Slavonic colleague. The Norwegian master is nothing if not Norwegian. He has inherited the spirit of those who in 1814 asserted the independence of their country, secured for her one of the most liberal constitutions in Europe and laid the foundations of an immense revival, not only in industry, but in literature and art. It seemed at that auspicious epoch that the stream of national life, long dammed back by foreign power, flowed in every channel full and free. Poets arose, such as Wergeland, who embodied the general enthusiasm in glowing verse; while, as representing music, came the picturesque figure of Ole Bull, who, with his violin under his arm, went through Europe and America proudly Norwegian, calling himself in pleasant moments "Ole Olsen Viol, Norse Norman from Norway." . . .

We have no right to say that had Grieg devoted himself to what may be called for distinction's sake the classical expression of music, he would have failed to make a name; but we dare venture to assert that he would now be occupying a position below his present popularity and renown. In the Norwegian musical dialect, in the lovely folk-tunes and deep feeling of the "dark and true and tender" North, Grieg had that which was not only his inheritance and congenial, but a powerful means of catching the ear and winning the admiration of the world. He has employed those resources with wisdom and devotion. No musician is less a composer of the study than he. His works have a large, open-air effect; they take us among the mountains and valleys and by the fjords of his native land; they seem instinct with the life of the people.

The paper went on to say that, though it had long been recognized that Grieg was on the way to attaining the greatest popularity in England, no one had known how popular he was till the enthusiasm with which he was greeted personally made it evident. The rendering of the A minor concerto was not sensational, there was no virtuosity, it showed a man who was composer first and pianist second. But it was good—nothing else could be said of it—clear, full of expression and intelligent. Of the elegiac melodies for string orchestra, the reviewer wrote that he could hardly remember having heard more beautiful ensemble playing than in these melodies under Grieg's magic baton. Towards the end the music died away so gradually that it was hardly possible to know when the last dying note stopped sounding and the stillness became complete. It was, in truth, marvellous playing.

The *Times* had also a long and elaborate account of Grieg's first appearance in London. The paper referred to the storm of applause which broke out in the packed hall the instant the composer appeared. Of the performance of the A minor concerto the paper wrote that Grieg played it in his own special way.

The French speak of a *voix de compositeur*; in the same sense there is a composer's touch on the piano which, when applied to his own works gives them a peculiar charm of their own, although there are no doubt many musicians who can no more play their own pieces than poets as a rule can read their own verse. Both in a technical and in an intellectual sense his rendering was perfect, and his rendering of the familiar work was a revelation, although it would be unjust to forget that Herr Edward Dannreuther, who introduced the concerto many years ago, invested it with the most poetic charm. After the concerto Miss Carlotta Elliott sang two of Grieg's songs, "Erstes Begegnen" and "Farewell to Tvindehaugen," the composer playing the accompaniment. Both are charming melodies but neither of them shows Grieg's lyrical depth to the degree we find it, for example, in the passionate "Du Mein Gedanke" or in the mysterious "The Swan," one of the most beautiful songs in existence. The composer next appeared as conductor of two melodies originally set to poems by A. O. Vinje but subsequently arranged for strings and admirably played by the Philharmonic orchestra. Once more the enthusiasm of the audience rose to the highest pitch at the end of the performance and Grieg at least will have no reason to complain of the impassive attitude towards modern music generally attributed to English, and more especially, Philharmonic audiences.

A fortnight later Grieg gave a concert of his own in the same hall —this time assisted by his wife and Fru Norman-Neruda. This concert too was described by the press as a decided success. The *Times* wrote:

The concert given by Edvard Grieg, the Norwegian composer, at St. James's-hall last night was well attended, but should by rights have been crowded to the last seat, for the performance was of its kind unique. Not that the compositions of Grieg, which made up the programme, were new to musicians and cultured amateurs, but they had certainly never been heard in London in the manner in which they were rendered by their originator. We previously tried to convey some idea of Grieg's playing by comparing it to what the French call *voix de compositeur*. The poetic and indefinable charm of his manner was again felt by the audience in such pieces as "On the Mountains" or the "Norwegian Bridal Procession," which even those most familiar with them thought they had never heard before, so instinct with individual life was the reading here presented. Almost the same remark applies to the singing of her husband's songs by Madame Grieg—a *voix de compositeur* in a different meaning of the words. Whether this lady could produce much effect in the works of other composers is a question we need not discuss. Suffice it to say that in such charming lyrics as "My Song shall be Thine" and the impetuous "Good Morning" she was—in the same sense and for the same reason as Grieg on the piano—unsurpassable. Madame Norman-Neruda in the violin sonata, Opus 8, and in the "Romance" and "Finale," from Opus 45, fully entered into the spirit of the hour, and materially contributed to the success of one of the most interesting concerts of the year.

There was no doubt: Grieg had conquered London completely. A couple of days after the last concert, we find him down in the Isle of Wight where he had gone to rest after his exertions. While still excited and full of thankfulness he writes to Beyer about the concerts. "Exhausted today," he admits. "Though here by the turbulent sea I shall pick up again." He had need of all his strength for he was not yet finished with the season.

On the way home the tour went by Copenhagen where in June he took part in the first Northern music festival. At the big orchestral concerts the piano concerto and "Taken into the Mountains" were performed with Erika Nissen and Thorvald Lammers as soloists and at the chamber concerts the third violin sonata and a selection of the Vinje songs were given. "A Norwegian artist pair of high rank brought the first half of the concert to an end," wrote Charles Kierulf in *Politiken*. "They were Fru Erika Nissen, led by the hand of Edvard Grieg. As soon as they appeared they were heartily applauded. Every music lover knew that in these two bodies, frail in appearance and not outwardly imposing, the holy fire of art burned with an exceptionally clear and brilliant flame. And yet the reception was as nothing to the cheering that broke out when Grieg's grand piano concerto in A minor had been played to the end with Fru Nissen at the instrument and the composer at the conductor's desk. It was undoubtedly the culminating point of the concert."

At last, towards St. John's Day, Grieg and his wife were home once more at Troldhaugen, after almost a year's absence. But now too only for a short time. In August there was again a tour in England, where on the 29th, at a music festival in Birmingham, Grieg conducted the first performance of the overture "Autumn" with great success. Even though he remained at home at Troldhaugen through the autumn and up to Christmas time, there was no peace to be had. The concert agents were beginning to stretch out their tentacles after him, and during the course of the autumn he received invitations to appear in Berlin, Prague, Moscow, and St. Petersburg. It is very understandable that under such circumstances it was difficult to concentrate on creative work. The only thing forthcoming from his hand in these two years, 1887 and 1888, was a new volume of lyrical pieces, the fourth in the series, Opus 47, which came out at Christmas 1888. It contains a Waltz-Impromptu, Album-Leaf, Melody, "Halling," Melancholy, Spring Dance and Elegy, all well-sounding music, beautiful though easy to play, but not showing any new sides of Grieg's talent and not to be compared with the previous volumes in freshness and originality. The pieces seem more to have been written for rest and recreation—to use with justice an expression Grieg himself had used *with injustice* of one of his most deeply inspired works—the *Album for Male Voices*.

About New Year 1889, they were off again out into the world, this time with Berlin, where Grieg was engaged to take part in two Philharmonic concerts on January 21 and 29, as their first objective. At these, his first appearances in Berlin, the overture "Autumn" and the *Peer Gynt* Suite, No. 1, the elegiac melodies for string orchestra, Opus 34, and the piano concerto, with Erika Nissen in the solo part, were performed.

Reading the Berlin criticism of these two concerts, one is struck by how much it differs from the English. Certainly, it is appreciative enough, and Grieg had no ground of complaint, but it has an objective placidity and balance that involuntarily chill one a little and form a decided contrast to the unreserved enthusiasm of the English criticisms. The reviewer of the *Berliner Tageblatt* wrote as follows: "In the concert overture, 'Autumn,' there is much that is blurred rather than exact in form, it is also too long. But there are many points which waken the attention of the connoisseur and show that a significant spirit dwells in it. There is, for example, a place where the brasses, in a chromatic passage, pass over from the first theme, which is held meanwhile by the lower parts: very clever and original. The transition theme is fresh and very well worked out. But the orchestral suite music to Ibsen's dramatic poem *Peer Gynt* showed itself to be of still greater significance than the overture. In these pieces the poem and its setting stand on the same level. The first, 'Morning Mood,' is a pastoral in which the flute and oboe begin the theme, which is then continued by the whole orchestra. Altogether enchanting is that part where in the upper register broken chords are struck while the theme in the lower sings out through them. The second piece, 'Åse's Death,' is in every respect an important composition. The theme is most appealing and full of emotion, the harmonizing unusually original and well-sounding. The effect was moving and overwhelming. The third piece, 'Anitra's Dance,' had to be given da capo. It is excellently and charmingly elaborated, the imitations in the orchestra are very happily and effectively contrived, but I am convinced that the composer himself does not set so high a value on this part as on the foregoing. Rubinstein has written several Intermezzos decorated with similar oriental turns of fancy but not one to equal 'Anitra's Dance!' The Finale, 'In the Hall of the Dovre-King,' where the trolls provoke and torment Peer Gynt, is a fine piece of fancy."

Nationalzeitung writes: "His composition combines the charm of tone painting with flowing form. Eagerly the ear follows the harmonic subtleties which give the simplest melodies the stamp of originality. All that seems to develop so easily and naturally is in reality the result of deep study and a manifestation of one of the most delicate talents of our time. As with all our greater instrumental music, his work too is based upon Beethoven, whom he has studied and understood and from whom he has learned the art of climax and the art of contrast as well as the finer effects of tone-gradations but of whom he never allows himself to be too reminiscent. The details are his own while in the art of form he follows Beethoven with veneration."

Also at his second appearance in Berlin, where Erika Nissen was soloist, Grieg had the best of receptions both from public and press. A fortnight's stay at Leipzig—and then off to new and tremendous triumphs in England. This time Grieg appeared in all at five concerts in London. He conducted the *Peer Gynt* suite, the elegiac melodies, and the piano concerto with Agathe Backer-Gröndahl in the solo part. All three violin sonatas were performed: the first he played with Fru Norman-Hallé, the second with no less a person than Joseph Joachim, and the third with Johannes Wolf. Nina sang a series of her husband's songs and in addition played the Norwegian dance duets with him. Finally, Grieg himself acted as soloist in a number of piano pieces.

It was clear by the end of the first concert that Grieg had taken London by storm and soon after the English papers wrote that in the musical world of London there raged for a time an out and out "Grieg fever." This time too, the London press gave great attention to Grieg, all the newspapers having long accounts both of his art and of his person; and to his publisher, Dr. Abraham, he wrote that Fru Nina had become to such an extent the darling of the public that he was almost jealous. In a word, it appears from the London press that Edvard and Nina Grieg had completely conquered the English public and could rejoice in a popularity rare in the artistic world.

The journey home this time was through Paris, where Grieg, during a short stay, concluded an agreement with Colonne for an appearance at the Châtelet Theater, at the end of the year. A concert was planned also at Pleyel's where Grieg was to perform his own works, assisted by Fru Nina and Johannes Wolf. Immediately before this first appearance in Paris, Grieg gave, on invitation, a series of concerts in Brussels, where at this, his first appearance in Belgium, he had an enthusiastic reception from both public and press. In Paris, Grieg appeared at three concerts of his own works, two orchestral concerts of Colonne's, in the Châtelet Theater on December 22 and 29, and a recital of chamber music at Pleyel's on January 4. In addition, the Parisian National Musical Society gave a concert in Grieg's honor at which, besides a selection of his songs, the string quartet and the Norwegian dance duets were performed.

All the Parisian papers commented on the Grieg concerts in the most flattering manner; and it appears from them that the enthusiasm and delight of the public must have been quite exceptional.

"The Parisian public gave Grieg a brilliant reception instantly, they greeted his entry with shouts and applause such as Mozart and Weber never heard," wrote the *Figaro's* reviewer, Charles Darcours. In a letter of January 5, 1890, Grieg told his publisher, Dr. Abraham, that after his last concert at Pleyel's the day before, he had a triumph to record, the like of which he never before had experienced. The English applause was certainly exceptional, he continued, but here, besides the tremendous applause and the innumerable recalls in the true Parisian fashion, there was such wonderful rapture throughout the pieces. "*My wife sang so from her heart* and so beautifully and could rejoice in a tremendous success; after the 'Bridal Procession' I had to go again to the piano—the people shouted 'Berceuse' and I played 'Berceuse' (I think Opus 38, No. 1). Again enormous applause—and again I had to go to the piano and played two dances from Opus 17. Afterwards there was a great levée, even greater than that of the Philharmonic Society in London. The third sonata caused a tremendous furore. I will send papers. Facit: very glad—and very tired," Grieg finished his account.

La Liberté's critic wrote as follows: "Grieg is the living, thrilling incarnation of Norway. I do not know how it is but somehow when I hear his music it seems as though I see and think of that land which I have never seen but which I feel I 'recognize' at once in his naïvely plaintive melodies."

Le Matin wrote after the concert on January 4: "Edvard Grieg's music waked at first the distrust of the conservative world. But, little by little, his fresh inspiration and the melancholy poetry of his works have conquered the old hearts one by one and now his works are known and loved in all the musical camps. Edvard Grieg is, before all, a Northern composer. Every movement glows with strong local color and we breathe a sharp scent of pine with every bar. Grieg is a poet. He dreams over great Sabbath-still inland seas and throws over us the spell of the midnight sun's mystic phantasies. The evening in the Salle Pleyel yesterday was one long homage to the Northern composer. But his wife too, who rendered some of her husband's romances with extraordinary charm, bore home a large share of the palms."

The Paris correspondent of the English paper *Truth* gives in an article so vivid a picture, not only of Edvard and Nina Grieg's art but also of their persons, that it may be of interest to quote a part of the article here. After having first related how it was not without much hesitation he put in an appearance at "an Edvard Grieg seance," the programme of which announced that Grieg himself would fill up the whole evening, and how, after having listened to Grieg and his colleagues for three hours, he became so fascinated that he would gladly have listened longer—the writer goes on:

The little great man (for he is a genius) has unlocked, to give to the world, the treasures of Norse song-lore and of the primitive music of Norway. His *Werke* take one's breath away by their freshness, pungent originality, variety, and at times deep sentiment—quite unlike any kind of musical sentiment we are used to. In the symphony in B minor he gave proof of strength of wing and sustaining power: anything more delightful in its wild freshness and originality than "A Norwegian Bridal Party driving through the Mountains," I never heard.

Grieg looks peculiar, and so does his wife. He has, in walking across the stage, a self-assured and concentrated manner. Thinking out his *Werke* and many other things to boot has set a stamp of meditation on him. He is not unlike Rangabe, who was for many years Greek Minister here, and who thought more of his poetry than of his diplomacy. Grieg and his wife are free from posture, genuine and, off the stage, as simple as a pair of children. She has a smile and glance bespeaking universal propitiation. As a singer of the Norse songs he has set to music she is matchless. Did you ever hear a prima donna, save Jenny Lind, carol a simple song decently? Their staginess and competitive style spoil them for this kind of vocal music.

I own to having been a little startled when Mme. Nina Grieg came on the stage to accompany her husband in a duet. Imagine a concert-singer free from all the conventionalities of "the profession"; without a bouquet, free from paint, indifferent to crow's feet, with a cropped head of hair, brushed any way, and a high-bodied brown silk dress, enlivened somewhat by a necklace and large pendant of filigree silver, made in the Norwegian style. She dropped a deep and reverential curtsey to the audience—the very same I am sure that she dropped to the Queen of Sweden—glanced round at her husband, and then began to sing. After a few bars I felt like crying *Ca y est!* She went straight to one's soul. Her eyes got eloquent, her retroussé nose took delightful piquancy, and the delicacy, the purity, the pathos that she infused into her song were beyond all praise. She was given up to the song, and did not trouble herself about Nina Grieg, or how she looked, or what people thought of her. Every verse was enthusiastically applauded, and whenever there was applause she dropped her court curtsey.

During the course of a very few years Grieg had conquered the great cities of the world with his art; the concert halls were filled with a public that did him honor and applauded him with enthusiasm. And the professionals too, in different countries, had given him a hearty welcome in full appreciation of the hitherto unknown and strange elements which through his works had been infused into "art music." The tonal spirit of the North—about which Schumann, enthusiastic over Gade's youthful works, had spoken prophetic words—had now become a reality. Ears were pricked when this tone was heard in the world's orchestra, easily recognizable as it was, bearing a message from the peoples and races which were as yet only at their dawning with all the elements for a rich and enterprising life. No wonder that all looked forward with the highest expectations to the fulfilment of the splendid promises of which this young art was the harbinger. It is, therefore, not without bitterness that we must record that Grieg, at the first visits to London, Berlin, and Paris, had already played his best trumps and that his programmes at all subsequent concerts were merely a repetition of what he had given when he first appeared. This is no doubt the reason for much of the ill will Grieg met with in later years from the professional critics and which we have seen expressed with great harshness, as in Debussy's comments after the Paris concert in 1903.

IN THE summer of 1889, Grieg, as already stated, orchestrated the three scenes of *Olav Trygvason*. Besides this work he completed two volumes of songs, Opus 48, to German poems by Heine, Geibel, Uhland, von der Vogelweide, Goethe, and Bodenstedt, and six songs to words by Holger Drachmann, Opus 49.

When we consider these two volumes of songs, and especially the first, we think involuntarily of some remarkable utterances of Grieg's in an interview given to a London newspaper some months before. He tells, with much detail, of his whole development as an artist and emphasizes especially the great and important influence of Norwegian nature on his art. When the interviewer asked whether Norwegian nature still had the same power over him and filled him with the same inspiration, Grieg answered: "Speaking personally, yes. There is no feature of Norwegian nature that is not for me as full of beauty as it has ever been. The blue inland seas, the waterfalls, the sky, the mountains and woods in all their pristine beauty are the same as before; but in my music I am no longer so exclusively Norwegian as I was once. There is a period in youth when in burning enthusiasm for a fixed idea, a fixed ideal, we say to ourselves: 'I must and will do that, just that.' But that time passes and we become calmer and less one-sided. My later work is not so markedly typical of Scandinavian music. I have travelled about and become more European, more cosmopolitan. These changes come gradually, we are hardly aware of them before suddenly they are there."

That these remarks were not the outcome of the mood of a moment is shown by Grieg's at that time much discussed "cosmopolitan declaration of faith," which he published a short time after in the Danish *Musikbladet* for October 8, 1889. The main purpose of this was indeed to disassociate himself from a remark attributed to him soon after his meeting with Nordraak. Grieg is supposed to have used the often quoted words: "We (Nordraak and I) conspired together against the Gade-influenced-by-Mendelssohn effeminate Scandinavianism and set our feet enthusiastically on the new way where the Northern school is now to be found." After having characterized the words quoted as an utterance of a long past period pertaining so much to his salad days that he feels it his duty to disavow it, Grieg continues in the article: "You will understand that from my present standpoint I *cannot* acknowledge a pronouncement which, to a greater degree than is desirable, bristles with youthful arrogance. I really must assure you that I am neither one-sided enough not to cherish all due piety and admiration for a master like Gade, nor superficial enough actually to announce myself as the most national among the nationalists, the Messiah of Norwegian composition, as the author expresses it. In regard to an assertion such as this, I venture to say that the writer lacks the most important requisites for judging me. Had the writer known my art as a whole, he could not have failed to recognize that in my later works I have been reaching more and more towards a broader, more general view of my own particular individuality, a view influenced by the great movements of the times—that is to say, cosmopolitan. But—and this I willingly admit—never could I find it in my heart to pluck up with violent hand the roots that bind me to my fatherland. As I regret that such misleading statements about my art have found their way into circulation in Denmark, may I beg for space for these lines in your esteemed paper." The article is dated Troldhaugen by Bergen, September 14, 1889.

But let us look a little at how this, his broader, more general view, this greater all-roundness, this reaching out towards the European, the cosmopolitan, affected his art. Was it able to liberate fettered powers in him, show forth new sides of his genius, renew its germinative powers?

On good grounds Gerhard Schjelderup in his Grieg biography has taken for granted that the six songs, Opus 48, written to German texts, belong to a long-vanished period. But Grieg corrects this in a letter to Schjelderup in which he informs him that the songs were written shortly before they appeared, in the summer of 1889, which may surprise others besides Schjelderup. Having followed Grieg from his early youth, from his Leipzig period when he stood with both feet firmly planted in the artistic life of Germany, followed his gradual development as a romantic composer through Danish lyricism in transition to Norwegian lyricism, followed him in his ever richer development through Björnson's and Ibsen's poetry till at last he attains in the Vinje songs that *really* broad and general view of his individuality only reached by an artist on the great heights from which there is a free, wide outlook to all quarters—one gets from these songs to German texts a depressing feeling that, in spite of everything, labor has been in vain. It is as though we have been climbing a mountain, the air has become purer, the view wider, freer, gradually we have begun to have glimpses of kingdoms and countries which give promise of very great things and then, suddenly, we find ourselves again at the foot of the mountain, just where we started. Again we are with Grieg in his youth when, still a pupil at the Conservatory and before his personality had begun to unfold itself, he wrote his songs to German verses. Now, as then, he leans upon German romanticism, speaks its language and now too speaks it very well. The first of the songs, "Gruss," to words of Heine's, is both well shaped and melodious, but it would not have surprised us had we found it in Opus 2, written twenty-seven years earlier. "Dereinst, Gedanke mein," "Der verschwiegene Nachtigall," and "Zur Rosenzeit" all three exemplify very clearly that a composer's task does not consist first and foremost in writing good music. Were that the problem, these songs might be named as in the front rank among Grieg's works, for they are as sterling in the musical sense as they are free from technical faults. But it is not only that they express experiences at second hand; the composer is carrying through here a piece of work that has already been done, and it does not help at all that he does it as well as his predecessors; his work is doomed, nevertheless. It is probably a sound and instinctive reaction against this breach of a fundamental law of the spirit which has led to these songs never being sung either at home or abroad, in spite of their being, as already stated, musically correct. There is a more personal touch about "Lauf der Welt" which, though not a song of any great importance, yet bears marks of having been written by Grieg, closely affiliated as it is with the finale of the cello sonata. The most important song in the collection is "Ein Traum" in which, in spite of the foreign garb and slightly bombastic melody, one is clearly conscious of Grieg's vigorous and decided personality. That it, unlike the others in the collection, has achieved considerable popularity is doubtless because extrinsically it is a singularly effective song which provides dozens of gifted singers, male and female, with a piece both vocally and elocutionally very telling.

Of the following Drachmann songs, one enjoys especially the fine nature impressions in "Julesne" (Christmas Snow) and "Forårsregn" (Spring Rain); the latter especially is an unusually subtle and delicate study in color. "Nu er Aftnen lys og varm" (Now is Evening Bright and Warm) and "Vug, o Vove" (Rock, O Waves) present many fine and delicately drawn traits of character, and if we are not entirely captivated by them, it is largely because Grieg has sacrificed two of his finest qualities, his precious melody and his equally exceptional and characteristic harmony. We follow him here out into spacious and frequented seaways which can well be pleasant and varied but in which it is never very exciting to sail. In the other two songs of the collection, we meet Drachmann very much at home. "Så du Knösen, som strög forbi" (Did You See the Lad Pass By?) and "Vær hilset I Damer" (Salute to the Ladies) are full of the theatrical lyricism and exaggerated pathos which could arouse the enthusiasm of the public of the Eighties and kept their hold till about the turn of the century, but which we now find it rather difficult to take seriously. Time has dealt hardly with this kind of lyricism, it has indeed eaten through the shell, and inside—inside there was nothing. It cannot avail, therefore, that Grieg has done a bad job with good grace and has written both fresh and inspired music. These songs too, with the exception of "Salute to the Ladies," are hardly ever seen on programmes, and one must agree with Grieg when, at the beginning of the article in *Musikbladet* already quoted, he writes: "I shall not, however, step forward as defender of national art in the general sense since the history of art has itself attended so thoroughly to the necessary defense that any further attempt on my part would be so much wasted labor." These songs and the whole of his life-work besides demonstrate the truth of what he says.

In October 1889, Grieg gave a series of concerts in Christiania. The principal work at these was *Olav Trygvason* which was performed for the first time on October 19 at the Musical Society under Grieg's baton. What certainly helped to enhance Grieg's happiness and delight in this performance of his youthful work was that Björnson came to town to attend the concerts and that these two at last, after sixteen years' separation, were again united in a friendship which endured now to the end of their lives.

At these concerts the new songs to German verses and the Drachmann songs were also performed, sung by Ellen Gulbranson and Thorvald Lammers, to whom they were dedicated. This time too Grieg received great ovations, and not less than three banquets were given in his honor. One of these was tendered by his friends at the Grand Hotel, where Björnson made a long speech in his honor. Grieg's speech returning thanks is noteworthy. In his later years he had been acclaimed time after time by the people of the capital and honored and fêted as perhaps no other Norwegian artist, yet it seemed to be impossible for him to overcome the animosity that had once established itself so deep in his mind in regard to Christiania and its denizens. Even during the cheering at the concerts and in the emotional atmosphere of the festivities, if the mere idea "Christiania" presented itself to him, he would seem to feel suddenly a cold gust of air that sobered him at once and wakened the old suspicions in his mind. In returning thanks he said, according to *Musik-Tidende*, that he had always regarded Christiania as a strange town, but lately it seemed to him it had really begun to be a wonderful town. Fundamentally it was and would continue to be strange, because there was something warm in its coldness and cold in its warmth. All the talented and gifted men of the country found their way here, took hold firmly and then slipped back. It seemed as if this town would not let them go without in some way crippling them. Either they had to flee abroad, or they got consumption or were damaged in some sort of way. He would wish that Christiania might one day become such that artists could live and thrive there. He drank to Christiania's becoming "a happy town."

Involuntarily we think of the classical opening sentence in Knut Hamsun's *Hunger*, which appeared some months later, in which he calls Christiania "this strange town which no one leaves without carrying with him the traces of his sojourn."

After the Artists' Society had held a very successful farewel festival on October 28, Grieg and his wife travelled to Copenhagen where *Olav Trygvason* was performed for the first time by the Concert Society on November 16. About the reception of the work in Copenhagen Grieg wrote in a letter to Iver Holter that it affected him like a cold douche after Christiania. This was partly due to the fact that the critics, misled by the "cosmopolitan confession of faith" which Grieg had publicly made, interpreted the work as an outcome of this and in their appraisement judged it on this assumption, which both annoyed Grieg and—made him think! In a long letter to Angul Hammerich, in which he explains that the work had been composed in 1873, sixteen years before, he complains about this and says that he cannot understand how anyone could imagine that he would choose a subject like that to substantiate a cosmopolitan confession of faith. He begs Hammerich to be so kind as to try, so far as he can, to prevent the word "cosmopolitan" being used as a slogan against him to signify a change of front. For such a thing was never meant (!). He draws attention also to the fact that in the article mentioned he had expressly stressed the presence of *both* elements, both the national and the cosmopolitan. Obviously a withdrawal, even though a very cautious one.

In February *Olav Trygvason* was performed in the Gewandhaus in Leipzig. This time too *Signale* produced a review which makes a worthy finish to the earlier consistent crying down of Grieg's works. Bernsdorf rails against the whole affair, the arrangement of the programme, the misplaced chasing after novelties, the wholly uninteresting thematic devices in the work, the total want of what a musician understood by work such as a composition of large proportions required; against the entirely superficial characterization for which the most objectionable devices had been employed as, for example, a perpetual thundering of kettledrums with blaring of brasses, muted horns, and tremolo in the strings—and further against its melodic and, still worse, harmonic barbarities (Atrocitäten). Finally, Bernsdorf fumes over Björnson's text which he says deals mainly with murder and fire and is so full of allusions that one would have to learn a whole compendium of Northern mythology to understand them.

But this time too Bernsdorf had to end his review with stating that the work was received with applause and that both the composer and the artists taking part were called before the curtain.

To Beyer Grieg wrote: "As you can imagine, it was a strange feeling to mount *that* conductor's desk for the first time to conduct *that* particular work. I think I may justly say that it was a fine performance. Sinding thought there had been more enthusiasm over the whole thing in Christiania and perhaps he is right. But the language, the language! That makes so much difference. The chorus parts sounded imposing and the Volva did her part with verve. For the rest, this performance has made me think a lot. Thanks for writing to Björnson. But I don't think he is able or inclined to do anything. He has moved far away from where he was then."

PEACE ORATORIO AND SECOND STRING QUARTET

IT IS probable that a continuation of *Olav Trygvason* would not have been successful so far as Grieg was concerned either, now that the habit of reflection laid its paralyzing hand on him every time he tried to attack a big work. But, cheered and stimulated by the warmth with which his opera fragment had been received all round, among other places in Stockholm where it was performed in April 1890, Grieg felt an uncontrollable desire for renewed collaboration with Björnson. After it had become clear during the summer that a continuation of *Olav Trygvason* was not to be thought of from Björnson's side, Grieg began to ponder over how he could best get work in collaboration started.

We see from a letter dated December 10, 1890, in which Grieg makes a direct proposal, what the idea was that had for long been occupying his mind and for the fulfilment of which the right occasion seemed now to have presented itself. He wrote in his letter:

"Dear Björnson,

"What do you say to the idea of taking those thoughts of peace which music can illumine and deepen, and putting them into a real Björnsonian poem—in a kind of cantata form, which would be suitable for solo voices, chorus, and orchestra? It has been one of my dearest thoughts these later years to write a requiem—a modern requiem, without dogmatic belief. But I have not found the words, though I have rooted about both in poetry and in the Bible. But when I read the peace speech you made to the Workers' Society I thought instantly: an apotheosis of peace, that is a requiem in a very special sense. There need be no lack of contrast —the great light of peace against the horrors of war. I believe in this idea. Think it over and if you get interested in it—then answer.

"Yours

"Edvard Grieg."

Björnson was, as usual, quick on the trigger; he both adopted the plan and answered at once. Now followed an exchange of letters between the two in which they discussed the matter in detail after Björnson had first sketched in broad outline what he thought the design of the work should be. Grieg was delighted at having

TROLDHAUGEN 1885-1900 301

got Björnson to take up his idea and wrote from Copenhagen: "For once I have had a happy thought. I have said No to being a patcher-up for all sorts of dramatic poets down here, because I want to be myself—and then I meet you in your innermost soul! That must lead to something!"

But already the sensitive plant was evident in Grieg—his excessive sensibility and the way in which he was bound to romantic ideals. He wrote in the same letter: "If you could avoid dwelling on things that to me individually are not musical, it would be fine. (I allude, for example, to the expression 'Factories further away' and later, 'Garrison life'). But—you understand what I mean: I want only what is tuned in a lofty key. And that I know I shall get. I am longing now like a child."

Only three days later all doubts seem to have been swept away in enthusiasm over Björnson's idea and Grieg then wrote: "I feel, as it were, a great beating of wings in your idea, and so I give no instructions, but leave everything to your inspiration—when you express yourself briefly. Whether the mothers' lament comes before or after Jesus—either way will be good. Do as you like. The bit about heritage can come in very well again in different stanzas in the war march—if I understand you here aright. If you are making new verses I can let the same musical motive sound through them. But here, too, do as you think best."

But in a letter of January 8, 1891, he is again full of the gravest misgivings. "You almost drove me crazy with your letter yesterday. I think either you overestimate what music can do—or what I can do. I will ask only one thing: that you don't try to put in too many features. Great simplicity in your design will make it possible for me to do well. If you try in your holy frenzy to put in everything, I grow afraid. When you shut up factories and banks and send telegrams (!)—'my courage withers straight.' But I believe you are 'imposing on my fancy' so that the surprise will be the greater when your noble poem comes!"

In the month of March Björnson made his appearance in Copenhagen, and the project was further discussed while Grieg in April stayed in Christiania, where portraits of him were painted by Werenskiold and Eilif Peterssen. On April 20 he told Dr. Abraham in a letter that he had just received a magnificent poem from Björnson for a big work to be called Peace, and that as soon as he got home to Troldhaugen he would begin work. The only thing that worried him was that the newspapers had already been discussing the work before a note of it had been written.

That now, as so often before, it was not easy for Grieg to get to work is plain from a letter to Björnson. On June 2 Grieg writes from Troldhaugen: "What splendid things there are in what you have written I am realizing more and more. But I am an idiot. I go round about like a cat round a plate of hot porridge and can't make a start. What I want to reach lies too high. When I try to touch it I fall back. I am too clumsy. But it will come. Send me some of your self-confidence. That is what I need." On July 23 he says: "If you want to change the beginning there is still time, for so far I have not got much further than 'to smell at' your words."

One month after another went by without a sign of any peace oratorio coming into being. Björnson grew impatient—and one cannot blame him for it. He had experienced almost exactly the same thing in the case of *Olav Trygvason* eighteen years before. In October he announced curtly that he would wait no longer but publish the poem. Grieg felt that this was not fair to him. Now anyone who liked could use the text, and the possibility of that would be no pleasant thought for him who had meant to sacrifice years of his life to the task. He wrote to Björnson: "It will no longer be what I had imagined. The text will lose for me the best, the ineffable, that which gives the shiver of ecstasy (that which gave it in *Olav Trygvason*)." He complains that Björnson does not seem to realize that the publication of the poem has a paralyzing effect on his creative power.

Reading today this arguing back and forth of Grieg's, we see clearly that all the obstacles which he piled up for himself, both the real and the imaginary, served really to hide—perhaps even from himself—the true reason why this joint work miscarried and we have no peace oratorio. Not till five years later did he, for the first time, write with complete frankness about it to Björnson in a letter dated July 1, 1896: "For some years I imagined that the peace oratorio lost its attraction for me when you let the poem be printed and the press got to know that I was to compose the music for it. Some truth there was in that, for there is something of the sensitive plant in me. But the chief reason lay deeper: I was not equal to the task. In part because the text was broader than I had imagined it would be, and especially because my health just at that time got the serious blow which shook the very foundations of my creative energy."

The few lines of the poem to which Grieg wrote music and which are published among his posthumous songs under the title "Jeg elsket—" (I Loved—) do not suggest that he had been in happy vein when at last he tried to fit his music to Björnson's words. The external characteristics that we know from so many of his best works are certainly here too, both the rich use of chromatics in the harmonic web and the typically Griegian intervals in the harmonic line: octave, seventh, fifth. But they have now a mannered and out of tune effect because the quivering inner life which once enforced these characteristic features of his musical language is wanting.

Yet another large work Grieg made plans for at this time. He had a great desire to give the somber and wildly passionate Lofthus quartet a bright and cheerful sister. In February he wrote in Copenhagen the first movement of a string quartet in F major and in March of the same year the second movement, but then that too came to a standstill. Time after time, as the years went on, he tried to complete the work—but in vain. Even as late as 1903 he wrote to his publisher about the quartet he had hoped to finish. The last years had brought so much that was sad and depressing, he had not been in the mood to finish the cheerful work which was to have formed a complete contrast to Opus 27, but he hoped, perhaps in the coming summer, to find the longed for peace and mood. The quartet was never finished and not till after Grieg's death were the first two parts, after having been revised by Julius Röntgen, published as a posthumous work.

It is not only the key that is the same as in the first violin sonata. In general feeling, the first movement of the quartet reminds one strikingly of the F major sonata, composed almost thirty years before. But it has by no means the freshness and spontaneous charm of that youthful work. And if the second movement, a scherzo in spring dance rhythm, brings to one's mind the second violin sonata, the likeness is of a wholly superficial kind. Just those things which specially characterize the two sonatas, sap, energy, excess of vitality, fertility of invention, rich and bubbling over, are lacking in the two movements of the quartet. Although there are many fine passages in the working out both as regards harmony and rhythm, they show that the causes for the non-completion of this work too were of the kind that lie deep. "Something lies locked up in me that no one understands"—to use Grieg's own words. The reason for this failure, as for so much else, must this time too be traced back to what happened in the fateful winter at Lofthus.

It was, no doubt, as a result of his bitter experiences with the peace oratorio that Grieg did not take up seriously a project for musical-dramatic work that came now from Ibsen himself. Even as early as their first meeting in Rome in 1866 they had discussed the possibility of working together to make *Olav Liljekrans* into an opera, and now the poet suggested *The Warriors of Helgeland*, a subject which might well be tempting for Grieg to tackle.

In a letter to Dr. Abraham, dated Grefsen Bad, near Christiania, June 19, 1893, Grieg writes: "Yesterday Ibsen was here. He is determined to prepare the text for an opera for me: *The Warriors of Helgeland*—stuff that he has used for a play and which is excellently adapted for setting to music." If only he were well, complains Grieg, and he ends by saying that he must think things over and above all see first what exactly Ibsen is aiming at. From what Ibsen told him, he would have one act ready almost at once, Grieg writes in the letter. How much reality there was in Ibsen's proposal it is not easy to say, but it is obvious at least from the foregoing that Grieg did not exactly grasp at the project with both hands, in spite of its being the dream of his life to write an opera and though, as we have heard, he found the text remarkably suitable for musical treatment.

NOTHING so restored, strengthened, and stimulated Grieg as wandering in the country. From the time when, as a fifteen-year-old boy, he made with his father a journey overland from Bergen to the Eastland and learned to know the fantastic beauty of the Norwegian mountains, a deep delight in nature was his most faithful companion throughout life. In letters to Beyer we see how it is this feeling that steadily buoys him up and helps him over the difficult periods when both mental and bodily oppression seemed about to exhaust his strength. And the blessed thing about this stimulus, in contrast with the wave of emotion which often swept him high in the excitement of the concert hall, was that it had no shadowy side, it was not followed by the reaction which often led down into the blackest depression. No, his joy in nature was in truth restorative—he never felt himself so free and happy and buoyant as after one of his mountain walking tours. He writes to Beyer that "one can love no great spirit so purely and completely as Nature," and he pities those who are not drawn to and fascinated by its deep mystery, "I think life must be a closed book for them." But he continues, "alone one cannot indulge one's feelings for nature beyond a certain point without melancholy knocking at the door, but in company with a sympathetic friend one's enjoyment may be infinite—unbounded." If he is alone with nature his excitement may rise to such a pitch that he is whirled away in it. No, if he is to get the full, reflecting delight out of his wanderings, he must have a friend who feels like himself and can share his happiness with him. It is not to be wondered at, therefore, that his best and nearest friend, Frants Beyer, was also his inseparable comrade on the mountain tours he made almost yearly in the Jotunheim. One of the reasons for the closeness of Grieg's friendship with Julius Röntgen was certainly that he was both an enthusiastic lover of nature and an eager walker. But other friends and colleagues also, such as Holter, Sinding, and the English composer, Delius, took part in these happy wanderings in the mountains.

To Holter Grieg wrote on August 11, 1890: "I am off tomorrow morning to Turtegrösæter, near the Skagastöl peaks—ascent from

Fortun in Sogn—to put steel into my nerves for the winter. Will you come there or shall I meet you somewhere else? Ich bin zu allen Schandthaten fähig! You have fished, bathed, and sailed enough now down there in civilized Norway. Now let nature have you for a little. You need to graft some mountain stuff too into your activities."

In another letter, also to Holter, we get a vivid impression of Grieg's gay and happy summer mood: "There will be a whole crowd at Troldhaugen. Brodsky, his wife and sister-in-law, Fru Piccard, Dr. Abraham, Delius, Holter and, I hope, Sinding. There will be a place for you all, N.B. if you are not too dainty. As for you, you are heartily welcome. Boathouse, fishing tackle in order. Frants has a sailboat. Good weather and ditto humor you must bring with you—that is an order. Let us know when you are coming!"

There was, however, no crowd at Troldhaugen that year, as most of those named in the letter were in some way or other prevented from coming. But Julius Röntgen and his family came on a visit to Norway, and with Röntgen and Beyer Grieg made a tour in the Jotunheim in August. "How I regret that you didn't come *this year*," Grieg writes to Dr. Abraham, August 25, 1891, "the summer was exceptionally beautiful and the Jotunheim incomparable. I made a tour with my friends, Beyer and Röntgen, and we have all come back ten years younger."

When in 1930 Röntgen published his Grieg letters he completed them with a short biographical sketch of Grieg's life and with some stories of the times they had been together, both abroad and in Norway. We find here a description of the mountain tour in 1891 on which occasion Röntgen first got to know Beyer. Röntgen relates:

In the year 1891 my wife was again well enough for us to think of a summer journey to Norway. We chose Lofthus again and went there in the beginning of July. Grieg had given us an introduction to the music-dealer Rabe in Bergen and when we were starting with him on a trip by the Voss railroad, a rather carelessly dressed gentleman at the station came forward to Rabe, said good-day to him and, as he turned to me, cried in a lively voice, "I am Behr," as if we were old acquaintances. On his side he seemed surprised that I did not recognize him. I didn't know what to make of him and took him for a rather shady musician who wanted to force himself on me. He attached himself to us and proposed that I, with him, should climb Lövstakken, one of Bergen's seven mountains, whilst the others went on by train. Good Lord, I thought— I hope nothing worse will happen than his begging for something from me. And so began our tour. On the way, my singular guide bought some bottles of beer which disappeared in the pocket of his coat. And on we went without my suspecting whom I really had to do with. Suddenly he looked into the distance and said, "There lies Troldhaugen!" I looked at him in astonishment and asked, "Do *you* know Edvard Grieg?" Now the astonishment was on his side. "What did you say? Our friend, Edvard Grieg?" Whereupon, half in desperation, I shouted, "But who are you actually?" When to this he answered, "I am Behr, Grieg's friend, Frants Behr!", at last the riddle was solved and I cried: "You are Frants *Beyer*!" Tempestuous embraces from my side were the immediate result. Now it was clear to me. How often had Grieg told me of his best, faithful friend, Frants Beyer! Through Grieg, Beyer knew me and so his greeting me as a friend was quite natural. We found one another in our common friend and in this way our friendship was cemented for life. In good and evil, in life's many dispensations he has stood at Grieg's side, faithful and ready to help, and better than anyone else he knew and understood the finest strings in Grieg's nature. He was himself musical, through and through (not indeed a musician by profession, he was a lawyer), composer of several songs, filled with the deepest feeling for Norwegian nature—how often had not I heard Grieg speak of him. "I have him alone to thank that I can climb mountains," Grieg had said once when the doctors remarked on the wonder of his being able to live so long with only one lung.

A beautiful monument to this friendship are the published letters from Grieg to Beyer. They cover the years 1872-1907. In one of the last letters to Beyer Grieg wrote: "I began a letter to Julius just now as follows: 'If I had a son he would be called Frants Julius or—Julius Frants.' For you both write me such dear letters that I become almost sentimental! Yes—so it is. It is splendid to have friends in youth. But indeed it is still more splendid to have them in old age. In youth, friends, like everything else, are taken for granted. In old age we know what it means to possess them."

But to go back to our first meeting. Frants Beyer showed me his own villa Næsset almost opposite Troldhaugen. The two friends always used a rowing boat to reach each other. In animated talk about Grieg we reached the top of Lövstakken and drank there to Edvard's and Nina's health. The empty bottle we buried there as a memento. That was our first trip to Lövstakken. How often did we not go back to it in recollections later.

The following day we visited the Griegs at Troldhaugen where we were received with the greatest kindness. Troldhaugen lies high on a hill that slopes steeply down to the fjord. From the tower of the house there is a wide outlook over the fjord with its small, pine-clad islands. The grey mountains surrounding Bergen form the background—a view as grand as it is beautiful! A flower garden lies in front of the house, from which small paths lead down to the fjord. They go along a steep wall of cliff which was chosen by Grieg to be his last resting place. Right down by the fjord lies a little boathouse with the boat belonging to Næsset hidden by bushes. Further along the shore one comes to a little one-roomed hut—Grieg's workroom.

Next day we went to Lofthus, where Grieg visited us later and where we planned a tour in the Jotunheim. Frants Beyer was with us on this tour. One of the principal points in the Jotunheim is Turtegrö and here our first stay was to be made. Grieg and I went from Lofthus to the Sognefjord in a "stolkjerre" (two-wheeled cart like a small dog cart), whence we reached Skjolden in a rowing boat. From Skjolden the way goes steeply up to Turtegrö. On the way we picked up a fiddler and took him with us in the wagon and he played country airs for us during the glorious drive. How that music suited the surroundings! Grieg listened enraptured, constantly nodding his head in time to the music. In his hand he held a glass of port wine which from time to time he proffered to the fiddler. "This is Norway," he said with beaming eyes. It was a warm August noon, the fjord was deep green and we lay stretched out on sacks of hay and let that splendid mountain landscape pass in review before our eyes. We rode on horseback over the mountains to Turtegrö, but before the journey began Grieg drank with me to our brotherhood. This solemn moment—our entrance into the Jotunheim—he had chosen for that. The Jotun mountains now rose up gradually before our eyes, Fanaråken, Ringstindene and, at last, the great Skagastölstind, the Norwegian Matterhorn. The dark mass of stone was colored red-brown by the evening sun. At last we reached the hut of the famous guide, Ole Berge, and were heartily received by him. Suddenly we heard Frants Beyer's cooeying and soon he was with us in beaming Jotunheim mood.

Besides Ole Berg's hut there were also two other huts where the sæter girls lived. We visited the girls the very first evening and Frants Beyer managed to persuade them, after a bit of hesitation, to sing for us. I heard here for the first time Norwegian folk songs in the surroundings to which they belong; what a performance they gave us! Frants Beyer told us how in the morning, when the cows were being milked and the girls were singing, he laid his notepaper on the back of a cow and so jotted down folk airs "fresh from the cow."

Early next morning I heard Ole Berge's sister calling in the goats and singing. Everywhere was that calling and singing. Among Grieg's posthumous manuscripts I found a sheet dated Turtegrö, 1893, with various motives from the Jotunheim.

For our first trip we chose the ascent of Dyrehaugstind. Frants Beyer was our guide. The way went first through ling, later through rockstrewn wastes, and finally over snow slopes. Grieg did not feel strong enough to clamber to the top, so remained behind with Frants Beyer while I climbed alone. Dusk had fallen when my friends and I came back. At Turtegrö they had become anxious over our long absence and had sent out people with food and drink to meet us. We were very glad indeed to see them and we strengthened ourselves with rum toddy, while Grieg spread his hands in blessing over Frants Beyer and me as we drank to our brotherhood. In exultant mood we continued on our way and it was not till late in the evening that we got back to Ole Berge's hut.

After some days we went from Turtegrö over the Kaiser pass to Skogadalsböen, a tourist hut at the mid point of the Jotunheim. Everywhere we had "peak weather." Grieg either walked or rode on horseback. Beyer sang on the march snatches of Mozart's string quartets, enjoying the music as if he heard it in the most perfect performance. By Gjertvasbreen, a huge, round glacier, we rested for a while. In what spirits! Those who have not seen Grieg in the mountains on such an occasion do not really know him. Only there his genial nature, free from all bodily constraint, could fully unfold itself.

From Skogadalsböen, passes and valleys lead in all directions. The tourist hut here is the best placed and also the most comfortable in the whole of the Jotunheim. It lies on a mountain knoll from which one sees deep into the richly wooded Skogadal, with its rushing river, which forms a magnificent contrast to the rest of the wholly treeless landscape.

At Skogadalsböen we had an unforgettable evening. The tourist hut was at that time looked after by Tollef and Brit Holmestad. The wife had, a short time before, had a child and her sister, Gjendine Slålien, was with her to help her. This Gjendine was born near Gjendin and called by her parents after this lake. She was the only person in Norway with this name. The first time we saw her she was rocking her sister's baby in her arms while she sang her to sleep with the beautiful cradle song Grieg has made use of in his Norwegian Folksongs, Opus 66, under the name of "Gjendine's Cradle Song." As she sang it, it made a wonderful impression—very rhythmically and yet with a free and natural style, towards the end more and more slowly and softly till it died away altogether. She sang readily and knew many folk songs. A charming dance of German origin was remade by her through some characteristic changes into a genuine Norwegian piece and thereby the original, rather banal melody became something entirely different, something quite fascinating. Gjendine could blow the goat horn also, an instrument that can only take the three first notes of the scale's minor. With these three notes she could produce the most original melodies. So passed the evening in the comfortable hut with song and gaiety and when we came out the mountains lay fantastically lit by the moon and from the depths could be heard the rushing of the river. Gjendine stood up on a rock and sang the cradle song for us once more. How thrillingly beautiful it sounded! Grieg said to me, "You are certainly in luck—a thing like this doesn't often happen in Norway."

Next morning, we left Skogadalsböen. When we had gone a little way we heard the notes of the goat horn on which Gjendine was blowing a tune for farewell—further and further away till it died completely in long notes. In Grieg's lyric piece "Hjemve" (Longing for Home), Opus 57, we find the same motive on the three notes.

Our next objective was Vettifoss, the highest waterfall in Norway. The guide, Anfinn Vetti, had his home near the fall and we spent a night with him. But then the tour was over. Frants Beyer went back to Turtegrö, Edvard to Bergen, and I to wife and children at Lofthus.

That the primitive conditions prevailing in the mountains could also offer experiences of a less agreeable kind to a delicately nurtured man is not surprising. After another tour, in 1893, Grieg wrote to Röntgen: "The Jotunheim is certainly wonderfully beautiful, but it is a pigsty for all that! On the way home I was suddenly overcome by a skin disease that is driving me almost crazy. I can hardly keep still as I write these lines. The cause of the illness lies in—*Jotunheim beds*! Now I am going to take a warm bath!"

Until three years before his death, according to the account of his doctor, Klaus Hanssen, Grieg went on with his yearly walking tours in the Jotunheim. When he became too weak for longer tours he continued his wanderings in the mountains round Bergen. The mere thought of that glorious open-air life in the Norwegian high mountains was enough to fill him with joy and rapture. "A mountain tour somewhere with Frants, what do you say?" he writes on January 12, 1896, to Johan Halvorsen. "When I think of such a possibility I shiver with joy and excitement as if I were about to hear Beethoven's Tenth Symphony."

IN THE summer of 1891 Grieg was again, after a two years' pause, in creative activity. From the summer of 1889, when he completed the two volumes of songs, Opus 48 and Opus 49, he had written nothing new. In a letter to Dr. Abraham, January 30, 1891, he says that "the manuscripts are not going well, the last while has been again a dead period." Why, he does not know, but it is his duty to state the fact, he writes.

His next work, Romance for two pianos, Opus 51, shows that it has not been easy, even now, to get into his stride. Here too, as in the cello sonata, Grieg experiments with breadth in design. The work, like the Ballad, is written in the form of variations on a Norwegian folk song, the fine old ballad about "Sjugurd og Troll-brura" (Sigurd and the Troll Bride), material well fitted to have an inspiring effect on Grieg. But in spite of beautiful and characterful details, the Romance suggests rather diligence and toilsome labor than inner experiences. This work shows the correctness of Grieg's words when in his "cosmopolitan declaration of faith" in the English interview he drew attention to the fact that he had become less one-sided, more European, more cosmopolitan. But it seems as though he found it considerably more difficult to make a figure as an independent European than as a highly individual and characterful Norwegian. Both Schumann and Liszt have been his diligent assistants in the working out—this can be seen especially in the technical treatment of the piano.

Two years before his death, Grieg orchestrated the Romance for full orchestra, but not even the luxuriant drapery of a symphony orchestra can cover up the inward shortcomings of the work, and in both editions the Romance must be reckoned the weakest of Grieg's works.

A quite other, much happier spirit and touch mark the six lyrical pieces, Opus 54, which were also written this summer. Here Grieg uses the little form which gradually became the only one in which he could express his intentions with complete sincerity and integrity. The six pieces are all gems of fine and individual music for the piano. "Gjætergut" (The Herd-Boy) certainly, with its richly chromatic setting, stands on the threshold of the drawing-room, but at the same time it is so intensely felt and experienced that it has become an arresting piece of poetry. Still more is this the case with the fresh, vital "Gangar" (Walking Dance) which shows how near is Grieg's relationship with our folk music. That "Trolltog" (Procession of the Trolls) has attained so great a popularity may be set down largely to its enticing title, but the music also has a compelling power, leading the imagination into kingdoms and countries where nature mysticism prevails and where Grieg is sole monarch. "Nocturne" shows the composer as the sensitive man of culture and shows also that his methods of expression lie very near impressionism. After a lively "Scherzo" with genuine Grieg rhythm and harmonies, we come to the last and also most original and valuable piece, "Klokkeklang" (The Chiming of the Bells). This is a study in sound, so bold and so striking in its effect that one can only marvel that it has not long since become a pet number of the pianists. It is understandable that in the Nineties its radicalism might have startled and deterred, but we have experienced since then such "sound phenomena" as Debussy, Ravel, and Stravinsky—to name only one or two—so a pianist can surely without risk worth mentioning include it in his repertoire. With its continual succession of fifths it has the effect of the chiming of church bells in a Norwegian mountain valley, a rising wave of sound pealing persistently among the mountains—until at last it merges into muffled organ-like sonorities, chords which are again succeeded by the ringing of the bells. To Julius Röntgen, to whom the volume is dedicated, Grieg wrote: "The last one, 'The Chiming of the Bells,' is quite simply mad. But you will at least find *something* here and there not altogether crazy."

Yet two more works Grieg finished this summer before he entered again into his usual two year period of silence. They are both adaptations of his own songs, the first, Opus 52, for piano and the second, Opus 53, comprising "My Goal" and "The First Meeting," arranged for string orchestra.

In the autumn they went as usual to Christiania, though this time not without hesitation. It was perhaps an inner voice that dictated the following lines in a letter to Holter: "What I most wanted to do was to stay at home and work in peace. Perhaps that would have been too lonely, spoiled as I have now become." For the rest, there was a special circumstance which induced Grieg to yield this time, in spite of doubts, to the temptation of concerts: in the autumn he was to celebrate his twenty-fifth-year jubilee as concert-giver in Christiania. So the tour started there in the beginning of October with a series of concerts. At the first, Grieg himself played his new lyrical pieces and, with Fru Gröndahl, the Romance for two pianos. Both works had a good, though not specially enthusiastic, reception, both by public and press. Winter-Hjelm wrote as follows in his review: "When I am personally most captivated by his earlier works in which the influence in respect to form of Gade and other masters goes side by side with his, at that time, new and enthusiastic proclivity towards national motives, I do not believe I am biased; it seems to be a feeling I share with the greater part of the public."

At the special jubilee concert, the second *Peer Gynt* suite was performed for the first time, besides *At a Southern Cloister's Gate*, *Olav Trygvason* and some of the quartets for male voices. There was not a vacant seat in the great Circus which held over two thousand people, and Grieg received a great ovation. Afterwards a dinner was given in his honor at which Ibsen, among others, was present and used the occasion to thank Grieg for having with his wonderful art been a good advocate for his work. They two had mutually supplemented each other, said Ibsen, and therefore he wished now to thank Grieg.

The students too did him homage with a great torchlight procession, which made a wonderful show in the still winter night, Grieg tells his publisher. "The whole festival was such as I had never experienced and will never experience again. I only hope it has not demoralized me, " he ends his letter.

After having given a concert with Nina of Sinding's Drachmann songs on November 28, they went back, in spite of everything, to Troldhaugen in the quiet hope that perhaps he might experience a happy and fruitful work period. But no. From a letter to Holter, dated Troldhaugen, December 21, 1891, we hear in what sort of spirits he is. The letter is as follows:

"Dear Holter,

"Thanks for your last. You make me think of the parable of the threads. So long as you played the Norn, everything went well. But since I came here you have evidently got the web into a mess. For now things are in a thoroughly bad way. For three days I've been sitting here with influenza, phlegm, and fever and twitchings all over. Not so bad as to make me go to bed but enough to embitter my whole existence. One gets nothing gratis in this world and a journey such as we made must be paid for. You can have no idea what a splendid tour we had. The greatness, quietness, and glory of the mountains are beyond description. And we had fine weather all the time. The evenings were perhaps the loveliest. We travelled till 9 or 10 at night and were not the least bit tired. The first day we reached Odnæs, next day Fagernæs, third day Skogstad, fourth day Husum, and fifth day Lærdal. Then we had to wait for the boat and it took a day and a half to Bergen. Scandalous!—If I wasn't feeling such a poor creature I would find it glorious in the quiet world around me here. It is like summer: 8-10 degrees above. Good influenza weather. Give me the 18 degrees below on the mountains, that was weather both for body and soul! Facit: To the mountains in summer!!

"Happy Christmas!

                                        "Yours
                                        "Edvard Grieg.
"Remember me to Sinding and Gade."

We see from his letters that he went the winter through without being able to get to work. He revised and corrected the fifteen-year-old *Sigurd Jorsalfar*. That is all, and for this work he set up his little work-hut, which lay damp and cold right down by the fjord—new plagues, new sicknesses. He wrote to Emil Hornemann on June 25, 1895: "Since the month of February, when I got rheumatism in my legs, I have not been able to write a note! I lose spirits, will, everything."

In a letter to Jonas Lie on August 3, he said: "All through the winter I have been practically an invalid with rheumatism in my feet. It is a strange thing: what we expect most from we get least out of. I built down in the valley at Troldhaugen a little turf-roofed hut where I could have peace and quiet and fastened all my hopes on it. But, if you please, it stood too near the wind from the sea and the floor was not two feet from the damp earth. The fact is I got some trouble in my feet which began like cramp and, as I have said, turned out to be genuine rheumatism. And that doomed my hut. I have not dared to set foot in it since."

But even now life had its bright spots. When Grieg and his wife celebrated their silver wedding on June 11, 1892, great homage and all kinds of attentions were paid them by their many friends and admirers, both at home and abroad. In his letters Grieg, obviously cheerful, describes the eventful day in great detail.

To his publisher, Dr. Abraham, who surprised him with a large gift of money, Grieg wrote as follows: "The very day chose to be exceptional for us and you must hear about it. The weather after a fortnight of rain was heavenly beautiful. Even before we had left our bedroom the brigade band struck up 'A Mighty Fortress is Our God' down in the garden, followed by a serenade composed for the occasion. The effect of the first notes in the wonderful still morning I shall never forget. Numerous gifts of flowers had already arrived and, as during the course of the day more than a hundred messages of congratulation arrived and flowers with them all, Troldhaugen was finally buried in a sea of flowers. And such masses of presents! Art lovers in Christiania sent a big picture by Werenskiold; artists in the same place, a huge bearskin rug, a very splendid specimen; lovers of art in Bergen, a Steinway piano; a music school in London, a beautiful silver writing set. From Norway, Sweden, and Denmark came furniture, silver, and other gifts. I hardly know my rooms again. Since, on account of trains, the morning visitors had to leave almost at once, before I had even had time to greet them all, I suddenly had the brilliant idea of inviting the whole company to supper. This was received with acclamation. But—the cuisine! We were prepared for fifty guests but this was a matter of one hundred and thirty! My friend, Fru Beyer, who has a special housewifely genius, arranged everything by telephone and telegraph in such a masterly way that by evening everything was there all at once, exactly as in a fairy tale. The tables were laid in the garden and lovely ladies acted as hostesses. At nine in the evening two hundred and thirty singers came, who performed a very beautiful festival poem to my music. In between there was talking, piano playing (by me), singing (by my wife) and, above all—drinking, for punch flowed like the Rhenish wine in Heine's poem. To add to all this, cannon thundered from the neighboring islands, while beautiful Bengal lights and St. John's bonfires mirrored themselves in the sea. The fjord was swarming with boats and wherever we looked the knolls were black with people. The whole thing was by happy chance a kind of popular fête and, as such, exceptionally successful."

But his happiness in this festivity too was to be followed by a reaction and a short time after we find Grieg ill and suffering. On
August 3 he wrote to Holter: "I have been a patient since we
parted. I managed to collect a capital catarrh of the stomach that
kept me steadily alternating between bed and sickroom. I have not
yet fully recovered, am still taking opium pills every day and keeping to the strictest diet, but I think now I am in a fair way to sur-
vive as I am at last allowed to go out of the house a little. In the
town I have not been for more than six weeks. I've grown most
horribly thin. The thing now is to get some fat on my bones and
strength in my middle. The other day I had the chance of a brilliant engagement for America in the winter. It came just at the
right time, don't you think! Naturally, I refused. I see that Svendsen has gone off to Vienna. I was baulked of that too. No—one
can't get along without health. If only I could be well enough to
get away next month I should be more than delighted."

And well enough he was. In autumn they went, as usual, to
Christiania, where Grieg first conducted the *Sigurd Jorsalfar*
suite and "Taken into the Mountains" with Lammers as soloist
at the Musical Society and then gave a concert where, besides
Nina, Johan Halvorsen took part in the third violin sonata. Then
they went to Copenhagen. From a letter to Holter from Copenhagen, November 26, 1892, we get a vivid impression that it was
not always easy to get through these concerts. "I came here poorly
and—thanks to concert nervousness—became worse and worse,
could keep nothing down, and half an hour before the concert was
so exhausted that I thought there was only one thing to do: cancel
the engagement. But then another voice made itself heard in me
and said: Is there a thing called energy or is there not? And with
that I started off. I made the carriage stop at a chemist's, took a
powerful stomach bitter, and as soon as I had got to work had
something else to think of for a while than my stomach. All went
so well that, besides repeating some items, we had to add things
not on the programme. But the reaction! That is worse. I was to
accompany Nina at a folk concert we promised to assist at, but
even that I have had to give up. A public life is poison."

But the tour went on, by Berlin to Leipzig, where on February
7, 1893, Grieg conducted his piano concerto with the Russian
pianist, Alexander Siloti, in the solo part and also his second *Peer
Gynt* suite. April and May were spent at the Riviera where, little

by little, his strength came back. The month of June Grieg spent at the Grefsen baths, near Christiania, where his health continued to improve—and finally towards St. John's Day he was home again at Troldhaugen, so strengthened and invigorated that not only could he undertake a walking tour in the Jotunheim with Beyer and Röntgen, but he began to think about composition again. From this summer date the Lyrical Pieces, Opus 57.

If one reflects on the many depressing experiences of the last years, when illness, time after time, stood hinderingly in the way and upset all his plans, we understand better the mild resignation that marks the first piece, "Svundne dage" (Vanished Days) full of melancholy, bitter feeling that swells to a violent outburst and on the background of which the lively subsidiary theme depicts for us carefree youth. Also the second piece, "Gade," which was composed indeed on the occasion of Gade's death, calls up vanished times, a backward glance to the happy youthful days in Copenhagen. In addition the collection includes "Illusjon" (Illusion), "Hemmelighet" (The Secret) and a graceful little waltz, "Hun danser" (She Dances)—all three good drawing-room pieces. But the finest is undoubtedly the last, "Hjemve" (Longing for Home). Here Grieg gives beautiful expression to the longing that gnawed at him constantly when he was out in the world. And so lively is his imagination that out of his longing the longed for land grows and rises up vividly alive before our eyes. Instinctively Grieg uses here the major scale with augmented fourths when he wishes to paint a picture of Norway, that is to say, the old Lydian mode from which the most characteristic of our folk dances derive.

In September he is off again, out into the world. First two concerts in Christiania in October, at which the new lyrical pieces were played for the first time; then two concerts in Copenhagen in November, when Teresa Carreño took part in the piano concerto and Laura Gundersen in "Bergliot." In February Grieg conducted the *Sigurd Jorsalfar* suite for the first time in the Gewandhaus in Leipzig; in March there were performances in Munich and Geneva; in April he was conducting at Colonne's in Paris where Raoul Pugno played the piano concerto, and finally on May 24 the season ended with a performance at the Philharmonic Society in London.

During the stay in Copenhagen, Grieg wrote as follows in a letter to Dr. Abraham: "It is hardly believable how much younger I am feeling these last months." The reason is not difficult to guess: he had begun to work again. In the hotel he had found a retired room where he could compose and in that room it was, for the time being, spring. "Ich meine Liederfrühling," he wrote in a letter.

Of the sixteen songs written in Copenhagen only the five to words of Vilhelm Krag are of interest today. The eleven Paulsen songs are among Grieg's weakest, which is not to be wondered at when one reads the generally unimportant, often utterly flat verses which could not possibly engage the deeper powers in Grieg. The important thing for musical collaboration is that the composer should be able quite instinctively to feel his way in to the emotion that dominated the poet before the words were born, in to the very springs of inspiration. Where, as here, everything is on the surface, where within the outer shell there is no kernel, not only is the work of the composer rendered unnecessary but also impossible. It is significant that the melodic line, which with Grieg can be both pure in itself and of great value with its singularly deep perspective in enforcing and illuminating his ingenious harmony, is weakened to an expressionless and poor melodic parlando. The most important of the songs is "Henrik Wergeland," but this too is marked by a self-conscious tone which made it hard for the lyricist Grieg to feel himself at home. It is difficult to understand how Grieg could be willing to set his name to a song like "Turisten" (The Tourist)— Grieg, whose self-critical sense was so alert. This song has almost the effect of a parody, decorated as it is with many of the purely external features characteristic of Grieg, his bass in fifths, for example, the fall of the melodic line from the octave to the fifth by way of the seventh, the alternations between major and minor, and the use of the stanza form which to Paulsen's words has the effect of a malicious caricature. These songs, taken as a whole, are new evidence that Wagner's influence, far from being stimulating, had, on the contrary, a paralyzing effect on his powers, even if the careful elocution may be placed to the credit of a diligent study of the Bayreuth master.

To turn from these songs to the five written to words by Vilhelm Krag, Opus 60, is to come into another world. If one did not know it to be so, it would be impossible to believe that they were written at the same period. Once again his musical language has life and color, his melody is rich and full of expression, and with his picorial harmo ny he paints the most fascinating pictures of Vilhelm

Krag's delicate and tender troubadour lyrics. Again we must admire his ability to let emotional experiences come to expression in
a frame of beautiful scenes from nature. "Liden Kirsten" (Little
Kirsten) and "Moderen synger" (The Mother Sings) have the subdued and gentle mood which brings to life the far-away picture
world of the new romanticism. How sparklingly gay and carefree,
how filled with sunshine are the following lines in "Mens jeg
venter" (While I Wait):

> Wild geese, wild geese in snowy flocks,
>   Sunshiny weather
> Ducklings strutting in yellow socks,
>   Fine feathers—

and "Der skreg en Fugl" (There Screeched a Bird) has the sharp
savor of the salt sea, while the opening bars on the piano give expression, true to nature, of the bird's pain-filled cry "in the grey
autumn day." It may be of interest here to explain that the bird
cry really seems to have been a study from nature. On the inside
of the cover in one of the many small account books Grieg always
carried about with him and in which he carefully set down his daily
outlays, great and small, we find this motive scribbled down and
under it "Seagull's cry heard in the Hardanger fjord."

"Og jeg vil ha mig en Hjertenskjær" (And I Will Have a Sweetheart) makes a glorious ending to the collection, a magnificent
song full of youth and rollicking humor, here too with nature impressions as an enhancement. "And over the dew-wet fields we go,
The beautiful night of St. John"—the modulation suddenly coming
in with these lines shows us one of the methods of surprise which
only genius knows how to use.

Considering the Vilhelm Krag songs, one understands Grieg's
happy and elated mood. They proved not only that he could still
create genuine art, but they showed also that he had new, unused
strings to his lyre. The songs were sung for the first time at a concert in Copenhagen on January 20, 1894.

Next winter Grieg lived in Copenhagen. Before leaving Norway,
after having spent the summer at Troldhaugen, he gave in October
1894 a series of five concerts in Bergen. It was ten years since his
last concert in the town of his birth and, as might be expected, the
greatest interest was taken in this series. During his stay in Copenhagen this winter we see from letters how uncertain and poor his

health was and how this hindered him in getting into regular work. He wrote to Beyer from Copenhagen on December 29, 1894, that if one day in thirty or forty he felt comparatively well, "then I am another man at once. Brighter outlook, desire to work, imagination, everything good suddenly knocks at my door. Then I say to myself: Now go ahead in the morning so as to use the mood while it lasts—and then in the morning I am again the old man, heavy and depressed, without the power to continue what has been begun."

Nevertheless, he wrote this winter, besides a number of lyrical pieces and "Nordische Weisen" for string orchestra, Opus 63, the enchanting *Children's Songs*, Opus 61, which Nina sang for the first time at a concert in Copenhagen on April 26, 1895. While some of these as, for example, "Du grönne glitrende Træ" (Ah, Green and Glittering Tree), "De norske Fjelde" (The Norwegian Mountains) and "Fædrelandssalme" (Hymn to the Fatherland) are of the nature of occasional pieces, there are, to make up, others which, in spite of their simple and unpretentious outer trappings, must be placed among the best of Grieg's songs. The most interesting, so far as style is concerned, is "Havet" (The Ocean) to words of Nordahl Rolfsen. A severe simplification, a purity of line, and a wonderful sureness in characterization make this song singularly fresh and living. Again Grieg uses the major scale with augmented fourths, the typical Norwegian Lydian mode, to give life to the following lines: "The Pilot lies with flag on top, outside the door and opens up for every ship that comes," or "Arctic, North Sea, and Atlantic! Snow and fog and shoal and grave, can be found in all." Also "Lok" (Call) to words of Björnson's and the lively "Fiskervise" (Fisherman's Song) of Petter Dass are among the best of the collection and last, but not least, "Kveldsang for Blakken" (Evening Song for Brownie) in which Grieg takes the opportunity to show how with an unexpected little harmonic change he can create a vivid and imaginative picture. I am thinking of the way in which he brings to life the following line in the poem: "Dream of it, old Brownie: Nothing to do but eat and rest, maybe to trot round the yard at most, with the little lad on your back." By a divergence from the ordinary major and the introduction of the minor seventh of the mixo-Lydian mode, this stanza is given matchless charm of coloring. To the headmaster and organist, O. Koppang, who asked to be allowed to put some of the children's songs in his school song-book, Grieg wrote in a letter dated Troldhaugen, September 7, 1895: "Of my children's songs I myself set 'Havet' highest because I think it is the freshest and most full of character. There is a C sharp that should sound like sea salt. I should like very much indeed to have this one in particular in the second arrangement, and indeed the first also, sung by your flock of school children, and so come onto the lips of those for whom it was meant. For that matter, any one of the children's songs in this volume."

A new collection of lyrical pieces also dates from this year. It has nothing new in its kind to show, but it contains fine and characterful strains such as "Sylfide" (Sylph), "Tak" (Thanks), "Fransk Serenade" (French Serenade), and "Drömmesyn" (Dream Vision). The most important is the richly colored, vividly painted picture of "Bækken" (The Brook) and the last, "Hjemad" (Homeward Bound), which gives expression to the rapture and excitement that filled Grieg's heart when at last the day and the hour were come out there in a foreign land when the journey home to sun and summer and life outdoors and everything glorious could begin.

BUT there was another work that occupied Grieg seriously during this summer at Troldhaugen. A short time before he came home there appeared a small, outwardly inconspicuous book by Arne Garborg entitled *Haugtussa*. Now too, as when he first got hold of Vinje's poems, Grieg was flung into a transport of enthusiasm and wrote in a very short space of time not only the eight published songs but a series of others which, deplorably enough, were never completed. Among his posthumous papers there were found sketches and rough drafts in various stages of completion with the following headings: (1) "Prologue" —Til Deg Du Hei og bleike Myr (To Thee, Thou Heath and Pallid Fen), (2) "D'er Haust, det ruskar" (It's Autumn, Rough Weather), (3) "Sporven" (The Sparrow), (4) "Vesleymöy dröymer" (Little Maid Dreams) and (5) "Ho Mor" (Mother). It appears from Grieg's correspondence that he thought of making a big work of *Haugtussa*, building the separate parts into a whole, but he could not quite make up his mind about what the form should be. That was one reason why almost two years went past before he gave out his *Haugtussa* songs. As early as June 10, 1895, he told Dr. Abraham in a letter that he had just written new songs to some magnificent Norwegian poems of very recent date, and from a letter soon after it appears, characteristically enough, that, thank heaven, he was feeling well and brisk, better than for a long time! On September 6, 1895, he wrote to Matthison-Hansen: "I have been studying how best to arrange my music to *Haugtussa*, because the text unfortunately raises difficulties which I have not yet been able to surmount. And in the whole of Norway there is no one I know who understands these things." It was not till autumn, 1898, that the *Haugtussa* songs came out under the opus number 67.

Not since "Taken into the Mountains" and the Vinje songs had Grieg reached so high in his vocal art as here. The *Haugtussa* songs were again proof that only poetry of genius could set his deepest and finest strings vibrating. As though in psychic communion he follows the poet's innermost thoughts, deepens and vitalizes his visions, and re-creates his picture world. What has gripped Grieg most directly, struck the fundamental chord in him and so to speak tuned his harp, made him sensitive and perceptive towards the changing moods and rich play of color of the poems, is undoubtedly the nature-mysticism that breathes out from Garborg's poetry and has been so thrillingly expressed in the very first of the songs, "Det Syng" (Song):

> Oh know you the dream and know you the song,
> Their music you'll hide so deep,
> Yet often recall it and ponder it long
> And always in memory keep.
> Oh weaver of spells!
> With me you shall dwell,
> Your spinning-wheel turn on the high blue fell.

Grieg has been harshly criticized, especially by the German music critics, because here too, as in the Vinje songs, he has used the stanza form. But if one goes deeply into the songs one finds this not only justified but even necessary—and that for two reasons. First, because the moods in the original text run parallel, and second, because Grieg's musical language here, as in the Vinje songs, possesses in so high a degree the folk song's intense and full emotional content that to compose such songs as unities would seem almost like an infraction of style.

The next of the songs is, in its special character, without parallel in musical literature. Like a Northern madonna, Veslemöy rises before us poetically rendered in music as simple as it is striking and full of character. Behind the unpretentious exterior one is sensible of all the mysterious longings and dreams, all the visions and enigmas that can ravage and torment a poor human creature. Through suffering she acquires that inexpressibly beautiful and pure look, that fineness of nature and expression which make one feel that it is the very soul of the people which has been crystallized in the individual form.

> She is slender and dark and slight
> With features sun-browned but clear,
> And grey, deep eyes: their light
> Through still dreams made more fair.
> It is half as if over her lay
> A faint, thin veiling of sleep,
> Her moving, her speech, her way,
> A dream-like quietness keep.

'Neath a forehead lovely but low
Shine her eyes as out through a mist,
'Tis as though to her vision they show
A world far other than this.
Only her breast heaves heavy and deep,
O'er her lips faint tremors pass.
She's tremblingly tender and weak
Though young and so fair a lass.

What is most fascinating perhaps in the collection are the brilliant nature pictures. Where in musical literature can one find songs so sparklingly clear and fresh, which mirror so wonderfully nature and peasant life, which are so filled with sun and summer as "Blaabær-Li" (Bilberry Slope) and "Killingdans" (Little Goat's Dance). Once again we must marvel at the way in which Grieg, with very slight deviations from the prevailing keys, obtains the greatest and most surprising effects which give his pictures fragrance and color. In "Bilberry Slope" by introducing the minor seventh of the mixo-Lydian mode at the following words: "The like I've never seen! There's something good on the hills," and in the "Little Goat's Dance" by introducing the same harmonic change at the words:

There's sun caressing
Laughing and blessing,
Green hills bird twittering
Green hills sun glittering!

In this song too he uses with the greatest effect the augmented fourth of the Lydian mode and by this means depicts with one single little stroke the whole of sæter life in its busy, cheerful activities. It is the Norwegian musical feeling for contrasts, its great craving for color that dictates these tonal deviations, which both here and in others of his works Grieg shows that he can use with mastery.

Of the love songs we single out specially "Elsk" (Love) with its mixture of archness and passion and its witching fascination. Though "Möte" (Meeting) is more objective, richer in outward sensation and outward effectiveness, "Vond Dag" (An Evil Day) on the other hand is an exceptionally moving song, among Grieg's very best and perhaps the most beautiful love song he has given us, filled as it is with inner life, inner experience. It is indeed a love song worthy of Veslemöy:

Like a bird wounded under its warm wing
So that the blood drips down as drip hot tears,
She seeks her bed, all sick and shivering,
And tosses the night through in grief that sears
And burns the heart and cheeks with weeping sore.
Now must she die; her lad is hers no more.

"Ved Gjætle-Bækken" (By the Gjætle-Brook) makes a consoling ending. Here too are expressed longing and pain, but it is as though Nature herself lays a softening veil over the whole, rocks the mind to rest, gives forgetfulness and peace.

The *Haugtussa* songs show that Grieg's vein was still as rich and deep as ever and that in his later years too he was able to create works which equalled the best in his production. But it has been with the *Haugtussa* songs as with the Vinje songs and "Taken into the Mountains": outside Norway they have achieved but little circulation and also—little understanding, owing to poor translations. The *Signale* critic, Bernsdorf, had at last come to an end of his activities, but he had a successor who clearly followed in the footsteps of his predecessor, for in a letter from Grieg to Finck we find the following remark in connection with the *Haugtussa* songs: "A critic in *Signale* a few years ago took six columns to show that he understood these songs about as well as a bull understands a red rag." In the same letter Grieg complains about the German translation, which gave no idea of the beauty and originality of the poetry, and says that those who were not in possession of "Ahnungsvermögen" would not be able really to appreciate the music.

We shall now, after this account of *Haugtussa*, follow Grieg through the remaining years of the Nineties. Since they were so much alike, there is no reason to give such a detailed description as before, but though we run briefly through these years, that is because it will become evident how extremely little of Grieg's time was employed in creative activity.

We take up the thread in the summer of 1895. In the autumn there was the usual journey to Copenhagen, where Grieg conducted in the Musical Society on October 24. From Copenhagen and Leipzig he went on to Vienna, where on March 24 he gave a great orchestral concert in conjunction with Ellen Gulbranson and Dagmar Walle-Hansen. On the way home he conducted in Copenhagen with Busoni as soloist in the piano concerto. Then came summer at home in Norway, the time when he really *lived*. After having celebrated his fifty-third birthday with relations and friends at Lofthus, he wrote enthusiastically in a letter of June 18, 1896, to Dr. Abraham: "I am now over fifty years old and for more than the years of a man's life I have yearly gone travelling in my native land. But I have never experienced anything like this. The world was like fairyland. The weather was heavenly, the light nights impossible to describe, and added to this hills and water-falls in their greatest splendor. The air was so wonderfully mild and salubrious that none of us (not even my eighty-two-year-old parents-in-law) felt like going to bed before four o'clock in the morning, and then only to rest for an hour or two. And no tired-ness as a result—rather the maximum of good health and spirits in both old and young."

But the short summer was soon over and they went out into the world again to new performances, new triumphs. First two con-certs at the Opera in Stockholm in October, then the Musical Society in Christiania in November, then concerts in Vienna in December and January, and finally Holland in February and March. Everywhere colossal success, tremendous applause, laurel wreaths, and all sorts of honors. From Amsterdam Grieg wrote on February 18, 1897, to his publisher: "I can tell you it's a life here! Ten sheets I could write on it. On the Dutch oysters alone, nine sheets! And on the excellence of the Dutch people twice as many. Sunday a concert of my works was given. I was among the listeners and was so often called to the platform that in the end I had to get up on a chair and make a speech. Great jubilation. I am so popular here that they ask me on the street, 'Perhaps Herr Grieg wants to know the way?' And in the shops I am met with, 'It is surely Herr Grieg with whom I have the pleasure'—etc. Saturday was a great day. Musical honors, laurel wreaths, and a rain of flowers. You should have heard *Olav Trygvason* here. At the place where you thought the end should come, cheering broke out in the middle of the music. You should have heard too the male choir in Opus 30, with Messchaert as soloist. The audience was completely elec-trified. Encores and shouting."

So run consistently the accounts of his triumphs abroad, and no doubt this is one of the reasons why he found it impossible to with-stand the temptations of the concert hall. And so he kept on steadily with his journeyings. In November-December 1897, he

was on tour in England and on this occasion was asked to Windsor
Castle to play before Queen Victoria. He gave concerts repeatedly
in Stockholm and Copenhagen, and in April 1899, with the assistance of Bergliot Ibsen and the Italian pianist Gulli, he gave a
concert in Rome once more after many years.

On September 1, 1899, with Ibsen and Björnson, he was at the
opening of the National Theater in Christiania, where at the gala
performance he conducted his music to *Sigurd Jorsalfar*. "Now I
am as a matter of fact conductor of the orchestra at the theater,"
he wrote to Beyer, "I press the buttons and make the curtain go
up and down. It's a more difficult job to manage than the music. I
had to have a private rehearsal of pressing the button with my left
hand and conducting with my right."

Immediately afterwards, he went with Nina up to Aulestad to
visit Björnson in his home for the first time. How stimulating now,
as always, was the effect on him of Björnson's positive and buoyant
nature, we see from a letter he wrote from Christiania on September 14, 1899, in which he says: "There is a glow in me of all that is
good when I think of the unforgettable days at Aulestad. It is as I
said, I have had my life framed, as it were: The home in Piperviken
(Christiania) and the home at Aulestad, that is the frame." And he
ends by saying, "Up there with you I got rid of such a huge load of
pessimistic ballast that I really believe now I shall be able to overcome the barren self-criticism that has too long repressed my art.
Yes, dear Björnson, it seems to me that the very moment we go
on one of our glorious woodland walks, the sighing of the pines
forms itself into thoughts and words.—And so: Thanks, thanks and
thanks again to you, to Caroline, and the whole Björnson conception from Nina and from your

"Edvard Grieg."

A happy event in this year was the Norwegian music festival
which, on Grieg's initiative, was held in Bergen in the summer of
1898. It is true that it entailed—like most music festivals—much
strife and bitterness because Grieg decided to invite a Dutch
orchestra to take part in the festival. As to the propriety of this
there could, of course, be different opinions. Grieg defended his
standpoint by saying that it was all the same to him whether Norwegian music was performed by Chinese, Japanese, or—Dutch!—
so long as it was *well* performed. For only when our music had the

best possible interpretation, would it really reach the people's heart, he wrote in the article with which he replied to the many and angry attacks made on him, especially by the Christiania press, on this occasion. But the main thing, the thing that is today of interest, is that the music festival was a brilliant victory, not only for Grieg, but for our young art of music as a whole. To Dr. Abraham, Grieg wrote on July 6, 1898:

"Dear Herr Doctor,

"The house is full of friends, tomorrow we are off to Hardanger, so only a few lines now to tell you how thankful I am. Grateful to the whole world! For the festival was in every respect ideal! Everyone applauded. I have never heard better performances—not even in the Gewandhaus. Everyone is rejoicing and all agree that I was right. Now they are saying in Bergen, as in Christiania, we *must* have a better orchestra. That is for me the greatest triumph!

"Yesterday I had a telegram from King Oscar, congratulating me. How much champagne has been drunk, I do not know, but in any case there is no more champagne to be found in the town. I have won wholly—I was reconciled even with Herr H. The festival was blessed by the gods, for I have not felt so well for a long time as now. The weather was and is magnificent! I have grown ten years younger—Svendsen too! All the Norwegian composers are happy, for they have achieved success!"

Of compositions, there came out in these five years two volumes of lyrical pieces, symphonic dances for full orchestra, and Norwegian folk songs for the piano, besides the *Haugtussa* already described. If in his later years Grieg cultivated so diligently the genre that in his early youth he had made a beginning with, the writing of lyrical pieces for the piano, it was not only because the short and manageable form gave expression to his intentions—without too great a strain. There was another factor, namely that these easily played and easily understood little tone poems had attained a really enormous popularity and were, therefore, it goes without saying, amongst the publishers' most coveted wares. In correspondence between composer and publisher, they are called characteristically "Semmeln" and with good reason, for they went like hot cakes. The present owner of Peters' publishing house in Leipzig relates that great joy reigned at 10 Thalstrasse every time a new volume of lyrical pieces came from Grieg. That meant a security as to the yield of which there could be no doubt, and on such days the flag was run up to the top to mark the happy event. We have some evidence that it was not always so joyful a matter for Grieg to provide the coveted wares. On July 18 he wrote to his publisher from Troldhaugen: "To my shame I must confess that once again I have been 'lyrical.' But I say now with Leporello (in Mozart's *Don Juan*) 'Ich will nicht länger 'Bäcker' sein, nein, nein, nein, nein!' Or in Heine's words: 'Ich trage weit höheres Verlangen.' But the 'Semmeln,' at any rate, taste good, that at least I may claim, not to be too modest." And on September 15 in the same year he wrote to Emil Hornemann: "About your summer, I only know that you were first near Stettin (?) and then in Espergærde, where you have been composing like grim death. So your silence will be graciously forgiven. My silence is unforgivable because, with respect be it said, I have done nothing but the so-called 'Lyrical Pieces,' which are collecting round me like lice and fleas in the country."

The set which dates from this summer is the eighth of the series and contains six pieces published under the opus number 65. "Fra Ungdomsdagene" (From Youthful Days), which opens the collection, is almost exactly like "Svundne Dage" (Vanished Days) written three years before. Here too we have a principal movement in elegiac mood, which is interrupted by a lively dance scene, after which the principal movement is repeated. The next, "Bondens Sang" (Peasant's Song) is written in quartet form and sounds like a devout, sacred air. "Tungsind" (Melancholy) and "Salon" can well be classed together under the second title. "I Balladetone" (In Ballad Style) is perhaps the best and most full of character of the pieces in the collection. The frequent breaking in of the Doric mode gives it a stamp of antiquity—like a breath from days long vanished. The collection ends brilliantly with the festive "Bryllupsdag på Troldhaugen" (Wedding-Day at Troldhaugen) which has justly become popular the world over. The piano is used in such a way as to give the executant a task which, without presenting too great difficulties, places his proficiency in the most flattering light. At the same time, Grieg paints a fresh and delightful picture which gives the most beautiful expression to his warm and rich nature as it could manifest itself on a sun-filled summer day at his dear Troldhaugen. The piece was originally called "Gratulantene kommer" (Friends Come to Congratulate Us) and only

got its present title when the proofs were corrected. It is dedicated
to Fru Nina and was presented to her as a chivalrous act of homage
on one of their wedding anniversaries.

The ninth volume of lyrical pieces, Opus 68, was written in the
summer of 1898 and contains a fresh and vigorous "Matrosenes
opsang" (Sailors' Shanty), a delicately depicted "Bestemors
menuet" (Grandmother's Minuet) which, in its slight, graceful
style and its mood reminiscent of lavender, bears a faint resemblance to the Holberg suite. "For dine Födder" (At Thy Feet) and
"Valse melancholique" are good drawing-room music. Deeper and
more personal is "Bånlåt" (Lullaby). But it is not till "Aften på
Höjfjeldet" (Evening on the Mountain) that we perceive the real
Grieg. In the simplest way, in the beginning merely through the
expression he contrives to put into the melodic line, he has cap-
tured the feeling of the high mountain world in a deeply moving
tone poem. Later it was arranged for oboe and string orchestra and
was often performed in this shape at Grieg's last concerts. From
Amsterdam he wrote in 1906 to Beyer: "But in 'Evening on the
Mountain' you were in my thoughts. It was a piece of complete
enchantment. I was carried away myself. I had seated the oboist
right behind the conductor's desk so that no one could see him. He
played so ideally, so spontaneously, so much as if he were improvising, that when the splendid, great orchestra broke in it was almost
as if it had been hypnotized into precisely the same interpretation
as the oboe's." The two other works from this time are written on
motives from Norwegian folk music. In the four symphonic
dances, Opus 64, Grieg again makes use of the large orchestra.
None of them show new sides of his talent, though in their highly
flattering and richly colored orchestration they rank amongst the
most effective things he has written. But artistically they do
not reach the standard of their nearest relations, the Norwegian
dance duets, Opus 35. Just what makes the latter complete masterpieces is lacking in the symphonic dances, they lack precision and
conciseness of form and have often, in this respect, a rhapsodical
character. The attempt at thematic development Grieg makes
here contributes to this impression. In the last of the dances it is
confined to a step by step displacement of the theme upwards,
always in new keys, a method which—so utterly unlike the treatment we know as typical of Grieg—gives the otherwise excellent
composition a conventional stamp.

In the 19 Norwegian folk tunes for piano, Opus 66, we get to know Grieg in the full strength of his genius. Although the form is compact in the utmost degree and the collection for the most part consists of a series of miniatures, yet we are here initiated into a whole world of emotions and feelings, thoughts and reflections, colors and visions which lay open for us all the most intimate traits both of the composer and of the Norwegian character.

Taking, for example, "Det var i min Ungdom" (It Was in My Youth), "Morgo ska du få gifte deg" (Tomorrow Wedded You Shall Be), "Liten va Guten" (Little Was My Boy), besides the musical cattle-calls and lullabies, one sees that they denote the highest degree of harmonic subtlety without any overstepping of bounds or taking refuge in exaggerations. At the same time, these little tone poems testify proudly to the high level of our folk art. They take us to the fountain head and they show how just were Grieg's words when in a letter he said: "No—into the mountains, into the mountains—only there is salvation." Or in other words, they tell of a musical soil in the people so rich, so suitable for everything, so fruitful and, at the same time, of so fine a nature that this work of Grieg's alone should suffice to lead us to the obvious conclusion that only in a systematic study of our folk music and in a serious cultivation of the values to be found there is there salvation and a future for the art of music in Norway. It should be obvious to all—and Grieg's life and works are irrefutable evidence of this simple fact—that Norwegian musical art must have a homestead, a soil in which it can take root and from which it can draw nourishment. If we consider this soil of Norway's, it seems infinitely rich and varied, virgin wilderness as yet almost untouched by the axe, virgin prairie scarcely marked by the plough. It should not be necessary to go prospecting from this wonderland among peoples and cultures where hundreds sit on every acre, so to speak, and struggle over such crops as an exhausted land can produce. It is this beautiful lesson Grieg teaches in the best of his works and not least in the Norwegian Folk Tunes, Opus 66. And should we open our ears and listen to his teaching, we know that no one would rejoice more over that than Grieg himself. He had tried what it meant to give in to the delusions which foreign cultures can so easily invite, and he knew the cost. In the last ten years, when illness began more and more to darken life for him, it was the rich treasures in Norwegian folk music that cast both light and warmth into his universe. Above all: it was with the help of these treasures that, to his very last year, he was able to create values which are not only among the best he has given the world, but which could sustain in him also that inner consciousness without which he could not live; that in spirit and in truth he was and would continue to be a creative Norwegian musician.

THE LAST YEARS, 1900-1907

INCREASING ILLNESS BUT CONTINUED CONCERT
TOURS—SIXTIETH BIRTHDAY

GRIEG'S health had, for a long time, been poor. Before he was forty, he contracted a chronic catarrh of the stomach which it seemed impossible to overcome. In the damp little work-hut at Troldhaugen he acquired a continually recurring rheumatism, and during all these years the least indiscretion brought on a bronchitis which often kept him weeks in bed. But now came a new plague, worse than the others: the one lung, which, after his serious illness during his student days in Leipzig, had hitherto done good service, now began to fail and the result was a shortness of breath, at times so distressing that time after time it would bring him to despair. Constant complaints over his poor health run through the letters from these years. More and more often he had to resort to sanatoria and hospitals to gain strength enough to live amongst other people again. Grieg seems to have liked particularly the Voksenkollen sanatorium near Christiania. He wrote from there to his publisher on November 21, 1900: "Before I leave this fairy castle, I must tell you how much I regret that it lies so far from Leipzig. For it is a fact—and I am in a position to say it after six weeks' stay—that no better place for bronchitis and asthma could be found. When I came here it was difficult for me to attempt any sort of slope. Now I am, in that respect, a new man."

From the same place he wrote enthusiastically to John Paulsen on December 29, 1900: "If I were a clever journalist, I would sing out the value of this place to the whole world, because it is a little fairyland, and it is not for nothing that the sanatorium has been christened Soria-Moria Castle. It is not only the gentleness of fairyland but also its harsh wildness one gets to know. Today a snowstorm is raging all round us, all is in a mist, and access is almost impossible. We live 1,600 feet above sea level and have today the feeling of being on a wild mountain."

But barely a couple of months later we meet him, sick and suffering, in Copenhagen whence he writes to Beyer on March 2, 1901, that he is down with bronchitis and has also other troubles to fight against. He says to himself: "Will you see Norway again? And if so, how? In what condition? I think my old age is coming with giant strides. I can endure nothing more and live quietly by myself awaiting what is to come. Concerts abroad are cancelled, those projected here have been postponed for the present."

A year later he wrote, also from Copenhagen, March 27, 1902: "It is ten days now since I had to go to bed and I have not once yet been allowed to go downstairs to the restaurant for dinner. But I will not be ungrateful. I am glad to escape all these parties, one every day in Easter and going on long after that. No, to study literature and music at home, that is for me the utmost—with now and again a concert or a dramatic performance. Men of large conceptions, in whose company one can learn something, those I thirst after, but—where are they to be found? All who come seeking me want something for their sick mothers or their still sicker selves. It is quite unbelievable how one is made use of, day in, day out. What Björnson says so beautifully: 'Give your strength and your deed where you nearest see need' would be splendid indeed, if there were any strength. But I have to guard myself constantly if everything is not to be merely frittered away. One person will come at 10, the next at 11, the third at 12, the fourth next day at 11, the fifth at 1 and so on. Then there are shoals of letters to write which must be composed with care, because they almost always are to be enclosed in official applications. What did Wergeland say: 'Give me a little hut and take my fame!' Obscure folk live more happily, especially in our time, when one is exploited by climbers and position-hunters more than ever before."

In August 1902, we find Grieg in the Bergen hospital trying to regain strength. He writes from there in a letter to Beyer: "At Maristuen I grew worse and worse every day. Distressed and exhausted, downcast, my brain almost going, I dared not risk the three days' journey to the East. So the idea of the hospital occurred to me and we came over there. Even by midday when we reached Husum I felt eased, at Lærdal more, and on board the *Commander* I got through the night without nightmares or breathlessness. The following day's journey by sea helped still more. Yesterday evening, Klaus Hanssen welcomed us at the hospital and I had a *splendid* night's sleep."

After having lain ill for a month in Copenhagen, he wrote on February 5, 1905, to Beyer: "I can hardly hold my pen and am unspeakably worn out. Can hardly walk across the floor. The last two days I have been up and a little better. Last night I slept for the first time without a sleeping draught. So now I begin to have some hope."

A month after he wrote on March 7, 1905, also to Beyer: "Only a few lines to testify to my existence. Since I left Bergen I have been in the hands of five doctors, but none of them have been able to—I had almost said—take my life. In other words: Things are in a bad way. Not only that I don't improve, but new things are added so that it all grows, oh, so hard to bear."

Now as always, Björnson has a powerfully stimulating influence on Grieg, it is as if Grieg were infected by his friend's buoyant view of life and his excess of energy. On January 4, 1904, we find in a letter to Beyer from Aulestad: "For the meantime we are here at Aulestad—in Paradise. It is true that there is a big flaw in our happiness. For Björnson is in bed with bronchitis. But luckily it doesn't take him so hard as it does me. He lies in there and is so good-natured and thinks only of us others. He has been in bed two days now. The last thing he did before he became ill was—to set my razor! Yes—he is in a class by himself. And he has the faculty of stimulating others. I am completely remade up here—ten years younger. Nina hardly knows me again. I let the bright sides of my nature take charge. And if you knew how much good that does! But the life up here fits me like a glove. Here there are no duties and conventions. Everyone follows his own nature. We are to stay on. Björnson absolutely insists on it. And I am more than ready to stay. I have much writing work to do and I have now an exclusive right to Björnson's wonderful workroom."

But only a fortnight later reaction sets in and he writes the day before leaving Aulestad: "The last week has been melancholy with breathlessness, want of sleep at night, and nervous weakness. Either the end is drawing near or I am going to have some years so heavy that I probably won't be able to bear them. . . . "Music must rest, in the name of all the gods," he writes. A concert tour to Russia and Finland had to be given up. "All that doesn't trouble me very much," he continues. "What goes to my inmost heart is the failing of courage for life and the thought of the last years' miserable existence."

It was in these circumstances that he began to think of going to the east country, buying a villa in the neighborhood of Christiania, and living there. He tried to persuade Beyer to do the same: "The

Westland will still remain with you as with me all the same," he wrote to Beyer in 1901. "It wakes a longing in the soul after a mysticism in nature only to be found in the Westland. And then there are the memories of childhood. So long as we can walk, ride, or drive it will draw us back on short, delightful visits. That *must* be made possible." But not long afterwards, faced with the possibility of leaving the Westland, he has come to have grave hesitations. "When I think about breaking camp for the rest of my life, something contracts internally. And that something I am not able to treat with proper coolness. Because it is twisted in with the finest roots of my heart."

The more he thought over it, the more difficult it became to make a decision. Two years after, in February 1903, he wrote to Beyer: "We are forced to fidelity to our dear Westland. Yes, yes, Næsset and Troldhaugen! We shall not desert you yet awhile. So let the first be also for me the last! I have the feeling of being more fond of Troldhaugen and Næsset, the Westland and all it bears in its lap than ever before."

The plan then was never realized, and Grieg did not forsake his Westland, even though the climate was anything but suitable for his health.

He writes very wisely to Dr. Abraham that he has evolved a kind of philosophy of health which he is trying to apply to his own life: "Just as in true music it is not a question only of crescendo and fortissimo, but also of diminuendo, so life too shows the same shading. We are done now with crescendo and fortissimo. Now we shall play diminuendo. And even a diminuendo *can* be beautiful. Nor is the thought of the coming pianissimo so unsympathetic to me, but for what is ugly in the diminuendo (suffering!) I have the greatest respect."

It is almost unbelievable that Grieg in these years, when illness time after time was on the point of breaking him down, was able to get through his many and exhausting concert tours. In January 1900, he played in Copenhagen with Fru Neruda-Hallé his three violin sonatas and was not a little proud that this experiment went so well in every respect, he wrote to Dr. Abraham. In March he gave a concert in the same place at which the Folk Songs, Opus 66, were performed. In April, he gave two concerts in Christiania, one in the National Theater with Erika Nissen and Cally Monrad as soloists, and six days later a concert, the proceeds of which were to go to a memorial for Rikard Nordraak. In October 1901, with Nina, he gave two concerts in Bergen for the same object, and as evidence of his great popularity it may be mentioned that while a collection in Bergen on May 17 for the Nordraak monument brought in only 437 kroner, Grieg's and Nina's concert produced nearly 2,000 kroner net profit. In April 1902, he gave a concert for the first time in Warsaw and was given a reception comparable only with that he had received on his first visit to London. "But what far excelled London," he wrote, "was how it piled up like a pyramid. Yes, much might be told. But you must hear at least that finally the audience, after having waited down in the entrance halls, went with me out into the streets. And the ovations were continued there with all sorts of wonderful sounds and shouts. It reminded one faintly of Ole Bull in Bergen in the old days! And how the orchestra played! That was lovely."

In the spring of 1903 he gave concerts in Warsaw, Prague, and Paris, everywhere to wildly enthusiastic audiences. In March 1904, he gave no less than eight concerts in Stockholm. Even before his arrival there, every seat for three of the concerts was sold. In between, he gave concerts both in Christiania and Copenhagen.

In October 1901, Grieg lost his only brother, John Grieg, who died under tragic circumstances. The brother's life had been anything but bright and happy. Originally destined for an artistic career, he had, for financial reasons, to turn to business to earn a living, a thing he suffered under for the rest of his days. Gerhard Schjelderup writes of him that his was a many-sided nature and that it was difficult to say where his greatest ability lay. As a boy he showed talent for drawing, and along with his musical studies he threw himself eagerly into the study of literature. He left behind him a whole volume of poems, many in German. In addition, he translated into German early in the 1860s Ibsen's *Kongsemnerne* (The Pretenders) and several of Björnson's poems. All his life he was true to music and played, as cellist and music critic, an important rôle in his native town. When the relatives were gathered together for the funeral, Edvard sat down at the piano and played Beethoven's C sharp minor sonata, his brother's best-loved piece of music. Grieg felt the tragic event deeply, as we see from a letter to John Paulsen, dated November 6, 1901: "I should have thanked you for the book long ago. But I could not, I was not able to. I am simply not a human being. . . . The leaves fall, sometimes quietly and sometimes, as here, in storm. I could wish to be a Buddhist the better to understand and sympathize with the thought of annihilation. The ideas of rest and peace should certainly be beautiful. But the Christianity we are brought up in has only a sympathetic shrug of the shoulders for the seeking soul whose way through life it has made so difficult. It will need hundreds of generations yet to free us from the yoke of Christianity. . . ."

But now too life had its bright sides and offered some happy events. On June 15, 1903, Grieg celebrated his sixtieth birthday with great festivities which lasted for several days. There was a reception at Troldhaugen, an excursion to Flöien, festival concerts where Grieg and Halvorsen conducted the National Theater orchestra which had come from Christiania for the occasion, folk concerts in the open air and, of course, banquets with endless speeches. But what shed the greatest glory over these days, which were blessed, moreover, with the most heavenly beautiful weather, was that Björnson for the first time paid a visit to Troldhaugen on this occasion, and made the speech in Grieg's honor at the banquet in the evening.

It was no ordinary oration, Grieg says in a letter to his publisher, and we must agree with him there. It was, indeed, so far from a festival oration that when we read it today we realize that it needed a Björnson's impressive and fascinating personality behind it in order to be construed as such. It was a magnificent historico-psychological survey of the Norwegian people and Norwegian nature, wrote Grieg, and that is true enough, but what makes it questionable as a festival oration is, in a word, that it sets out to show us our weaknesses and arraign us for them—especially that we do not set ourselves the *far goal*.

Out of these dangerous waters Björnson, however, steered his festival oration safely and beautifully to land. In an exceptionally brilliant address he showed the intimate connection between Grieg's music and the Norwegian landscape. He described his journey from the East over to the Westland as he came along Rauma down into Romsdal, and he painted a marvellous picture of the scene that met him. "Over the mountain plateau comes water, there come rivers, there come rivulets, there come threads of water, the very slenderest. But without ceasing! The spray is thrown back like a delicate bridal veil. I saw some headlong brooklets that had not gone many fathoms before they became at variance and so split into two—and then, if you please, the two parts split again! I saw water in masses, waterfalls which fell from ledge to ledge to ledge to ledge. There was a rushing—a leaping in it all! There has never been a madder youthful ardor than in what I saw." He had to think back to the time when he felt that Grieg's pictures in melody stopped too abruptly, they were too short. He wanted then to have that put right, but now he saw that it was exactly like the Norwegian landscape. He went on to say that Grieg had got more into tune with nature and man's life than anyone else among us. Psychologically he had got a little bit further in. . . . He had brought Norwegian feelings and an impression of Norwegian life into every music-loving home the world over. In the concert halls where the nations sit together in the great light of art there was Norway in the midst of them. Björnson ended his speech with the words: "Yes, it is grand—what you have won for us out there, but it is as nothing to what you have won here at home in the taking of our finest and highest emotions and giving them us again as illumined and as near ideal perfection as you could make them. Finally: This I say because I think it is so—if one would measure a great man one must measure not only what he has done but also what he *has made possible!*"

A festival oration it was indeed and, in addition, a sound, serious, and warning address—worthy of Edvard Grieg upon his day of honor.

LAST ROMANCES AND PIANO PIECES

THE winter of 1900 Grieg spent in Copenhagen and wrote there his last romances, ten songs, Opus 69 and Opus 70, to verses by Otto Benzon.

Naturally, in his treatment of these Danish poems Grieg gave up his national characteristics. Nevertheless, we may marvel at the freshness and versatility of his genius and the striving towards a revival to which the best of the songs bear witness. "Der gynger en Båd på Bölge" (A Boat on the Waves is Rocking) with its rocking movement in the piano, its fresh youthful feeling and its splendidly built up climax must be counted among Grieg's most effective songs. "Til min Dreng" (To My Boy) is charming in its feeling—full of tenderness, archness, and humor. "Ved Moders Grav" (At Mother's Grave) Grieg himself seems to have thought highly of. In a letter to Lammers he wrote of it: "I meant it to have the sound of an Amati violin—or better, violoncello. Somber—moving." If it seems to us today already a little passé, it is again principally the text that is to blame.

"Snegl, Snegl!" (Snail, Snail!) requires an interpretive artist with imagination if it is to be effective, taking rise as it does more from reflection than direct experience. In these songs too, Wagner's influence is visible—it can be seen most clearly in "Drömme" (Dreams) which could hardly have come into existence without help from the German master. Much the same may be said of "Eros," but this song is far more personally felt and experienced, although it is planned to make its effect through external and superficial devices and an extravagant pathos and breadth which are unlike Grieg otherwise. "Jeg lever et Liv i Længsel" (I Live a Life of Longing) is one of the songs in the collection that Grieg seems himself to have rated highly, since he wrote to Lammers that he hoped he would like it "with all its wild, concealed passion and pathos." "Lys Nat" (Light Night) and "Se dig for" (Take Care!) are both rather commonplace, even though fine and full of feeling. Of "Digtervise" (Poet's Song) which concludes the collection, Grieg wrote to Lammers: "But the 'Digtervise' above all is the one for you. That about sitting up in Olympus and scoffing at the Philistines down below, that is exactly the thing for you." But from Grieg's music we get the impression that all the jovial mockery and grim humor are a little strained, at which we are not surprised when we see how the poet has given expression to his thoughts.

That Lammers found difficulty in making this poetry his own, even with Grieg's music to help him, is shown in a letter of September 1, 1904, in which Grieg, while making some suggestions for a concert programme, writes: "And among the songs with piano if possible *something* new at least. For example, Benzon's 'Poet's Song' but mind, only if it has become flesh and blood with you. For on one thing we can agree at once: it must go *con amore* or to the devil with it altogether." Even by this time it does not seem difficult to foresee that posterity will choose the latter alternative.

In the summer of 1901 Grieg wrote at Troldhaugen the last volume of the lyrical pieces, Opus 71, which he dedicated to Fru Mien Röntgen. Perhaps that is the reason why in the first piece, "Der var engang" (Once upon a Time), he adopts a motive from Swedish folk music. Fru Röntgen was a Swede. This piece too is built up in the same manner as many described before, since on the background of an elegiac principal theme from a Swedish folk tune, strongly reminiscent of "Ack, Värmeland du sköna" (Oh, Värmeland Thou Beautiful) there is inserted an allegro in Norwegian spring dance rhythm. In a richly colored dance scene there is conjured up yet once more the gay joyfulness of youthful days— in hurrying chase, as in a vision—and we are again back in the fundamental elegiac mood. In the two nature pictures, "Sommeraften" (Summer Evening) and "Skogstilhed" (Forest Stillness) we meet Grieg again with eyes turned to the south, and though they contain many fine features which we recognize as genuine Grieg, they do not give in their somewhat cold peacefulness any satisfactory expression to Grieg's vehement delight in nature. A true inspiration, amongst the best of its kind, is "Småtrold" (Little Trolls), rhythmically and harmonically as brilliant as it is original. The collection includes besides a "Halling" (Fling Dance) and a little tone poem "Forbi" (All Is Over) in which Grieg's rich use of chromatics once more scores a triumph. With "Efterklang" (Echo) he gives his lyrical pieces a charming ending. From "Arietta," the very first piece he wrote in his early youth, he has built up now with great dexterity a fine and graceful little waltz which, after a series of delicate but most effective modulations, slowly dies away.

When Grieg, in letters to his publisher, asserted so positively that this was the *last* volume of lyrical pieces and that this genre must not be repeated any more, events were to prove him mistaken. Five years later he gave out yet another volume of piano pieces, *Stemninger* (Moods) Opus 73, which can only be regarded as an eleventh volume of the lyrical pieces. But if we except the wonderful treatment of a folk tune from Valdres, the six other pieces show that Grieg's judgment was sound when he decided that the genre should not be pursued any further. He expressed this himself in a letter to Matthison-Hansen, dated Troldhaugen, August 29, 1905, in which he wrote: "I cannot manage to get back my strength, and feel a hundred years old at least! Nevertheless, I have hauled and dragged at Pegasus' mouth so much that he had to get going. But the result with me was as Emil Hornemann in his time said of Johan Selmer after the performance of 'The Spirit of the North.' He said, 'The mountain shook and brought forth a mouse.' " And my mouse is, moreover, a very little one, so small you need spectacles to see it. It is only a volume of piano pieces to throw into the maw of Mammon. It is to be a bait to Peters in Leipzig to make him print two orchestral scores without a murmur. But through this 'mouse' I have realized for the first time that I have grown old. Pegasus had to be treated in a very special way merely to make him docile enough to move at all. There are a couple of year-old Norwegian pieces that I like, otherwise it is not my heart's blood that has flowed here."

FOLK DANCES

JUST after he had finished the last volume of lyrical pieces, Grieg had a letter from one of the first fiddlers in Telemark, Knut Dale, asking if Grieg could not do something to ensure that the old folk dances should be preserved. In the letter Knut Dale pointed out that he (Dale) was now the only person who had learnt from Möllarguten himself and when he was gone the tunes also would be gone. Those played now were in every respect different, wrote Dale. It is because of that letter that we are today the happy possessors of some of the most beautiful, most fantastic and original works that piano music can show.

Grieg welcomed the suggestion gladly. Knut Dale was sent in to Christiania where Johan Halvorsen took down seventeen tunes for the fiddle, which Grieg later adapted for the piano. On November 21, Halvorsen wrote to Grieg: "I shall be more than happy to put the fiddle tunes on paper! I have wanted to do it for many years. Send Knut Dale in here at once if possible! I take it that he is the right person."

On November 8 Halvorsen wrote: "I am expecting Knut Dale any day now," and on November 17: "Knut Dale has come. Today we rescued two tunes from oblivion. It is not so easy to write them down. There are small turns and trills in them like a trout in a rapid—when you try to get hold of them they are off. Knut Dale is an intelligent and sound fiddler. Now and again he had some rhythmic turns, a blending of two-fourths and six-eighths time that made me laugh aloud with delight—and that does not happen often. He seems to have many dances in his storehouse. I must have him here for a fortnight or three weeks. He sends greetings and thanks for the money."

In a letter of November 25, Halvorsen wrote as follows: "Divinely genuine are the fiddle dances and you will find many things to rejoice your heart. I should so much like to play them for you before you begin to transcribe them. There are certain rhythmic turns that cannot be recorded. Some splendid wedding marches are good enough to eat. Also 'Tussebrurefærda på Vossevangen' (Bridal Procession of the Gnomes on Vossevangen). Knut Dale is a capital fellow. Exceedingly modest and clever. He is delighted that the tunes will be preserved. When I take the fiddle from him and play it, his eyes shine with a musician's delight."

On December 3, Halvorsen sent the seventeen recorded fiddle dances and wrote the following letter: "Dear Grieg! I am sending with this the result of Knut Dale's stay in Christiania. I hope you will find something you like. I have tried to put everything down as carefully as possible. Repetitions there are in plenty, but that is very easy to put right. As regards the key, there is one curious feature—that G sharp is almost always used (at the beginning of the D major tunes). Not till towards the end (on the deeper strings) comes G. For myself, I find the G sharp fresh and delightful where G would have been insipid. Then there were the trills and the grace notes. These trills are the soul and adornment of the fiddle dances together with the rhythm. They are produced often by only a vibration of the hand and give the effect of a kind of 'quivering.' An exception is the trill on the open A which sounds out clear and fresh. I noticed that even the most complicated grace notes or trills did not take away in the slightest from the rhythmic lines of the tunes. I am practicing every day on the Haring fiddle[1] and have managed to achieve not a little of the 'real thing.' A fiddle like that chuckles and chatters and whines and quivers. And how beautiful it can sound, for example, Möllarguten's wedding march. Of the walking dances I think 'Skuldalsbruri' takes the prize. I ought to get hold of Sjur Helgeland and Ole Moe and all the rest of them now that I have begun the job."

In a letter dated Troldhaugen, December 6, 1901, Grieg sent his thanks for the tunes. "This is what I call a real Saturday night, dear Halvorsen. Outside a storm from the south is thundering, shaking the house, and on top of it a proper deluge is pouring down from Heaven. But in the sitting room it is cosy. I have just received your tunes for the fiddle and have this moment finished reading them through, chuckling inwardly with delight. But at the same time, I have been raging and burning over not being a player of the fiddle. How I do hate that Conservatory in Leipzig!— But to business: Those 'singularities' you speak of regarding G sharp in D major was what used to send the blood running wildly and madly in my veins in the year 1871. Naturally, I stole it at once in my folk-life pictures. That note is something for the re-

---

[1] The Haring fiddle (Hardanger fiddle) is a special sort of violin with two sets of strings, the lower set continuously sounding like the drone bass.

search worker. The augmented fourth can also be heard in peasants' songs. They are revenants from some old scale or other. But which? Incomprehensible that no one among us takes up research in our national music, since in our folk music we have such rich wellsprings for those who have ears to hear, hearts to feel, and understanding to write down. At present I am feeling as if it would be a sin to adapt the tunes for the piano. But that sin I shall come to commit sooner or later. It is too tempting. I send the heartiest thanks for your work, which has given me a very great happiness, and the future will show that you have done more than that. It won't be before summer that I can get down to them. Would you like me, when the time comes, to place both your work and mine with Peters?"

It would seem from letters to Beyer that Grieg first began on the folk dances in August 1902, and that the work occasioned him much trouble. "It interests me tremendously," he wrote, "but it is a hell of a job. Why? Well, because I have grown more critical than before in the direction of keeping the style correct. Here is quite another kind of difficulty than in the treatment of Lindeman, that of deciding what is to be kept of what was originally noted down for the violin, having regard to the lower part." And later in the letter he wrote of the tunes, "How easy it is to take the flavor from them! Truly it is a question here of having kept unimpaired one's most delicate sensibilities."

Not till the end of February 1903 had he finished his work and could send the folk dances for printing. In a foreword, he explained his personal view of the material, giving at the same time an account of the principles he had followed in his adaptation. He writes here:

Those who have a feeling for these harmonies will be carried away by their great originality, their blending of pure and delicate grace with bold strength and untamed wildness in regard to melody and still more to rhythm. They bear the mark of an imagination as audacious as bizarre, these relics from a time when the Norwegian peasant culture was isolated in remote mountain valleys from the world without and, precisely because of this isolation, preserved all its originality. My task in arranging the tunes for the piano was to attempt through what I might call stylized harmonizing to raise up this folk music to the plane of art. It is in the nature of the matter that the piano must relinquish many of the small adornments that have their foundation in the character of the Hardanger fiddle and the peculiarities of its bowing. As an offset, the piano has the great advantage that through dynamic and rhythmic versatility and through new harmonizing of repeats it is able to avoid too great a monotony. I have striven to draw clear, easily followed lines and, above all, to create a concise form. The few places where I have thought it artistically right to build further on the motives in question can easily be detected by comparing my adaptation with the first record taken down by Johan Halvorsen (published at the same time by the same publishing house), which is to be regarded as the original score. Although the folk dances sound on the Hardanger fiddle a minor third higher, I have decided, so as to get a more satisfactory effect on the piano, to keep to the key in which the original was taken down.

Of all the Norwegian folk music Grieg has taken up for artistic treatment, this is the most individual, that which stands most sharply in contrast to ordinary European musical feeling in respect both to harmony and rhythm. In the treatment of this material a composer would be helpless, even though he had acquired all the technical ability which the study of the whole of European art-music could give him. This was a question of a folk art which could show methodical cultivation and point towards values bearing witness to an unusually highly developed and refined musical culture. But it was, at the same time, a folk art which had never been the subject of conscious *theoretical study*. No one understood its laws—hardly anything was even *known* of them. In other words, an art which demanded that *instinctive sureness of perception* which was precisely Grieg's strength. With the most highly sharpened sensibility he seems here to feel his way in to the very wellhead, the mystic source of the creative faculty in Norwegian music. Without taking from it anything of its own special characteristics he lifts it up in the glorified light of art-music and makes its exclusive values accessible to all. There is no question here of mere "transference" as he himself modestly calls it. It is a free rewriting, rather, with holdfast in the given material. Never has his genius revealed itself more richly or more characteristically than with this process, never has his own complex, schismatic and yet so monumental creative ability come to expression in a more comprehensive and arresting way. Look only at "Giböens bruremarsj" (Giböen's Wedding March) which opens the collection, how all the resources of the modern piano have been exploited in its re-creating. Or "Jon Vestafæs springdans" in its tripartite form, in which each part shows the material in a new light as it were, and which develops and unfolds itself in pure sound to rise finally to an unbelievable greatness and power. In "Bruremarsj fra Telemark" (Wedding March from Telemark) (No. 3) we meet a harmony so bold and a leading of tonal lines so ruthless in its uncontrollable impetus towards freedom that it seems on the point of bursting the tonal frame and starting out into atonality's anarchistic realm. And yet what colorful charm, what harmonic delicacy, even tenderness! In "Haugelåt" (Dance of the Gnomes) and "Rötnamsknut" (Rötnam's Hill) Grieg builds up a transition movement in the same way as he did earlier in, for example, the Norwegian dances and some of the quartets for male voices. He introduces a tranquillo by carrying the theme in augmented notes over into the minor and brings out a whole world of beautiful and characteristic harmonies. Not least must we admire the expression and the character he succeeds in putting into a simple accessory part. "Gangar efter Möllarguten" (Walking-Dance after Möllarguten) (No. 6) and the second of "Knut Luråsen's Hallinger" (Flings) afford splendid material for the study of extreme rhythmic differentiation. Those who have had the good fortune to hear Grieg's own interpretation of these folk dance tunes found the experience unforgettable. Has any artist ever succeeded in giving expression to a virile, living, buoyant and yet extremely *subtle* rhythmic feeling more richly and convincingly than Grieg?

Last, "Möllarguten's Wedding March" must be mentioned— last, because involuntarily one shrinks back at the thought of attempting to describe in words the meeting between these two geniuses in Norwegian music, these two geniuses who in spite of all external unlikeness in outward circumstances yet, broadly speaking, experienced in their inmost being the same fate. That which is fundamental to and lies at the core of our creative ability, that which in its abundance could mirror both heaven and earth, which could, indeed, in occasional blessed moments give the intoxicated tone poet the feeling that he had the power to bring *heaven itself down upon earth*, this rich and beautiful faculty was in modern culture without the means of expression which could render its treasures available for all—all! That was Möllarguten's tragedy, and that was Edvard Grieg's tragedy. Is it perhaps because of this that we perceive in Grieg a matchless delicacy and devotion when he takes up Möllarguten's own tragic wedding march? "According to a well known fiddler in Telemark, this march was composed by Möllarguten when his sweetheart, Kari, jilted him to marry another," a footnote says. Eight times the same motive is repeated, merely set off with new decorations. Grieg's harmonic treatment gives us the sensation of penetrating steadily deeper and deeper into the material, as he seems continually to uncover new strata until at last we seem to perceive the living, vibrating nerve—the very spirit of tone poetry. And there is peace and sublimity in his treatment, there is purity and, perhaps above all, dignity. Only once does Grieg weave an elegiac line into the harmonic web in which pain threatens to break through, before he goes over into the classically pure coda in which quiet resignation is beautifully expressed.

Has tragic fate been anywhere expressed with more sublimity and dignity than by Möllarguten and Grieg in combination? Involuntarily we remember Grieg's comment on the Norwegian national character in his autobiographical notes to Finck, where he writes: "The deeper the movements of the spirit are, the more reserved and enigmatical the expression should be." And further: "It was considered brutal to show one's best feelings. As to these the expression is as concise as it is chaste." Especially against the background of the genius displayed in his harmonic treatment of the folk dance tunes do we understand his words when he writes: "The kingdom of harmony was always my dream world, and my harmonic way of feeling was always a mystery to myself. I have found that the obscure depth in our folk music results from its unguessed harmonic possibilities. In my treatment of folk tunes, Opus 66 and elsewhere, I have tried to give expression to my guess at the hidden harmonies of our folk tunes."

But it has been with the folk dances as with "Taken into the Mountains" and the Vinje songs: it is only the very few who are capable of giving them exact and complete artistic expression. Our numerous professional pianists do not seem to have a sense for this exquisite and aristocratic piano art. Otherwise it is inexplicable that these treasures which it ought to be our dear duty to keep alive for our people should, year after year, lie unused. We shall hear more fully later of Grieg's own interpretation and we shall hear also of his great delight and rapture when finally, in the last year of his life, he met a pianist who was able to give his dear folk dance tunes adequate expression.

THE DREYFUS AFFAIR—POLITICAL AND SOCIAL INTERESTS

THAT Grieg was an excellent letter writer the reader will already have realized vividly. In shoals of letters to correspondents at home and abroad he writes at length on his views of nature and mankind, on art and artists and in addition on political, social, and religious questions. When at some future time there is published the fullest possible edition of Grieg's letters, they will help to complete the picture of his rich and complicated personality, his keen powers of observation, and sensitive intelligence. Besides the already printed collections of letters to Frants Beyer, Julius Röntgen, Dr. Abraham, and the letters to various correspondents which Gunnar Hauch has published, there are many letters to Iver Holter, Thorvald Lammers, Johan Halvorsen, the editor O. Thommessen, the Utne family, and several others, which have not yet been published, but which have most kindly been placed at the disposal of the author. One of the things that impresses one most in reading these letters is Grieg's warm love for his fatherland and the interest with which he followed our people's political development, which be it said he always regarded as intimately connected with the life of the spirit. And we have frequent proof that he was an attentive observer of the great world movements. Almost startling is a remark in a letter to Beyer on the occasion of the death of Kaiser Wilhelm I in which he forecasts, as it were, the social revolution. The letter is dated Leipzig, March 21, 1888, and he writes: "It is quite touching to see how the Germans to all appearances cling to their royal house. But I say to myself: Don't you believe it. And just wait; the future will show that I am right. It is from this country that revolution against iron repression will come, since no other country suffers under it to the same degree as Germany. The moment must come when the poor people simply cannot pay their taxes and then the play will begin; but that will not happen till despair cries aloud, for it is unbelievable how servile and well disciplined the people are. It seems to me that wherever I look, at home or abroad, political interests merge into mere humbug, discord and squabbling and exaggeration, so that one turns away from it all—to the Jotunheim!"

The same feeling as to deep and growing national unrest he expresses ten years later in a letter to Dr. Abraham, September 30, 1898, where he writes: "I have just read that the old lovable Queen Louise of Denmark is dead, a more peaceful death certainly than that of the Empress Elizabeth of Austria. What do you say to that? It is assuredly more than a way of speaking to say that we are dancing on a volcano. What a pity that you cannot read Prince Kropotkin's letter to Georg Brandes in *Politiken* in Copenhagen. The letter was indeed written in French but, alas, translated into Danish. One thing in the letter is worth remarking. He says: When the higher and highest strata of society have no hesitation in butchering thousands—nay hundreds of thousands—of peasants and workers to obtain the peaceful and comfortable conditions these highest grades of society desire for themselves, how can one wonder if this utterly and entirely unenlightened social stratum turns the tables and says: 'I do not care whom I strike down of the higher grade. That will give people something to think of and then perhaps the better conditions we hope for will come at last.' Kropotkin considers that the one is as bad as the other. But enlightenment must begin some time: So first recognized butchery from above must be discontinued. Utopia! isn't it? But believe me: Other times *will* come. Through blood or intelligence! Through the latter it is to be hoped."

Grieg had his lively sense of justice to thank that, very much against his will, he was in a way mixed up in the Dreyfus affair in France. Greatly disturbed over the result of the case, he refused, in September 1899, an invitation to conduct a concert of his own works at the Châtelet Theater in Paris. In his answer he wrote to Colonne that after the outcome of the Dreyfus case he could not bring himself to come to France. "Like all other non-Frenchmen, I am shocked at the injustice in your country and do not feel myself able to enter into any relation whatsoever with the French public."

When Grieg wrote that answer to Colonne he was at Aulestad on a visit to Björnson, whose son-in-law, Albert Langen, translated his letter into French. To Langen's request that he be allowed to publish the letter in a German newspaper, Grieg at first answered No, but when in the course of conservation he asked Langen if he thought such publication could do any good and was answered: "Yes, undoubtedly!" he agreed to the publication. The result was that all the great European newspapers quoted Grieg's letter and he had the whole of official France on top of him. He duly received threatening and libellous letters, some anonymous, some signed, and when, a few months later, it got about that he was to write a great work, *Peace*, to Björnson's poem, destined for performance at the world exhibition in Paris in 1900, the French newspapers lifted up their voices and said: Let him look out! And when the English newspapers remarked that by all accounts France meant for a time to boycott Grieg as Wagner in his day was boycotted, Grieg remarked with his characteristic humorous self-irony that the comparison was no doubt flattering, but he hoped all the same that the English were mistaken.

A few months later he had a letter from de Greef telling him that he had played Grieg's piano concerto at Lyons. As a result he had received threatening letters and the police had to be ordered to the concert hall to prevent a scandalous scene. But the concerto went well and at the end there was tremendous applause. "But when things go so far with a mere interpreter, how would it be with the old man himself?" wrote Grieg in a letter.

This he experienced three years later when he was again proposed as conductor in Paris and was invited to come. Even before he arrived the newspapers had called for demonstrations and when on April 19, 1903, he mounted to the conductor's desk in the Châtelet Theater, which was packed from floor to ceiling, he was received with hissing, shouts, and general hubbub. "Now I have achieved the honor of being hissed off the stage," he wrote to Johan Halvorsen. "I was prepared for anything, since the press had been calling for demonstrations. But in the morning I had taken five drops of opium (on the advice of the Danish Professor Rosving) which had such a brilliant effect that I was perfectly calm. When I came in, the applause, in spite of hissing, was so tremendous that I had to bow again and again. But when I turned towards the orchestra to begin, the hissing and shouting '*A la porte,*' '*des excuses*' and from above most amusingly '*Pas encore! Pas encore!*' in chorus in the rhythm of the Troll King's Daughter) got so uncontrollable that I had to put down the baton, step down, and wait quietly to see what would happen. There was a wild fight, but the whole thing was drowned in the most tremendous applause, while meantime the worst disturbers of the peace were thrown out by a *trebled* police force. When peace had been restored for a moment, I went up to the desk again but, good Lord! if they didn't begin again. But now I had had enough of it. The thing was not to let the shouting get started. I gave an energetic sign to the orchestra and as the overture 'In Autumn' fortunately begins *ff*, the situation was saved." The concert went on with steadily increasing sympathy from the audience. Ellen Gulbranson and Pugno took part as soloists. Finally came the *Peer Gynt* suite. "It produces the same infallible effect on every audience," writes Grieg, "by the end of the first movement, great applause. After 'Åse's Death,' prolonged cheering. After 'Anitras Dance,' ditto and so mixed with *bis, bis* that I had to repeat it. After 'The Hall of the Dovre-King' complete madness. I came on to the platform four or five times, but that wasn't enough. So that had to be repeated also. And afterwards ovations such as—they say here—no French composer has ever had. . . . The proudest moment was when Nina and I were about to get into the carriage which was to drive us home. Because it was surrounded by a trebled cordon of police! It was a great comedy! But the press the day after—such fury over the great success! Anything more despicable I have seldom seen. There were some noble critics, among them Gabriel Fauré in *Le Figaro*, but as a whole it was mud-slinging and had nothing to do with musical criticism."

So Grieg experienced the triumph of art over politics and was strengthened in the opinion he expressed in the midst of the worst attacks that "right always continues to be right," since in 1906 he witnessed the complete establishment of Dreyfus' innocence and his obtaining the reparation for which Zola, Björnson, and Grieg had been the most ardent fighters.

From his earliest youth Grieg had been a zealous republican and it is natural, therefore, that in the battles in Norway about the Union with Sweden he was always to be found on the extreme left. This too was one of the reasons why he always had a grudge against Christiania—that nest of Tories, as he called it. Remarks in letters to Iver Holter, Jonas Lie, O. Thommesen and others show his standpoint clearly.

After he had written one of his songs in the service of political agitation, we find the following purely radical standpoint in a letter to Dr. Abraham, dated Meran, Schloss Labers, May 3, 1893: "The last day in Mentone I wrote a song for male voices which is to be sung on our Independence Day, May 17. Our honorable, free Con-

Edvard and Nina Grieg in 1904

stitution, which the Swedes will no longer respect, requires that every Norwegian according to his ability should rush to help. It is shameful to see what lying telegrams the Swedes are sending out to the world. They reckon with the ignorance of foreign countries as to the real facts of the case and so they deliberately misrepresent the truth. Today I read that in Sweden 'recourse must unfortunately be had to suspending the Constitution.' What? *Our* Constitution, which we have not received as a gift from Sweden, but which we have made ourselves and with the help of which we have steadily advanced and prospered, this it should be in the power of another nation simply to suspend? That is an impossibility. And if Europe should allow it, I will not die of my bad stomach but either with a pistol in my hand—a musket is, unfortunately, too heavy for me—or what I should like much less, in captivity. Truly Ibsen was justified when he wrote his pessimistic masterpieces, if the Norwegian people have sunk so deep that they will not as one man drive the enemy out of the country."

But the Norwegian people were not standing ready like *one* man to drive the enemy out of the country. Not at least for the time being. In fact, so little unanimity was there that it was sometimes difficult to get a choir to sing a song intended to stimulate feeling for freedom and independence. A letter Grieg wrote to Lammers on January 12, 1894, shows this: "It is no good any longer singing 'I am from Norway and I am good.'[1] For if these so-called singers will not take up an out and out patriotic song, they are neither from Norway, nor are they good. I will not recognize them as Norwegians and much less as 'good' Norwegians. But don't let us see ghosts in broad daylight! Such an occurrence is surely unthinkable. The conservatives you have in your choir will not let themselves be ruled by 'the Swedish sword!' I feel sure that the song will be rendered with great strength and tenderness. It is these two contrasting qualities in the song which give it relief, contrasting qualities which, joined together, I call love of the fatherland."

In 1894 Grieg was asked to conduct two concerts of his own works at Stockholm. How he received this invitation we see from a letter to Lammers of January 12, 1894: "I have also had an invitation from the court theatrical director in Stockholm to conduct

---

[1] The opening stanza in Selmer's "Tollekniven" (The Sheath Knife), one of Lammers' most popular concert numbers.

two concerts there. I do not need to tell you what I answered! It only wanted that! The asses!"

Two years later he had again an invitation from Stockholm and this time he accepted. In a letter to Lammers of March 6, 1896, he explained his altered standpoint: "Well, this is a nice sort of muddle we have got into. Soon the whole nation will be asleep. Let us artists at least keep awake. It is unquestionably our mission to keep alive the national feeling and God knows that is needed now. I was before too furiously angry to give my art to the Swedes (I was asked to). But now I have changed my tune because I feel it is a duty to undertake in this way a 'promenade' to Stockholm in the new conditions. If nothing unforeseen happens, I will risk it in autumn. Werenskiold and Thaulow have for a couple of years been pioneers here and I admire them for it, though so far as Werenskiold is concerned, at any rate, it did not come about without a struggle."

In Stockholm, Grieg received so hearty a welcome and his music was performed by orchestra, choir, and soloists with such warmth and understanding that he was quite taken by storm. At a banquet at the Grand Hotel after the concert there were, of course, speeches made in his honor to which he replied. "I must say they came spontaneously and well just after the splendid performance of 'Ja, vi elsker'[2] (Yes, We Love the Land that Towers). Wonderful moment to hear these words from these throats. But this I tell you: That nothing will make me believe any more in hatred between peoples, for the people's wish is towards good understanding, that is the very strong impression I received."

We see from a letter he wrote only a few months later, February 21, from Amsterdam to O. Thommessen, the editor, that in spite of all the warm understanding which met him in Stockholm, Grieg did not therefore "go into the service of Sweden" as he once feared Christiania was ready to do. "Here there is a capacity for enthusiasm one does not often find. On the first evening at the choir rehearsal of *Olav Trygvason* (three to four hundred people), the piece was received with almost southern excitement. And when I came up on to the conductor's place and let my glance glide over the great gathering—then my Norwegian heart was touched!

[2] Norwegian national anthem with words by Björnson and music by Nordraak.

Everyone—ladies, gentlemen—had small Norwegian (pure)[3] flags on their breasts! I had already lifted the baton when I saw it but was so moved that I had to lower it again and say a few words. More cheering. But listen now: The day after came a letter from a Dutchman suffering from Swedish influenza, who is a teacher of the Swedish language here, in which he called upon the conductor of these concerts to make a public apology for this scandalous insult towards Sweden. Yes, he shall have his apology—You bet he will! The same man stated recently in a paper here that 'Yes, We Love the Land That Towers' was stolen from a Swedish-Finnish poet of the name of Runeberg. I had already written a protest that had beak and claws. But so well is Norwegian literature known here—the Dutchmen stole a march upon me! And the editor announced later that there was a steady stream of protests. The gentleman in question, naturally, sings small now, but if he dares the slightest word of remonstrance he shall have a broadside and I will use the opportunity to tell the Dutch what this 'Man schreibt uns aus Stockholm' of which the European papers are full really amounts to. There is good soil here for an understanding of Norwegian independence. Naturally! The nation which put up the famous fight against Spain to which its folk songs still bear witness, and the nation which at last since 1830 has become itself, knows through the eloquent facts of experience how to appreciate our struggle."

As the political situation came gradually to a crisis, we see from Grieg's correspondence with what vivid interest he followed the development of events. In 1905 there is hardly a letter from him in which political events are not discussed at length. On June 7, Grieg was the first to telegraph congratulations to the Prime Minister, Michelsen, and after the Karlstad agreement he wrote him the following letter:

"Dear Prime Minister Michelsen:

"Let me be one of the first to congratulate you and thank you as warmly as any Norwegian can. You know better than I how much work and self-denial have been put into this Karlstad convention. But I will take leave, as a man of today, to say that twice as many frontier fortresses would not have been too great a sacrifice for

---

[3] The "pure" flag was the one from which the sign of union with Sweden had been removed.

Norwegian independence. My instinct for the ideal rejoices. For the spirit of the future and of progress hangs over this work.

"Hearty greetings and sleep well,

"Yours,

"Edvard Grieg."

After the processional entry of the King and after having conducted some of his works—among them "Landsighting"—at the Festival Concert of the Musical Society, Grieg wrote a letter to Beyer on September 12, 1905, which shows how stimulating and cheering the whole thing had been to him: "There were thousands of things I meant to write to you about. Don't know where to begin or end and naturally forget what I wanted most to say. First and foremost in my thoughts is that old Norway is saved. We older ones can feel nothing but gratitude that we have lived to see it. And admiration. The more I think about it all, the more astounded I am that it is true. As I go up the hill towards the palace I stand still in a dream over the King's banner floating so splendidly up there on the palace, over the sentries, over the lively, cheerful movement in everything. It has actually become warmer, cosier to be here. I have been, as I think you have too at bottom, a republican from my youth up, but I do not doubt for a moment that considering the circumstances the right course has been chosen here."

The successful development of political events was also the occasion for Grieg's beginning to keep a diary. At the festival performance in the National Theater on November 28 when *Sigurd Jorsalfar* was given, Grieg and Björnson were called to the royal box and presented to the King and Queen. "I felt this first meeting with a free Norway's first King and Queen as something beautiful and significant and therefore chose this day to begin the long planned diary," wrote Grieg in his first entry.

On December 31 he finishes his diary with the following words: "Now passes the year 1905, the great year, to its rest, and I part from it in deep thankfulness that I lived to see it! And yet: without the youthful dreams which this year made realities, my art would not have had its right background. Longings have formed personality in music. Had June 7 come in my youth, what then? No. It is best as it is. The long life-struggle for the individual as for the nation has been the greatest good fortune. Freedom, that is: the fight for freedom."

Seldom has an artist been so loaded with distinctions and honors as Edvard Grieg. But with his fresh and liberal outlook, both on art and mankind, he was not able to receive all this homage with suitable reverence and solemnity. He was good-natured enough to accept a string of orders—both at home and abroad—he was given the Grand Cross of the Order of St. Olav—but he never *wore* any of his orders; it would have been contrary to his nature, he declared that he would simply feel like a monkey if he showed himself with an order on his breast. When he was awarded the French Legion of Honor and a friend wrote to congratulate him, Grieg replied: "Thanks very much for your friendly congratulations. My being named as a member of the French Legion of Honor is, however, an 'honor' which I share with 'legions' so let us waste no more words on it." When after his great success in Amsterdam in 1897 he was awarded two Dutch orders, he wrote to his publisher: "As you know me you will understand that I was overjoyed. The two orders lie very nicely in my trunk. The customs officers are always very amiable when they see things like that." Even his title of "doctor" he found it difficult to take seriously—he was "doctor honoris causa" of the Universities of both Cambridge (1893) and Oxford (1906). The pianist, Oscar Meyer, relates that Grieg had laughingly flung out his hand when he called him "Herr Doktor."

The honors which came from academies and institutes of art, on the other hand, really did give Grieg great pleasure. In 1872 he was made a member of the Swedish Academy, in 1883 the Academy in Leyden appointed him corresponding member, in 1890 he was elected to the French academy, and in 1897 to the Academy of Art in Berlin.

BESIDES the already discussed letters on music to *Bergens-posten* from Bayreuth in 1876 and an article on Halvdan Kierulf in *Musikalisches Wochenblatt* for January 1879, Grieg published three essays on music. The first, on Schumann, is to be found in *The Century Illustrated Monthly Magazine*, New York and London, for January 1894; the second, on Mozart, in the same journal for November 1897, and the third, on Verdi, in *The Nineteenth Century*, London, March 1901.

The first two essays must be regarded rather as apologia than as real appraisals. Grieg goes vigorously to war against the Wagner-smitten musicians who permit themselves a shrug of the shoulders over the beloved masters of his youth. He criticizes especially those conductors who rehearse most carefully the work of Wagner, while often producing a Mozart opera hurriedly and carelessly. Today it seems strange that it should have been necessary for Grieg to appear as defender of Mozart, for example. But those who think back only twenty to twenty-five years will realize that there was justification enough. Remember, it was the time of great orchestras. Realistic programme music, rendered possible mainly by Berlioz and Wagner, set its mark both on concert hall and opera. And it was difficult in the midst of all the loud-voiced declamation, the shrill, charlatanic propaganda, to win a willing ear for a Mozart's delicate, lucid, rococo art or a Schumann's sensitive, romantic mind. But reaction will come some day, said Grieg, and Wagner will get his due and Mozart his. Wagner's works too it will one day be possible to regard from a distance and judge historically, and only then will it be seen whether Wagner, in spite of changing times, will stand as high as Mozart. When in 1906 Grieg was asked to write an article on the occasion of the 150th anniversary of Mozart's birth, he wrote in his diary for January 14: "Have had a request by telegram to write a Mozart article for the master's 150th anniversay, January 26. I have two days to write it in. The article must be sent on Monday morning at latest as it must be out on Friday, the 19th. I thought of Falstaff: What is honor? For this is undeniably an enormous honor, that from

Mozart's own town I, a far away Northerner, am asked to do what a hundred others could do. But I remembered Falstaff's philosophy of life and telegraphed: Yes! Now we shall see. This means two days at my desk. I shall lock my door and do my best. Good God! Life is so short! What happiness to be allowed to do reverence to my immortal master, the beloved of my youth, Mozart, in his own Vienna!"

A Norwegian pianist, who had studied in Germany, had come home and made his début with Schumann's A minor concerto, brings forth from Grieg the following reflections in his diary: "And now even Germany has travelled so far from sound nature that her modern performers produce pure caricatures of her own masters. So bad has been the effect of the art of the Wagnerians (herein comprising Bülow) on present-day musicians that they feel all music in a Wagnerian (I say advisedly not Wagner) manner in the sense that they cannot create or render four bars in the same tempo. But that was not Schumann's intention. He wanted to have his music rendered in the tempo indicated without any attempt being made to improve it. Why cannot a passage marked tranquillo be rendered so that its *character* is quiet while the tempo remains essentially the same? With Bülow at the head, everything must be exaggerated nowadays where the piano is concerned, thanks to the above-named school. The first and part of the second parts of Schumann's A minor concerto, rendered as they were rendered yesterday, should make the noble master turn in his grave. It was like one of these indiarubber faces drawn out on all sides till unrecognizable. It was like the music of a drunken man. It reeled and raved—it didn't walk. Allegro became presto and passages quiet in character adagio, the splendid harmonies in the ensemble were scarcely heard at all, they were so hurried over. Though there is a sure tradition here. Schumann died in 1856, I came to Leipzig in 1858 and a few months later heard Clara Schumann play the concerto, and every tempo stands indelibly marked in my soul. Such youthful impressions do not lie. The brain is soft as wax to receive them and what is stamped on it remains for life."

Of the two great contemporaries, Tschaikovsky and Brahms, it is clear that the first stood nearest Grieg's heart. After having met Tschaikovsky in Leipzig in 1888, Grieg wrote to Beyer on January 29: "In Tschaikovsky I have acquired a warm friend of my art. He has as much sympathy for me as I for him, both as artist and man." Of the *Symphonie Pathétique* he says in a letter to August Winding, December 13, 1895: "You speak of Tschaikovsky's *Symphonie Pathétique*? And God help you if you have not rejoiced in it! Is it not remarkable! Though I have to use my powers of reflection to understand the unity in the whole work, yet all four movements have genius. It is so wholly Tschaikovsky and so altogether masterly."

When a bust of Grieg was to be set up in the foyer of the Gewandhaus in Leipzig on the occasion of his sixtieth birthday, Grieg wrote to his publisher: "How is the bust getting on? Has it been put up beside Reinecke? It only wanted that! Well, it would at least be a reconciliation in marble! Very significant for our mutual relations. But I hope I may have the luck to stand near my honored friend, Tschaikovsky. He is a master after my own heart."

To understand Grieg's remark about Reinecke it must be explained that, when a pupil at the Leipzig Conservatory, Grieg had already reacted against Reinecke's stiff-necked, conservative attitude, the same that manifested itself all through his thirty years' activities as conductor in the Gewandhaus, as many a young composer was made to feel. Grieg's German biographer, Richard Stein, relates that when Grieg had written his piano concerto he submitted the manuscript to Reinecke in the hope that perhaps the work might be produced in the Gewandhaus. After having waited for a very long time, he finally called on Reinecke to see if in this way he could get to know the fate of his work. He was received very amiably and Reinecke conversed for a long time with his former pupil. But the piano concerto was returned to Grieg without a word having been said about it in the course of conversation!

But to return to Tschaikovsky. If Grieg felt a warm sympathy for his Russian colleague, both as man and artist, Tschaikovsky's letters show that the feeling was in a high degree reciprocal. He describes his first impression of Grieg in the following manner: "Into the room came a very little, middle-aged man, very thin and with shoulders of unequal height. His fair hair was brushed back high and he had a thin, almost youthful-looking, beard, also side whiskers. The features of this man, who so instantly won my sympathy, were not in themselves specially striking, they are neither beautiful nor exceptional. But on the other hand, he had uncommonly attractive blue eyes of medium size, irresistibly fascinating, like the gaze of an innocent, noble child. I rejoiced to the depths of my soul when it appeared on our being introduced that this person who drew me so strangely was a musician and none other than he who with his deeply felt notes had long since conquered my heart. It was Edvard Grieg." In another letter, Tschaikovsky wrote: "Grieg and his wife are so droll, sympathetic, interesting, and original that it is impossible to describe it in a letter."

In Grieg's diary for December 31, 1905, we find the following remark: "Have read much in Peter Tschaikovsky's *Life and Letters of Modest Tschaikovsky*, English edition. What a noble and genuine personality. And what a melancholy pleasure to continue in this way the personal acquaintanceship of the unforgettable Leipzig days of 1888. It is as though a friend were talking with me."

To Beyer Grieg wrote on January 6, 1906: "I am struggling in the evenings with an English book: Tschaikovsky's *Life and Letters*. It goes to my very soul. Often it seems as though I were looking into my own. There is so much I recognize from myself. He is melancholic—almost to madness. He is a fine and good man but —an unhappy man. The last I did not think when I met him some time ago. But so it is; one has either oneself or others to contend with."

His admiration for Brahms was more reserved. In a letter to Finck, Grieg blames him for seeming to undervalue Brahms and at the same time expresses his own opinion of the German master in a way as poetical as felicitous: "For me there is, as regards Brahms, no doubt whatever. A landscape, torn asunder by clouds and mists, where I can perceive towns with ruins of old churches and also of Greek temples—that is Brahms! But this placing him absolutely by the side of Bach and Beethoven is for me as ununderstandable as the tendency to reduce him to the absurd. The great must be allowed to be great and a comparison with other great ones is not and never will be permissible." On another occasion he writes to Finck: "Schumann is the *poet*, there he forms a contrast to his greatest disciple, Brahms, who in every line—even in his songs—is the *musician*."

While staying in Leipzig in January 1896, at the same time as Brahms, Grieg wrote to Beyer: "I do not understand why so one-sided—I mean in his greatness one-sided—a nature as Brahms can have sympathy for my art, which so far as I can see goes in a very different direction. But sparing in words as he is, he showed me that he had it. His 4th Symphony in E minor was performed in the Gewandhaus, a work I did not know before and which has a first movement that is amongst the most beautiful things he has written."

In December of the same year, Grieg gave a concert for the first time in Vienna and while there he was much with Brahms. "It was a wonderful sensation for me when I went with Grieg up the well known stair in Carlsgasse," Röntgen relates. Brahms received them with great cordiality. They lunched with him at his favorite restaurant, Der rote Igel, and in the evening went together to the concert. Brahms sat with Grieg on the platform and here Grieg for the first time made the acquaintance of a Viennese audience. Grieg's own concert was a sensational success. The cheering was interminable and the people of Vienna excelled themselves in enthusiasm. At a celebration in the hotel afterwards, Grieg made a speech for Brahms so warm and beautiful that all were deeply moved. "Not a word on his own triumph, with which we were all so enraptured, passed his lips," says Röntgen. "Brahms listened with bowed head and when Grieg had finished, he got up, went to him and pressed his hand without saying a word."

To Beyer Grieg wrote on December 27, 1896, about Brahms: "Ill as he now is, poor fellow, he has been exceedingly kind to us. While I was ill he came personally three times to enquire how I was and at the orchestral concert he was present all through, from first to last, a thing he never does in these later years; he was even with us at a social gathering in the hotel after the concert. This gives my stay in Vienna its greatest value, because though I may not be such a very great admirer of the latest Brahms, I am so much the more an admirer of the earliest. Above all, he is Germany's greatest, perhaps, alas! her only really great man in our days."

On April 4 Grieg wrote to his publisher: "*Brahms is dead*. Now the critics have their work cut out for them to take his measure. He can be glad. He had not outlived himself and he died without suffering. How poor Germany has now become in music!"

This view of the future of German music Grieg held till his death. He thought that with Brahms the last of what was really great in German music had gone. As regards Richard Strauss, for example, there was only one work of his, *Tod und Verklärung*, which had his complete sympathy.

In his diary for January 13 he wrote as follows: "Have just come from the general rehearsal at the theater concert and was moved to tears over *Tod und Verklärung*. Why, why did not Strauss continue to build further in this, which is the way of poetry, instead of going over to what is the way of sensationalism and empty virtuosity? No conjuror's art with the orchestra can make up to us for want of inspiration and imagination." He was so carried away by this work of Strauss that after the concert he sent the composer a greeting by telegraph. The letter he received from Strauss on this occasion, after a long wait, led to the following reflections in the diary: "One can speak of concealed enemies as of concealed fifths. They are hidden here under the garments of courtesy. But it is certain that if Strauss had had a grain of sympathy for me he had the opportunity here to express it. Though far be it from me to imply or expect anything of the kind. My art lies so infinitely far from his that I dare not reckon on his understanding. Obviously I cannot compare myself with a master like Strauss in the kingdom of technique, but as there are other things in art than virtuosity, one might hope to find in a Richard Strauss an awareness of that fact, if it were not that the representatives of the small countries have the priceless advantage over those of the great, that we, the small, who must know everything, acquire a wider horizon than they who are stuck right in the middle of their own one-sided culture. Therefore, I have better chances to understand what is of significance in Strauss than he has to see what may possibly be good in me."

Of *Also sprach Zarathustra* Grieg wrote to his publisher: "I have just been reading the score of *Also sprach Zarathustra*. But the future does not lie there. This is not music. Only a fiery play of sound and technique." And after having heard several of Strauss' songs in London he notes in his diary on May 15, 1906: "They did not please me, however much I wished that they should." *Salome*, which he heard in Berlin under the personal conductorship of the composer, produced the following strong comments in a letter to Beyer: "Yes—Good Lord, you should have heard it! There is something of 'the great harlot' of Revelation in it. It is the evangel of decadence, in spite of a technique which is a thing of genius. I would still take my hat off if I knew it was written with conviction. But the pinch is here. A doubt insinuates itself that sensation is what is aimed at. And then the thing becomes criminal at once. How has the art of music fallen into such error? Wagner is pure

Mozart in comparison with this. For the people who fill the house night after night it's a case of 'the Emperor's new clothes.' I don't understand what they feel, since I, who listen with two musical ears, am so nearly driven mad that I long to run out as fast as I can."

In the same letter we hear Grieg's opinion of the other big man in German music, Max Reger: "Just come home from lunch at Hinrichsen's [Peters] where I met one of the modern 'famous,' even suddenly famous, German composers, Max Reger, who serves us up a mash of turnips and sausages for the first course and plum pudding for the second. The strange thing is that Julius has fallen for him. He is indeed accommodating. Yet I like, as you know, his liberal and advanced outlook and have my own strivings in the same direction! But here I cry off."

In a letter to Röntgen, June 21, 1906, he gives in detail his reasons for this dislike of Reger. He says here: "Your admiration for Reger is bound up with your 'German-ness' ['Deutschheit']. Peters has sent me a piano quintet of his which is so warped that *I* at least cannot assimilate it. I have always regarded polyphony as a *means*, not as an *end*. So it is with the great masters; there polyphony and homophony harmonize most beautifully. That is and always will be my ideal. That Wagner's arrogant lengthiness should be brought even into chamber music! To impress by means of length is really too cheap! Or through complication either! But perhaps I understand simply nothing because I am a Norwegian, that may be the secret. What is to come now will not be, God knows, the complicated stuff! I am ready to take my oath on it! And with that I conclude."

When in Holland he had heard Mien and Julius Röntgen play Reger's variations on a theme of Beethoven's for two pianos, he noted in his diary for May 8, 1906: "That this music is acclaimed in Germany as genius is a sad sign of decadence. It is leaden, heavy constipation—nothing else! It is outrageous to thrust oneself forward at the expense of sound nature. I am liberal to the uttermost and do not judge after the first hearing. But here I make an exception, for this pretentious stuff made me furious. What is technique except a means? And what sort of technique is this? Congested with polyphony, lacking light and air. What is the good of a solitary gleam in this desert?"

Speaking generally, Grieg considered that German music after Wagner should rest for a time as a meadow must rest before it can again give good growth, as he puts it in an interview in *Berliner Lokal-Anzeiger* in April 1907. The future will show if he was right.

Was Grieg, then, what is called conservative? Had he not the ability to look ahead, to follow the development of music as it manifested itself at the furthest outposts? Most assuredly he had! But we must remember that his reaction against certain phenomena in German music dated right back from his student period in Leipzig and followed him all through his life. The reason for the seriousness of his reaction here was probably that the German school, German technique, the German spirit in music, in spite of all he owed them, had not been able to release the powers that lay bound *deepest* in his nature. And when Grieg, in spite of his very limited acquaintanceship with French music, showed his sympathy, in words warmer than he had ever employed in the case of German music, his German biographer, Herr Stein, had no right to interpret it as if Grieg had grovelled before the Frenchmen. He had no reason to do so. Quite the contrary. In the case of Debussy, for example, we know that he had reason rather to do precisely the opposite. Against the background of Debussy's almost blackguardly article after the concert in Paris in 1903, it is of interest to hear what Grieg wrote in his diary after a performance of *L'Après-midi d'un faune* at the National Theater in 1906, interesting because it shows both the fineness of his nature and his wideawakeness. On December 8 he wrote in his diary: "To learn to know Debussy was indeed for a Feinschmecker the real Schmaus. There is genius in the orchestral web he weaves. Wonderful harmony, severed from all tradition, but genuine and felt—though exaggerated. As the experiment of a personality created for it, I find these things in the highest degree remarkable. But no school should be formed on these lines. Unfortunately, that is precisely what will happen, as here there is just something for the professional copyists to imitate."

To Johan Halvorsen he wrote, after the concert: "Thanks for our last meeting! And thanks again. Both because you played Debussy and because you did it so that I should have liked to hug you for it."

In a letter to Röntgen of February 6, 1907, he described the performance in the following words: "Have I written to you about the performance here of Debussy's orchestral work *L'Après-midi d'un faune*? Extravagant music, but very full of talent and to me ten times more sympathetic than the New-German plum pudding."

When Peters' publishing house in 1905 had decided to produce the orchestral score of Bizet's opera, *Carmen*, Grieg wrote to Herr Hinrichsen: "When is the score of *Carmen* coming out? I am looking forward to it like a child and I hope I shall live to see the publication." When he had got the score he wrote: "I must thank you especially for the *Carmen* score. A real work of art is there accomplished! I can't let it out of my hands. What a masterpiece! How one admires anew, in studying the score, its clarity and lucidity! If only I had got to know it thirty years earlier!"

No—there were other and much more deep-lying reasons for Grieg's sympathy with French music than those Herr Stein imputes to him. These were above all the qualities he so admired in Bizet—clarity and lucidity in respect to style—qualities which he loved also in Mozart. Further, the plastic, concise, and concentrated form which has distinguished French music from Couperin and Rameau to Debussy. And last, but not least, the *delight in color* it expresses, a quality Grieg could only very occasionally find in German music. May not his reserved attitude towards Brahms for instance be due principally to the want of this element? We must remember that Grieg, from the time he began to reflect over the problem of technique, suffered infinitely from the feeling of having stuck fast, of being fettered, the feeling of being left with material matchless in its richness which he could not find the technique to express. Even in his "stipendium" report to the government after his second journey to Rome in 1869-1870, Grieg drew attention to the fact that "it is of the greatest importance for a Norwegian musician who has received his elementary education in Germany to have his ideas clarified by a later stay in Italy and purified of the narrowness that sees no other source of renewal than the study of German music. A dweller in the North has in his national character so much that is heavy and self-conscious, and this is not really counter-balanced by the *exclusive* study of German art." And almost forty years later he expressed the same view. In his diary for January 20, 1907, we find the following reflections on the problem of technique: "Jeremiads might be written on our art conditions which force the young out to Germany *at too early an age*, or rather, too early a stage of development. All of us have become spoiled by the German sentimentality, which is far removed from our Norwegian nature. The Norwegian artist nature is still capable of producing naïve, sound, single-minded art if only it is shaped out of the national disposition and not out of the foreign."

Whether a transference of the field of study from Germany to France would have been as beneficial and fruitful for Norwegian music as it has been for Norwegian painting it is now difficult to say. That Grieg was no stranger to the thought his open letter to the French musicians, published in the *Figaro*, clearly shows—the confession which roused such wrath in his German biographer, Richard H. Stein. If we take away what is exaggerated in the article, it shows, nevertheless, that Grieg looked to the French school in music as the one which could help us to set free much of the powerful stuff that still lies locked up in Norwegian music. The article runs thus:

Allow me to use this opportunity to say aloud and plainly a word about the debt of gratitude Norwegian musicians owe to French music. No doubt the same is the case with all the other nations, but we in the far North are in a special position in this respect. We are north-Teutons and in common with the Teutons have a tendency to dreaminess and melancholy. But we do not, like that race, feel the desire to pour out our souls in broad rivers of words; we have always cared only for what was clear and pregnant. Therefore, it is hardly profitable for our young composers to intoxicate themselves in the color orgies of the modern German romantic school and try to equip themselves with the technical weapons of this school as well as its breadth of form and architecture. They will have only the greater difficulties when they try to break away from all that to find characteristic expression for their own individual and national personality. And it is just at this critical moment that a study of French music will help them to find their way back to themselves. It is French art, with its light, charming, and vivid composition, with its crystal clearness which saves the Northern tone poet. . . . The Norwegian artist who has learned the secret of expressing what is in his heart will never forget that it is France which has taught him this secret and therefore we cherish a real and deep sympathy for the artists of France.

Of his Norwegian colleagues, Grieg felt himself most drawn to Johan Svendsen. Under the section "Christiania Period" the relationship between Grieg and Svendsen has been described in detail and will therefore be supplemented here only by one or two separate remarks of Grieg's. After having described his own great difficulties with the work of composition, Grieg wrote on December 20, 1882, to Matthison-Hansen: "This is perhaps a suitable occasion to speak of my great countryman who has precisely all that I have not. He is in my opinion the greatest *artist* (as opposed to *poet*) that the North possesses and one of the few great spirits in Europe. It astonishes me, therefore, that you pass over something so important in so few words. Was Svendsen really celebrated chiefly as a conductor? If so, one can only say that the Danish musicians have let themselves be imposed upon by his brilliant ability in this direction. For he is every bit as good a composer (inventor, formalist, instrumentalist) as he is a conductor, but his power here is greater." When in 1895 a new conductor was to be appointed to the Gewandhaus in Leipzig, Grieg wrote to his publisher: "I should be very glad if Nikisch were to be the new man in the Gewandhaus, but still more glad if they chose Svendsen. Nikisch is not German either and as a conductor I place Svendsen at least as high."

As is well known, Svendsen, after he had been appointed conductor at the Royal Theater in Copenhagen at forty-three, composed only one work, *Andante funèbre*. Grieg kept on hoping that he would produce a third symphony, he speaks of it several times in letters to Dr. Abraham. But, alas, he had to wait in vain. In 1896 he wrote to Björnson, who had asked Svendsen to write music to *The King* and had received no answer: "I weep inwardly when I think what he is and what he might have been with his splendid talent. One can say of the Norwegian character what Peer Gynt said of Our Lord: 'He may be a very fine fellow but—a good manager, that he is not.' It is terrible what Norway loses because so many of its best people behave like madmen towards themselves. It is the something untamable in us that defeats its own ends. But to compensate we have material from which people may be made and which we will some day try thankfully to develop."

Towards performers Grieg was not, as a rule, very merciful. Pianists he often gave a good drubbing and female singers put him almost always in such a rage that he used really abusive language in speaking of them. And the source of his irritation was that he almost always got the impression that they thought first of themselves and second of art. A couple of random extracts from his diary will make this clear. On the occasion of a Norwegian woman singer's concert he wrote on January 7, 1906: "Here for example is one of these highly gifted ones who have no greater joy than knowingly and willfully to do precisely the opposite of realizing the composer's intentions. Why? To be original—to be sensational." And after he has gone through the whole gamut of her sins comes the following conclusion. "What are prima donnas? They are the quintessence of vanity, stupidity, ignorance, and dilettantism. I hate the whole lot of them. 'And your wife too?' it will be objected. But I answer: 'Excuse me, she is fortunately not —a prima donna.' "

In January 1907 he wrote of another Norwegian singer after having first, from the purely vocal point of view, described her voice which, in spite of everything, had kept its good quality: "But what has all this to do with the solution of the problem under consideration: the singing of ballads? Unfortunately that has never been her gift and never will be, in spite of all her will power. To see a face that always expresses something quite other than the substance of what she is singing makes one desperate. We learn from her that the art of singing romances is something by itself. It is good if it can include also bel canto. But this bel canto alone, isolated as here, is no use at all. And then this eternal sameness, these false rhythms, and this clear, yes but vulgar, articulation. It was a misery. . . . This I call dilettantism. And that is its right name even though the person concerned imagines herself to be the world's first artist! (Nor is she so far from it, alas!) She is a real master in one thing—in managing to achieve a success by the skin of her teeth. After the most feeble applause an extra number or a da capo. Oh, you prima donnas! I say, as Ole Bull did about the directors of the theater in Bergen: 'May the devil pickle them!' "

When in Amsterdam Grieg had played accompaniments to twelve of his ballads for Julia Culp, he noted in his diary May 1, 1908: "She sings them with much talent but, as a whole, there is too much gloom and monotony for me. And to that is added an insufferable complacency which I notice more and more. Of course, she is a singer. Ergo, first herself—and then her art! I had hoped, after the description of her, for an exception. But no—it was the rule. I have said it so often and I repeat it. I hate the whole lot of them, famous or not famous—perhaps the famous ones most!"

All the greater was his joy and delight when occasionally he met a woman singer to whom he could accord his full admiration. On February 19, 1907, he noted in his diary: "Last night Madame Cahier. At last! A splendid singer. Great art, excellent technique. And all infused with soul. She could express everything. No—there is no dividing line between lyric and dramatic. Ballad and stage presentation must have both. But—woe is me! I forgot that I hate all female singers! Hate turned to admiration and sympathy. And naturally, not a trace of the prima donna! Let herself go naturally and straightforwardly. She was gifted enough for that."

After having heard Teresa Carreño play Chopin's E minor concerto in the Gewandhaus, Grieg wrote to August Winding: "The devil take these virtuosos with their improvements. In the first part of the concerto she decided to play the passages more slowly, so élan was wiped clean out, and in the finale she suddenly made up her mind to take the second theme more slowly still. That sort of thing should be punished. And then she boasted of it. That was the worst of all. But then I told her what I thought and added, 'Nun, Chopin ist ja todt, er hört es nicht!' What Weingartner says of tempo-rubato conductors applies equally well to executive artists. They all suffer from virtuoso—or self-complacency—sickness. And yet Fru C. is so sweet a personality it vexes me that she should be infected."

A foreign pianist who was to play his piano concerto brings forth the following general pronouncement in Grieg's diary for April 4, 1907: "These soloists!—they should be exterminated. They should be used to stamp each other out. A pack of egoists. First themselves—then art!"

Nevertheless it was an executive artist who with his deep understanding perhaps did most to bring sunshine and warmth into Grieg's last years. After having met Percy Grainger in London he noted in his diary for May 21, 1906: "Finally Percy Grainger played two of the folk dances most brilliantly. Yes—he has genius—that is certain enough. I am happy to have won a young friend like this." On May 24, the entry in his diary reads: "But I missed Joh. Wolf and the splendid Percy Grainger who turned the pages for me at the concert and whom I love almost as if he were a young woman. It is a dangerous thing to be very greatly admired, but when one admires in return as I do here, the one balances the other. I have never met anyone who understands me as he does. And he is from Australia. What about the way the critics have blamed me for my music being too Norwegian! Stupidity, ignorance it is and nothing more." How intensely he rejoiced in this understanding is shown also in his letters to his publisher, Herr Hinrichsen, where he says that "in my present condition the memory of these performances has the effect of the sun breaking through the clouds."

THE last two winters Grieg lived in Christiania, where he stayed at the Hotel Westminster from September 1905 to April 1906 and from October 1906 to March 1907. That hotel life with all the unrest that goes with it did not suit him is apparent both from his letters and his diary. It was certainly anything but good for his delicate constitution and his extremely sensitive nerves. Added to all were the annoyances that a famous artist living in an hotel room in Christiania in our days is of necessity exposed to and against which it was difficult for him to guard himself. Even the letters, which increased in numbers month by month and which he tried conscientiously to answer; and the people of all kinds who came to see him on the most unbelievable errands, most of them probably to ask his help and make use of his great name and influence! "The hotel is a perfect exchange where the doors swing from morning till night," he wrote to Beyer. "Even if they are told 'not at home' there are plenty of them who consider themselves privileged to go in all the same." In another letter he wrote: "Sometimes I feel a sudden longing to be a troll on a mountain top and let everything go to the devil. Look at Svendsen, for example. I have often thought: Should I take him as my model? He never by any chance answers a letter. If I had not a growing horror of seeming ostentatious I would announce in the foreign newspapers that I must be excused, that neither my time nor my health, and so on and so forth. Liszt did that once and, tempting as it is to do it too, the very fact that a great man like Liszt did it is a reason for my *not* doing it. The reason I waste so many words on this subject is really that I am borne down by the oppression of it if I don't complain of my fate to a friend now and again!"

The least noise or commotion from his neighbors disturbed him also—sensitive as he now was—put him off his sleep, and in the end upset his nerves altogether. He moved up to the Holmenkollen sanatorium to get away from the bustle of the hotel and, if possible, get rest and sleep. But in vain. In the diary for March 19, 1906, he notes: "Have just got home after a fortnight's stay at Holmenkollen Sanatorium. It did not answer its purpose. I had poor nights—with breathlessness and hallucinations. One thing my stay there

has taught me. I cannot live at a height, and that piece of knowledge will be of use to me when I come to live in Christiania in
autumn as I have now definitely decided to do."

Yet he took on engagements for concerts abroad, to appear as
conductor, solo player, and accompanist. That he did not start on
his concert tours in a happy frame of mind an entry in his diary
for March 19, 1906, shows: "A great mountain in the form of a
concert tour to Prague, Amsterdam, London lies before me and
obstructs the view to the glorious quiet time I dream of. Will this
tour be my last? And shall I end my life out there? Dark apprehen-
sions obscure my outlook. But I shall not complain. I shall go
thankfully, wherever the end may be. Though God knows my
choice would be to lay myself down to rest at home!"

Before he began his journey he gave a concert at the Hals
Brothers on March 21, 1906, assisted by Fröken Borghild Bryhn,
later Borghild Langaard, who made her début on this occasion.
This proved to be Grieg's last concert in Christiania. From his
diary it appears that he looked on this concert mainly as a trial of
what he was able to do in the way of public piano playing, since his
breathlessness had so increased. He was astonished himself at how
well he got through it, indeed Nina thought that he had *never*
played so well, he writes in his diary, and this gave him courage for
the coming concert tour. But there is bound to be a dark spot in
everything and the dark spot now was that the folk dances, which
he played in public for the first time on this occasion, were not received with the warmth and understanding he had expected and
had good reason to expect from his countrymen. It is not without
bitterness that he notes in his diary after the concert: "What disappointed me was that the folk dances did not take as they should
and ought. I played them with all the love and witchery I was
capable of. But—the people at home here are not with me where
my development has now led me and that is hard to bear. Here
they are all holding to my youthful standpoint, which on appropriate occasions is lauded at the expense of my present one.
But—I mustn't let that hinder me. If only I may continue to develop so long as I live. That is my greatest desire. The understanding of the public will come when the time is ripe."

It was not only the general public but the Norwegian musicians
also who greatly lacked understanding, as Grieg discovered when
six months later he heard a Norwegian pianist play some of the folk

dances. In his diary for October 3, 1906, he writes: "When he played 'Folk Dances,' 'Dance of the Gnomes,' and 'Bridal Procession of the Gnomes' my teeth were set on edge. Why in all the world does Percy Grainger, an Australian, play these things perfectly in rhythm and modulation while a Norwegian cannot grasp either? It's quite the wrong way round."

This is why he was filled with such profound gratitude towards Percy Grainger who not only gave the folk dances a magnificent rendering but who, in youthful enthusiasm, made propaganda for them in foreign countries. In an entry in his diary of May 30, 1906, Grieg writes in greater detail about Grainger's rendering of the folk dances and goes on to say: "There is no Norwegian at present who can touch him. And that is significant in more than one respect. It shows both that we do not yet possess a Norwegian pianist who has understanding enough to grapple with such tasks as that, and that though understanding is not found where it should be found, in our own country, it can be found abroad, yes—even in Australia, where the wonderful Percy Grainger was born. All this talk about its being necessary to be a Norwegian in order to understand Norwegian music and especially to perform it is so much twaddle. Music that counts, however national it may be, is yet lifted high up above the purely national level."

What delighted Grieg even more perhaps was that he heard from Paris that the folk dances had been discovered by the young musicians, who were in raptures over them, had indeed gone crazy over "the new Grieg," he writes to his publisher. "I tell you this," he adds, "because it really has pleased me very much and because I feel very sure that you will share my happiness. Youth—that is the future. Nothing is more certain than that."

But to go back to the concert in Christiania. Joy over its successful result was short-lived. After having repeated the same concert in the Calmeyergaten Mission House before a full house, he notes in his diary for March 30: "Reaction set in as I feared. Asthma, sleeplessness, with breathlessness, and the most dreadful hallucinations left me with but one wish: Away, away from it all. No one knows how little existence is worth in such suffering. No one understands that there is then only one friend to be found— death."

Yet he began his tour and left Christiania on April 5. The day after he noted in his diary: "During the night at Göteborg such an alarming attack of asthma, breathlessness, and hallucinations that I thought of going back home. But went on to Copenhagen where in the Hotel Bristol I had, thank God, a good sleep." The tour went on through Berlin and Leipzig to Prague, where at the concert on April 16 he was received with such extreme enthusiasm that at last he had to appear in his greatcoat to induce the audience to go away.

After the concert in Amsterdam he was filled with gratitude over his warm reception and the brilliant artistic result. "I must say, over and over again, like Vinje: 'More have I had than I deserved,' " he wrote in his diary, "A good star shone over the whole concert last night." Of Fridtjof Backer-Gröndahl, who played the piano concerto, he said that "he takes everyone by storm with his magnificent art, his noble and modest character."

After yet one more concert in Amsterdam, along with Julia Culp and Casals, with whom he played the cello sonata and whom he designates "an incomparable, a great, great artist," he went on to London where in May he gave a series of concerts, this time too to crowded houses and with tremendous enthusiasm on the part of the public. The homeward journey was through Copenhagen and Christiania and at last, on June 21, he was again at Troldhaugen.

Summer did not, unfortunately, bring the so intensely longed for rest and peace. His diary shows how he suffered from steadily increasing breathlessness and sleeplessness. He tried a trip up to Myrdal with Frants Beyer, but the result was—complete inability to sleep. After an interval of about three weeks he notes in his diary for July 31: "All the time since I have been greatly depressed. Continual breathlessness (though fortunately without hallucinations) and on top of this a wretched rheumatism. And that in spite of a week's magnificent weather, about 22 degrees Reaumur in the shade. No—Troldhaugen—indeed the whole Westland—is a passion that costs me dear, for it takes my life. But—the Westland gave me life, enthusiasm for life, the voice to reproduce it in music. The gift has been a loan only. I must pay it back again when that is required of me. If only I could take the step, tear myself away from Troldhaugen, and live the rest of my days in the dry air I need. But I have not the heart for that. I blame myself for my sentimentality, and yet, there must be something real in it, since it is unshakeable and sits there demanding its rights."

In August he had a welcome visit from Adolf Brodsky and his wife, who came from England for the sole purpose of paying their respects to Grieg. In the diary we see how stimulating had been the effect on him, he even slept better during this time. But hardly are these dear friends gone before reaction sets in. "The strung up nerves must slacken again. It is a damnable process," he writes in his journal.

It is hardly believable that Grieg at this period should have had the strength to write some of his most beautiful and deeply inspired work, the chorales for mixed choir a capella, Opus 74, his last work. Three of them were composed this summer at Troldhaugen while the fourth or, more rightly, the first was finished in the autumn at the Hotel Westminster in Christiania. In the diary, September 15, he noted: "Finished three chorales for mixed choir and soloists, a free adaptation from Lindeman's Norwegian Folk Songs. They are so beautiful, these melodies, that they deserve to be preserved in artistic clothing. This small piece of work is the only thing my wretched health has permitted me through all the summer months. This feeling: 'I could, but I cannot' makes one desperate. I fight in vain against heavy odds and must soon give in altogether." To Beyer he wrote on December 2 from Christiania: "Yesterday I finished the fourth chorale, 'How Fair is Thy Face,' and if there wasn't so much writing I should copy it out for you. There is something fine and touching about it, something I think that you will like. I hope it will sound well. I should like to have a try at string instruments. But it is a mistake to talk of what one wants to do, even to one's best friend, for then I am superstitious enough to expect to find a lion in the path."

The religious element is strongly represented in many of Grieg's works, intimately bound up as it is with his feeling for nature and his conception of nature as a whole. In nature he saw the divine and through nature he felt his connection with the divine wellhead and source of all things. To illustrate his religious awe and delight in nature it is enough to refer to the slow movement in the piano concerto and some parts of the Ballad, besides many songs, among them several of the Vinje songs. To Beyer Grieg wrote in the summer of 1905: "For me, mystery always prevented simple joyfulness taking the upper hand. The free life I could rejoice over inwardly. But Nature herself? Before her I stood in silent veneration and awe as before God Himself."

It is very seldom that Grieg touches in his letters on religious topics and in the diary we find religious questions mentioned only once. That is in an entry on November 1, 1906: "Björnson was with me at dinner the day before yesterday at Advocate Helliesen's. At coffee time he began to talk about the idea of immortality and a long conversation ensued, in which Björnson naturally was the chief speaker and defended his standpoint, but in which the others, especially the hostess, took part. As a Unitarian I stand near Björnson, but his conception of God is not quite clear to me. Primitive force, yes—very well. But behind its inexorable manifestations—cause and effect—which often appear like the work of an evil demon, to be able to see a great love, that is the great art, the great problem and the great division between many free-born, truth-seeking people. The fine thing about Björnson is the great tolerance that leavens all he says. Of this we should all be studious. For what we do not know—that know we not."

Only a few days before his death he wrote to a friend in Switzerland in a letter dated Bergen Hospital, August 28, 1907: "To express my views on religious questions I need better health than I now have. And yet—not many words are needed. During a visit to England in 1888 I was very much impressed by Unitarian opinions (trust in God alone—belief in a three-in-one God and in a son co-equal with Him is barred) and in the nineteen years that have passed since then I have stood by this conclusion. Pure science? As a means, excellent, but as an end—at least for me—utterly unsatisfying. The conception of God I must maintain, even though it so often comes into collision with the conception of prayer."

Yet one last time it is Norwegian folk music which liberates the powers lying fettered in his nature. Yet one last time this is the means through which Grieg can make known to us an inner richness, inner beauty and strength. Yet one last time it is the meeting with the Norwegian folk-soul with all its hidden powers which, so to speak, forces out the most beautiful and richest flowers of Grieg's art. Even when compared with the chief works of his most vigorous creative period, the four chorales show a heightening of artistic power, a greater depth in subject, a yet more many-sided elucidation of the material, a greater subtlety and complexity of the means of expression. These are religious meditations which in individuality and originality are without parallel in church music.

The most remarkable in every respect is "Guds Sön har gjort mig fri" (God's Son Hath Set Me Free) to words of Brorson's. Never has the dualism in Grieg's personality been more clearly expressed than here. After the first verse, in lively march rhythm, aglow with cheerful assurance of faith and victorious joy, Grieg in the next verse brings in a baritone solo which, supported by a solo quartet of male voices, carries the thematic material further. Already the tone picture shows the conflict situation which has arisen here, as the chorus is changed over into B minor, while the soloist continues to sing his part in B major! It is the conflict between the assured faith of older times and the religious unrest of our own days which has here been taken up for musical treatment. It is the distress of the modern man of culture, his suffering, his searchings of heart, and his abandonment to religious mysticism which are here expressed in a way that is as daring and original as it is moving. It is a musical parallel to the extremely complex and subtle religious reflections which we meet in literature in the Russian poets and especially in Dostoievski. When, in the midst of the choir's tormented harmonies which almost all the time border on the extreme, we hear the solo sustained in the bright, confident B major, we think involuntarily of Grieg's words: "The conception of God I must maintain, even though it so often conflicts with the conception of prayer." He could not have illustrated these words better or brought out their depth of meaning in a more convincing way. The words which have produced this remarkable confession of faith read thus in Brorson's vigorous and picturesque language:

> God arms me thousand-fold
> Against the serpent old.
> Stay snake, and see
> Me, royally
> Pass in the purple of the free.
> How greatly we rejoice
> Who follow Jesus' voice,
> Truth's path hold fast,
> All evil past,
> To reach glad Heaven at last.
> What though the whole world tries
> Again to blind my eyes,
> Nay, nay,
> For aye
> Out of the mire I stay.

Too dear my price has been
To try the game of sin;
I his decoy
Spurn scornfully
And look to heaven with joy.

In the last verse, the lively march rhythm is again taken up and the bright, buoyant tone of the first verse. The hymn finishes with the opening stanza, "God's Son hath set me free!" which through changing keys is forced steadily higher and higher up into the light to give expression to an ecstatic joy before it sinks down into the mighty organ chords in which the stanza is once more repeated and ends.

"Jesus Kristus er opfaren" (Jesus Christ Is Risen)—words by Hans Tomisön, who died 1573—is formed like a liturgical antiphony between soloist and choir. This beautiful piece of folk music from Valdres has, through Grieg's harmonic treatment, attained a marvellous peace and sublimity. It sounds like a devout thanksgiving in a Gothic cathedral. Only in the choir's repetition of the Kyrie Eleison does pain break through, expressed in a way that has a strong resemblance to the middle part in "God's Son Hath Set Me Free."

"Hvad est du dog skjön" (How Fair Is Thy Face), with words by Brorson, is also formed like an antiphony between choir and soloist. Here too we remark the infinite delicacy of the treatment and the intensity of feeling which show better than all words Grieg's religious resignation and devout seriousness.

If we think of all the bodily suffering and spiritual anguish Grieg in this year had to endure, we understand better the longing for eternity expressed in the last of the chorales, "In Heaven." In these last days he was quite familiar with the thought of death; his diary, where time after time he dwells on it, shows this clearly. Suffering and tormented to the breaking point of his endurance— yes, even to the verge of madness—he had only one wish, one longing, one thought, to reach the rest, the repose and peace that were not vouchsafed him in this world. "It feels to me as if the great migration were not so far away. Yes—yes!" he writes resignedly in his diary. And so his farewell to us, his artistic testament to us is, most naturally, the last of the chorales, "I Himmelen" (In Heaven) to words of Laurentius Laurentii (1573-1655). Gerhard Munthe twists the words of the Scriptures a little and says, "One

must become as a little child to enter into the kingdom of art,"
and Grieg's whole life-work shows the rightness of that sentence.
But we can now, towards the close both of his life and his art,
choose rather to repeat the words in their original form: "Except
ye become as little children ye cannot enter the kingdom of heav-
en." Grieg preserved throughout the whole of his life this, the
surest mark of true genius, he preserved the capacity for childlike
devotion. Therefore, in full religious devotion, he could make the
poet's words his own and sing:

> To Heav'n above, to Heav'n above
> Where God, our Lord, doth reign,
> What blessedness to come where love
> And joy have vanquished pain,
> And there for ever in amaze
> On God in His white radiance gaze,
>   Lord God of Sabaoth.

> And this poor frame, and this poor frame,
> Laid crumbling in the mould,
> All bright and shining has become
> As is the purest gold,
> Now all its wounds and pain are past
> And face to face it sees at last
>   Lord God of Sabaoth.

> Adornment too the soul shall wear,
> The promised crown of light,
> The bridal crown of righteousness
> And robes of spotless white.
> Oh God! What bliss to dwell with Thee,
> And in Heav'n's light Thy face to see,
>   Thee, God of Sabaoth.

In 1906, the German composer and writer on music, Walter
Niemann, published his book *Die Musik Skandinaviens*. At last
Grieg received from a responsible German source full understanding and recognition. The book, which is dedicated to Edvard Grieg,
brought forth the following remarks in a letter to the author dated
Troldhaugen, August, 6, 1906: "I feel it as a great satisfaction,
as a sign of the times that now, precisely when Norway has at last
achieved the happiness she has so long looked for of having a self-
dependent and independent position among the nations—pre-

cisely now our musical art also has won for itself recognition from abroad. And, in truth, it is none too soon that Norwegian art should be received in Germany at least with understanding. And to speak plainly—especially *my* art. How many times have I not had to suffer the cheap banality 'Norwegerei, er norwegert' and so on, directed as a complaint against my works. No one would permit himself to use the expression 'Deutschtum, Deutscherei' as a term of abuse towards any German composer. And yet it is a fact that German music critics have remained distrustful and unsympathetic, not only towards Norwegian, but also towards *all* national movements in the art of music *outside Germany*. How petty —how prejudiced that is." This view he emphasized still more strongly in the interviews several German newspapers and magazines had with him during his last visit there in the spring of 1907.

In October we find Grieg again in Christiania, where he remained till the middle of March. On January 12, 1907, he conducted his A minor concerto at the Orchestral Society's concert and on March 6, with Nina, he assisted Julius Röntgen at a concert in the hall of the Brothers Hals. This was his last appearance in Christiania. With Röntgen he played his Norwegian Dance duets and also accompanied Nina in a series of songs. "The dances went splendidly and had an enormous success," he noted in his journal, "and after Nina's songs, wild cheering—thank Heaven I had no need to repent my deed of daring. We would do anything, anything, for Julius. As an extra, she sang 'Hip and Hoppe' and when that was loudly cheered, finally 'Wood Wanderings'— old youth! But that youth conquered, the audience showed to the full!!"

And so the last tour began. On March 21 there was a concert in Copenhagen. Both for the concert and the public general rehearsal Grieg had packed audiences. On April 7 there was a concert in Munich and on the 12th and 14th at the Philharmonic in Berlin. For both the Berlin concerts all the tickets were sold long before. Of Halfdan Cleve, who played the piano concerto, Grieg notes in his diary that "he played like a real artist."

During this stay in Berlin he paid a visit to Nordraak's grave. In the diary he notes: "I laid a laurel wreath by his splendid monument and thought as I did it: forty-one years have gone since last I stood at this grave, that is to say: my life. It was as though I stood for a moment face to face with all I have experienced—and of it, first and foremost, the Nordraak time—the glorious!"

The journey home was through Kiel, where on April 26, Grieg conducted his last concert. After a stay of six weeks in Denmark, where he tried a cure with Finsen light baths without getting any relief, he travelled home in the middle of June to Norway, to the last summer at Troldhaugen.

THE SUMMER OF 1907—DEATH AND BURIAL

THE two months Grieg had still to live were grievously heavy for him. In these last years he had been well accustomed to suffering, well acquainted with grief, but in this last summer at Troldhaugen it seemed, time after time, as though bodily as much as spiritual oppression threatened to drive him to despair. The diary speaks its own clear language here and Grieg experienced the bitter truth of Björnson's words:

> That the last pang
> That is the sharpest.

It is simply heartrending to follow him in the comparatively few entries in the diary from these last weeks, when his strength, under a constantly increasing breathlessness and sleeplessness, was slowly ebbing away. Now, as before, it was the visits of dear friends that helped to lighten a little his weary existence.

On July 13 he noted in his diary: "Ten dreary days which have convinced me that I am going more rapidly down hill than I had thought. The breathlessness is increasing in spite of two weeks' massage; brain and digestion together enough to drive one mad. Anything rather than that. If only there was some way of sleeping quietly away into the great sleep when I cannot bear it any longer."

The same day he had a visit from his youngest sister, Elisabeth, the one among his sisters he cared most for and felt nearest to. In the diary he wrote: "This morning came the dear Bet with the *Kong Sverre* from Christiania, after having finished twenty-nine years of work as an elementary school teacher. Few deserve rest as she does, the faithful and indefatigable, hard-working creature. She brought sunshine, both outward and inward sunshine, with her. If only summer would come at last after unceasing rain and cold for such a long, long time."

About a week later, Grieg had a visit from his old friend, Julius Röntgen, and soon after Percy Grainger came also to Troldhaugen. From the diary we see what a stimulating, cheering effect the visit of these two artists had on him, though they evoked melancholy too with the thought of his own condition.

On June 22 he noted in his diary: "And summer really came. At first, certainly, with cold north wind, but sun and a clear sky gave freshness and courage and the dear Bet gave peace and security. And at last, yesterday afternoon, came the excellent friend, Julius Röntgen, filled with Jotunheim warmth and enthusiasm. And, in addition, ideal summer with 18 degrees Reaumur and the real, bright fairy-tale atmosphere with hill-fairies and the tinkling of bells in the air. Although I have never before felt myself so completely outstripped as at this meeting, yet in the midst of sadness there is so much joy that I am grateful for it all the same."

On July 27 he notes: "And so the beautiful Röntgen days are over. Yesterday evening we all went with him to the steamer that carried him to Copenhagen. From the artist as from the man there was again much to learn. And in his new violin sonata there is again development. On the 25th, in the morning, came Percy Grainger and so I had the great joy of bringing together these two splendid men, who would, I knew, understand each other. Such width of outlook as Julius has is rare. What is important in Grainger's talent he recognized at once in spite of all foreignness and listened with enthusiasm as much to his music, his magnificent piano playing, as to his masterly and so deeply original treatment of folk tunes. For my own part I can say that I had to reach the age of sixty-four to hear Norwegian piano music interpreted with so much understanding and genius. His playing of the folk dances and the transcriptions of folk songs break new ground both for himself, and for me and Norway. And what a fascinating natural, deep, serious and childlike disposition! To win such a young friend, what joy! I could forget the oppression of the body if it did not by contrast announce itself so much more emphatically and, as it were, write upon the wall for me: He is $<$, you are $>$. And to look at this truth objectively is difficult."

Grieg had promised to take part in September in a music festival at Leeds, where among other things he was to conduct his piano concerto with Percy Grainger in the solo part. Although his condition grew worse during the summer, he had made up his mind to go. But this time fate willed otherwise.

For August there are only three entries in the diary. They shall be quoted here in their entirety.

August 5: "Yesterday evening we went with the dear Percy Grainger to the steamer which was to take him to his mother in Denmark. What an artist, what a man! What a high idealist, what a child and, at the same time, what a broad and developed outlook on life. A future socialist of the purest water. The words, 'Aus Mitleid wissend, der reine Thor,' fit him exactly. His work on folk music is of the greatest importance, since in him are combined musical excellence, skill in the science of comparative languages, historical and poetic vision, and a colossal enthusiasm for the task. And not only enthusiasm, but it would seem also a practical grip of the subject. It looks as if he would do all his best work in folk songs, which I regret very much because it implies that under-valuing of his talents as a pianist, which he shows only too plainly. The old story: 'Willst Du immer weiter schweifen?' As a piano player I do not know to which of the very greatest I should liken him. But all comparison is futile when greatness is the question. He is himself. Possibly I am partial to him because he has ac-tually realized my ideals of piano playing. If I had had his tech-nique, my conception of the nature of piano playing would have been exactly the same. Like a god, he is lifted high over all suffer-ing, all struggle. But one feels they have been there, but are over-come. It is a man, a great and distinguished man who plays. May life go well for him!"

The second entry is from the 25th and runs as follows: "From the 6th to the 25th has been one continuous suffering. Breathless-ness and sleeplessness increasing. The 20th, 21st and 22nd we spent with Beyers and Elisabeth at Voss. I hoped that the inland climate might bring me sleep. But no. Only of my general condition can I say that it is a little better. We had a still, warm day of sunshine. I might almost say the *only* one in the whole summer and I felt that that was what I needed. But next day it poured again and has gone on pouring since. Yesterday evening, Klaus Hanssen and his wife came up to us and, oddly enough, just at the same time as my new masseur who was to give me massage and 'packs' à la Skodsborg. Klaus examined me with the greatest kindness and superintended the whole performance. The result is that the massage is to be dropped, as it is too much for my nerves, but the packs to be con-tinued, as they did me good and brought me a little sleep at night—at least in the first part of the night. Wretched today, the 25th, after breakfast, don't understand why, it may be the strain of the massage yesterday evening."

The last entry is from August 31 and runs: "27th-30th spent in the hospital at Bergen under Klaus Hanssen's observation. Under worsening of illness, too, alas. The first night was without sleep, the 2nd and the 3rd under chloral. Today, the 31st, everything impossible as the isopral had no effect whatever and I lay awake almost the whole time. The whole thing is terribly depressing. Nevertheless, we must prepare for our overland journey on the 3rd. It is a question of getting away from this climate, though the journey to England these days seems to me more than doubtful."

Here Grieg's diary ends on Saturday, August 31.

On Sunday, September 1, Beyer and his wife were at lunch with the Griegs at Troldhaugen. Dr. Klaus Hanssen was there also. Grieg was then very weak, but would not give up the idea of the journey. To Klaus Hanssen, who had grave doubts about it, he answered that he thought himself strong enough still for a concert tour to England. "These concerts give me energy," he said. On Thursday, the 3rd, according to the arrangement, he was to take the steamer from Bergen to Lærdal and from there drive to Christiania. The last night before going on board he was to stay at the Hotel Norge in Bergen.

On Monday, September 2, Beyer rowed over in the afternoon to Troldhaugen and found Grieg "very, very ill." But the carriage was ordered and with his family and Beyer's Grieg drove to the Hotel Norge in Bergen. Arriving at the town in the afternoon he went to his tailor's and arranged about his outfit for the journey. Afterwards he drove to the house of an old friend and relation, stationer Riis, to say good-bye. Grieg was too weak to go into the shop and Riis, therefore, went out to the carriage and said good-bye to him. His friend felt, though he said nothing, that it was the last farewell. Grieg drove now to the Hotel Norge and when he got out of the carriage gave the coachman detailed orders about the start next morning. He looked now so ill that it struck the people of the hotel. "He looked like a man marked for death."

The day after, September 3, his condition had changed so much for the worse that Dr. Klaus Hanssen had to forbid the journey and insist on Grieg's going to the Bergen hospital. At about 7 in the evening Beyer visited him there. "He looked more ill than ever before," Beyer relates, "and had hardly strength to ask me to take his greetings to my wife as I held his hand in mine for good-bye. But though I was infinitely anxious about him, I did not think that death was drawing so near. I thought that his collapse came as a result of his sleeplessness and I hoped to find him better next morning."

Edvard Grieg, from a Painting by Erik Werenskiold,
Troldhaugen, 1902

But by the evening the doctor saw that there was no hope. Grieg realized it himself and observed, "So this will be the end."

The first part of the night passed as usual. Grieg could not sleep and he said to the nurse, "It is as usual with me, I shan't be able to sleep tonight either."

Fru Nina Grieg stayed at the hospital at night but had her room in another part of the building. The last words Grieg said to his wife were, "Well, if it must be so."

A little after three he fell into a doze. Fru Grieg was warned at once and put on some clothing to go to her husband. But when she came death had been before her. Edvard Grieg had fallen asleep— quietly, peacefully.

Doctor P. H. Lie, who undertook the post mortem, has given the following explanation of the cause of death. "The unfortunate issue of the inflammation of the lungs in his youth ruined his left lung and entailed consequences which impaired the working capacity of the right lung also. This reduction in the breathing surface of the lungs could, to a very large extent, be compensated for by a powerful heart. And Grieg's heart remained strong for a surprisingly long time. But difficulties increased when the healthy lung became emphysematously enlarged and danger came when the age was reached at which as a rule changes which weaken the heart develop in the blood vessels. These changes had not, however, occurred in the blood vessels of the heart but to an unusual extent in the vessels of the lungs so that the circulation in the lungs became more difficult and the demands upon the heart were increased. Finally, these became too great. The nourishment of the heart suffered on account of the poor circulation of air in the lungs and paralysis of the heart supervened."

The funeral service took place on Monday, September 9, an immense number participating. Not since the burial of Ole Bull had Bergen seen anything like it. From near and far, from home and abroad, from musical societies and academies of art, from kings and emperors and, of course, from colleagues and admirers everywhere in the world came letters of condolence and telegrams in hundreds.

From Amsterdam came his friend Julius Röntgen to follow Grieg to his last resting-place; from London came Adolf Brodsky and took his place amongst the first violins in the orchestra to render the last honors to the master, and from Christiania came Johan Halvorsen to conduct the funeral music.

The Swedish authoress, Annie Wall, in her book *Människor jag mötte* (People I Have Met) has drawn a vivid picture of the ceremony, from which the following extract is taken:

The funeral ceremonies for Grieg and his last journey were amongst the most solemn and impressive at which I have ever been present. I can only compare with them the committal to earth of the great Polish poet, Sienkiewicz, in the Catholic church of Vevey in Switzerland. In the hall of the Westland Museum of Industrial Art in Bergen all was prepared for the ceremony. The walls were hung with black draperies and the hall decorated with palms and large wreaths between high candelabra and burning candles. In the background, at the top of the entrance stairs, could be seen a marble bust of Grieg, surrounded by laurels and cypresses. On a dais in the middle of the hall stood the coffin completely covered by flowers, mainly pink roses and white lilies.

Besides Fru Nina and the nearest mourners there were about five hundred people assembled in the hall. Among them were many of high station and representatives of many corporations and societies at home and abroad. Kaiser Wilhelm had also sent a representative.

But outside the Museum and along the road by which the dead was to be carried there surged a crowd which must have numbered thirty to forty thousand. For the whole of that old Bergen which Grieg loved so well wished to honor its master in getting a glimpse of his coffin. There was no boat in the harbor that day but flew its flag at half-mast, no house in Bergen or its neighborhood that did not hoist the national colors with the sign of mourning.

When the clock struck twelve, the bells from all the church towers in Bergen tolled over the sleeper, pealing with a melancholy clang in the rain-heavy air. But in the hall of grief, Kapellmeister Johan Halvorsen had lifted his baton and the great orchestra, in which the Russian violinist Brodsky who had come for Grieg's funeral had taken his place among the first violins, began to play Grieg's "Spring." Silver pure, the first notes met the ear. When the music died away in a soft pianissimo, there was a breathless stillness in the hall and tears stood in every eye. It was one of these exalted moments granted sometimes in life to mankind and which can never be forgotten. Dr. Klaus Hanssen, the dead man's doctor and personal friend, then walked forward to the coffin and described in clear and simple words Edvard Grieg's life and development as an artist. He counted that generation fortunate which had lived at the same time with Grieg. One simple passage from the speech will be quoted here. These words of Klaus Hanssen will be held in remembrance by artists in Norway both now and for all the future:

"But above the genius of the man, above his outward activities, stands the man himself, his personality and its development. Acquaintanceship with this is not given to every man. But all who had the good fortune to come into close touch with Edvard Grieg learned to set as high a value on the man as on the artist. I am not thinking of his great intelligence and sparkling brilliancy, I am thinking rather of his qualities of character, his utter rectitude which never yielded in the least degree to the spirit of compromise—his great conscientiousness and austere demands which never permitted any half measures, his staunch disposition and his warm heart."

A large male choir under the leadership of Ingolf Schiött and with him as soloist broke into Grieg's "The Great White Host," after which the laying of wreaths on the coffin began. Among the masses of flowers that were heaped up round the coffin there were several bunches of heather, for like Ole Bull Grieg had a great fondness for this flower of the wilderness. From Bergen four laurel wreaths of silver were laid upon the coffin.

When at last all the flowers and wreaths had been arranged, Grieg's funeral march for Nordraak sounded out. It is like a great ancient lament over a departed hero. After the last note had died away, eight of Grieg's nearest friends lifted the coffin and bore it out to the hearse drawn by four horses. When the coffin came into sight at the door of the Museum, all heads were bared and Bergen's brigade-band struck into Chopin's funeral march. The long, mournful procession moved off. Next to the hearse walked Fru Nina Grieg with her sister and two of Grieg's sisters. Fru Grieg had all the time preserved an admirable composure. Beside me in the procession walked a peasant woman in the beautiful, becoming Hardanger dress. It was Brita Utne from Hardanger. As she went she now and then dried a few tears and said quietly, "How good Grieg was, how bright he was and happy!"

When the procession reached Möllendal churchyard the coffin was lifted by the hands of other friends and carried into the crematorium which was decked with greenery and flowers. After the casting on of earth, the coffin sank soundlessly and was committed to the flames.

"At Troldhaugen there is a wall of rock that looks to the west, out towards the fjord," writes Frants Beyer. "Its top is crowned with small birch and spruce trees. At the foot of the wall the rock-strewn ground is thickly clothed with a carpet of bracken. Bird cherry, rowan, and birches shelter the place. Grieg had talked to me many times of this spot as his resting place, the last time only a few weeks before his death. 'Here it is,' he said as we went slowly past. Fru Grieg had his wish fulfilled, and a grotto after a design by his architect cousin Schack Bull and as simple as Grieg himself was hewn in the rock." Beyer describes the placing of the urn in the grotto in a letter to Fru Grieg, who was at the time in Denmark. And with these simple words of his friend the story of Grieg's life and work shall close. Beyer's letter is dated Bergen, April 7, 1908, and reads as follows:

"Dear Nina!

"And so Edvard's ashes have now come to their last resting place. I deeply hope that you will feel satisfied with the grotto and the whole thing. It was a quiet, soft spring day when in the afternoon Schack and I brought the urn from the fireproof room in the museum buildings and drove in a closed carriage to Troldhaugen. I set the urn in the grotto and then the stone was put in place. A blackbird sang in the spruces above. Just at that moment the sun went down behind clouds edged with gold and cast its last rays over the water upon Edvard's name.

"Dear Nina, it will be so dear and precious to you to have the grotto so near, and there is a wonderful peace and beauty over the spot Edvard himself has chosen.

"May his ashes rest in peace!"

ACKNOWLEDGMENT

OF those who have helped me in the preparation of this book, I must first and foremost, acknowledge my debt to Fru Nina Grieg. Besides talking things over with me, Fru Grieg also showed the interest and confidence in me to put at my disposal the collection of Edvard Grieg's posthumous papers kept in the Bergen Public Library, consisting of family letters, letters on art, manuscripts, entries in his diary and so on.

I have to thank also for information given by word of mouth several of Edvard Grieg's relations and a number of persons who stood near to him. I name: Fru Marie Grieg (Edvard Grieg's sister-in-law), Fru Mimi Grieg Bing (his brother's daughter), Consul Joachim Grieg, Fru Brita Utne, Director Johan Bögh, Herr Iver Holter, Herr Henri Hinrichsen (Peters' Publishing House, Leipzig).

The following have very kindly lent letters from Edvard Grieg: Fru Brita Utne, Fru Hulda Garborg, Johan Halvorsen, Iver Holter, O. Thommessen, also Thorvald Lammers' and Knut Dale's heirs.

Supplementary information I have received with kind courtesy from, among others, the proprietors of Wilhelm Hansen's Music Publishing House, Copenhagen, the head of the Peters' Library of Music, Dr. Kurt Taut, Leipzig, Dr. Rolv Laache of the Records Office, Oslo, and the University Collection of Manuscripts, Oslo. I must thank also Herr Victor Smith, the librarian of the Bergen Public Library, for his constant helpfulness and kindness.

Of published sources use has been made of *Breve fra Grieg*, selection by Gunnar Hauch, Copenhagen, 1922; *Breve fra Edvard Grieg til Frants Beyer*, published by Marie Beyer, Christiania, 1923; *Grieg*, Door Julius Röntgen, Gravenhage, 1930; *Edvard Grieg, Briefe an die Verleger der Edition Peters*, Leipzig, 1932; *Richard Nordraach, Hans efterladte breve*, published by Wladimir Moe, Christiania, 1921.

DAVID MONRAD-JOHANSEN

INDEX

INDEX

PUBLICATIONS OF
THE AMERICAN-SCANDINAVIAN FOUNDATION

—

FROM THE OLD NORSE

The Poetic Edda, 2 vols. in one	$3.00
The Prose Edda	2.00
The King's Mirror, with an Historical Introduction by Laurence Marcellus Larson	5.00
The Saga of the Volsungs and of Ragnar Lodbrok	1.50
Four Icelandic Sagas, with an Introduction and Notes by Gwyn Jones	2.00
Norse Mythology, by P. A. Munch and Magnus Olsen	2.50

HISTORICAL

Axel Olrik: *Viking Civilization*	3.50

PUBLICATIONS OF
THE AMERICAN-SCANDINAVIAN FOUNDATION

(*Continued*)

LITERARY CRITICISM

Topsöe-Jensen: *Scandinavian Literature*. Illustrated	**$3.50**
Sigurd Bernhard Hustvedt: *Ballad Criticism in Scandinavia and Great Britain*	5.00
Halvdan Koht: *The Old Norse Sagas*	2.00
Margaret Schlauch: *Romance in Iceland*	2.00

DRAMA

Holberg: *Comedies* (*Jeppe of the Hill, The Political Tinker*, and *Erasmus Montanus*)	2.00
Sigurjónsson: *Modern Icelandic Plays* (*Eyvind of the Hills, The Hraun Farm*)	2.00
Ibsen: *Early Plays* (*Catiline, The Warrior's Barrow, Olaf Liljekrans*)	2.00

ART

Laurin-Hannover-Thiis: *Scandinavian Art*, with 375 Illustrations	8.00

PHILOSOPHY

Sören Kierkegaard: *Philosophical Fragments*, with an Introduction by David F. Swenson	2.00

BIOGRAPHIES AND MEMOIRS

Hans Christian Andersen, by Himself (*Story of my Life*)	2.50
Halvdan Koht: *The Life of Ibsen*, 2 vols. Illustrated	7.50
Jon Sörensen: *The Saga of Fridtjof Nansen*. Illustrated	4.50
Fredrika Bremer: *America of the Fifties*. Illustrated	2.00

POETRY

Tegnér: *Poems* (*Frithjof's Saga*, and *The Children of the Lord's Supper*)	2.00
Björnson: *Poems and Songs*	2.00
———: *Arnljot Gelline*	2.00
Stork: *Anthology of Swedish Lyrics from 1750 to 1925*	2.50
Runeberg: *The Tales of Ensign Stål*	2.00

TRAVEL

Hjalmar Lindroth: *Iceland, a Land of Contrasts*. Illustrated	3.50